MADAME RESTELL

Madame Restell

THE LIFE, DEATH, AND RESURRECTION OF OLD NEW YORK'S MOST FABULOUS, FEARLESS, AND INFAMOUS ABORTIONIST

BY JENNIFER WRIGHT

hachette
BOOKS

New York

Hachette Books
Hachette Book Group
1290 Avenue of the Americas
New York, NY 10104
HachetteBooks.com
Twitter.com/HachetteBooks
Instagram.com/HachetteBooks

First Edition: February 2023

Published by Hachette Books, an imprint of Perseus Books, LLC, a subsidiary of Hachette Book Group, Inc. The Hachette Books name and logo is a trademark of the Hachette Book Group.

The Hachette Speakers Bureau provides a wide range of authors for speaking events.

To find out more, go to www.hachettespeakersbureau.com or call (866) 376-6591.

The publisher is not responsible for websites (or their content) that are not owned by the publisher.

Print book interior design by Jeff Williams

Library of Congress Cataloging-in-Publication Data

Name: Wright, Jennifer, author.
Title: Madame Restell: the life, death, and resurrection of old New York's
    most fabulous, fearless, and infamous abortionist / by Jennifer Wright.
Description: New York, NY: Hachette Books, [2023] | Includes bibliographical
    references and index.
Identifiers: LCCN 2022032437 | ISBN 9780306826795 (hardcover) |
    ISBN 9780306826818 (paperback) | ISBN 9780306826825 (ebook)
Subjects: LCSH: Restell, Madame, 1811–1878. | Abortion services—New York (State)—
    New York—History—19th century. | Abortion—New York (State)—New York—
    History—19th century. | Women in medicine—New York (State)—New York—
    Biography. | Patent medicines—New York (State)—New York—History—
    19th century. | Restell, Madame, 1811–1878—Trials, litigation, etc. |
    Trials (Abortion)—New York (State)—New York—History—19th century.
Classification: LCC RG734.R47 W75 2023 | DDC
    362.1988/80973—dc23/eng/20220708
LC record available at https://lccn.loc.gov/2022032437

ISBNs: 9780306826795 (hardcover); 9780306826825 (ebook)

Printed in the United States of America

LSC-C

Printing 1, 2022

FOR MY DAUGHTER, MADELINE

CONTENTS

ℙROLOGUE

WINTER, 1878

ℯ﹏﹏﹏

ᴬLTHOUGH IT WAS 10:45 P.M. WHEN MADAME RESTELL OPENED the front door of her Fifth Avenue brownstone, her face seemed unsurprised by what she saw: a strange man in a black suit, shivering on her landing, the harsh puffs of his breath lingering between them in the cold January air. After all, how many men like him had found themselves hovering upon her doorstep over the past forty years? These men knew of Madame Restell's reputation as a woman of skill and discretion. Perhaps this man had just come from supper with his mistress, who had informed him of some unwelcome news. Or he might have been a husband whose wife was in the kind of ill health that would prevent her from having more children. Perhaps he already had more children than he could afford to feed.

"May I speak to Madame Restell?" he asked.

"Do you wish to see her professionally?"[1] Her voice lilted with a hint of its original West Country accent.

He nodded. The woman beckoned him inside.

Winding her way through her drawing room, Restell walked—according to the man observing her—with "a stride that was firm, for all advancing years, and a bearing that flaunted a callous defiance."[2] She hardly resembled the part of "hell's representative on earth," as her nemeses liked to call her; rather, the elderly Restell looked more like the regal grandmother she was.[3] She had been beautiful once, even her harshest critics acknowledged, like Countess Ellen Olenska moving among the glamorous circles of Victorian New York. Gone now were the luxurious frocks and diamonds that had accentuated Restell's once curvaceous figure. In their place—albeit still glittering with jewels—lay a black silk mourning dress, worn in memory of the husband she'd lost the year before.

At sixty-six years old, Madame Restell had begun to strike people who saw her as a "careworn woman."[4] Her brown hair, impeccably styled as ever, was now flecked with gray; yet, after all these years, her elegance hadn't dimmed. Her dark brown eyes remained as keen and piercing as ever.

And neither did her magnificent Fifth Avenue brownstone look—as some protesters had been known to shout from the street—as though it were "built upon a mound of baby skulls." The house itself, mere feet from the construction site of St. Patrick's Cathedral, imposing with its Corinthian columns, looked like the home of someone as refined as they were powerful. The interiors were as sumptuous as any of the rooms in Edith Wharton's novels, full of oil paintings, artistic bronzes, and statues. The marble floors were covered with Turkish rugs. Marble columns flanked the stairways. Ladies could gather around two pianos to play and sing in the evening if they so desired.

Restell and her newest guest made their way downstairs to her basement office, where she and her granddaughter Caroline, by then her apprentice, conducted their business. She invited him to take a seat.

The stranger was still shivering, face pinched with anxiety beneath his great beard and mutton chops. A scar on his left cheek gave him a particularly pitiable air. Once settled, he informed her that he'd seen her advertisements and wanted something to prevent a woman from giving birth.

Restell asked him whether the woman he'd come for was married or unmarried. "If unmarried, it's a case of needing immediate action," she told him sternly. "If married, there's less necessity for hurrying."[5]

This was Madame Restell's indirect way of making sure all her clients actually wanted an abortion. She lived down the street from an orphanage; sometimes, she told female patients that she could help them find a family to adopt the baby if they wished. Indeed, in cases where the pregnancy was especially advanced and abortion seemed unsafe, she pressured her patients to opt for adoption over an operation. Some did. Most did not.

The man before her refused to say anything more about the pregnant woman he represented. Restell assured him that she did not need to know her name. He muttered only that it was a "delicate situation."[6]

Knowing the grave urgency that this understatement typically conveyed, Restell gave the man some pills, telling him that the directions were inside the bottle as it was illegal—and therefore unsafe—to have them on the outside.

"It is not infallible," she advised him. "No medicine is. In nine cases out of ten, however, it is effective."[7] If the medicine did end up working, it would act by Thursday.

In the middle of their conversation, another caller knocked on the door. Madame Restell went upstairs to see who it was, and the man later reported that he could not help but be curious upon hearing a female voice. He listened to their conversation, catching certain phrases. The woman said something about her husband having been away for two months. She already had two children. She'd been… "indiscreet," as she put it.

Before long, Madame Restell returned. With a sigh, she remarked, "Poor little dear…she has been unfortunate, and has come for relief. Many such ladies come here for such relief."[8] Restell's remark was likely intended to reassure her other customer: She knew what she was doing. The only people Restell saw more of than anxious men were distraught women.

Restell told the man once more that the pills she had given him ought to be safe. She also reminded him that if they did not have the intended effect, he should bring his lady friend by the house for an appointment that would cost him $200—or $5,000 in today's currency. That would be a surgical abortion.

Thanking her, the man clutched the pills to his chest and headed back out into the cold night air. Restell never expected to see him again. But if she had pulled back one of her lace curtains and gazed after him as he departed, she might have noticed his lips flicker into a victorious smile. As it happened, he would return to the steps of her lavish abode. But not with a lady friend.

Two weeks later, on February 11, 1878, Restell's gentleman caller came back, this time with a group of policemen and a warrant for her arrest.

"You've brought quite a party with you," Madame Restell deadpanned as she opened the door.[9]

Ever the dramatist, Anthony Comstock relished in his big reveal: He was no anonymous, terrified sinner requesting Restell's services on behalf of a mistress, but in fact the head of the New York Society for the Suppression of Vice. That society attempted to ban all that they considered obscene—whether it was pornographic pictures or birth control pills. Its members also attempted to jail anyone who defied them. Comstock was the very man who had created the 1873 laws that forbade using the US Postal Service to send out anything even *mentioning* birth control, let alone supplying it. Many before him claimed that Madame Restell was too powerful to pursue. But who was laughing now?!

To his annoyance, Restell seemed to find the affair absurd. She was not dissolving into the puddle of tears he had expected.

Madame Restell knew about Comstock. Of *course* she knew about him. Likenesses of him ran in the papers regularly. She shook her head upon realizing who he was, remarking, impassively, "You [are] Mr. Comstock? I thought he was dark complexioned." For a moment, her sangfroid gave way to the sensational interest of a tabloid media connoisseur as she asked, "Are you the man who was injured in the face by the prisoner?" He was. A New Jersey pornographer had not responded to Comstock's interference with the same bemusement Madame Restell was exhibiting.

Comstock had already developed a reputation as somewhat of a controversial figure, and his treatment of Madame Restell would lead to questions about his character as well as hers. In mere months, newspapers would begin wondering whether he "transcend[ed] his duty by leading innocent people into temptation in order that he may convict them."[10]

But Madame Restell was no innocent. She knew the risks inherent in her line of work. A policeman had been patrolling outside her mansion for years in an attempt to intimidate her. He had not done so. So why should these men?

Comstock's officers began their search of the premises. Restell casually told them to go ahead, insinuating that they'd find nothing to convict her. Less casual was the woman they found recuperating in one of the lace-curtained bedrooms upstairs: upon seeing them, she burst into tears, announced that her husband was rich, declared that she was the mother of four children, claimed that she was only there on behalf of a friend, and wailed that she was going to kill herself if they arrested her. She was also wearing a veil to protect her identity.

Amid this commotion, two new women arrived at the door. Restell calmly sent them away, gesturing to the policemen and remarking, "You must excuse me, ladies. These gentlemen are acting in a very officious manner and will not allow me to see you."[11]

Comstock ushered them in nevertheless and proudly declared that he was searching for evidence of *abortions*. At that, the twosome turned pale and ran out the door.

As the officers continued to search, making their way to her basement, Restell informed them that they were merely searching her wine cellar. As for the pills and powders they found, she was adamant that they were no more than could be provided by any druggist. Still, the men seemed satisfied that they'd found enough medicine and contraceptives to arrest the infamous Madame Restell on the grounds that she was distributing articles used for "immoral purposes."

"Where am I to go?" she inquired.

"Before the judge!" Comstock said.

"With these men?" Her eyes said: *hell* no.

"How, then?"

"In my own carriage. It's at the door. At least I am entitled to that courtesy."[12]

Once assured she could travel to court in her famously lavish carriage, drawn by two gray horses and driven by a purple-clad coachman, she agreed without objection. Just before leaving, she asked if she could "take oysters." After all, she complained, "I've had no lunch, yet."[13]

The police agreed that they would wait until a lovely lunch was served and accompanied her into the kitchen.

Gazing at the men icily, she lowered one oyster after the other into her mouth and swallowed each one down. She'd spent a lifetime ensuring she had enough money to afford such delicacies. Now, she would need her energy for what lay ahead.

This is the story of one of the boldest women in American history: a self-made millionaire, a celebrity in her era, a woman beloved by many of her patients and despised by the men who wanted to control them.

An immigrant who came to the Lower East Side of Manhattan lured by the promises of the American Dream, Madame Restell soon found herself a widow attempting to raise a toddler.

It didn't take Restell long to learn how horrifically hard single motherhood was in the mid-1800s. "Why," she wondered, "should women have no say over if and when they became mothers?" Before long, she was producing pills made of tansy seeds, which could induce miscarriage. Then she learned how to perform surgical abortions, offered on a sliding scale so as to accommodate poorer women while still allowing her to amass a fortune.

Restell's profession eventually took her from the fringes of Five Points to the heart of Fifth Avenue. She became one of the era's savviest businesswomen, writing editorials in the big city newspapers and publicizing services her competitors merely whispered about. Her adversaries were at least as upset about the idea of a woman making that much money and consuming that much attention as they were about the very idea of abortion. Each time they advanced an argument decrying abortion—women would become prostitutes! Men wouldn't know if their wives had been faithful! The white race would be decimated!—Madame Restell published another rebuttal.

Her pen wasn't always enough to keep her on the right side of the law, but she didn't let that slow her down. When Restell was finally arrested and sent to jail, for a year, she began using the warden's office for her work affairs. She employed three prisoners to act as her servants—they did her washing, cleaned her cell, and made sure she was supplied with fresh fruit (she preferred peaches). However, she never forgave the police for her imprisonment. She later cut ties with her own daughter after said daughter—to her horror—married a cop.

The only thing Madame Restell hated more than cops were the moralizers determined to destroy her business. When the Catholic Church spoke out against her, she outbid the archbishop of New York for the land he wanted to build his house on. There, she built a mansion, and from it she doled out birth control to her many patients. She did not ask for any man's opinion, for she was not interested in hearing it.

Restell was a businesswoman, a scofflaw, an immigrant, and an abortionist. She made men really, *really* mad. She deserves a place in the pantheon of women with no fucks left to give. But, despite her impact, she has been largely lost to history. Most Americans don't know her name at all, and those who do have a less-than-accurate impression of who she was. Every existing record of her life reduces her somehow: to *only* an activist, *only* a villain, *only* a campy show woman, *only* the tragic victim hounded to death by Anthony Comstock.

Madame Restell was so much more than any one thing. She was unrestrainable. Unapologetic. A survivor. The kind of woman who has always existed in America, and always will.

CHAPTER ONE

S HE WAS NOT FRENCH.
And she was not even called Madame Restell—until much later.
The heroine of our tale entered this world in 1811 as Ann Trow.
The "lucky star" under which one of her future clients claimed she
was born hung over a small English town called Painswick. Those who
would later allege she was sent by devilish agents could hardly have
picked a more perfect birthplace.

Today, Painswick, with its Cotswold stone cottages, is known primarily as being "the epitome of an English town." It is one possessed
of an idyllic beauty, standing on a hill overlooking one of the Five Val-
leys of Gloucestershire, a land of rivers and streams. Anne Boleyn and
King Henry VIII once hunted in its woods; ironically, Boleyn's eventual
executioner, William Kingston, also hailed from the region.[1] In 1643,
during the First English Civil War, King Charles I and Royalist forces
stayed in Painswick for a time. According to a walking tour guide, "tradition has it that [King Charles I] went up to the Beacon and, seeing
the beautiful valley to the east, said, 'This must be Paradise.' Since
then that valley, and the hamlet on its western side to the north of
Painswick, have been called Paradise."[2]

Yet there was also another side to the splendor of Painswick. During
Ann Trow's childhood, the townspeople possessed an unusual fondness for pagan customs, celebrating a yearly festival to the Greek satyr
god Pan. Until around 1830, citizens of Painswick staged an annual
procession in honor of this pagan god, who was most typically associated with sexuality.

The tradition appears to have originated with Benjamin Hyett,
a member of the local gentry. In the mid-eighteenth century, Hyett

1

erected a classically styled woodland pavilion, called Pan's Lodge, where he and his friends could celebrate "nocturnal orgies," according to the historian Timothy Mowl. Disinclined to let nobles have all the fun, it seems, locals soon got in on the action. *Gentlemen's Magazine*, in 1787, described the town's festival as one that "would have disgraced most heathen nations," as it was filled with "drunkenness and every species of clamor, riot and disorder."[3]

So, Ann was born into an uncommon place with particular—and particularly libertine—customs. But she was far from the only woman to grow up with a similarly blasé outlook toward sex during the period of her youth. While eighteenth- and early nineteenth-century society admired virginity, actual attitudes toward everyday premarital sexual activity at the time were more relaxed—both in Europe and even in supposedly puritanical America—than they're often portrayed as being in modern media.

As the historian Jack Larkin stated, "Into the 1820s, almost all Americans would have subscribed to the commonplace notion that sex, within proper social confines, was enjoyable and healthy and that prolonged sexual abstinence could be injurious to health. They also would have assumed that women had powerful sexual drives."[4] Premarital sex between couples was common. So common, in fact, that one pastor, in South Carolina in 1847, claimed that most brides—"except for two or three"—were pregnant when he performed their weddings.[5] In some northeastern American states, *bundling*—in which two sweethearts would snuggle, supposedly chastely, in bed, with the consent of their parents—was a common custom during courtship through the 1700s.[6] The "chaste" part of the practice, however, was notoriously misleading—which may help explain why, in the 1790s, one-third of rural New England brides were already pregnant by the time they walked down the aisle.[7] Women were seen as enjoying the practice of bundling as much as, if not more than, men. A poem from 1785 captures the spirit of the tradition:

> *Some maidens say that, if through the nation,*
> *bundling should go out of fashion,*
> *courtship would lose its sweets, as they*
> *could have no fun til wedding day.*

The concept is hardly that different from modern attitudes toward courtship. A 2002 study found that by the age of forty-four, 99 percent of Americans had sex. Ninety-five percent had premarital sex, making premarital sex nearly universal.[8]

As the lewd poem implies, many considered sexual impulses in women to be natural, not shameful. Indeed, popular magazines advocated punishment for men who had premarital sex with women and then left them, but sympathy for the women, who were perceived as unfortunate victims in that situation.[9] It may seem incredibly obvious to say "you should sympathize with a woman who had sex with a man and got dumped after"—until you realize that there are still messages today likening women who choose to have premarital sex to worthless, chewed-up gum.

Ann had the strange fortune to live during a period of great change regarding sexual attitudes. In modern times, we're sometimes guilty of assuming that one sexual ideology dominated a previous century— thinking everyone from the nineteenth century was prudish, for instance. Or else we theorize that all of history is one long, uninterrupted upward trajectory from utmost prudery to utter hedonism. In truth, dominant attitudes regarding sex shift decade to decade. Consider the laissez-faire approach to sex during the early aughts with those considered acceptable a decade and a half later, in a #MeToo era. The attempted rapist character on *Gossip Girl* in 2007 who became the show's romantic hero in later episodes would not have been given that story line fifteen years later—indeed, in *Gossip Girl* 2.0, characters now ask, "Do I have your consent?" before sex.

Over the course of her life, Ann watched public sentiment slide from being moderately permissive toward female sexuality to being more constrained, culminating in a time when doctors were convinced that "good women" did not have a sex drive *at all.* The change must have felt a bit bewildering, especially to someone who grew up in a place where residents partook in "every species of clamor, riot and disorder."

Sexual permissiveness aside, Ann's upbringing was simple. Her father was a laborer who worked at the local woolen mill, as did her mother. Her schooling consisted of basics: she might have learned how to read, most likely from the Bible, so as to recite the catechism, though religion was not a large part of her upbringing. Judging from records concerning Ann Trows, who was born in Painswick during this period, Ann wasn't baptized until the age of 16, perhaps in preparation for her marriage.[10] While (male) country doctors sometimes came from humble backgrounds, certainly she and her family would have had no such aspirations for her. They never expected that one day she would go on to buy all her family members houses, in spite of the fact that from an early age it was clear that Ann possessed "an acute intellect and a determined will."[11]

Like many young girls from lower-class families, Ann was sent into domestic service at the age of fifteen. Servitude at the time was a brutal business, no matter how charming BBC shows persist in making it seem. Dismiss any *Downton Abbey* notions you might have about this period of Ann's life. Young Miss Trow was not serving tea to nobility.

Instead, she worked for a middle-class butcher's family. Given her age, and the fact that she was unskilled, and came from a poor family, it's likely that she was a maid of all work. As such, she'd be required to do any and all chores around the house. Her day would begin before dawn. She might awake in an attic—which would be freezing during the winter—and creep downstairs at around 5:00 or 6:00 a.m. to make sure all the fires were lit before the family came down for breakfast. Then she would spend the day scrubbing floors, carrying water into the house from a well, emptying chamber pots, dusting the rooms, changing the beds, polishing the brass, scrubbing the laundry, cleaning the rugs, and serving the family's meals. Her work would continue until after nightfall—perhaps around 9:30 or 10:00 p.m., at which point she'd collapse, exhausted, only to begin again the next day.

Domestic drudgery of the lower orders was work that most of us would find physically and emotionally exhausting. However, Ann was naturally someone who enjoyed being busy. There were to be few periods of her life where she appeared to relax, and she always seemed a bit bewildered by those who enjoyed a life of idleness. She was also tireless.

Ann would never forget this time in her life. Nearly a lifetime later, her servants would live in nicer conditions than those of her neighbors, and she'd go out of her way to help them. And, just as she'd never forget the grim physical work that accompanied being a maid, she'd remember, too, the sexual peril inherent in being a teenage girl living in a near stranger's house.

Despite most households' insistence that maids not have gentlemen callers, her work as a servant would hardly have insulated Ann from sexuality, both her own and that of her peers. Many ladies took great care to keep their female staff from meeting with men from outside the house. But they often forgot about the men inside the house, especially those within their own families.

If well off, these men could assault household maids with little or no repercussions, legally or socially. And they would. This was sufficiently common in the eighteenth century that the Irish satirist Jonathan Swift advised the household maid "to get as much out of her master as she possibly can and never allow him the smallest liberty, not the squeezing of your hand, unless he puts a guinea into it.... [N]ever allow him the last favor for under a hundred guineas." He urged particular caution around the family's eldest son, as, from him, the maid would "get nothing from him but a big belly or the clap, and probably both together."[12]

Swift meant for readers to take his comments humorously, as any maid would have known that there was not much room for negotiation. If a maid did have sex with a male member of the family who desired her, she risked becoming pregnant and losing her job. People may have been happy to marry women of their own class whom they'd already impregnated, but if they impregnated a maid, they weren't going to keep paying her to dump out their chamber pots. If she refused sexual favors, however, she was likely doomed anyway: She could be fired immediately. Most chose the former option, compliance. A memoir written by an anonymous wealthy man, most likely Henry Spencer Ashbee, who grew up during the mid-1800s, *My Secret Life*, stated, "As to servants and women of the humbler class...they all took cock on the quiet and were proud of having a gentleman to cover them. Such was the opinion of men in my class of life and of my age. My experience with my mother's servants corroborated it."[13] The author further discusses impregnating some servants and, perhaps fortunately for them, procuring abortions.

Ann may or may not have experienced these assaults herself, but even so, she was likely well aware of their prevalence. If none presented in her household, she would certainly have heard stories about other maids who had been seduced or outright raped by their masters. Young girls hoped to follow the example set in *Pamela: Or Virtue Rewarded*—the

popular novel of the period in which a young maid thwarts her master's near constant attempts to rape her (at one point he leaps out of
her closet; at another, he kidnaps her) only for him to marry her. Ann
may well have even read about these experiences in the popular advice
guide *A Present for a Servant-Maid*. Published in 1744 and still referenced throughout Ann's own era, the manual was divided somewhat
evenly between good recipes and warnings about the terrible men who
would try to sleep with the help. That list included their masters, male
servants, sons of the household, and guests. As for what to do, the manual suggested it was probably best to keep away from men as much as
possible, to remind married men of their wives, and to avoid smiling at
single men, as it would "the more inflame him and render him more
persevering than ever."[14] The *Servant-Maid* guide was, to its credit, candid about the fact that avoiding these inflamed men would be incredibly difficult, and, in some cases, even impossible. It also stressed that if
a young woman became pregnant, the man would probably not marry
her, a situation that could lead to prostitution. At best, because life was
not a romantic novel, it mentioned, he would marry her, and then all
his friends would sneer at her for being poorly born.

It is a shame that this book did not contain any effective suggestions
for birth control—something Madame Restell would end up attempting to remedy later in life.

In any event, trying to avoid a master's wandering hands while also
dumping out his chamber pot seems stunningly degrading. Whether
Ann had to fight off advances is lost to history. But for the rest of her
life, she would show the utmost sympathy—and often offer vastly lowered prices for her services—to women who had been impregnated by
their employers.

At this time in her life, Ann's options seemed to be either to marry
or remain in service. She had little desire to remain a maid.

So, Ann married.

It was hardly unexpected. At sixteen years old, she was pretty and
popular, and known to be "a favorite among the cloth weaving population of Painswick."[15] One of her suitors was a twenty-two-year-old
man named Henry Sommers. As a journeyman tailor, Henry had completed his apprenticeship. He was considered fully educated and qualified to work in his field. With such a useful skill he could expect to
have steady employment. At the time, Painswick was well known for

its cloth and weaving industry. By marrying him, Ann's own fortunes would improve, and she could stop hauling water for her employers' laundry.

But as many women who live in the real world ultimately discover, married life is not always a fairy tale.

Shortly after her nuptials, Ann found out that her new husband was less a Prince Charming and more of a charming alcoholic. She discovered that she was "no better off after marriage than before."[16] As a result, "to support him, and herself, she had to do the tailoring work that he should have done."[17] Ever the hard worker, she soon became very proficient, and within a few years she was a talented dressmaker.

By 1830, she was also a mother to a daughter named Caroline. Supporting her family in Painswick was a constant challenge, but "she heard that in America she could get good wages for the trade that her husband's dissipation and idleness had forced her to learn."[18]

So, in 1831, Ann, Henry, and their toddler set sail to New York. Had she known how fierce the competition would be, she might never have left home.

Chapter Two

T HE VOYAGE TO NEW YORK FROM ENGLAND WAS A BRUTAL ordeal for the poor in 1831. Immigrant ships were considered, according to the *Quebec Gazette* in 1834, to be "the worst of all the merchant ships of Gt. Britain & Ireland." "With few exceptions," the paper said, "they are very old, very ill-manned, very ill found."[1] The passengers were crammed together on bunks for the monthlong voyage with little or no regard for their comfort. The more immigrants the ship owners were able to accommodate, the more money they made. The close quarters allowed disease—whether colds or flu, or more serious ailments, such as typhus—to spread easily and quickly. The health of the passengers was not helped by the fact that the food was appalling, if present at all. Until 1842, the British government did not mandate that the ships going to America provide passengers with adequate food and water. Before then, starvation on immigrant ships was not uncommon, especially if the journey was longer than expected due to bad weather. In 1836, a ship by the name of *Diamond* traveling from Liverpool to New York took one hundred days to make the crossing, due to poor weather, rather than the thirty days the passengers had anticipated. As a result, seventeen of the one hundred and eighty steerage passengers starved to death onboard. Captains and other employees would barter food in return for sexual favors from female passengers. Even after 1842, the food allotted to passengers was "not sufficient for the sustenance of any human being."[2] The immigrants had to cook their own food, and fights were known to break out as people jostled for access to a fire for this purpose. Furthermore, the water given to voyagers was often stored improperly. It had, according to one immigrant, "a rancid smell that...was enough to turn one's stomach."[3] The

8

water was also limited; what the ship could hold had to be reserved for drinking—there was little, if any, left over for washing. Passengers would defecate in buckets, which were known to tip over in rough weather. The stench on the ships was, consequently, overpowering.

What a relief it must have been for Ann and her family, hungry and filthy, to step off that ship and be met with a vision of New York. When Frances Trollope traveled there in 1827 and saw the city in all its grandeur for the first time, she later wrote, "Situated on an island, which I think it will one day cover, it rises, like Venice, from the sea, and like that fairest of cities in the days of her glory, receives into its lap tribute of all the riches of the earth."[4]

How infinitely different this city was from Ann's pastoral hometown! How exciting to be in such an American city, filled with the bustle of horses and carriages and buildings being rapidly constructed.

And how full—truly full—of people it was. Already New York's population was 185,000, and it was growing rapidly. By 1840 it would be 327,000.

Until her arrival in New York, Ann Trow Sommers did not realize that she was only one of thousands of women who thought they might make a good living through their sewing skills in America. In 1830, the economist Mathew Carey estimated that in New York, Boston, Philadelphia, and Baltimore there were already between 18,000 and 20,000 working women, many of those working as seamstresses.[5] Just as with the population, that number would continue to rise.

The mid-1800s saw a distinct shift in America, from being a country where people gathered primarily in rural areas to one where people were flocking to urban industrial areas for work. In 1800, 83 percent of the US labor force was in agriculture. By 1850, that number had decreased to only 55 percent.[6] This new labor force, made possible by industrialization, included women. The migration to the cities offered promise to many, but the appeal was especially strong for portions of the female population. For example, mill towns—which had sprung up during the 1830s—offered women financial independence away from their homes. That lure was strong enough that by 1840, women made up three-quarters of the workforce in these areas. Many hoped to earn enough money to provide for a relative, pay a brother's tuition, or save for their own dowry and then return home. Others intended to get a better education, or to buy the things they wanted for themselves—books!

pretty dresses!—with their own money. At least one went because she "hate[d] her mother in law," which seems fair.[7]

At the mills, women would earn wages as well as food and accommodation in a nearby boardinghouse with six to eight women to a room. But employment conditions were far from ideal. Workers labored from sunup to sundown. According to an 1849 issue of *Operatives* magazine, the boardinghouses were so "absolutely choked with beds, trunks, bandboxes, clothes, umbrellas and people" that it was "difficult to stir, even to breathe freely."[8] At the mills, fiber particles wafted in the air, making it hard for workers to breathe.

But while the environment itself was dismal, it also presented women with the possibility of exhilarating new intellectual challenges. Corporations offered lecture series to employees: twenty-five cents for twenty-five lectures. Workers had access to libraries that they might not have seen in more secluded areas. Factory towns like Lowell, Massachusetts, published literary magazines composed of the women's writing, such as *The Lowell Offering*. Industries often boasted proudly of the "literary mill girls" who had improved themselves while away from home. In actuality, many women found the work and long hours so exhausting they had no energy for lectures or penning pieces. Still, the poet John Greenleaf Whittier discussed how "here, at last...the work of her hands is adequately rewarded; and she goes about her daily task with the consciousness that she is not spending her strength for naught."[9] Being paid for labor can be intoxicating, especially in an era where women from more rural backgrounds were expected to labor for free. By the 1850s, one writer bemoaned the tendency of women to work away from home: "The most intelligent of the farmer's daughters become schoolteachers, or tenders of shops, or factory girls. They contemn the calling of their father, and will, nine times out of ten, marry a mechanic in preference to a farmer.... [T]hey remember their worn-out mothers."[10] At least some young women seemed to agree with this assessment. After they had been relatively independent in the mills, many women who returned to their family's farms in the 1840s complained somewhat snootily of "nice folks" who were sadly "countryfied in their ideas."[11]

By 1845, there were approximately fifty thousand working women in New York City—around one-seventh of its total population. Most of them were employed in factories, where they typically worked

13 to 18 hours a day and earned less than $3 per week. For perspective, in modern terms, that equates to a salary of $33 to $96 a week for as much as 126 hours of work. This amount was only about one-quarter of what men at the time received for equal work.

Still, competition for the limited jobs available to women was so keen that, as the *New-York Tribune* reported, women were happy to "snatch at the privilege of working on any terms."[12]

Ann likely felt fortunate to have her husband with her when they landed in America, especially as the streets where she was living were not exactly paved with gold. Upon their arrival, Ann and Henry lived on Oliver Street in Lower Manhattan, near the notoriously dangerous immigrant neighborhood of Five Points, a far cry from the quaint charms of Painswick.

If the streets of Five Points were paved with anything, it was vomit and horseshit. The stench alone was brutal, and the insect problem was notable. That was due to the fact that the neighborhood's spring-fed Collect Pond had been filled in to become a new residential area in 1811. This initially seemed like a fine solution to a problem that had developed: the pond had become contaminated by the growing factories of the area dumping their waste in it. And so, "Paradise Square" was constructed.[13] The houses were lovely. But the workmanship that had gone into filling the pond was not. By 1820, the pond began to reassert itself, the land became marshy, and the houses began to crumble. In the summer, mosquitoes swarmed the neighborhood, bringing with them malaria. The pools of stagnant, contaminated water also became breeding grounds for cholera.

This scenario did not attract a particularly nice class of residents. The neighborhood became known for crime, prostitution, and the gangs later made famous in Herbert Asbury's 1927 book, *Gangs of New York*. Asbury's tales, by his own admission, grew somewhat in the telling. It's doubtful, for instance, that Hell-Cat Maggie, a female fighter, really filed her teeth into points and kept all the ears she ripped off her opponents pickled in a jar at her bar. Or that Mose, an Achilles-like figure who was said to have led the "Bowery Boys" gang, was eight feet tall and once ripped an oak tree out of the ground to beat members of a rival gang to death. But Asbury did capture the colorful spirit of a neighborhood that horrified and fascinated many in equal measure. In 1834, the frontiersman Davy Crockett visited the area; he later said,

"I think I saw more drunken folks that day than I ever saw before." The denizens of the neighborhood were, in his estimation, "too mean to swab Hell's kitchen," and after interacting with them, he decided, "I would rather risk myself in an Indian fight than venture among these creatures after night."[14]

It follows then that Ann, a young mother who probably walked through that neighborhood every day, must have been a good deal braver than American folk hero Davy Crockett.

During her time in Painswick, she had become accustomed to the notion that sex was a fact of life—sometimes good, sometimes bad. But it was only now that she would see the desperate situation into which that unavoidable fact plunged American women.

By the mid-1800s, the streets of New York teemed with an estimated 30,000 homeless children. The miserable conditions they lived in were startling at best, but more often appalling. In 1849, the *Brooklyn Daily Eagle* begged people to look to Lower Manhattan, five minutes from the Fulton Ferry, where they'd see "ragged children crouched and huddled together like swine...greedily devouring the contents of their filthy baskets: all day long they have been wandering up and down the streets gathering half picked bones and rejected food; cast from the swill tub into the gutter." The paper described a scene of "six wretched, starving, freezing children" huddling around their mother, who was "ragged and filthy in the extreme, her dress in rags and tatters, her hair is matted in wads, and she is, indeed, an object of loathing."[15]

European countries had prepared for children born out of wedlock. As one physician noted in 1847, "In England, there are foundling hospitals, where unfortunate mothers can hide at once their offspring and their shame. In every large town in France, there are similar establishments; and in Vienna, still better, there is a government hospital, to which any woman may go, and in absolute security, await the birth of her child, whom the laws of society does not allow her to cherish and protect as a blessed gift of heaven. Here, we have nothing of this kind."[16]

It's important to understand that there was a difference between society's treatment of foundlings versus orphans. Orphans were children who, while they may have come from respectable homes, had lost both of their parents, perhaps due to an epidemic or some other act of God. They were considered pitiable. Foundlings, however, were children who had been abandoned immediately after their birth.

They were considered, in the words of New York's first chief of police, "embryo courtesans and felons."[17] Fans of feminist history and the musical *Hamilton* will know that Eliza Schuyler helped found the first private orphanage in New York, called the New York Orphan Asylum Society, in 1806. While that's laudable, it was also lacking; orphanages did not admit foundlings. The Infant's Home, New York's first foundling asylum, would not open until 1865.

And so, foundlings were left on street corners and doorsteps. One of the more heartbreaking aspects of these stories is how hard many mothers strove to find the "right" door at which to deposit their baby, one which might open to a kind person who would take their child in and care for it. They rarely did. When one baby was delivered at the doorstep of the former New York City mayor Philip Hone in 1838, he claimed that "it was one of the sweetest babies I ever saw."[18] He was tempted to keep it, but his friends informed him that if he did, he'd soon have twenty more babies abandoned upon his doorstep. He sent it off to the almshouse with a servant.

That was the fate of most such infants. Almshouses were where cast-off infants were supposedly cared for, but it's hard to say that they experienced much "care" there. A report from 1856 by a committee appointed by the Senate of the State of New York found that these places were "for the young the worst possible nurseries."[19] The state hired women as nurses to tend to the infants until they were two years of age, but sadly, many of those women were ill equipped and untrained, and funds were insufficient for even basic care in terms of food or clothing. From 1854 to 1859, nearly 90 percent of the infants in those institutions died.[20] Even at a time when it was estimated that a third of children died during their first year, the statistic was shocking.

Poor people trying to provide for their children couldn't even rely on basic compassion from their fellow New Yorkers, let alone help from government-funded institutions. In 1850, one newspaper, the *Buffalo Commercial*, was almost hysterically unsympathetic to the poor. It published an opinion piece from an author who was fed up with the "hundreds of suffering children who are perpetually rapping at our doors...[as] few if any of them have been taught their accountability to God or Man."[21] The author of this piece did not propose any charitable solution—he just, like many of his fellows, regarded these destitute, literally starving children as a real nuisance.

In the new urban environment, relative anonymity gave people the freedom to be awful. Back in the country, a pregnant and abandoned woman might suffer a good deal of social criticism—depending upon how seriously her neighbors took the advice that magazines gave to be kind to women who had premarital sex and were then abandoned. She could certainly be fired if she was employed anywhere. New York state law did dictate that the mother and baby be "supported at the expense of the county where such bastard should be born."[22] This may have proved somewhat easier, however, for a small, close-knit community, even if the assistance was provided begrudgingly, than for a sprawling metropolis such as New York City, where the babies supported by the city often died.

Still, while the scenes that surrounded her might have made Ann clutch her daughter, Caroline, slightly closer as they walked through the street, she had reasons to be optimistic that first year in New York. Henry soon found work as a tailor. During at least this period of his life, family friends would later claim, he was industrious and hardworking.

That in and of itself is praiseworthy considering that he was said to be a very heavy drinker, and that drinking served as a universal pastime among the very diverse residents of the Five Points neighborhood. Certain bars in the Five Points offered a kind of primitive keg stand. Lacking glasses, the proprietors poured beer from the keg through a tube into a person's mouth. For three cents, one could have as much beer as they could drink in one swallow. People, understandably, became excellent at holding their breath.[23]

While Henry was presumably making a beeline past these temptations on his way to the tailor shop, Ann continued to work from home as a seamstress. She was skilled as ever in her craft. Ann might have begun to dream of a home in a nicer part of the city, and a better future for their young daughter.

And then, Henry died.

Later journalists were surprisingly adamant to note that his death was *not* because of his drinking; rather, he died from typhoid fever. The disease, which is spread through contaminated food or water, was rampant in the slums of New York at the time. If he got it from drinking water, ironically, it might have been to his benefit to have consumed alcohol instead.

So in 1833, at age twenty-one, Ann found herself a widow in a rough neighborhood and a strange country, entrusted with the care of a toddler. This was a terrifying position to be in, both for herself and her child, at a time when one-third of the deaths in the city were of children under five.[24]

If Ann had been childless, it's likely she would have either returned to domestic service or begun working in one of the textile factories around town. With a child, however, both of those options were impossible. A maid with a child would typically find her baby unwanted in the family's home and would have to send her child away to be cared for by "baby farmers," who would take in children and raise them for a fee. As for factory work, the sheer number of hours demanded by those jobs made caring for a child inconceivable, and besides, it didn't provide enough money to entrust the child's care to anyone else.

That didn't mean that women with children didn't take on factory work. It just meant working women resorted to drugging their children.

In an 1859 cartoon, *Harper's Weekly* reported that opium served as "The Poor Child's Nurse." Opium, a pain reliever with effects similar to heroin, was popular among virtually all classes by the mid-1800s. While wealthy upper- and middle-class people might enjoy its effects upon their own disposition, working mothers found it to be a virtual necessity in terms of childcare. Advertised in New York in 1833, the hawkers of the infant sedative Godfrey's Cordial promised it was "most useful for young children who are weakly and restless": "[It] may be taken with perfect safety and success by children from birth."[25]

Godfrey's Cordial was as good as advertised at keeping infants asleep. That's because it contained laudanum, a tincture of opium, in a sweet syrup. An 1857 article in the *Brooklyn Evening Star* said it could "explain away your charitable wonder that the frequent beggar women who hold out imploring hands, and roll up patient eyes at Broadway stoops, should be blessed with brats of such accommodating sleepy headedness, by showing... that those infantile objects of your admiration are brought up to scratch with laudanum—fuddled continually and permanently stupefied at last."[26]

The permanent stupefaction part is important. It had become clear by the late 1850s that in many cases, Godfrey's Cordial was keeping children asleep forever—overdoses could kill them, and constant use weakened their health, leaving them susceptible to other ailments. By 1860, the *Philadelphia Inquirer,* writing about overdoses, implored mothers to "be more than careful of the sacred charge of little children. Do not, to ease your cares, sink them into unnatural slumber."[27]

Not drugging your infants to keep them quiet seems like a reasonable directive for mothers who were at home with their children. But it ignored the way the Industrial Revolution had changed women's lives. These mothers weren't drugging their kids because they wanted to; they were compelled to do so because they literally *couldn't* be at home with their children. And there was no money for anyone else to care for them. Single mothers like Ann found that, if they took time off from factory work to care for their child, they risked unemployment and starvation.

Essentially anesthetizing children was the only way to keep them calm for the hours parents had to be away from their families.

But couldn't an older child care for a younger one? Certainly there were women who attempted that solution. One excerpt from the *New-York Tribune* in 1844 describes a mother who left her infant in the care of his older brother with instructions to put the infant to sleep if he woke. When she returned, her toddler proudly reported that the baby woke up crying, but he put it back to sleep. "The mother, thinking it had slept long enough, went to take it up, when she discovered its head, horribly mangled. It appeared afterwards the boy, quite unconscious of the crime he was committing, had taken a hammer and beat the child on its head until the poor little thing fell asleep in death."[28]

In return for taking such risks, so as to give their full attention to work at a given factory, women were barely compensated. In the 1830s, Mathew Carey found that about 60 percent of women working sixteen hours a day could not earn more than $1.25 a week. That equates to $39 a week today. The economist Helen L. Sumner Woodbury noted in 1910 that women actually fared far better financially in work that was typically done by men, such as cigar making, as opposed to textile work. However, when "they have entirely displaced men, they have soon lost their economic advantage."[29]

Prostitution, understandably, struck many women as a better alternative to factory work. The journalist William Lloyd Garrison recalled an incident where a missionary attempted to dissuade a woman from the trade and she replied, "Instead of coming here you had better go around to some of these factories and shops that grind a poor girl down to $2 a week, and get them to pay better wages. It's no use; a girl can't live on what she gets."[30] Sex work allowed for both better wages and a freedom that factory and menial work did not offer. The hours were certainly more forgiving; frankly, the fact that sex workers could expect to get a good eight hours of sleep was something that many jobs at the time did not permit. Plus, a prostitute could earn enough money to have *someone* competent take care of her offspring, or even to send them to school. The money a woman could make—perhaps $50 a week as a prostitute—was substantially more than she could ever earn at a factory. Little wonder, then, that there were approximately 10,000 prostitutes in New York City by the 1840s. In 1846, the *New-York Tribune* quipped that there were "about as many prostitutes [in New York] as there are soldiers in the United States Army."[31]

For some women, sex work truly did prove superior to the alternatives, and it wasn't always as socially damning as one might expect. In the 1840s, Julia Brown, a former prostitute turned madam of New York's most elegant brothel, was not only accepted by high society but beloved by the wealthy. "Princess Julia" attended all the best soirees and maintained a friendship with Charles Dickens. Fanny White, another famous New York prostitute of the time, traveled abroad with a gentleman friend to meet Queen Victoria. There was also Helen Jewett, who "swept like a silken meteor through Broadway, the acknowledged queen of the promenade."[32] In addition to being a sex worker, Helen was a prolific letter writer, a talented seamstress, and a woman who didn't hesitate to take men who sexually harassed her to court. Her life was a rich and captivating one. The *Herald* described her as a "fascinating woman in conversation, full of intellect and refinement, with talents calculated for the highest sphere in life."[33] It is worth noting, however, that they were describing Helen as such after she'd been brutally beaten to death with an axe. She was likely murdered by one of her clients, Richard P. Robinson, who would defend himself of the charge by claiming, "I am a young man of only nineteen years of age yesterday, with most brilliant prospects!"[34] Infuriatingly, this sort of defense is still employed two hundred years later to defend young men who have committed crimes against women. Despite testimony from women in the brothel, Robinson was found not guilty. Helen's brilliant prospects were deemed unimportant.

All this to say—prostitution also had its disadvantages.

As James Miller explained in a paper on prostitution that ran in *The Edinburgh Medical Journal* during this era, "to the majority of women, the state of prostitution proves a grave, not a chrysalis-shell."[35] By the 1850s, Dr. William Sanger estimated that in New York, a woman would only work as a prostitute for, on average, four years before dying.[36] It was similarly estimated that only 2.35 percent of metropolitan prostitutes survived fourteen years in the business. It was a dangerous profession, because of the clientele, because of the squalor of many prostitutes' surroundings, and because of the potential for exposure to then untreatable sexually transmitted diseases. In July 1832, a New York paper reported that "a prostitute at 62 Mott Street who was decking herself before the glass at 1 o'clock yesterday, was carried away in a hearse at half past three o'clock. The broken-down constitutions of these miserable creatures, perish almost instantly on the attack."[37] Venereal diseases, such as syphilis, took a toll during a period when medical care, especially for the poor, was very limited. Half the prostitutes in New York at this time reported that they suffered from syphilis.[38]

This outlook also didn't bode well for the very children whose mothers had turned to prostitution. Children born to and raised by prostitutes were likely to enter the profession themselves. Given the short life expectancy of their mothers, they might do so at an early age, and so child prostitution became a problem in New York, as it was in other major cities. In his 1885 exposé, the journalist W. T. Stead talked to a brothel keeper in London who claimed, "Many women who are on the streets have female children. They are worth keeping. When they get to be twelve or thirteen, they become merchantable." Stead found that girls of this age were often drugged, whether by snuff or chloroform or laudanum, and then sold to men who wished to sleep with a virgin. When Stead remarked, horrified, to a police officer, "The very thought is enough to raise hell," the officer replied, "It is true and although it ought to raise hell, it does not even raise the neighbors."[39]

If Ann had chosen to moonlight as a prostitute, no one could have blamed her; a study by William Sanger in 1859 found that a quarter of the prostitutes in New York had tried working as seamstresses before turning to sex work.[40] Soon, Ann moved to Chatham Street, still on the outskirts of the Five Points. There, in 1850, as George Templeton Strong wrote, "after nightfall, amid the theaters, saloons, dance halls, and cheap lodging houses, the thoroughfare overflowed with 'members of the whorearchy in most slatternly deshabille.' "[41]

And it was there where she worked as a seamstress. Unless Ann was truly masterful—at a veritable Coco Chanel of Lower Manhattan level of mastery—she would not have been able to earn enough to support herself and her daughter. Helen L. Sumner Woodbury noted that women trying to make a living sewing during this period were in a particularly competitive situation. The fact that it was one of the few skills women were trained in meant that, in her words, "clothing trades...served as the general dumping ground of the unskilled, inefficient, and casual woman workers," creating "a condition of almost pure industrial anarchy."[42] The average seamstress made even less than a woman working in a factory—about $1.12 a week, *if* she was constantly employed. If you've ever encountered a novel from this period where a woman is in massive debt to her dressmaker and wondered why the dressmaker was allowing clients to run up absolutely insane debts, well, this is why. If you were at work as any kind of seamstress, you were lucky if people were offering you money at all.

Ann's situation looked desperate. During the day, she took in whatever clothing her neighbors might need mended. Every evening, she passed dozens of prostitutes, trying to make their way in a world that had abandoned them. It seemed likely she would join their number, and her daughter would probably have to do the same.

All this would surely have been the case, had Ann not been friendly with her neighbors.

CHAPTER THREE

VERY NEAR ANN'S NEW HOME ON CHATHAM STREET, THERE lived a pill compounder by the name of Dr. William Evans. He was, to put it mildly, a character. Being a successful pill compounder—rather like being someone who sells supplements today—was more dependent on having a big personality and being an excellent salesman than on having pills that worked. In an age prior to medical regulations, you could package more or less any powder in a pill and claim it was a miracle cure. Evans's numerous advertisements promised that his "chamomile pills" would relieve everything from "low spirits" to "constipation." "Hypochondriacism" was also on the list of ailments he promised to help—which is at least one malady that can be cured by sugar pills.[1] Most of the diseases he said his pills would relieve were, like "low spirits," things it would have been difficult to objectively assess. He claimed that he was "singularly effective" and that his pill formulas came from "the research of the most eminent medical men in the world."[2] He might have been, at the very least, prone to exaggeration.

Ann Trow Sommers was not a bit fazed by this. Throughout her life, she would appreciate men with big personalities. And if Evans was faking it until he made it, well, he was still doing better in his trade than she was as a seamstress. Before long, she began helping him with his work; in return, "to her he imparted many secrets of the business."[3]

It didn't take Ann long to figure out that she could produce her own wares. Soon, she was making pills that promised to help relieve liver, stomach, and lung ailments, the latter largely brought on by consumption, a bacterial disease that destroys the patient's lung tissue. The efficacy of this medication is, frankly, dubious. Consumption, for instance, can only be cured by a course of antibiotics that were unavailable until the 1940s. That said, even if Ann's promises were ambitious and overblown, people in the neighborhood believed that her pills worked. And she began to gain renown for them.

Soon after Ann began manufacturing pills, one woman came to her with a request for a medicine that would help induce an abortion. Ann knew what happened to women in her neighborhood without contraception. Unwanted pregnancy was a disaster for them, and for any other children they might already have. Ann could see the effects outside her window every day of her life. So she didn't hesitate to provide a service. Whether it was to prevent pregnancy or end one, the pill seemed to have served its purpose. Unlike "low spirits," which may naturally fluctuate, you can tell fairly easily whether you are pregnant.

And just as Ann Trow Sommers wasn't the only woman who had planned to make it in New York as a seamstress, that woman wasn't the only one who desperately needed birth control options. Ann quickly found that her new pills "speedily sold so extensively that she gave up tailoring."[4]

What Ann was doing in providing a version of an abortive pill was by no means revolutionary in itself. For as long as women have been expecting, there have been methods to end a pregnancy. The first clear written description of abortion dates back to 1550 BCE in Egypt, when women who wished to abort turned to one of the remedies described in the *Ebers Papyrus*, an ancient medical text, which suggested that following its protocols would "cause all to come out which is in the stomach of a woman."[5] Its advice included inserting warm oil and fat into the vagina, or inserting a plant-based pessary, much like a tampon or suppository. The pessary was coated in "unripe fruit of acacia, colocynth, crushed...and 6/7 a pint of honey." Remarkably, this isn't as outlandish a treatment as it might seem. During fermentation, the acacia plant produces lactic acid, which kills sperm and is still used in spermicides today. According to Vicki Oransky Wittenstein, the author of *Reproductive Rights: Who Decides?*, this is an abortion method "modern researchers think may actually have worked."[6] It seems at least preferable to another recipe for abortion pessaries, mentioned in the *Kahun Papyrus*, in which crocodile dung mixed with dough was inserted into the vagina.[7]

Pessaries like these were decried by the Greek physician Hippocrates in the fourth and fifth centuries BCE, whom antiabortion advocates frequently reference in their defense. After all, the Hippocratic Oath states, "I will give no deadly medicine to anyone if asked, nor suggest any such counsel; and in like manner, I will not give to a woman an abortive pessary."[8]

Some suggest that this language, in addition to the oath's admonition to "do no harm," means that Hippocrates regarded fetuses as people to whom no harm should be done. In truth, though, claiming that the Hippocratic oath is antiabortion because it is anti-pessary is a bit like claiming someone is anti-beverage because they don't believe in drinking poison. *Diseases in Women*, a treatise attributed to Hippocrates though likely the work of numerous physicians, explicitly explains how they could produce disastrous results: "Suppose, after an abortion, a woman receives a serious lesion or that she causes ulcerations in her uterus with harsh pessaries (such as women produce in treating themselves and others), and her fetus is destroyed and the woman herself is not cleansed, but her uterus becomes very inflamed and closes?"[9] Pessaries weren't very good for the women themselves. They could die or lose their ability to become pregnant in the future.

Pessaries rarely produced a "clean" result. They were effective precisely because they were harmful. They were not made of sanitary materials. For instance, some contained, among other things, beetles that produced a toxic substance called cantharid. Others included "a head of boiled garlic."[10] Surely the thought of inserting either beetles or boiled garlic into one's vagina is enough to make a modern woman shudder. These ingredients were intended to irritate a woman's insides, often causing infection, which was what ultimately destroyed the fetus. In the process, they could cause great impairment, increasing a woman's risk of vaginal infections, including toxic shock syndrome. TSS would account for the descriptions of women dying with very high fevers in ancient Greece.[11]

Hippocrates and physicians like him didn't recommend the kind of abortive attempt they knew produced poor results for their patients. Doing so would have gone against the code of ethics. *Diseases in Women* did, however, recommend alternative means to induce miscarriage, such as strenuous exercise, including leaping so that a woman's heels touched her butt, or "shaking [a woman] under the armpits."[12] In a less exercise-based approach, it prescribed Queen Anne's lace, a wildflower herb that could be an effective means of contraception and abortifacient. Ingesting seeds from Queen Anne's lace prevents the production of progesterone, which is necessary for pregnancy. Women in Appalachia, India, and other underserved regions still use the seeds today as an (imperfect) kind of herbal morning-after pill.[13]

Queen Anne's lace isn't the only plant with a supposed ability to prevent pregnancy. Pennyroyal served much the same purpose. Like Queen Anne's lace, its use dated back to ancient Greece, where a play by Aristophanes, *Lysistrata*, describes a desirable young woman as being "trimmed and spruced with pennyroyal."[14] The implication being, not only was that woman good-looking, she was also free to have sex without fear of pregnancy—a combination that has been desirable in virtually any time period. Herbs such as rue and gingerroot were commonly used to achieve the same end. Abortive remedies have also long been part of American society. Benjamin Franklin even included a recipe in his book of general knowledge, *The Instructor.* It suggested that "unmarry'd women" suffering from a "suppression of courses" (today better known as a missed period) consume pennyroyal mixed with twelve drops of spirits of hartshorn.[15]

It is likely that the preventative powders Madame Restell marketed were composed of these varied natural ingredients. She may even have suggested they go into a tea.

Her pills, though, were more popular, likely because the powders cost $5 a package while a box of the pills, or a vial of liquid, could be purchased for only $1.[16] The pills were meant to be employed if the powders—which were intended to act like a birth control pill—failed.

While her admirers clamored for them, her detractors scoffed that the pills contained nothing of value. Some men believed that a young and barely educated immigrant woman must be a scam artist. One of these critics, a man named Dr. Jacobi, later claimed that Madame Restell's wares were nothing but "bread coated with sugar" that she sold for $100.[17] This doctor may have been attempting to do Restell a favor or to save his own skin, though her professional pride would certainly not allow her to appreciate it. As he made this assertion, he was on trial himself for performing abortions. His defense hinged upon the notion that everything abortionists sold was a mere "humbug" and that members of the profession were charlatans, not murderers. Still, even more recent historians, such as Clifford Browder, likely due to a reasonable level of skepticism regarding homeopathic cures, have claimed that Restell's products "were ineffective if not downright fake."[18]

This would appear to be an unfair assessment.

Certainly, no birth control or abortifacient used in the mid-nineteenth century came near to being as effective as today's methods. However, two hundred years from now, chemotherapy—with its array of often miserable side effects—might seem like a horribly primitive way to attempt to cure cancer. But in the absence of a better method to eliminate the disease, it does not mean that people who receive chemotherapy now are foolish or being conned.

At least through the 1830s, Madame Restell's pills appear to have been made of ergot of rye and cantharides. Ergot of rye is a fungus that develops specifically on rye plants. The primary source of cantharides is the dried bodies of blister beetles, also known as Spanish flies (*Lytta vesicatoria*). Both of these ingredients were considered effective abortifacients at the time. One journal from 1844 wrote that "cantharides in [small] doses...would not endanger life, but would be likely to produce an abortion....Ergot of rye would be the most efficient medical agent to procure abortion by acting specifically on the uterus."[19] Later, in the 1840s, Madame Restell seemed to have refined her methods. An examination prompted by the doctor of one of her more reticent patients found the vial she'd been given to be filled with "oil of tansy and spirits of turpentine."[20]

Now, there is a wide gulf between wholly ineffective, on the one hand, and effective and safe, on the other. For example, swallowing turpentine, which is often used as a paint thinner, might seem like a bad idea. It is in fact a *terrible* idea. Pregnant women (or anyone, for that matter) absolutely should *not* swallow turpentine or, for that matter, tansy oil. Even doctors at the time were aware of this peril. The doctor who examined the mixture Restell was selling declared that he thought they were "among the most dangerous preparations that could be taken."[21]

However, the fact that these remedies were dangerous doesn't mean the ingredients were combined without reason. Because, like ergot of rye and cantharides, the combination of turpentine and tansy oil was thought to be successful in ending a pregnancy.

Sadly, these are still ingredients that women with few legal options use to induce abortions to this day. One doctor told the *Guardian* that, within the world of DIY abortions, "turpentine became a kind of harrowing motif."[22] The same doctor recalled a woman in the 1970s injecting turpentine directly into her abdomen. As recently as 2006, the mother of a teen in Columbus, Ohio, was accused of forcing her daughter to drink turpentine in order to induce an abortion. Regarding the case, a local doctor said that turpentine "is a known substance that has been used in abortions. The problem [is] it will cause an abortion and it will cause you to die.... [F]or the fetus to die the mother has to be dead or near death."[23]

Tansy oil is less well known for its abortive properties. Coming from a yellow flowered plant, the oil was traditionally used to embalm bodies. While it can be safely used to treat skin ailments and as an insect repellent, it can be extremely deadly if taken orally. As little as ten drops might be fatal.[24] It is considered especially dangerous for pregnant women, as it can cause uterine contractions and lead to a miscarriage. Which, of course, is what some pregnant women want.

In 1839, the *New York Daily Herald* reported that a woman by the name of Sarah "wished to procure an abortion without the aid of Madame Restell." She proceeded to take a quarter of an ounce of tansy oil. Doctors would later claim this was "too much by half"; she died a few hours after ingesting it.[25]

As with turpentine, prior to the legalization of abortion in America, many women intentionally drank teas that contained herbs such as tansy, pennyroyal, and rue in order to provoke a miscarriage. Even today, while less common, this practice has not vanished. In 2012, the *New York Times Magazine* published a harrowing account wherein a woman drank tea composed of herbs (including tansy oil) to induce her second abortion.[26] She did so while composing goodbye letters to her loved ones in case the tea killed her.

In regard to Madame Restell's clinic, what's remarkable is not so much that women flocked to her door, but that Madame Restell seems to have managed the dosage of these incredibly dangerous ingredients in such a way that her patients not only survived but became repeat customers. One woman even claimed that Restell's pills successfully caused her to miscarry five times.

During this period, Ann's brother, Joseph Trow, followed his sister to New York. He found work located near her as a sales assistant at a pharmacy. In addition to providing him with stable income, it ensured he had ample skill with which to help his sister in the production of her pills when demand began to outstrip her individual ability.

But Joseph wasn't the only supportive man in her life.

In late 1835, Ann met Charles Lohman, the man who would become her second husband. Twenty-six years old, he was a Russian immigrant who, after moving to the Lower East Side, had found work as a printer for the *New York Herald*. Charles was later said to be "a fine looking man of very genial disposition, joyful nature, and very fond of conviviality and a good glass of wine."[27] Another paper posthumously declared him "just a good, ink-fingered, hard drinking fellow."[28] Ann may have been very kind to people in need, and a charming conversationalist, but it's hard to consider someone of her professional determination to be as easygoing as Charles was made out to be. At a time when her work was consuming much of her days, it might have been a relief for Ann to spend time with an upbeat fellow. The biographer Browder speculates that literary inclinations might have brought them together—George Mastell's bookshop, which carried works by figures such as Voltaire and Thomas Paine, was located at 94 Chatham Street, near Ann's home. This is by no means certain, but it's pleasant to imagine their hands touching as they reached for a volume of *Eugene Onegin*.

But while her fondness for reading may have been part of Ann's appeal to Charles, her greater lure may have lain in the fact that the young widow was clearly unwilling to remain poor. Like Ann, Charles was drawn to America's promise of prosperity for all. As an atheist he was also attracted to America's Enlightenment philosophy and the idea of a country where church and state were separate. In this, he may have vastly overestimated America's tolerance. But then, so did Ann. Ann would eventually join an Episcopalian church for the social access it provided, but Charles would remain a staunch nonbeliever. Even so, the pair found themselves, at least initially, excellently matched. They both believed in a future where they could cast off outmoded ideas and get rich, and were mutually frustrated that, despite making the arduous journey to America, "the iron grip of poverty still continued to bear relentlessly upon them."[29] By 1836, Ann Trow Sommers had become Mrs. Ann Lohman. In the same year, Charles, excited about the promise of his adopted country, became a US citizen.

Many newspapers credited Ann's second husband with launching her career as an abortionist and birth control provider. Some claimed he was surely "a professor of her art," and that he must have "school[ed] the woman in her uncanny art."[30] Clearly, it must have been he who produced the pills and taught her how to perform the abortions. This was declared despite ample evidence to the contrary—Charles was a good-natured printer at a newspaper with no medical training when he met his wife, and she had learned about pills from an entirely differ-ent man whose trade she immediately surpassed. Some of those writers believed that women were utterly inept; others imagined that a woman in a field they regarded as wicked must be compelled by a Svengali-like man who controlled her.

It's a tiresome and, unfortunately, still true fact that, if men like something a woman does, they assume another man must have helped her do it. If they hate something a woman did, on the other hand, they assume a man must have *made* her do it. There's no indication that Ann was coerced in any way by her second husband; what's more, there's no indication she was anything but obstinate when it came to people telling her what to do. Whatever one thinks of her actions, she deserves the dignity of autonomy so often denied to women in history.

There was plenty in Ann's background and circumstances to indi-cate that her decision to induce abortions stemmed entirely from her own worldview. She'd lived her whole life in poverty, and she had seen what happened to women and children trapped within it. She was empathetic toward other working women's concerns. She also wanted to make money, and the profits from her pills were undeniable. Last but certainly not least, she was not puritanical in her attitude toward sex. So, let us say she did not take up her trade because a man forced her. In all likelihood, she took it up because she was good at it, people had a need for it, and her business quickly became lucrative. After the challenges she experienced while married to her first husband, it's also doubtful she was eager to rely upon a man for her income ever again.

Regardless of his role in its origins, it was Charles who took Ann's career to a whole new level. In many ways he would prove to be the man behind the woman. While Ann was no longer working as a seamstress, the pair still lived with daily financial concerns. It's true that the threat of penury and prostitution no longer hovered over Ann's head, but they were still living in fairly miserable conditions. If both of them desired the level of wealth that had at least partially motivated them to come to America in the first place, then Ann's business had to expand beyond catering exclusively to the residents of Lower Manhattan.

During his time working at the *Herald*, Charles came across many advertisements in the newspaper for pills like the ones his wife was producing. Ann likewise had seen her mentor Dr. Evans's profusion of ads filled with outlandish claims. She and Charles realized that they had to start advertising. Seemingly deciding that Ann's actual life story might not be enough to inspire confidence among the wealthier denizens of the city, they thought about what sort of woman people with money to spare *would* visit.

So, they dreamed up a woman from France. Specifically, a female physician who had worked at hospitals in Paris and Vienna, two very romantic cities that it seems extremely unlikely either Ann or Charles had ever visited. They even claimed she had inherited the craft. It had been her French grandmother who had devised the recipe for her pills, which, in France, had received accolades for their "efficacy, healthiness and safety" for thirty years.[31] Anyone who met Restell and noted her British accent could probably tell this was not true. But then, as often now, Americans viewed Europeans, and especially the French, as being more advanced and sophisticated in their sexual mores than their countrymen. If anyone was going to help manage one's birth control and abortive needs, you could do far worse than going to a nonjudgmental, worldly Frenchwoman with many lovers.

Gradually, Madame Restell came to life.

Her creation proved to be a dazzling, and very effective, lie.

CHAPTER FOUR

C REATING THIS PERSONA AND HAVING A RELENTLESS ADVERTIS-
ing campaign would prove essential to Madame Restell's success in a growing industry. Despite her medicine's almost immediate
popularity, she was not the only person—let alone woman—of this
age to offer abortions and abortive pills. This was a time when abortion was, if not quite legal, still commonly accepted. Some states had
passed laws against it, New York among them, but the punishment,
if convicted for inducing an abortion, either through instruments or
drugs, was a year in jail or a $100 fine. Considering that practitioners
could charge up to $100 for an abortion, the fine was not a sufficient
deterrent. More challenging would be putting aside the money for
advertising; by 1839, Madame Restell was paying around $1,000 a year
for advertising in two of the city's most popular papers: the *Sun* and
the *Herald*.[1]

There was no shortage of others doing the same. A Dr. Bell promised to cure "irregularity of females," and a Dr. Ward promised to put
an end to "female obstruction" while a Dr. Vanderbaugh offered "an
effective remedy for suppression."[2] A Dr. Leroy, meanwhile, offered
pills that he said "seldom fail to produce regularity."[3] Even Madame
Restell's own Dr. Evans, by 1837, was promising pills that could treat
"female debility."[4]

But Restell's primary competition from other women came from
two particular providers: Madame Costello and Mrs. Bird. By 1837,
Mrs. Bird's business was well underway at 7 Division Street, not far
from Madame Restell's location. In the *Herald*, Mrs. Bird advertised
her "celebrated aperient [laxative] and tonic renovating vegetable
pills." With these she promised to cure everything from headaches to

rheumatism, including, most notably, "the sickness incident to females in delicate health." Coupled with her promise to provide midwifery and assurances that she had been "duly qualified in a lying-in hospital in Europe," savvy readers could deduce that she was offering birth control.[5]

By 1840, Madame Costello, who operated from an office at 31 Lispenard Street, began promoting a "female monthly pill" that she said was "acknowledged by the first physicians in the United States as the very best medicine that ladies laboring under a suppression of their natural illness can take."[6] Put simply, that suppression meant not getting your monthly period. Like Madame Restell, "Madame" Costello had been born with a different name, Catherine Ames, and had adopted a more European-sounding one. Unlike Madame Restell, she wasn't even *from* Europe; rather, she was from Boston.

Neither of these women had more credentials than Madame Restell, and they certainly had not been trained in Europe. No one grinding out abortive pills in Lower Manhattan had trained in Europe. But all these women were ambitious and competitive, and determined to eliminate their rivals at any cost.

However, with Charles's help, Madame Restell would craft the kind of ad that would grab people's attention as none of her competitors could.

While Mrs. Bird and Madame Costello ran advertisements that would be understood by anyone who could read between the lines, Madame Restell's statements were unmistakably direct. Her ad in the *Herald* was addressed "to Married Women" and announced that "Madame Restell, Female Physician," was "happy to have it in her power to say that since the introduction into this country, about a year ago, of her celebrated preventative powders for married ladies whose health prevents too rapid an increase of family, hundreds have availed themselves of their use, with success and satisfaction."[7]

Not only did she explicitly promise family limitation, but her ads took it a step further: They argued that it was *moral* to limit the size of one's family. After describing the pill's success both in America and abroad, the ads pondered the matter (in text that seemed to owe a great deal to Robert Dale Owen, a writer who preached the benefits of family limitation):

Is it not but too well known that the families of the married often increase beyond the happiness of those who give them birth would dictate? In how many instances does the hardworking father, and more especially the mother, of a poor family, remain slaves throughout their lives, tugging at the oar of incessant labor, toiling to live and living but to toil when they might have enjoyed comparative affluence?... How often, alas, are the days of the kind husband and father embittered in beholding the emaciated form and declining health of the companion of his bosom ere she had scarce reached the age of thirty—fast sinking into a premature grave—with the certain prospect of himself being early bereft of the partner of his joys and sorrows, and his young and helpless children of the endearing attentions which a mother alone can bestow?... Is it desirable then, is it moral, for parents to increase their families regardless of the consequences to themselves or the wellbeing to their offspring when a simple, easy, healthy, and CERTAIN remedy is within our control?[8]

These arguments were, in all likelihood, not entirely novel to people at the time. Even today, having numerous children is expensive. And, as anyone who has given birth can tell you, it takes a toll physically. But it would have been astonishing to see the case laid out so clearly in 1839. Finally, someone not just saying aloud but putting into print what many had long felt.

Restell's ads made clear that, if you were pregnant and did not wish to be, well, here was a woman who would not only help but applaud your decision.

When the editor of the *New York Star* criticized Madame Restell for offering birth control, claiming that she was "violating the decrees of divine providence, every law of social order and trampling upon the institutions of society," she was quick to offer a public retort in the *Herald*. She first reminded him of his privilege, declaring, "If the Editor of the *Star*, on entering into married life was either already possessed or had come into possession, by doing so, of the comfort and affluence necessary to the proper enjoyment of life, he must remember there are thousands of others not so fortunate." After casting him as an out-of-touch elite, she explained that if she was violating divine providence, "every attempt to arrest the march of pestilence or death, every endeavor to ameliorate the social condition of the human family, or counteract or prevent the destructive consequences arising from the rage of the elements, to erect lightning rods to thwart heaven's artillery, decries the protection and bounty of Divine Providence."[9]

To this day, likening birth control and abortion to a social good akin to a lightning rod in an article *that ran on Christmas Day* would be a pretty bold claim. But, as one of her ads stated in April 1840, "Madame Restell need offer no apology to her sex in urging the absolute necessity of using remedies which have proved to be safe, mild and efficacious."[10] She also doled out pamphlets free of charge titled "Suggestions to the Married," detailing methods of family limitation.[11] These pamphlets, dressed as thinly veiled advertisements, further encouraged women to buy her preventative powders.

The editor of the *Star* wasn't the only one outraged. Restell's ads were denounced as "obnoxious" by newspapers as far away as Lancaster, Pennsylvania. Her ads, needless to say, did not run in these papers. Critics doggedly persisted in claiming, also in print, that her ideology was "a gross outrage against society and nature."[12]

However, those ads also made Madame Restell famous—almost overnight.

In a world of polite, discreet abortionists, Madame Restell stood out. She became widely known as *the* abortionist of New York City, despite the fact that Madame Costello and Mrs. Bird had taken to their trade at about the same time.

Never content to rest on her laurels, Madame Restell then started denouncing her competitors as con artists.

She began by stressing that her signature was on each box of her pills, giving the impression that any other similar pills were knockoffs. Customers should accept no substitutions. She further cautioned readers of her ads against "the innumerable worthless if not injurious compounds continually thrust before public notice, accompanied with spurious letters and certificates of cure."[13]

Madame Costello and Mrs. Bird didn't stand a chance. Mrs. Bird, perhaps realizing there was no way to compete with someone practically shouting for women to use birth control *now*, expanded her business to cater to women with children. By 1840, she was advertising herself as "a blessing to mothers" and selling a soothing tonic "for children cutting their teeth," as well as "Mrs. Bird's Nipple Salve."[14] She did not stop performing abortions at her lying-in hospital, where she could tend to women "however distressing may be their complaints."[15] She just thought she might be able to distinguish herself as a female physician who also catered to mothers.

And despite her best efforts, she failed.

That was not merely because Madame Restell had superior advertisements, but because she never had Madame Restell's skills. The most remarkable aspect of Madame Restell's practice is that, despite some accusations, there's little evidence that any patients died in her care. The same can't be said of Mrs. Bird. In 1841, she was found trying to clandestinely dispose of a coffin that contained the body of a seventeen-year-old patient who had died after hemorrhaging.[16] Mrs. Bird would go on practicing medicine, but, unlike Madame Restell, she was never able to attract an upper-crust clientele.

Madame Costello was more tenacious. She was a forty-year-old widow when she entered the health-care profession, and she had no intention of being outshone by a recent immigrant in her twenties. Even after Restell's business started taking off, Costello continued to perform abortions, but it was said that she was "a humble imitation of Madame Restell, without her genius, and also without her wickedness."[17] By "wickedness," her critic from *The Polyanthos*, a New York newspaper, likely meant Madame Restell's absolutely unapologetic nature. By December 1839, Restell claimed to have four hundred letters from grateful customers. Costello gamely continued to advertise her Female Periodical Pills with a coded approach, explaining that they were for cases "where monthly periods have become irregular from colds, etc." Optimistically attributing a missed period to a cold is certainly a different approach than the Malthusian panic Madame Restell evoked in her ads. Madame Costello also assured prospective clients that she had hundreds of satisfied patrons as if to stress that Madame Restell was not the only one with appreciative customers.

Madame Restell did not take kindly to Madame Costello's claims of great success. Years later, in 1843, directly next to one of Madame Costello's ads in the *Herald*, Restell ran her own ad, headlined "Caution to Females." In it, she detailed her expertise and personal care for her patients as authentic and impossible to replicate asserting, "She [Restell] does not wish to be classed with the pretenders continually appearing and disappearing, advertising as 'Female Physicians' who, too ignorant and incompetent themselves, are obliged to get some scarcely less ignorant quack to experiment instead."[18]

It never seemed to occur to Madame Restell that instead of trying to eliminate each other as competition, these women could have banded together to become a collective of like-minded professionals. In retrospect, this seems wildly shortsighted of her. Sharing information as respectful colleagues, at the very least, would have helped them refine their skills. Better, more reliable products might have meant more patrons for all of them as the word of successful abortive pills spread. They could certainly have divided up the city, and each agreed to serve certain neighborhoods. Beyond the short-term benefit, if they had come together as a unit working toward a common goal—widely accessible birth control and abortion to limit family size—and spoken out as a collective, recruiting other women to that cause, history might have run differently. But how could Madame Restell have focused on such ideas when she was still just trying to climb her way out of poverty? After all, she wasn't an activist trying to get people to rally around a cause. She was just trying to find a way to afford a better life for her family. If business kept up, she could afford a nice house in a lovely neighborhood. Perhaps she could make enough money to, eventually, send her young daughter to a good school.

Mundane concerns like these are usually the ones that make the world run.

At the end of the day, Madame Restell was still young. If she saw any dark clouds forming over America regarding the industry of abortion and those who opposed it, she likely imagined these concerns would pass. She was earning far more than any fine she might have to pay, and that was the worst outcome she was worried about. She was not interested in making friends or allies in the business; she was interested in making money. Eliminating her competitors by shaming them and causing people to doubt their skills helped. Her ads may have had the airs of a moral philosopher, but she was—at heart—a businesswoman.

Chapter Five

B Y JUNE 1839, BUSINESS WAS BOOMING.
The advertising and the persona Madame Restell had so carefully crafted served their purpose. If you were a New Yorker who read newspapers at all, you were acquainted with her as Madame Restell's ads were running continuously in the *New York Daily Herald*. They were so numerous that, in response to a Dr. Carpenter canceling his advertising, as he did not feel he was being respectfully served, the editor jokingly responded, "To lose Doctor Carpenter, under the circumstances, is to lose one's best and oldest, kindest friend. In my heart I estimate him as much—no, not as much—but very nearly as much as I do that pretty Madame Restell, female physician to the human race, for improving the offspring by limiting their number, and bettering the breed, office at 160 Greenwich Street."[1]

This address, to which she'd moved earlier that year, was already a step up from Madame Restell's original office. Her new workplace was outfitted in such a way as to inspire her customers' confidence in her medical expertise. The lighting was subdued, and the walls were decorated with "anatomical plates, specimens of anatomy...and other curious and instructive illustrations of her particular doctrine."[2] Visiting a doctor's office adorned with "specimens of anatomy"—perhaps a skeleton in the waiting room—might strike some as unnerving, but such items were doubtless helpful in explaining her methods. The average person's anatomical knowledge at the time would have been extremely limited, and having visuals on hand to illustrate her approach would be useful. Madame Restell also had staff. The door to her office was said to be manned by an elderly woman, to whom patients stated their case before being introduced to Madame Restell. This may have served as an early screening system, though it would be years before Madame Restell was beset by blackmailers or undercover journalists. Right now, her industry was only beginning to expand.

Even in the short term, 160 Greenwich Street would not be her only business address. Restell's advertisements bragged that she sold over two thousand boxes of pills in New York City in only five months. This was probably somewhat exaggerated, but she was undeniably having a great deal of success. Sensing growth opportunities, she expanded to Philadelphia, where she opened a satellite office at 39 South Eighth Street. She explained to the citizens of Philadelphia that she had done so "in consequence to the great demand for her medicines in this city, and the great inconvenience, as well as expense of sending for them from New York."[3]

By age twenty-nine, Madame Restell was well on her way to creating an empire. But it was one that required more than pills alone.

Madame Restell may have been very good at her pharmaceutics, but her pills were not infallible, and she was known to be performing surgical abortions as well. One patient in need of a surgical abortion would be the same woman who said she had miscarried five times after taking Restell's pills. Madame Restell informed her, "I can probe you, but I must have my price for the operation."[4] The patient asked what she would use for this probe, and Restell replied, "A piece of whale bone." The woman elected to probe herself with whalebone rather than paying Restell for the operation.

This was a poor decision on her part; afterward, she had to have a hysterectomy.

The notion of using a sharpened whalebone to cause an abortion is eerily reminiscent of the way coat hangers have been employed to a similar end. Indeed, a whalebone might also come from a woman's closet and achieve the same shape if she were to pull one from her corset and sharpen it. The procedure would likely be much the same with either device. The whalebone would have to be inserted through the cervical os (the opening to the uterus). Doing so would require a remarkably steady hand, as well as knowledge of the appropriate amount of force to use. Even the smallest error could perforate the bowels (which can kill a woman) or the uterine artery (which can also kill a woman). If the procedure was a success, this wouldn't happen, and the woman would miscarry in two or three days. Yet, even then, she ran the risk of becoming septic, and dying as a result of the infection.[5]

Again, what is truly extraordinary here is that, despite extensive investigations into Restell's practice later on, as well as an eagerness on behalf of the public to track down the names of women who died at her hands, there is little evidence of Restell losing patients. Which begs the question—how did she learn to perform such a complex operation so effectively?

Restell's public résumé alleged that she had learned from French relatives. Newspapers would go on to parrot this, with a *New York Daily Herald* piece (surprisingly, not in one of her own advertisements) declaring that "her [Restell's] Grandmother was an eminent female physician in Paris, and she has studied the science under the first medical minds, both male and female, of France."[6] It is a very glamorous story. This would have been comforting to many people, not simply because French people seem sexy and sophisticated, but also because France was thought to be on the forefront of surgical innovation. While American doctors flocked to different cities in Europe throughout the nineteenth century to gain knowledge of medical techniques, the period from 1820 to 1860 was known as the "Paris Period" because of the medical innovation that occurred there. Within the City of Lights, doctors could follow Parisian physicians through free clinics, watch various operations, and attend lectures on medical subjects at renowned institutions, including the Sorbonne. American schools, by comparison, lacked the large hospitals with hundreds of patients where doctors could gain firsthand knowledge. Most American medical schools through the 1840s did not even require their students to go to hospitals, and only about half required students to dissect a human cadaver.[7]

If Madame Restell had studied in France, as she claimed, it would connote a level of knowledge about the body and its functions that many of her American peers lacked.

Regrettably, this claim was a lie.

What we do know is that Madame Restell—or Ann Lohman—was a British immigrant who had worked as a servant and seamstress prior to her career as an abortionist. For her assertion about being trained in surgical and abortive arts by a French grandmother to be true, there would have to be unaccounted-for years in Restell's life story. Much though she might have wished, she simply did not have time to train in France and learn medical arts. She was extremely busy taking in people's laundry and trying to keep herself and her young child alive on New York's Lower East Side.

But surely, she learned how to perform abortions from someone.

Restell was certainly well read—and took immense pride in reading a great deal—but she wasn't someone who taught herself skills from books. In the case of her work as a seamstress, she learned from her first husband, a tailor, and then quickly exceeded his skills in the arena. The same can be said of learning to make pills from the pill compounder who lived near her. She surpassed her mentors routinely, but she did typically have a mentor.

As for such a medical mentor, there are a few possibilities.

First, it's hard to overstate how unglamorous surgery was during the early 1800s. In 1796, it was stated by Lord Edward Thurlow in the British Parliament that "there is no more science in surgery than in butchering." This comment prompted one surgeon, a Mr. John Gunning, to reply, "Then I heartily pray your lordship may break your leg and have only a butcher to set it."[8] As sassy as this response may have been, Thurlow wasn't entirely wrong. That's because surgery, prior to the invention of anesthetic in 1846, was a positively terrifying process. Up to 50 percent of patients undergoing surgery died during their procedure—which is one reason hospitals made them pay in advance. Patients knew they might leave with fewer body parts than they'd had· upon entering. Even Robert Liston, considered one of the finest surgeons of the period, once accidentally sliced off a patient's testicle in addition to the leg he was amputating.

Surgery was rarely performed unless the patient seemed likely to die anyway, although some changed their minds when they saw the operating room. Patients would be bound with leather straps to a blood-soaked table, and, as anesthesia did not exist, they would watch while surgeons employed a saw on their extremities. This was so terrifying that in one instance a patient Liston was about to treat for a bladder stone leapt off the table and locked himself in the lavatory. As Dr. Lindsey Fitzharris wrote in *The Butchering Art*, "Liston, hot on his heels, broke the door down and dragged the screaming patient back to the operating room. There, he bound the man fast before passing a curved metal tube up the patient's penis and into the bladder." Needless to say, surgeons were not held in the high regard they are today.[9] In fact, prior to the educational reforms that began in 1815, surgeons were not even considered respected members of the medical establishment. Fitzharris noted that "many surgeons...didn't attend university. Some were even illiterate."[10]

In her youth, Madame Restell had worked for a butcher. Doing so meant seeing the cadavers of animals, if not humans. Depending on how much the butcher liked to demonstrate his methods to his employees, it's possible that she had a very vague understanding of anatomical composition. Again, considering that some of her fellow surgeons had no dissection experience at *all*, this background would have stood her in good stead. Of course, animal cadavers are not human ones. Any attempts to educate yourself about body composition from them would be a process filled with errors, but it's a technique that has been used before. Galen, the well-known physician and surgeon of the Roman Empire, based his study of human anatomy entirely on animal corpses. This led to some serious missteps—for instance, he believed the female uterus was divided into numerous chambers and looked something like a dog's. Still, if Madame Restell were literate and versed in a bit of anatomy, she might have been almost on par with some of her less esteemed peers. However, as far as actually performing abortions, her notable success rate would imply a method of trial and error that should have left more of her patients dead or injured than is generally thought to be the case.

What is most likely is that Dr. Evans, the man who taught Restell the art of compounding pills, was doing more than just serving as an apothecary. Fitzharris remarked that "a man who had been apprenticed to a surgeon might also act as an apothecary.... [T]he surgeon apothecary was a doctor of first resort for the poor."[11] This was probably the case with Evans. His advertisements declared that his "knowledge of medical and surgical practice has been derived from the best schools in England and Scotland." While the notion that he attended the best schools may have been the kind of exaggeration he was prone to, the claim that he possessed serious surgical skills was probably not. In fact, the same advertisement noted that some of his patients visited him because of "the deviations of the infatuated from morality."[12] It's reasonable to assume he performed surgical abortions. If Madame Restell became more popular than her mentor, it may have been primarily because she was absolutely more public about the services she provided. It also seems entirely possible that women were more comfortable seeing another woman about their birth control needs than a man. Or perhaps she was just more skilled and innately possessed of a steadier hand than Dr. Evans.

Ultimately, Madame Restell offered her female patients medications and treatments that were as effective as anything the age had to offer. More importantly, she was providing them without any sense of shame or secrecy. For women in need of her services, that made her simply irresistible.

CHAPTER SIX

G IVEN HER BACKGROUND STORY AND HER PROLIFIC MEDICAL practice, it was only a matter of time until Madame Restell became famous. When the newspapers began profiling her, they found her to be exceedingly charming. On June 21, 1839, the *New York Daily Herald* cheerfully declared that the city was experiencing "Another Move in Philosophy—a Beautiful Female Physician." The physician at the heart of this article was none other than Madame Restell, whose looks, as much as her work, would be commented upon for years to come.

The paper noted that, in addition to being beautiful, "Madame Restell herself appears, from her writing and conversation, to be a woman of great scientific acquirements—of a remarkable knowledge of medical science—and withal beautiful, accomplished and ladylike in her manners and deportment."[1] The *Herald* further stated that Restell's methods were "directed towards the improvement, the elevation, the amelioration of the human race." Searching back through history, the writer determined that "the wonderful physical and intellectual superiority of the Egyptians, the Hebrews, the Persians, the Greeks, the Romans, during their periods of culmination were produced and caused by a similar process and system now used by Madame Restell."

That last note of praise was not *entirely* correct. While many of those civilizations did employ methods of birth control and abortion, that's not true of the Persians. In fact, they were so firmly opposed to abortion that, if a woman was found to have procured one, she would be sentenced to death, as would her sexual partner and any midwife who helped her. If a woman miscarried for any reason, she was whipped four hundred times before being made to drink cow's urine, to "wash over the grave in the womb."[2] But then, ancient Persia supposedly

possessed a truly overwhelming treasure trove of terrifying punishments (for instance, according to the ancient historian Herodotus, a
judge who accepted bribes was flayed and his skin made into a chair
for future judges to sit on), so it's possible that their punishments
regarding abortion did not stand out to the *Herald* writer.

That minor mistake aside, the article was problematic in other ways:
the notion that you could employ birth control to breed a superrace of
humans, for example, is an aspect of eugenics. A staggering number of
Americans would go on to embrace this outlook in decades to come,
but it doesn't seem anywhere close to Restell's intent. If Madame Restell was trying to improve the race, she did not mention as much in
her advertisements. But her advertisements were very clear in their
assertion that having too many children could bankrupt families and
kill women.

The fact that effusive praise came from the *New York Daily Herald*
wasn't entirely surprising, given how regularly she was advertising in
its pages. But even if her ads hadn't been a source of revenue for the
paper, Restell might have found an enthusiastic, intrigued champion
in the *Herald's* editor, James Gordon Bennett.

Like Madame Restell, James Gordon Bennett Sr. was an immigrant.
He was born in Scotland in 1795, and his family originally sent him
to seminary school with the hope that he would become a priest. Bennett was not remotely interested in that idea; he found that he loved
literature but regarded religion with contempt. By 1819, inspired by
Benjamin Franklin's autobiography, Bennett immigrated to America, where he spent the next sixteen years writing, editing, and trying
(and failing) to start his own newspaper. He finally succeeded with the
launch of the *New York Daily Herald* in 1835. The paper would be
shaped by Bennett's philosophy that "the object of the modern newspaper is not to instruct, but to startle and amuse."[3]

The *Herald* was thrust into prominence after its coverage of the
Helen Jewett murder in 1836. The murder of the high-class prostitute
with an axe was one that many papers struggled to cover as it dealt
with a societally taboo topic of discussion: not merely murder, but sex.

Bennett did not have any qualms about discussing the events that
had transpired. He downright fulsomely described the details of the
murder, writing, upon observing the victim's body, "Slowly I began to
discover the lineaments of the corpse, as one would the beauties of

a statue of marble.... Not a vein was to be seen. The body looked as white—as full—as polished as the pure Parian marble. The perfect figure—the exquisite limbs—the fine face—the full arms—the beautiful bust—all—all surpassing in every respect the Venus de Medicis."[4]

Within weeks, the paper was selling all fifteen thousand copies of its daily run.

Bennett continued to fill his newspaper with deliberately provocative headlines. One story declared, "Five hundred dollars reward will be given to any handsome woman, either lovely widow or single seamstress, who will set a trap for a Presbyterian parson, and catch one of them flagrante delicto."[5] That doesn't seem like news so much as an entirely unnecessary honeytrap—it would still be attention-grabbing today if the *New York Times* ran a piece asking any woman to go out, have sex with a priest, and then report back to them on how they pulled it off. If the *Herald*'s reporters could not find the news stories they wanted, they were determined to *make* them happen, and this was exactly the kind of item that got people talking. And the strategy *worked.* Suffice to say, the *New York Daily Herald* was not your grandmother's newspaper. Bennett intended the audience to be a group of people sophisticated enough about the world and the city to understand that sex was a part of cosmopolitan life—and therefore shouldn't be considered off limits. By 1845, only ten years after it launched, the *New York Daily Herald* became the most popular newspaper in America.

Madame Restell—a young, irreligious woman who ran scandalous advertisements facilitating sex—would have been adored by Bennett under any circumstances. She was all but emblematic of the world that fascinated Bennett and his readers.

But that wasn't a world that everyone was about to embrace.

On the opposite end of the spectrum, there was Samuel Jenks Smith, who was among Madame Restell's most vocal dissenters. The editor of the *New York Sunday Morning News* was a man of more conservative tastes. While Bennett may have been something of a libertine, at least in his outlook (he was supposedly a lot crankier in life than he was on paper), Smith was a family man and a devout Christian. Lest that seem too wholesome, conjuring the image of a man harmlessly reading to his twin boys before a fire, keep in mind that the phrase "traditional"

in the 1830s meant that he fervently supported slavery. As he wrote in what is one of his more infuriating passages, "You say you do not consider slavery a monstrous evil—I do! But the monstrous evil is to the owners; they are the real sufferers. The slave himself never was, and never can be, so happy as when he has a master....No free African on his own native soil or among another people can be, in my opinion, so happy as the careless, indolent, and indulged slave of our Southern States."[6] Remember, enslaved people in the United States at this time were beaten, hunted by dogs, routinely raped, and tortured in other ways at the discretion of their masters. Harriet Jacobs, who was born into slavery, described one fellow slave being tortured to death in a cotton gin, a woman being shot through the head, and others having their flesh torn off by dogs. She noted that the master who committed those atrocities "boasted the name and standing of a Christian, though Satan never had a truer follower," adding, "I could tell of more slaveholders as cruel as those I have described. They are not exceptions to the general rule. I do not say there are no humane slaveholders. Such characters do exist, notwithstanding the hardening influences around them. But they are 'like angels' visits—few and far between.'"[7]

Samuel Jenks Smith said, regarding slavery, "My feelings are entirely southern—tempered possibly a little by our colder climate—but disposed, when the necessity occurs, and is inevitable, to war against the hypocritical sappers of our holiest institutions."[8]

"Holiest institutions." Men like Smith can oppress a whole lot of people while simultaneously touting their holiness.

Smith intended the *Sunday Morning News* to be a conservative, holy paper. There was one issue per week, delivered at 8:00 on Sunday morning, and intended to be read after returning home from church. In 1835, he declared that in his publication "the principles of sound morality will be earnestly maintained; and it shall contain lessons of instruction, mingled with sufficient humor, to make it an agreeable companion for the family circle."[9] Essentially, its stated goal was to be a family-friendly newspaper. The only problem with that business model was that a very moral newspaper struggles to be as interesting as a newspaper that's willing to rhapsodize about the nude body of a murdered sex worker when not encouraging women to seduce religious men for the funny story it would provide.

For such a strategy to remain relevant, there needs to be someone not family friendly to deride.

Madame Restell fit the bill. She was interested, as Bennett was, in a world governed, not by religion, but by Enlightenment-era principles. Little wonder then that by July 7, 1839—less than a month after the *Herald* piece declared Restell to be a beautiful and promising female physician—Samuel Jenks Smith voiced his objections to her and her profession more generally. He was horrified that Restell, this "practical political economist," thought families might decrease their expenses by having fewer children. He was even more aghast that Restell was telling women "sexual enjoyment may be granted without the results." He lamented that her profession "strikes at the root of all social order—is subversive of family peace and quiet—will generate jealousies and hate—will demoralize the whole mass of society and make the institution of marriage a mere farce." He certainly credited Madame Restell with a great deal if she was so easily able to undermine all of society. It's surprising that her contemporaries providing similar medical treatments, such as, perhaps, her mentor Dr. Evans, hadn't already done so. Then again, they were not being written about in newspapers. Smith continued with the more compelling argument that what Madame Restell was doing posed a danger to her patients. He noted, "We scarcely believe that any woman can be so abandoned as to undertake, publicly, to perform what physicians declare to be impossible without jeopardy to the lives of those that are willing to submit to such a course of treatment."[10]

But then, Madame Restell had many fully alive former patients recommending her course of treatment.

Smith was trying to make Madame Restell a compelling target and representation of licentiousness in the modern age. And this quarrel, while ostensibly about Madame Restell, was at least as much one between two men with vastly different ideas of what the world, and what newspapers, should look like. As Bennett and Smith were sniping at each other's philosophies in their papers, Madame Restell was doubtless back at her office, perhaps admiring one of the many moderately creepy anatomical drawings she'd hung up there.

Her life would have been much more peaceful if she had quietly stayed in that office, operated on her many patients, and ignored

Smith. But when she paused her work to read what was being written about her, she became furious. It's possible that if she had ignored the spat, she wouldn't have become quite so controversial a figure. Then again, it's very easy to tell people to ignore the haters. It's hard to manage that restraint when the hatred is directed toward you. It was not in Madame Restell's nature to sit back quietly while she was being publicly insulted. If she were alive today, she would be fighting with people on Twitter constantly, likely in front of a massive following. Within days, she was penning an article in reply to Smith's indictment.

On July 15, Madame Restell published her retort in the *Herald*. Here, she laid into Smith, claiming that Smith had written, "Mrs. Restell knows very well that the business she is engaged in is improper." She replied, "This is false. As everyone is fully aware, who has read my circular, wherein my reasons are given to show [family limitation] is of the utmost benefit."[11] As for his claim that her preventative powders were harmful, she offered one hundred dollars to whoever could prove that any individual had been harmed by taking them. She pointed out that the *Sunday Morning News* also contained birth control advertisements, noting that the advertisements in his paper promised to treat "certain delicate diseases" with "the most honorable secrecy observed." "Such moral advertisements," Madame Restell wrote, "are gladly inserted if they can be obtained. These, I presume, *if paid for* are, of course, very conducive to morals, piety, and virtue." As for herself, she claimed she was singled out solely because "I did not deem your scurrilous sheet of sufficient importance" to be worth advertising in.[12]

Smith quipped in return that she *had* offered to advertise in his paper, and he had turned her down.

Over at the *Herald*, Bennett was unabashedly delighted by this turn of events. While an editorial claimed the *Herald* would maintain "perfect neutrality" regarding the clash between Smith and Restell, it also noted that "[Madame Restell] has on her list a thousand fair patients already beautified, cured and improved in health, looks, husbands, and happiness. Can the Rev. Doctor show such certificates?"[13] In a fashion that was very much in keeping with the *Herald*'s sensational style, the paper also accused Smith of "offering [Madame Restell] some curious pill." To drug her? Rape her? Poison her? It's not relevant because this outlandish accusation was completely made up. So much for perfect neutrality.

The media back-and-forth might have gone on for some time had Anne Dole not come forward. Dole was one of Restell's many patients. Hoping to miscarry, she had purchased thirty-one pills from Madame Restell. Feeling sickened by them, she took the pills to her doctor, in an effort to ensure that they were not going to kill her. He was surprised to find they contained ergot and rye (apparently, she had not told the doctor these were pills for the purpose of inducing a miscarriage), and insisted she go to the police.

On August 17, 1839, Madame Restell was arrested and charged with providing an abortion. A decade earlier, in 1829, laws had been passed in New York ruling that pre-quickening abortions (those performed before twenty weeks' gestation) were misdemeanors. Performing a post-quickening abortion was a felony. So, while at the time, the fact that Restell had provided Anne Dole with abortive pills was only a misdemeanor, it still meant that Madame Restell faced a fine of up to $500 and a year in jail.

Following her arrest, Restell was quickly bailed out of jail by her husband and her mentor, Dr. Evans, for the sum of $1,500 (which would equate to about $41,000 today). This may not have been much money to Restell, who was charging her wealthier clients $100 for appointments by this time, but officials surely hoped it would be sufficiently large to dissuade others who were thinking of following in her footsteps.

Fortunately for Restell, her accumulated wealth meant that she had the funds in hand to hire a talented lawyer, in William Craft. For the first time, but not the last, she prepared to go to court.

No one was more excited about the impending trial than James Gordon Bennett. It promised to be a sexy legal battle, the kind he loved to cover. Practically salivating, on August 21, the *Herald* declared, "The youth, beauty, black eyes, raven hair, and singular physiognomy of the accused and the surprising display of…legal acumen, and forensic evidence would be, in themselves, enough to attract half the city to the halls of justice." News of a beautiful woman and her wily lawyer was enticing enough, but Bennett and the *Herald* may have been even more excited by the continuation of the battle with Samuel Jenks Smith. The *Herald* warned that if Restell lost in court, it would represent a kind of spiritual victory for Smith, and if that came to pass, society would have "exchanged beauty for ugliness—a scholiast for an

ignoramus—a belle for a bully, a little good-looking humbug in petti-
coats for a fat bull-headed one in breeches."[14]

The *Herald* even seemed eager to offer legal strategies to exonerate Restell within its pages. It suggested that Anne Dole might say
that she never took the pills. Or Restell could say that the pills contained nothing dangerous at all. Or that she was a mere quack. All
in hopes of so "flabbergasting the astute Dr. Samuel Jenks Smith and
make the grand jury laughingstocks for the next generation—besides
proving this female philosopher to be one of the most splendid hum-
bugs the world has been honored with, since the days of Mahomet the
prophet."[15]

This was terrible legal advice. People knew the pills contained
ingredients widely accepted to induce abortion. Anne Dole's doctor
had examined them and could testify to that effect. All Anne had to
do was stand up in court and say that she had taken the pills in order
to have an abortion.

But she declined to show up in court.

There are many very understandable reasons why a woman who
came to Madame Restell would not want to appear in court saying she
had tried to have an abortion. Doubtless, even having her name in the
papers was an absolute nightmare for her. Without her testimony, the
case was dropped.

Anne Dole proceeded to die of puerperal fever—an infection
that can present in the uterus following childbirth—in March, seven
months later. Taking Restell's pills as intended might have saved her
life.

If there's a victim in this story, it is Anne Dole. Madame Restell, who
often adopted a motherly attitude toward patients—even telling them
that they could call her mother—may have felt the worse for it. But
it is not clear whether the more prominent male protagonists in this
tale noticed at all. They just continued the fight among themselves. If
childbirth was dangerous, well, that was only natural—and certainly
not newsworthy.

The fact that seemed to inflame Samuel Jenks Smith the most was
that Restell had not gone to jail. In September 1839, a month after
Restell's arrest, he not only wrote articles speaking out against her in
the *Sunday Morning News,* he penned a poem denouncing her and her
male clients. It detailed such a client's outlook, saying:

But finding that some had no faith in his humming
He hinted a way to prevent babies from coming
Referred to his excellent friend Mrs. Restell
Who the Virtue of Women Was Making A Jest All
Affirming that all with full safety could pair
Like the beasts of the field and the birds of the air
From which you may gather this doctrine at least
One man was a brute, and the woman a beast.[16]

The poem, about a brutish man who wishes to procure an abortion for the woman in his life using Madame Restell's services, is admittedly not very good. At the *Herald,* Bennett sarcastically sniped that while the poem was clearly a poetic triumph, "the fact that the sentiments [about pairing like birds and beasts] attributed to the individual [Restell] were never entertained either in speech or in print makes no matter of difference to this truly grand poet. And besides—it is sometimes necessary to *lie.*"[17] He further noted that Smith's own paper continued to run advertisements "in reference to 'delicate diseases' 'cured in three or four days,'" and suggested, again, that Smith's bitterness still stemmed from Restell not advertising in his paper.

This bickering between the newspaper men might have gone on for years. Both Bennett and Smith seemed to be savoring it, as did their readers. But in 1840, Smith became ill.

His doctor suggested that he sail to Europe to seek treatment. The editorship of the *New York Sunday Morning News* was passed to a Mr. E. Barnett in late February 1840, and Smith departed on his voyage. On March 3, after only a few days at sea, Smith died. The *Ladies Home Companion* reported that "the cause of the death was inflammation of the brain, which was exceedingly painful until a few hours before his death."[18] The *Sunday Morning News* would linger on for just a bit longer, but only until 1844.

Smith did not leave much of a legacy, but he did make it clear that Madame Restell was someone who could be attacked in the press. Furthermore, if people chose to attack her in public, she would probably respond, and that could increase a paper's circulation. The time when Madame Restell could have gone about her business quietly was now over. She was famous, or infamous, depending upon how someone felt about birth control and which newspaper they preferred.

Other newspaper editors were more than happy to pick up where Smith had left off.

The most enthusiastic among them would be George Washington Dixon.

Samuel Jenks Smith had been a deeply retrograde man. He had believed in a world where Black people obeyed white people, women obeyed men, and men obeyed a very Christian God. Nowadays, these views may seem unpleasant. But in this regard, he was not so different from some of the men you might even encounter today.

George Washington Dixon was a complete lunatic.

To his credit, Dixon was a very confident lunatic. In 1841, he claimed, in the fifth volume of his newspaper, *The Polyanthos*, that "we prophesy that the latest descendent of the youngest newsboy will animate his hearers with the desire to emulate the enviable fame of Dixon! Our name will be handed down until the end of time as one of the most independent men of the nineteenth century! Our very hat will become a relic. Every fold of our sternly disciplined raiment will contain a moral lesson, and our very old shoes will be a sight for sore eyes."[19]

Try describing yourself that way at a job interview. See how it goes.

If it seems disturbing to modern readers that Samuel Jenks Smith would have enthusiastically signed up to fight for the Confederacy had he lived to see the Civil War, consider also that George Washington Dixon was a blackface performer. After teenage years spent in the circus, he became known for performing songs such as "Jim Crow," "Cole Black Rose," and "Zip Coon."

By 1835, Dixon had started his first newspaper, *Dixon's Daily Review*, based in Lowell, Massachusetts, the land of literary mill girls. He was accused of trying to collect money using a forged note for $23.50 in 1836. It was said that, in regard to why you could not cash bad checks, his "understanding was somewhat deficient."[20] Witnesses were hard-pressed to say whether he was of sound mind. One remarked, "In reply to a question of whether Dixon was non compos mentis, I consider him as being on the frontier line—sometimes on one side, and sometimes on the other, just as the breeze of fortune happens to blow."[21]

So, not exactly a "yes."

Dixon was later found not guilty—as the jury was unable to tell whether he knew the document he used was a fake—but fellow newspaper editors were not so kind. In response to a piece Dixon had written trying to exonerate himself, the *Spirit of the Times* stressed that "the writer attempts to exculpate himself from being acquitted by a Boston jury of the crime of forgery on the ground of being deemed non compos mentis.... Mister Zip Coon is at his old tricks again. So far from possessing the ability to write a letter Miss-Nancy-Coal-Black-Rose cannot begin to write ten consecutive words of the English language."[22]

Dixon didn't care. He went on to publish a newspaper in Boston before moving to New York to launch *The Polyanthos* in 1838. This new paper seemed intended largely as a platform by which Dixon could lash out at anyone whom he deemed promiscuous. It was not well regarded; it was even harshly described as "a disgrace to the New York Press."[23] Not long after its inception, its reporting was blamed for the death of a sixteen-year-old girl involved in an affair. Papers declared that the girl (by the name of Miss Missouri) died as a result of "inflammation to the brain caused by great mental excitement, induced jointly by the violent conduct of her mother, and the publication of an abusive article in *The Polyanthos*."[24] Whether or not getting shamed in print can actually kill a person, that apparently wasn't the only incident. A man featured in Dixon's press pages, who had also allegedly had an affair, became extremely depressed and committed suicide by jumping off his roof. In addition to antagonizing people socially, Dixon's determination to expose and denounce people's sex lives didn't work out well for him legally. After two lawsuits, one of them involving a clergyman, Dixon was convicted of libel in May 1839. He was sentenced to six months in jail on Blackwell's Island (now known as New York's Roosevelt Island).

But Dixon remained shockingly undeterred. Jail time did not cause him to shut down the "vile penny sheet called the *Polyanthos*," or to rethink its reporting approach.[25] He genuinely believed that people having sex—in virtually any context—were immoral, or at least far inferior in their morality when compared to him. His time in prison only seemed to make him more confident in his own virtue. In 1841, Dixon's paper quoted an anonymous (and possibly fictitious) religious figure who claimed that Dixon was "eminently qualified for the position which he has so boldly taken as moral censor of New York. The stern chastity of his own life (unlike those of his brethren in the press) allows him with a good grace to inveigh against the immoralities of others."[26]

Few readers—if any—were keen to crown a moral arbiter from a narcissistic, libelous, supposedly virginal blackface performer who kept getting arrested. While many were likely against people having affairs—the majority of people, historically and currently, don't approve of cheating on one's spouse—the populace didn't view Dixon as a deeply moral man. They viewed him as a smug busybody who kept butting into people's private business and ruining lives.

It is hard to overstate the animosity people felt toward George Washington Dixon. Take this condemnation from the *New York Dispatch* from 1839: "That he [George Washington Dixon] is disgusting, a nuisance, and a bore, we know," the paper noted. But it urged New Yorkers to try to temper their hatred, explaining, "So is a spider," and "nobody would dream...of extinguishing the latter insect with a park of artillery, though all the city seem to have fancied that George Washington Dixon could be conquered with no less."[27] People wanted to kill him—and more than that, they actively tried. In 1838, he was "assailed by a man named Johnson who undertook to castigate him with a cowhide": "The melodist [Dixon] drew a pistol and shot him in the leg, somewhat impairing the gentleman's understanding. The wounded man, however, nothing daunted, again renewed his attack, when Dixon aimed a second pistol at Mr. Johnson's seat of honor and gave him such an argument a posteriori, as tore open his unmentionables, and plowed a passage through the flesh, tracking its way with blood."[28]

To sum up: Dixon shot a man in the ass because that man would not stop trying to attack him after only one bullet.

Later on, in 1841, Dixon was "badly wounded" by a blow to the head that someone dealt him outside his New York office.[29]

Somewhere amid these attacks, Dixon must have realized that he had to find something to publicly rage against that people hated more than they hated him. And he could do that by decrying loose women, with a special focus on abortion and birth control.

And thus his campaign against Madame Restell began.

Like so many high school gym teachers bewilderingly tasked with teaching sex ed, Dixon wished people to know that the only way to prevent pregnancy was abstinence. Anything else was an affront to God. Regarding Restell's ads for preventative powders, he claimed, "Preventative powders! There is no such thing in nature. There is but one preventative, and it is abstinence.... [T]his unprincipled creature

[Restell] knows better than God or man how married people ought to behave."[30] As was often the case, the fact that Restell's preventative powders were made from natural ingredients that women through the ages had employed to discourage pregnancy was not seen as relevant.

In February 1841, Dixon wrote that if Madame Restell was allowed to continue her practice, the result would be disastrous—for men. He urged them to consider:

> Seamen, you are going to a three years voyage, and gave the security for the good behavior of your wife; certain acts have consequences, the flow of blood proves that a blow has been given or received. Not at all—all this is at an end. Madame Restell shows your spouse how she may commit as many adulteries as there are hours in the year, without the possibility of detection. Young man, you took to your bosom the image of purity, a thing upon which you think the stamp of God has been printed, that virgin bosom, that rosy cheek, that sparkling eye assure you the treasure is yours—yours alone. Not so: Madame Restell's preventative Powders have counterfeited the handwriting of Nature; you have not a medal, fresh from the mint, of sure metal, but a base, lacquered counter, that has undergone the sweaty contaminations of a hundred palms.[31]

As a reminder: less than a century before this was published were the days where a third of New England brides were pregnant on their wedding day. Madame Restell did not invent premarital or extramarital sex. Even if she had, her powders and pills were often taken by married as well as unmarried women, not out of any desire to deceive their spouses, but because they felt they already had enough children. This was a fact unbelievable to Dixon, who scoffed, "Madame Restell addresses married women only! What an insult to the sex. No married woman in the land is without a spot for her distress; no married man is so utterly destitute that he cannot provide for it; if there are any such the law allows them refuge in an almshouse. It is a more honorable refuge than Restell's house."[32]

Dixon himself was not married. Nor did he have children. Telling people that if having a child is going to bankrupt them, then they should move to a homeless shelter, where the child they've been forced to birth will almost certainly die, is not an especially convincing argument. And, as for the idea that all married couples would have children if they could—77 percent of fertile, married women in America use contraceptive methods today, now that they are widely available.[33]

Nevertheless, Dixon continued to press his message. In March 1841, a grand jury looked into Madame Restell's advertisements for pills. They found them to be a public nuisance, defined as anything that negatively affects the safety or morals of a community—operating a house of prostitution is one such example. In this case, Madame Restell's ads were grouped with a series of annoyances, including "the piles of furniture and old clothes outside of auction stores... [and] the facilities afforded juvenile thieves by junk shops."[34]

Dixon was naturally delighted by this turn of events. Madame Restell was predictably less than thrilled. She'd held her tongue to a surprising extent throughout Dixon's attacks on her, perhaps assuming that most of the city held him in contempt and nothing would come of his criticism. Besides which, she had been incredibly busy keeping up with her expanding business while Dixon had been mounting his campaign. By 1840, her operation spanned multiple cities—with her pills now being distributed in New York, Philadelphia, and Boston. In addition to Restell's new office at 148 Greenwich Street, the Lohmans also purchased a workshop around the corner at 129 Liberty Street, devoted solely to compounding pills.

The rise of her business and income had not gone unnoticed. Success breeds imitators. And so, by 1840, much of Restell's attentions had been taken up with her rival Madame Costello.

Around this time, Costello was not merely competing with Restell, she was pretending to *be* Restell. She took out an ad claiming that she was the real Madame Restell, the other one was a mere imitator, and that patients should visit her address at 34 Lispenard Street. It was honestly a very bold—and sly—move in an age where people might not have been familiar with what certain individuals looked like, even those frequently written about in the newspapers.

Madame Restell was understandably furious that someone was not only muscling in on her business but attempting to steal her identity. She focused her ads on instructing people to "beware of fraud," noting that her signature would now be on each box of pills she distributed.[35] Given that her medicines were so popular that people were now passing off fraudulent versions of them, Dixon's newspaper allegations probably didn't seem like they should be a priority for her. She might have heeded the advice not to go after a spider with heavy artillery. Now, with the grand jury's stance, she had been proved wrong. Public opinion *could* impact her business.

And so, as she had in the past, Madame Restell took her problems to the press. She did so with a letter plagiarized almost entirely from the arguments laid forth in Robert Dale Owen's 1841 treatise "Moral Physiology," seemingly hoping that newspaper readers would not read the tome as closely as she had.

She directed her letter not to Dixon, but to the members of the grand jury. "As you have thought proper to overstep the strict bounds of your duties," Restell wrote, "and graciously, and no doubt disinterestedly, have stepped forward to take under your guardian and fostering care the 'public morals' of this 'noble city,' you will not, I hope, deem it impertinent in me to examine the premise." She claimed that, far from having an immoral influence, her birth control powders had a decidedly moral one. Her argument was three pronged. First, she contended that birth control might increase the rate of marriage. With her powders, "young people seriously attached to each other who might wish to marry, would marry early, merely resolving not to be parents until prudence permitted it. The young man, instead of solitary toil . . . would enjoy the society and the assistance of her he had chosen as his companion, and the best years of life." Second, if this did not make a dent in the gentlemen of the jury's perception—and it likely did not, if they could think of reasons that young men might enjoy birth control that had nothing to do with early marriage—Restell was quick to remind them that she was also saving lives. "It is well known among physicians (of which fact you should have acquainted yourselves) that there are some women who cannot, except at imminent peril of their lives, and the certain sacrifice of that of their unborn, give birth. Is it not moral for those to have the 'preventative powders' to save their health—their lives? Many weakly wives have been saved from a premature grave to be a succor and a blessing to those near and dear to them."[36]

Both of these arguments contained, though in moderately well-hidden fashion, the fairly rebellious notion that marriages could be fulfilling without children. Restell's own marriage seemed, at least in their early years, to bear this out. She and Charles Lohman did not have children of their own, raising only the daughter from Restell's first marriage. However, they were bound by a similar outlook, goals, work ethic, and other commonalities that can make a marriage joyful and satisfying. It's also worth noting that Madame Restell was a widow when she married Lohman, and that he did not seem as horrified as Dixon by the idea that his bride had been contaminated by sweaty palms other than his.

While that germ of an idea may have irked those who believed the purpose of marriage was to "go forth and multiply," both arguments still acknowledged a certain deference to the social order. People could not argue that couples getting married at younger ages, as Restell rather optimistically suggested, would be bad. Nor could they say, at this point in history, that they were in favor of women dying in childbirth so long as it meant those women were trying to have children.

But Madame Restell's third argument made a larger case, which hinged upon more divisive ideas:

> I cannot subscribe to the monstrous doctrine that there is no moral principle, no consciousness of right, no instinctive perception of virtue, that actuates female conduct, instead of the "fear" and "restraint" you allege. I cannot conceive how men who are husbands, brothers, or fathers, can give utterance to an idea so intrinsically base and infamous, that their wives, their sisters, or their daughters, want but the opportunity and "facilities" to be vicious, and if they are not so, it is not from an innate principle of virtue, but from fear.... What! is female virtue, then, a mere thing of circumstance and occasion? Is there but the difference of opportunity between it and prostitution? Would your wives, and your sisters, and your daughters, if once absolved from fear, all become prostitutes?[37]

What Madame Restell was exploring here was a fairly modern feminist view insofar as it meant that if women were loyal to men, it should not be because of fear of dire consequences, but because they liked them. A woman who knew she'd be beaten, penniless, and possibly pregnant if she cheated would probably be faithful to her spouse out of fear. However, one who regarded her male partner as her best friend, enjoyed their intimacy, and hated the idea of hurting him would be loyal out of love. Of course, this meant that men had to render themselves likable and be a good friend to their wives and prospective wives in return. This would eventually come to seem intuitive to every decent man, and bewildering to every man who felt he was owed unquestioning obedience from his wife because she was one of his possessions. For men who had never considered the notion that a wife was not his property, the effect was to make them panic. Without fear of consequences, *would* their wives go ahead and become prostitutes? What else would stop them? Many of them did not seem to know.

If Madame Restell thought men would be more trusting and openminded in the face of her reasoning, she was overly idealistic. This was not an era when most men thought about entering into equitable, respectful relationships with women. They did not consider women to be their equals. Some regarded such intellectual equality as physically impossible. In 1847, Dr. Charles Meigs declared that "the great administrative faculties are not [woman's].... [S]he has a head almost too small for intellect and just big enough for love."[38] If women were viewed essentially as children with breasts, then there was reason to think they wouldn't be governed by reason or restraint.

If Madame Restell was not stopped, men reasoned, they would have far less power over their wives. Hell, even Madame Restell had posed the possibility that their wives might start taking lovers if they had access to birth control, even as she promptly dismissed it. Playing into men's already misogynistic attitudes about women was more successful in turning public opinion against Restell than Samuel Jenks Smith's contentions had ever been. Dixon's facts might have been wrong, but he stirred his audience's fears in a way that was effective.

Years earlier, Smith had been shocked by Restell's flouting of norms and assumed other Christian men would share his dismay. Dixon went one step further, making it clear that Restell's behavior was a personal threat to each of them, individually. Inadvertently, through her response, Restell had bolstered his argument.

Unfortunately, before long, Madame Restell's problems would cease to be only with her enemies in the press. Three days after her response ran in the *Herald*, she found herself in a worse predicament. And it was one she could not even attempt to write her way out of.

CHAPTER SEVEN

ANN MARIA PURDY WAS DYING. HER PHYSICIAN HAD INFORMED her that the end was imminent. Doubtless in pain and likely enraged that she was dying at the young age of twenty-one, Mrs. Purdy didn't want to go without unburdening her conscience—and perhaps passing the blame.

As her husband, William Purdy, knelt by her bedside, she told him that Madame Restell was responsible for her illness and death. We will find this was likely untrue.

As such, there may be some inclination for readers of a book about Madame Restell to think poorly of Mrs. Purdy. Her accusations would obviously present obstacles to Madame Restell's business, and Madame Restell is, after all, our protagonist. But the journalists who described Mrs. Purdy's death during the era itself didn't have such an excuse, and they treated her with utter disdain. Deaths of women during this period were treated cavalierly, especially by the press. Women had abortions and died all the time. Or they failed to have abortions and died in childbirth. Or they tried to give themselves abortions and *then* died. The press seemed to surmise it was their fault for getting themselves into a situation where they needed an abortion in the first place. Or else they were stupid for going about it in the wrong way. If these women were not going to be mothers and procreate, journalists often seemed to imply, their lives weren't worth much anyway.

But how unbearable to know you are dying at twenty-one! Imagine yourself at twenty-one, and then imagine how angry and frightened Mrs. Purdy must have felt. With her life entirely ahead of her, how unfair it must have seemed to die before she had the chance to experience any of it. Seen from such a point of view, perhaps whatever inclination caused Mrs. Purdy to lash out was sympathetically under-standable.

Two years prior, in May 1839, Mrs. Purdy had gone to Madame Restell for an abortion. She was already the mother to a ten-month-old child. The newspapers would later rather callously report that Purdy had sought the abortion because "the prospect of having another child, while one was so young, was extremely annoying to her."[1] And that may have been so. No one should have to have a child they do not wish to have. Unexplored, however, are other reasons why Purdy might have felt ill equipped to have another child. For example, she might have suffered from postpartum depression following the birth of her daughter. She might have found the experience of giving birth to have been deeply traumatic. She might have been concerned about the family's finances or her own health. The point is: She was never asked about her reasons for seeking abortive services, and, following her death, the public didn't seem especially interested in them. Easier for a male newspaper writer to dismiss her as a frivolous woman than to investigate why even the dangerous business of seeking out an abor-tion might seem preferable to childbirth for her.

Whatever Purdy's fears, she kept them secret from her husband, though not from many others. She went to multiple neighbors hop-ing to find advice on how to handle her situation. It was a laundress named Rebecca who first suggested that she visit Madame Restell. Rebecca "not only urged Mrs. Purdy to go to the Mrs. Restell, but pro-cured for her a *Sun*, containing the advertisement, which she read and explained, as Mrs. Purdy was wholly ignorant of what was the meaning of the publication."[2]

It's worth noting here that Rebecca was a Black woman.

The fact that Rebecca knew where to find Madame Restell, and could also advise Mrs. Purdy on the type of services she provided, might merely indicate that Restell's advertising was effective as it was meant to be. However, it also suggests the possibility that Restell, who often catered to servants, especially in her early days of practice, operated on patients of color in addition to Caucasian women. In 1839, an article in the *Herald* suggested that a Black woman who worked in a brothel should have gone to Madame Restell rather than try to induce her own abortion, which killed her. Of course, this may have been a bit of wish-ful thinking on the reporter's part. Still, at a time when doctors like

James Marion Sims were using enslaved Black women as gynecological guinea pigs, and when others considered Black and white people to be entirely different species, the notion that Restell would have provided equal care to all women is commendable.

At the time, however, all this background meant was a general conviction that Mrs. Purdy had been "overcome by the persuasions of this colored woman."[3] Much of the reporting hinged upon the idea that Mrs. Purdy was a woman of almost childlike intellect, who had somehow been tricked into an abortion by Rebecca or Madame Restell, or both. Papers acknowledged that Madame Restell was intelligent. However, intellect in a woman such as her wasn't necessarily laudable— it could easily be perceived as canniness. Rather than use her mind for good, as a man might, she might use it to manipulate the feebler-minded members of her sex, in the manner of a witch. So it wasn't shocking that Purdy's doctor described Purdy as a woman of "fickle disposition, not illiterate for her station, but easily influenced."[4] Maybe she was. But there's much detail regarding what upset Mrs. Purdy at the end of her life. She was angry and blamed her abortion for the subsequent illness that led to her death. She was troubled by the knowledge that she had lied to her husband. She was even fearful about the possibility of damnation. But there's no evidence whatsoever that she expressed regret about not having a second child.

Whether influenced or not by Rebecca, Mrs. Purdy sought out Madame Restell's help, and bought some medication from her to induce a miscarriage. However, after taking one dose the first night, and another two the next day, she felt ill. This would have been a consequence of the medication having the desired effect. Many medications taken today still produce temporary discomfort. But when modern patients take those medications, they more often than not have the comfort of knowing they are prescribed by a reputable doctor and overseen for safety by the US Food and Drug Administration. Mrs. Purdy had no such assurances when Rebecca suggested she visit a woman on Mulberry Street who'd had an abortion, likely to discuss whether the discomfort she was feeling was normal. But that woman refused to talk about or even admit to her abortion. Even more anxious, Mrs. Purdy then went to a doctor to see what was in the medication she had been given by Restell. Her doctor told her it contained tansy and turpentine, and correctly pointed out that this was a dangerous combination.

Still eager to procure an abortion, Purdy returned to Madame Restell, who informed her that, for $40 or $50, she could do a surgical procedure that would certainly rid Purdy of her unwanted pregnancy.

That sounded fine to Purdy. The only problem was that she did not have the money. And so, as often seemed to be the case when it came to lower-income clients, Madame Restell reduced the cost to $20.

Still not low enough.

Ann Maria Purdy wasn't destitute. Her husband was employed: first he had worked smoking fish and meat, and then as an agent at a railway company. The couple had lodgings, albeit at a boardinghouse. Prior to her marriage, Mrs. Purdy had worked in a confectionery shop. Together, the couple likely could have found some funds for the procedure. The real problem was that Purdy didn't want to inform her husband of her condition, and, like most women of the period, did not have access to her own money. Even if she had worked in a shop or office, she could not have opened a bank account without her husband's permission, something that would not have been permitted until over a century later, in the 1960s. Madame Restell understood that situation and was sympathetic to Mrs. Purdy's plight, but she still needed some form of payment.

So, Mrs. Purdy pawned a gold watch, a chain she'd owned prior to her marriage, and some rings, all worth $16 combined, and gave Madame Restell the pawn shop ticket to hold until she returned with payment. According to the *Evening Post*, she "also gave her one dollar, being all the money she had with her, and which Madame Restell insisted on being given to her along with the ticket."[5]

Perhaps this makes Madame Restell sound unreasonably greedy, but the charge for performing a very specialized operation had been lowered from the modern-day equivalent of $1,400 to some unseen pieces of jewelry. There was often an implication by the press that the services Madame Restell was providing were unholy, immoral, and poisonous—and that she really ought to be providing them for free. The only thing more unnatural than a woman not wanting to be a mother was a woman wanting to be paid for doing her job.

When Mrs. Purdy returned for the procedure, she was said to be surprised to find that a man, not a woman, would be handling her case. This "excited her fears, lest a violation of her person be intended." Despite her fears, "Mrs. Restell and the man together assured her she would be kindly treated and relieved, and urged her to take off her hat, and recline on a blanket on the floor, with her head on a low stool.... [B]y the persuasions of the man and woman, Mrs. Purdy finally consented and submitted to the operation."[6]

This was the one part of Mrs. Purdy's story that Madame Restell would dispute. Not that the operation had been performed, but that a man had performed it. She later wrote regarding the Purdy testimony that "in no case do I engage a 'man' or physician for the simple and all-abundant reason that, whatever I undertake, I feel myself competent, as well by study, experience, and practice, to carry through properly. So far from me requiring a physician in my practice it is not unusual for me to be called instead of a 'doctor' in confinements where proper delicacy forbids the presence of a male practitioner."[7] Essentially, Madame Restell did not feel a need for a man to assist her because she was quite sure she was the more skilled physician. The male medical establishment would eventually get around to feeling attacked by this conviction, but not just yet.

Mrs. Purdy went home on the bus, in pain, and her miscarriage was completed within two or three days. Her physician, a man named Dr. Marvin, suspected that she had induced the miscarriage, and she confessed, making him promise not to tell her husband. To people who were not her doctor, she said she had delivered prematurely due to "severe exertion in washing."[8]

Mrs. Purdy claimed that following the abortion, she never enjoyed a single day of good health, up until her death two years later. The papers claimed that her decline into illness was attributable to "the injuries she then received, and the brutal violence done to her nature."[9]

It's true that abortions done in the conditions that Restell was using were dangerous. Mrs. Purdy lay down on a blanket in a back room in a time before germ theory and sanitation were popularized, so it's reasonable to assume the conditions were not sterile. This is one of the reasons it's so astonishing that Restell's patients did *not* die with regularity. But the complications that can result—say, a punctured bladder or sepsis—would not generally take two years to kill someone. Indeed, following the operation, Mrs. Purdy was said to have recovered, and then she was active until 1840, when she was confined to her bed.

Mrs. Purdy's death, on April 28, 1841, was officially caused by "pulmonary consumption."[10] The term "consumption" was often used to refer to tuberculosis, a potentially deadly disease that infects the lungs and damages other organs. It is spread through droplets in the air; you might be exposed to it by an infected person coughing on you, for instance. It was prevalent in large cities during the mid-1800s, where close quarters made it easy to spread. In 1840, a New York City inspector announced that "from pulmonary consumption alone, 1,315 people have died."[11] Among foreigners, the city inspector claimed, the disease accounted for 25 percent of deaths. Tuberculosis often causes patients to lose weight and expire slowly over the course of years, which foolishly caused some prominent figures to regard it as a very romantic disease. The poet Lord Byron once remarked, "I should like, I think, to die of consumption…because then the women would all say, 'see that poor Byron—how interesting he looks in dying!'" He did not mention that, by the end stages of the untreated disease, people were not delicately coughing drops of blood into handkerchiefs in an operatic manner. They spit up cups' worth of blood while writhing in agony, their stomachs distended, unable to keep down food or liquid. Admittedly, that may be "interesting," but it's definitely not appealing.

Tuberculosis is a horrible way to die. It is horrible that any woman would expire this way. That said, barring the possibility that someone at Madame Restell's office infected with the disease coughed on Mrs. Purdy, her death likely had absolutely nothing do with Madame Restell or the abortion.

However, the plausibility of the theory that the operation caused Purdy's ultimate demise did not matter to the people who were intent on labeling Restell a murderess. To be fair, they did not know how consumption was spread, and they would not, until 1882 when the tuberculosis bacterium was discovered by Robert Koch. Theories ranged from the idea that it was hereditary to the notion that it was brought on by "bad air," or that beautiful women were especially susceptible. In which case, why not attribute it to abortion? Today, those opposed to abortion tout a nonexistent link between abortion and increased rates of breast cancer, so it's hardly surprising that nineteenth-century opponents decided it could cause tuberculosis.[12]

Shortly after Mrs. Purdy related her story to her husband, he filed a complaint with the police. A warrant was issued by Justice Henry Merritt, and the officer Gilbert F. Hays went to Madame Restell's office to arrest her. Madame Restell, perhaps hoping to turn some of the confusion Madame Costello had created to her benefit, claimed that she was not the lady in question; she was simply Ann Lohman. It was a bold move, albeit not a particularly successful one.

Mrs. Purdy was still alive when Madame Restell was arrested, and Restell agreed to visit her bedside. This was necessary, as her prior accusation had been made without Madame Restell present, so it was not admissible in court. Mrs. Purdy clearly identified Madame Restell, saying, "This is the woman who said she was Madame Restell, and who gave me the medicine, and caused my miscarriage."[13]

And so, Madame Restell was indicted for a misdemeanor—that of producing a premature birth—but many newspapers claimed that "this wretched woman has been indicted for manslaughter."[14]

She had not been, but she was taken to a prison in Lower Manhattan, and her bail was set at $5,000. Her lawyer claimed this amount was absurd, considering that she would only be fined $1,000 (and spend a year in jail) if found guilty of the misdemeanor. Bail was eventually lowered to $3,000. While Madame Restell had friends in high places by this point, they would not pay such a fee knowing they would be publicly named as her benefactors in the press. And so, Madame Restell stayed behind bars.

The prison, which was known as "The Tombs," was originally called the Halls of Justice. The moniker stemmed both from the fact that it was built in the style of an Egyptian mausoleum, and because it was built on a swampy pond (New Yorkers during this period had a truly regrettable tendency to build on swampland). Five months after its opening in 1840, it began to sink into the ground. The effect was, predictably, depressing. Thomas McCarthy, a retired city public information officer chronicling the history of the jail, noted in the *New York Daily News* that "mentally [the prisoners] had sunk so low, and now they were in a room that was damp and cold, and dark and dank, that was sinking into the ground, just like a tomb."[15] The sight was a source of great public shame; in 1842, the author Charles Dickens remarked that "such indecent and disgusting dungeons as these cells, would bring disgrace upon the most despotic empire in the world!"[16]

Madame Restell ended up spending two months in The Tombs.

She did not seem overwhelmed with despair. But then, she had seen worse. She had been a servant in rural England. She had taken a boat to America. She could withstand The Tombs. Besides, there were some privileges that made the time tolerable. Prisoners were only allotted an hour of exercise per day, but they could spend their time inside their cells according to their wishes. Friends and family were allowed to bring books, food, and changes of clothing. Prisoners could even smoke, at least until nighttime, when no light was allowed in their cells.

And Madame Restell was not alone. In 1839 the *Herald* had wryly predicted that if she was ever imprisoned she would be visited "every week" by men seeking "discussion on the best method of improving the breadth of the human race." This proved accurate.[17] Reports claimed that she "received hourly visits of the rich and the great," as true in prison as when in her home or office.[18] Most of the visitors were gentlemen. It's possible that some of them liked her and visited out of genuine friendship. Others might have reasoned that, even as she was in jail, she was able to offer them advice on birth control for their wives or mistresses. And many were likely there because they were frightened that she might name them as clients, and so wanted to offer whatever they could—short of publicly bailing her out—to dissuade her from doing so. Some might have even tried to threaten her, though threatening Madame Restell seemed to fail with shocking regularity.

While many women would have been intimidated by The Tombs, Restell received some female visitors as well. Members of the American Female Moral Reform Society reported, "We would fain have pointed her [Restell] to Him who has said to the truly penitent, 'Though your sins be as scarlet, they shall be as wool, though they be red like crimson, they shall be whiter than snow' but her heart was harder than a nether mill stone. She rejected the tract, saying she had plenty of good reading, pointing at the same time to a lot of novels with which she was supplied; and, turning her back in anger, said, 'I will hear nothing from you—I fear neither God nor man, nor care for heaven or hell!' "[19]

This was not a special visit. Members of the Reform Society paid a call on everyone in the prison. Likely others just politely took their pamphlet and threw it away if they weren't interested. But then again, Madame Restell always had a flair for the dramatic.

On May 11, Madame Restell was finally bailed out of jail. Her bondsman was said to be a man of some note named Selden Brainard.[20] Prior to moving to New York, he had been a resident of Boston. There, it was said that "every fair day an elegant private equipage would be seen standing in front of a large stone mansion...it was Selden Brainard's. An extensive broker in State Street he was esteemed a man of opulence and integrity."[21] That esteem didn't last. By 1851, he was in Sing Sing prison on counterfeiting charges. However, his presence is a reminder of how thoroughly Restell was, by now, straddling two worlds—one of opulent patrons in elegant carriages who thought nothing of spending thousands of dollars on bail, the other of people who traveled by omnibus and were reluctant to part with even one dollar.

Madame Restell's trial commenced at the Court of General Sessions on July 14, 1841, where she was represented by attorneys John A. Morrill and Ambrose L. Jordan. She was charged with giving Mrs. Purdy medication to induce an abortion, as well as using instruments for the same purpose. Maybe she did derive some inspiration from the ladies of the Reform Society after all as she appeared in court that first day looking like a model of propriety. An account of the trial observed that she was "attired in the most elegant manner, in a black satin walking dress, white satin bonnet, of the cottage pattern and a very elegant white veil of Brussels lace. In her hand she carried a parcel of printed papers, which made some persons mistake her for the Lady Presidentress of the Tract Society."[22] Modern viewers might imagine her in the outfit from the famous painting of James McNeill Whistler's mother. Madame Restell was always a very stylish dresser, and so her choice of a court ensemble seems more akin to when one of today's modern sexy starlets (arrested for DUIs or the like) arrives in court dressed in an outfit Queen Elizabeth II might have worn fifty years ago.

The style was intended to depict Madame Restell as a prim matron, especially since much of her lawyers' approach hinged upon showing Mr. and Mrs. Purdy to be less than moral. This might prove to be a tricky prospect, given that Madame Restell was very public and very unrepentant about her work. As one account of the trial claimed, "within a year, Madame Restell has committed several hundred abortions, she has committed several hundred crimes...we do not say so, she says so herself."[23] If they were immoral themselves, perhaps the jury would be less inclined to see them as victims of Madame Restell's actions. Ideally, they might even dismiss the couple's testimony if they seemed to be pursuing Restell for financial gain or other less-than-noble purposes.

Since Mrs. Purdy had died by the time the trial began, that meant a great number of questions regarding her character came when Mr.

Purdy was called to the stand. The attacks on her character cast an extremely wide net. If there was any trait that might make a jury member think poorly of someone, the lawyers tried to show that Purdy possessed it.

After Mr. Purdy mentioned he was no longer married, Restell's lawyer asked, "Do you live with a woman, or are you in the habit of sleeping with one now?"[24] Mr. Purdy declined to answer. At one point, the lawyer seemingly mocked Mr. Purdy for being short. The testimony read:

JORDAN: How large a woman was your wife?

WITNESS: She was not so tall as me by a head and a half.

[The witness himself is considerably under the middle size.]

JORDAN: That's all.[25]

There was no follow-up to this. There was no medical reason to ask Mrs. Purdy's height. For instance, it's not because an adult woman of average height would respond negatively to Madame Restell's medications. Jordan simply asked the question to paint an image of Mr. and Mrs. Purdy as an unattractive, somewhat stunted couple, two tiny dorks trying to cash in on Restell's fame. When Purdy attempted to answer Jordan's questions, Jordan accused him of letting "his tongue with the rapidity of a mill tail."[26]

Restell's lawyer similarly wondered:

JORDAN: Did she [Mrs. Purdy] ever go out without you?

WITNESS: Yes, sometimes.

JORDAN: Had she company when she went out?

WITNESS: Well, I believe she went out alone.

JORDAN: Did she ever go out with company to your knowledge?

WITNESS: Once she did, when I could not go; she went with a young man of my acquaintance, of the name of Mowbray.

JORDAN: What was he?

WITNESS: A painter.

JORDAN: Oh! then we have it at last. Young painter Mowbray went out with her![27]

To modern-day readers, this barely seems like an accusation at all. Especially as, from the rest of the testimony, it appears Mowbray and Mrs. Purdy only went out one time, and she and Mowbray were accompanied by Mowbray's girlfriend, whom he later married. At the time, however, there was a clear implication that Mrs. Purdy was a slattern. Because obviously the only reason a woman would ever interact with a man—a painter, no less!—without her husband would be to have illicit sex.

No one in any period of history has ever had as much sex as men thought briefly unchaperoned nineteenth-century women had.

If the couple could not be condemned for their approach toward sex, Restell's lawyers conceived that perhaps they could be condemned for their approach toward money. Various witnesses were brought forward, including one Lucinda Van Buskirk, a friend of Mrs. Purdy. Her testimony seemed to indicate that Mrs. Purdy's quarrel with Madame Restell was primarily financial. Following Mrs. Purdy's miscarriage, she and Buskirk went back to Madame Restell's office. Buskirk claimed she went in part "to gratify an idle curiosity in seeing Madame Restell."[28] She was also there to support Mrs. Purdy, who, after miscarrying, now wanted her watch and various rings back. With her problem now eliminated, it was easier to feel that it should not have cost so very much to resolve. Why should Madame Restell demand payment at all? Shouldn't she just help her as she was a fellow woman?

Let this be a lesson to always get all the money you're owed up front.

Madame Restell explained, fairly politely, that she did in fact need to be paid, and was not in the habit of doing abortions for $1. She told Mrs. Purdy that she couldn't return the pawn ticket for her jewelry until she (Restell) was given money of equal value to that ticket, especially as "we have done it much lower [in cost] than we are in the habit of doing it." It's not clear what made Mrs. Purdy think she was entitled to have an abortion for $1. Perhaps she was an extremely optimistic woman. Finally, perhaps a bit frustrated by this situation on a day when, according to Buskirk's account, numerous other patients were in the office, Madame Restell closed the discussion by reminding her that "if you'd gone your full time [and given birth to a baby] it would have cost you a good deal more."[29] She was surely correct in this regard; babies, as every parent finds out, are surprisingly expensive.

Undeterred, Mrs. Purdy countered that she was going to tell her husband. Perhaps she thought this would intimidate Madame Restell. It didn't. Madame Restell cautioned her against this action, noting that it could result in "a state prison offense for you as well as me."[30] This threat wasn't actually based in truth—at the time, only the abortionist would be prosecuted—but Mrs. Purdy didn't know that. Finally, the women agreed that Madame Restell would send to the boardinghouse where Mrs. Purdy lived for the money, and then return the jewelry. This did eventually happen, though the watch that had caused so much Sturm und Drang was, almost immediately, accidentally ruined by quicksilver leaking onto it and destroying the mechanism.

Mrs. Purdy wasn't the only one who sought to take financial advantage of Madame Restell. When Huron Betts, a friend of William Purdy, was called to the stand, he recounted a scheme to blackmail Restell. He claimed that, prior to the trial, William Purdy had requested that Betts visit Madame Restell and "ask her if she would give him so much money to keep his witnesses away from Court."[31] Purdy did not specify the amount of money, which seems like it ought to be the first thing to mention when blackmailing someone, but these were not criminal masterminds. Moreover, this attempt did not seem to be effective. Trying to blackmail Madame Restell was not generally destined to be effective, as she was candid about her work, though she later stated that she felt this act alone should have been enough to find Mr. Purdy guilty of extortion and perjury.

Restell's lawyers' approach—even the part where they got very upset that Mrs. Purdy once went on a walk with a painter—was called "brilliant and powerful."[32] But their vigor and frank enthusiasm for depicting Mr. and Mrs. Purdy as disreputable also allowed the Purdy team to play upon the jury's sympathies. Mrs. Purdy was dead, and the members of the jury would naturally feel sad for her husband. In his closing argument, Mr. Purdy's lawyer likened Restell's lawyers' descriptions to an attack of a hyena upon the sacred bodies of the dead. Furthermore, he claimed that unless New York cast Madame Restell out, it would have "no parallels in history but those of Sodom and Gomorrah."[33]

Despite all those efforts by Purdy's lawyer to paint Mrs. Purdy as an innocent who "fell into the snares of the prisoner," and Mr. Purdy as a man who "dares to vindicate the loss of a murdered wife and child," there was plenty of evidence to suggest that these were not perfectly honorable people.[34] Mrs. Purdy was certainly assertive enough to haggle with Restell, which seems contradictory to the depiction of her as a childlike, easily influenced woman who didn't know her own desires. It's also possible that Mr. Purdy was deeply aggrieved by the situation and his wife's illnesses—but not so grief-stricken that he didn't hope to make a profit from it.

It was all also irrelevant. The charges at the trial did not pertain to the niceness of people's character. Although the lawyers tried to shame either Restell or Mr. and Mrs. Purdy, the only question before the jury was whether or not Madame Restell had provided the wife with an abortion, and the means by which she did so.

The jury was told all the counts of the indictment; the first two involved providing an abortion with drugs while the third and fourth (somewhat more serious charges) concerned providing a surgical abortion. It took the jury five minutes to deliver a guilty verdict. Madame Restell was indicted on the third and fourth charges.

Many newspapers were apt to write about Restell's conviction not as a matter of technical accuracy but as a great moral victory. The *Brooklyn Evening Star* happily remarked that "this is a jury that has been found firm enough to stand up firmly to the rigor of their duties." That virtue was necessary, as the paper felt that Madame Restell was "a woman without a woman's nature, who aimed to make herself wealthy by foul and unnatural practices": "When Madame Restell is arrested," the paper said, "we hope no other of her race may arise to outrage morality and pander to vice."[35] No matter that plenty of others were already, in New York, practicing the same trade as Restell. They were just not doing it as publicly or as well.

George Washington Dixon was, predictably, ecstatic. He considered Restell's conviction to be not just a vindication of his outlook on the world but also of his newspaper's frequent indictments of Restell and her work, especially as Mr. Purdy's lawyer congratulated *The Poly-anthos* and its editor for speaking out against Restell. The *Sun* came close to defending her. When the *Weekly Zion*, that June, marveled that any Christian could read a paper that ran advertisement's like Madame Restell's, The *Sun* reprinted its criticism and wrote, "it gives us pleasure, as far as we are individually concerned, to meet these spiteful attacks from fanatics, hypocrites, and corrupt partisans…it gives us strong assurance that we are doing our duty to the public, that truth is making its way in triumph."[36]

As for the *Herald* and the *Sun*, where Madame Restell's advertisements ran, well, her advertisements continued. But the days of the *Herald* mounting impassioned defenses about what a fascinating, glamorous character she was had come to an end. Even someone who enjoyed flouting decorum as much as Bennett didn't want to be seen as mocking a dead twenty-one-year-old. When writing of the trial, the *Herald* opined, "We regard the arrest of this woman...to be an interposition of Providence to crush the whole corrupt fashionable society of this city to atoms. Madame Restell has been an accomplice with the demoralized portion of society in violating the laws of God and man."[37]

So much for being a beautiful female philosopher.

In response to this public backlash, Madame Restell would later write, with immense annoyance, that each newspaper "deemed it necessary or polite to say something about 'the woman' and thus lay claim to a proportion of morality, since this was an opportunity to gain it cheaply, supposing, doubtless, that he who prates loudest and longest against 'iniquity' will be sure to be considered excessively virtuous."[38] In her estimation these writers were "either the veriest saints or the veriest hypocrites in Christendom."

She had not attended court herself during the summation or the reading of the verdict. Immediately after the verdict was issued, her lawyers obtained a suspension of judgment until the case could be heard by the New York State Supreme Court.

It would take another year before the case was heard.

During the same year, Mr. Purdy was arrested in a bar fight. According to witness accounts, he attempted to fight a Mr. Crandell, who had remarked that Mr. Purdy was too small to fight, picked him up, and laid him on the bar. Then Crandell retired to a couch, where he tried to go to sleep. That is the most adorable ending to a bar fight one can imagine. If, of course, it had ended there. Mr. Purdy, seemingly unhappy about being laid on the bar like a toddler, announced that he would either "murder him [Crandell] or be murdered."[39] He appeared to have punched Crandell two or three times before being arrested.

To be fair, Purdy had lost his job after the publicity regarding the case. Public sentiment may have gone against Madame Restell, but he didn't come off well at the trial. He had also lost a wife and a potential child. He would hardly be the first man to get in a bar fight rather than deal with his grief. Especially in 1842, when a great many men in New York were trying to use vigilante justice to solve every problem, whether it was insecurity about their height or not liking newspaper editorials. Nonetheless, Restell's lawyers must have *wished* they could have used that anecdote at her original trial as testament to Purdy's disreputable character.

The case finally brought before the state's Supreme Court hinged upon technicalities. Madame Restell's lawyers said the law required witnesses to appear in court, so the accused had a chance to confront them. Mrs. Purdy never had. Her testimony about Madame Restell had been taken when she was ill and lying upon her deathbed. Restell's lawyers allowed that there were some cases where depositions taken out of court could be used as evidence. However, they said, "it must be taken when the defendant was present and had the opportunity to cross-examine the witness." They argued that the ramifications of failing to do so stretched far beyond this case, and that "the great principle that the accuser and the accused must be brought face to face, and that the latter shall have the opportunity to cross-examine, can never be departed from with safety."[40] Now, some might note that Madame Restell *had* met with Mrs. Purdy. She'd been at her house. However, when Madame Restell had visited, it had only been to allow Mrs. Purdy the chance to identify her, not to question her. Questions were posed—of course Madame Restell, never a shrinking violet, tried to talk to her—but at that time, Mrs. Purdy had not been under oath. So, according to Restell's lawyers, "she did put questions, but if the witness had answered falsely, she could not have been convicted of perjury."[41]

As for what Madame Restell asked Mrs. Purdy, the justice, Merritt, claimed Madame Restell "put the same question over and over again." Now, it's possible that Madame Restell just shouted, "Why the hell are you doing this, Ann Maria? Why the hell are you doing this?" in the dying woman's face a few times. If her treatment of the members of the American Female Moral Reform Society is any indication, that would not be out of character. However, as her lawyers pointed out, it might have been "a very material inquiry." Whether it was a great question or not we will never know because it was never recorded. Even though, according to Restell's lawyers, "the Justice did not deny that the questions and answers were pertinent, but he thought it was not material to put them down."[42]

Now, at long last, it was Madame Restell's turn to rage in print, which she was more than happy to do. Her husband and lawyers had probably had to use considerable energy to stop her from mounting her own defense sooner. As it was, a year's worth of pent-up ire and condemnation came spilling out of her in the *New-York Tribune*. She accused the papers of using "every variety of opprobrious invective the language afforded" to defile her. "No epithet was considered too gross, too vile to express the holy horror entertained by the truly pure and virtuous writers of the newspaper anathemas." She reminded readers that it was not murder, or arson, or any kind of major crime that prompted this, but only a misdemeanor that "caused this mighty newspaper volcano to burst upon her devoted head." Still, she vowed, "I will venture to afford that not one press in ten, loud mouthed in my abuse, will even lisp that the Supreme Court have decided that the evidence upon which a conviction was obtained against Madame Restell was illegal, unauthorized, and inadmissible."[43]

She was correct.

Madame Restell went free. The case against her regarding Mrs. Purdy was dropped. She would continue to work and advertise in New York, and she would continue to be visited by the rich and great. She would become one of them herself. But in public opinion, she would not be seen as a woman guilty of a misdemeanor. As far as many were concerned, after this case, she was a murderer.

CHAPTER EIGHT

The public backlash against Madame Restell, and the perception that she had gotten away with something egregious, caused the politician and playwright Major Mordecai Manuel Noah to bemoan the fact that she had been granted her freedom:

> Now she nearly rides over one of her judges, tosses up her beautiful head, and says, in effect, "behold the triumph of virtue!" Instead of a linsey woolsey petticoat, a bodice of the same cloth, fitted closely to her beautiful form, her lap filled with oakum and her tapering fingers filled with tar—she is gloriously attired in rich silks and laces, towers above her sex in a splendid carriage, snaps her fingers at the law and all its pains and punishments, and cries out for new victims and more gold. Can that woman sleep?[1]

She was, it cannot be stressed enough, sleeping just fine, although probably not with Mordecai Noah, no matter how much he fantasized about her breasts in a tight prison uniform. As he pointed out, Restell's wealth was only growing. Her elegant wardrobe was commented on—she'd come a long way from hemming other people's gowns. Her businesses were bustling, and her advertisements were running regularly, not only in the New York papers, but also in the *Boston Post* (where she directed clients to her office at 7 Essex Street).

Her empire was continuing to thrive because the opinion of men like Noah was offset by the many women who seemed to love her, or at least need her. If the testimonials of her patients are to be believed, her services remained essential. Letters, supposedly from women who had undergone Restell's treatment, made for popular journalism fodder—such as one allegedly from an actress published in *The Polyan-thos* during the Purdy trial:

> It was a lucky star for me under which you [Restell] were born. I
> could no more live without you in my theatrical connections than
> a fish without water. Fair words butter no parsnips, however, and
> what is worse, kill no babies. Send me a hundred dollars' worth of
> the powders immediately, or there will soon be a groaning worse
> than the last one. God bless you dear madam, you have taken
> off the primal curse denounced upon Mother Eve in Eden. I am
> bound to pray for you every night of my life.[2]

Dixon published this woman's letter in an attempt to expose Restell's horrifying business, but, as in many cases, it served as an inadvertent advertisement for her. And it wasn't only actresses or servants who turned to Madame Restell. The *Herald*, her erstwhile defender, noted that "young unmarried females moving in the highest circles have applied to her for aid, and she has the evidence of the fact under their own hands."[3] Perhaps among the most notable accounts of abortion during this period was the death of Mary Rogers, a famed beauty of the period who worked in a cigar store. The body of the twenty-one-year-old woman was found in the Hudson river in July 1841, shortly after the conclusion of Restell's trial. By 1842 the *Buffalo Courier* claimed that "the prevalent opinion now is that her death was occasioned by an attempt of a medical man to induce an abortion."[4]

Surprisingly, suspicion fell more upon Costello than Restell in this case. However, the *Gazette* suggested that Costello might have performed the abortion at Restell's behest, which seems unlikely, as the two were rivals, and the evidence to support this theory is lacking.

The amplified publicity only increased the level of fascination surrounding Madame Restell. Following the Purdy trial, she had now reached what might have been the height of her fame—or infamy. Everything she did—or did not do—would be reported on and published before the masses.

Some other reports about Restell's involvement in activities and operations during this time, interestingly, did not revolve entirely around her. In November 1843, a woman named Amelia Norton, who had two abortions performed by Madame Restell, tried to kill her ex-lover,

Henry Ballard, out of a sense that he had ruined her. While he was on the steps of the Astor House, she grabbed him by the collar and drove a knife into his chest. It "would have proved fatal had it been an eighth of an inch lower," reported the *Brooklyn Evening Star*.[5] This apparently wasn't even the first time she had attacked him; Amelia had beaten Henry with her parasol in Nassau Street just a few months prior, in August 1843.[6] She absolutely did not handle her breakup in a healthy fashion. However, her trial jury was sympathetic. She was acquitted. The jury seemed to buy strongly into the idea that you should sympathize with spurned women, so much so that Amelia's counsel during the trial claimed that, "if Mr. Ballard could not live, as he said, in New York in safety, unless the accused was in prison, why then, let him leave the city, for we have enough villains here without him."[7] This overlooks the fact that she was the one doing the villainous stabbing in this case. But if there is anything to take out of this trial regarding Madame Restell's business, it is that Amelia Norton, for one, still seemed physically quite strong following her abortions.

In most of these reports, however, Madame Restell would remain the focus. In March 1844, she was arrested again, after two married women charged that they had gone to Restell and taken her medicines "for the purposes and with the effects of avoiding the inconveniences of maternity." The *Star* noted, somewhat sensibly, that in this case, "it seems to us their guilt is even greater than Mrs. Restell's."[8] No one fully thought anything would come of the case, as, according to the *New-York Tribune*, by now Madame Restell had "made enough money to drive a horse and six carriages through the elastic meshes of the law."[9]

There is that mention of her carriage again.

An astonishing number of reports mention Madame Restell's carriage, or allude to the fact that she was a person with a carriage. One might sense that it mattered an undue amount to reporters, and their interest in her carriage might even strike us as surprising. Although if you were reporting on a successful person engaged in an illicit trade today, you might possibly note that this person had a nice car, most articles, barring those in automotive magazines, would probably not mention the car. However, there is a great difference between having a carriage in the 1840s and having an expensive car in the 2020s. If you were to buy a car today, even a very high-end one, the bulk of your outlay, excepting occasional trips to the mechanic, would end with the purchase. But having a carriage did not just mean Restell could afford to buy a carriage. It also meant she could afford to maintain a team of horses to pull it, a carriage house in which to keep the carriage and the horses, and the salary of a coachman to drive the carriage. It spoke to an ongoing, continuous stream of income. For this reason, most New Yorkers did not—could not—have a carriage simply for their own use. As is the case today, in Restell's time one of the benefits of living in an urban center like New York was that residents could walk to most of the places that provided for their daily needs. They could also travel by public transport. Hundreds of horse-drawn omnibuses, like the one taken by Mrs. Purdy on her way home from her operation at Madame Restell's, plied their routes—indeed, they were said to pass "every five minutes" on the streets of New York in 1827. By 1832, horse-drawn streetcars, which ran along steel tracks, had become even more popular than omnibuses, owing in part to their lower fares and in part to the comparatively smoother ride, due to those tracks. The *Herald* wrote that people were "packed into [the streetcars] like sardines in a box, with perspiration for oil."[10]

Any individual who could own a private carriage was taken note of and assumed to be doing very well financially. This had been the case for some time. It's for that reason, in an attempt to tax the rich, that George Washington instituted what's often considered to be the first federal wealth tax on private carriages. (It's worth noting that Washington's personal carriage was an extremely glamorous model painted a flashy white with gold trim. As roads were often muddy and unpaved, this color combination required a slave to clean it virtually every time it was driven.[11]) Many upper-class or upper-class-aspiring Americans, predictably, hated that tax, some because they actually owned carriages, and some because they thought of themselves as carriage-owners-in-waiting. Owning a carriage was, even more than owning a car like a Ferrari or a Jaguar today, the ultimate sign to everyone that you had made it in America.

And carriages, like most symbols of success, were supposed to be for men. Or men's wives. Women were not supposed to have the kinds of careers that enabled a carriage-owning level of personal success. Under an inherited British law known as coverture, a married woman in North America could not own property, enter into contracts, or earn a salary. This stance was to change around 1839, when states began allowing women to own property in their own name. This was so, for example, in Mississippi—not because of fledging feminist sentiments in that state, but because women sometimes brought an unusual amount of "property" into marriage, in the form of enslaved people. It would take until 1848 for the Married Women's Property Act to go into effect. It was only then that the property women brought with them into marriage was not subject to their husband's disposal and could not be seized in order to pay off his debts.

The passage of the Married Women's Property Act was not universally well received. It took some time to pass, because, as one journalist argued, "[men] will die for the women, but they will not part with their chance of a life lease in their property. So they dismiss all legislative action by calling the 'fair petitioners' angels, and bidding them go scrub."[12] That reporter concisely described benevolent sexism and "get back in the kitchen and make me a sandwich" dismissals about 170 years before there were tweets about them. Other men were eager to have people know that they were not motivated by greed but by fear of a *total societal breakdown* if women had their own money. In 1846, the *Herald*, whose editorial staff once proclaimed that refusing a woman a right to her own property when she was married was a "relic of barbarism," ran an article from a dissenter lamenting that, by allowing women the right to their own property and income, "marriage will degenerate into concubinage, and discord, confusion, litigation and meddling will take the place of unity, peace, affection and happiness."[13] This gentleman may have confused his wife's inability to complain due to complete financial dependence upon him with unity, peace, affection, and happiness. He may have subconsciously realized this as he wrote, "Should not the bill now before the legislature have its name changed to 'a bill to enable married women to leave their husbands at pleasure?'"[14] Maybe! But that is only upsetting if you believe women having the financial freedom to leave a husband who makes them miserable is atrocious.

Madame Restell, throughout this controversy, remained married. There were efforts to paint Charles Lohman as a masterful figure, but Madame Restell was too outspoken for that portrayal to ever catch on. It was clear to everyone that it was Madame Restell's carriage, not her husband's. She had bought it. She was riding in it. Many people might have disliked the services Restell was providing, but they *really* hated that she was enjoying the fruits of her labor and not getting back to scrubbing. The fact that she was reveling in the money she earned spoke to a new financial independence for women that scared the hell out of certain people.

There was a new reason to attack Madame Restell when information on Eliza Ann Munson's abortion broke on April 15, 1844. The story was remarkable in its similarities to Ann Maria Purdy's case. Like Purdy, Eliza was on her deathbed when her abortion came to light. She was described as "a very beautiful girl, about 26 years of age," and though she was said to have "some highly respectable connections in New Haven, Connecticut," she worked for a tailor in that city repairing gentlemen's pants.[15] Like Purdy, she accused Madame Restell of having caused the infection that ultimately led to her death. Madame Restell was subpoenaed to appear before Munson for identification. Madame Restell, imagining that, if Munson was on her deathbed, she could lay low for a few days and avoid being identified, fled to a house on Varick Street. This move wasn't successful: "Threats of arrest succeeded in making one of the many women in [Restell's] house disclose the direction Restell had taken."[16] So, at 2:00 in the morning, she was arrested and brought before the ailing Munson with two other women, who were "dressed in all respects like Madame Restell"—the equivalent of a police lineup.[17]

Eliza Ann Munson did not look well. "At this moment, the hue of death was overspreading her countenance, and her eyes were fast closed," a newspaper reported, "and it was only at the urgent request of the Coroner, continued for several minutes, that she at length opened them, and at once fixing a look upon Restell, raised her finger, and pointing directly to her whispered—that is her!"[18] She died immediately afterward. Madame Restell was, once again, sent to prison.

Some months prior, in December, Munson had found herself pregnant. She was familiar with Madame Restell's advertisements and made the journey from Connecticut to New York to see her. She first tried taking tansy oil at Madame Restell's instruction. When that didn't work, on December 14, Madame Restell performed an abortion.

Following that procedure, Eliza went to work in a shop in New York; a coworker there later said she had been in good health and had never complained. She did add that on March 1, Eliza had told her she was disappointed; she had been expecting to see a man from New Haven by the name of Frazer, who had promised to marry her, and who had initially convinced her to come to New York. He did not appear, and she left the city in late March. When her friend wrote to her in New Haven, assuming she'd gone back home, Eliza never replied.

But Eliza Munson didn't go to New Haven. She went to the home of a Mrs. Bird, one of Madame Restell's competitors. This was most peculiar; when people are recovering from an abortion, they do not typically go to a different abortionist's house months later.

At the trial, it was revealed that Munson first went to Mrs. Bird's house on March 29. She had been taking tansy oil for several days. According to a physician who subsequently examined her and diagnosed a uterine hemorrhage, "there was but little attention paid to her at the house of Mrs. Bird, who left her to go to New Jersey without the assistance of a nurse or even a candle during the night while she was absent."[19] He also claimed that, following the inferred operation, she had been given improper food, which likely means meat or vegetables that had spoiled.

This was a stark contrast to the way Madame Restell treated patients. When women recuperated at her residence, Madame Restell provided round-the-clock food, drink, and care. Sometimes she even slept in their bedrooms at night to make sure nothing went awry. This was much more compassionate than the treatment offered by her competitors. If something had gone wrong, it's uncertain how much she would have been able to do, but she certainly would have caught a decline as early as possible. As brash and gleefully combative as Madame Restell could be, she was extremely cautious when it came to caring for women post-abortion.

The physician was then asked why, if Miss Munson had been operated on in December by Madame Restell, she was taking tansy oil when she arrived at Mrs. Bird's house. The doctor suggested that perhaps the placenta had not been removed and became inflamed, but "the placenta had not undergone the state of decomposition I should have supposed it would if the operation had taken place December last."[20] He claimed the look of the placenta indicated that the abortion had taken place only a few days prior to when he saw Miss Munson in March.

He continued, "The anxiety evinced on the part of Mrs. Bird to make me believe that Madame Restell had committed the abortion that led to the state of disease in the body of the deceased induced me to think that Mrs. Bird might have produced the abortion herself.... [A]n abortion may have taken place in December, and another one been produced at a later period of time."[21]

It seems that Madame Restell performed a first, competent abortion on Eliza Munson in December, and then, in March, Eliza was subjected to a far less competent one by Mrs. Bird. The coroner's office reported as much on April 18 in the *New-York Tribune*. Mrs. Bird would be tried for Eliza Munson's second abortion in September. At that trial, Munson's sister claimed that she had visited Mrs. Bird's house, where Eliza appeared to be dying. As her health was clearly deteriorating, Mrs. Bird went to Eliza's bedside and instructed her to "tell your sister you came here to recover from the effects of the treatment you received at Madame Restell's and that you have had no operation performed on you here."[22] Munson's sister further alleged that her sister had said nothing of the kind before these instructions.

Mrs. Bird was likely panicking. Madame Restell *was* more famous than her. Trying to blame her failure on a woman that people, and juries, were likely to be more familiar with was a monstrous thing to do, but it might have worked. Even now, expecting upstanding behavior from people who are involved in technically criminal enterprises is perhaps a little too optimistic.

Once again, Restell did not seem to be guilty in causing a young woman's death. But it would be a mistake to think that Madame Restell emerged from this episode unscathed. In May 1845 an act was passed that ensured abortionists would suffer more serious repercussions. Using drugs or surgery to induce an abortion was now categorized as a felony, and anyone found guilty could go to jail for two to five years rather than the previous one-year sentence. The new law also specified that women who had abortions could be sentenced to three to twelve months in jail and that unmarried women who attempted to conceal a miscarriage were guilty of a misdemeanor.

Madame Restell's wry statements that she had been publicly shamed for nothing more than a misdemeanor had all at once become a thing of the past.

Even as the stakes grew higher, possible conviction did not deter women in seeking abortions. Modern estimates state that by the mid-nineteenth century, as many as 20 percent of pregnancies ended in abortion.[23] Women might be married and "respectable," or unmarried and desperate. One 1860 medical paper, written by the physician Edwin Hale, "safely asserted that there is not one married female in ten who has not had an abortion, or at least attempted one." The doctor further noted that, in his own practice, he had seen women who had given birth to "eight, ten and thirteen children, and [had] at least as many abortions." Hale was not necessarily horrified by this; he believed that "in no instance should the life, or even the *health* of the mother be sacrificed to save that of an impregnated ovum before the date of its 'viability.' "[24] Horatio Storer, an antiabortion activist, later came to a similar conclusion, about the frequency of abortions, if not the moral merit of performing them. He claimed in 1868 that in New York, there was approximately one abortion for every four live births. Rather than stopping women from having abortions, the law passed in 1845 would merely make women more inclined to keep quiet about them. Women were already disinclined to discuss the procedure, for fear of social censure, so they certainly weren't going to discuss it if the procedure meant going to jail. This hesitancy, predictably, made it harder for authorities to find those who were actually performing the abortions.

Restell, who had been so happy to threaten Ann Maria Purdy with jail time when no such punishment had existed, may have cringed to see it made real. However, as a result of her obvious love of well-placed publicity, she probably took particular note of the part of the act that made it a misdemeanor to even *advertise* abortive drugs. Not only the people placing the advertisements but the publishers of newspapers that did so were now indictable for a misdemeanor. This did not mean that such advertisements would cease entirely and immediately. As the *New-York Tribune* noted, "means will ultimately be found of evading the law by advertising covertly and indirectly the abominations which have hitherto been paraded conspicuously."[25] Ultimately, Madame Restell would have to begin using coded language and exercising a level of discretion and subtlety that was far from her forte.

If she was itching to issue a response—to state, in print, once again, that the services she offered were a public good—she restrained herself. She might have known that doing so at this moment, following the death of Eliza Munson, would only inflame the situation.

She could, however, leave town—and she did. In July 1845, Madame Restell departed back home to England. The *Herald* reported that she had sailed back along with other "fashionable travelers," including

Chevalier Henry Wikoff (the *Herald*'s bon vivant undercover reporter) and the Prince de Solms-Braunfels, who, around this time, was establishing colonies of German immigrants in Texas. The paper expected that they would "doubtless create a prodigious sensation in the Tuileries, Buckingham Palace, St. Petersburg, Berlin, Baden-Baden, and all the fashionable resorts of the old world."[26]

A great deal had changed for Madame Restell in little over a decade. No more would she have to endure the frightening conditions she saw during her voyage to America. Although it's unclear which ship Madame Restell boarded on her return to England, grouped as she was in the company of princes and chevaliers, she went first class. She picked a magnificent time to do so. The 1840s and 1850s are sometimes referred to as "the golden age of sea travel"—for people who could afford it. The poor were still eating moldy bread in the lowest compartments of the ships, but accommodations for the wealthy were markedly different. By 1840, steamships were making the voyage from Britain to America— the Cunard Line's RMS *Britannia* being the first. In an advance that, at the time, seemed quite innovative, a ship could now make a transatlantic crossing in two weeks. Previously, a monthlong journey had really only appealed to intrepid travelers or those desperate to relocate. A two-week voyage was more—or even less!—manageable. Why, it might even appeal to wealthy American gentlemen and ladies who wanted to visit London and Paris just for fun. It became clear to some shipping magnates that while money might still be made by packing in lower-class passengers, ships could gain prestige by offering finer accommodations to the wealthy. Although the ships were not as elegant as they would become by the end of the century, first-class passengers could expect to travel in comfort by 1845. For instance, the SS *Great Britain*, completed that year, boasted cabins that contained not only a bed but also a sofa. A ladies' lounge, where female passengers could change into their nightclothes, was connected to the cabins. Perhaps most impressive, the ship had a dining salon that could handle 360 people at the same time. It was adorned with painted columns and gilded embellishments, and mirrors hung on the walls to create the illusion of greater space. This salon was, according to *The History and Description of the Steam-Ship Great Britain*, authored by Captain Christopher Claxton (who seemed far more comfortable describing the iron used to make the ship than the interior decor), "really a beautiful room."[27]

No more would Madame Restell have to fight her fellow voyagers for food. But while Madame Restell was presumably enjoying her time abroad, the tides were turning further against her profession back in New York. Madame Costello, the rival who had once claimed to be Madame Restell, was arrested and sent to The Tombs after operating on an unwilling seventeen-year-old girl at the behest of the girl's lover. The *Evening Post* celebrated this incarceration while also reminding readers that "there is another woman of like kidney still practicing this infamous business": "We refer to Madame Restell.... [The public] demand that their families shall be protected against the insidious evils of this woman, and if the officers who have this matter in charge fail to perform their duty, the public will hold them to a fearful reckoning."[28]

With laws changing and the newspapers calling for her arrest, it might have occurred to Madame Restell that she should simply stay in Britain. By this point, she could have retired comfortably wheresoever she chose, and never trouble herself with work again—and her family welcomed her as she returned to lavish them with gifts.

Yet she returned to New York. There are a few reasons why she might have chosen this path. First and foremost, America was where the money was. The class mobility that was possible in America based solely on wealth, not breeding, didn't exist in Europe. She could probably climb higher in America than she ever could back home. Moreover, she was ambitious, and she hadn't yet fulfilled all her goals; she would have been very reluctant to leave behind a business that by 1845 spanned multiple cities. Madame Restell, now in her thirties, was just starting to *become* wealthy. She was still not wealthy enough to dominate the top echelons of New York society and bend them to her will, no matter how many of its members would visit her secretly.

Not to mention, she *liked* her work. She believed in it as a social good. She took very justified pride in being excellent at it. She had no desire to retire when she was at the top of her profession—and she was furious that anyone, let alone the men she considered intellectually inferior, would try to tell *her* what to do.

And so, even as the papers were calling for her immediate arrest, the *Herald* reported that by October 1845, she was, once again, "on the ground again in this city."[29]

Predictably, Madame Restell celebrated her grand return by buying a brand-new and, by all accounts, *splendid* carriage.

CHAPTER NINE

MADAME RESTELL BELIEVED SHE WAS SMARTER THAN MOST OF the people around her. Although some who fancy themselves to be intellectually superior are narcissistic, that's not true of everyone who holds this belief: A person may simply be acknowledging reality—and in the case of Restell, a woman who ran an underground birth control empire and performed successful operations time after time without any formal medical schooling, it could very well have been true. However, that sense of superiority defined her treatment of her patients as well as her adversaries. Given that she felt she was smarter, she also felt entitled to make decisions for them, just as the men in their lives often did. That was especially true if she felt her patients were making stupid decisions, or if there was a financial benefit to acting against their wishes. And her shortcomings in this regard were never clearer than when she stole Mary Applegate's baby.

In November 1845, Mary Applegate, a young woman in Philadelphia, revealed she was pregnant. The father was Augustus Edwards, a twenty-eight-year-old stockbroker. Mary worked for his family as a seamstress and had been occasionally having sex with him for about five years. However, this was the first time she had become pregnant.

She dutifully went to Augustus and explained her predicament, perhaps hoping he would marry her or at least offer to support her child. He initially refused to do anything. Then she threatened to expose the situation to his father. That didn't inspire any paternal devotion on the part of Augustus, but it seemed to frighten him. He conceded that he was willing to pay for Mary to board at Madame Restell's house until she gave birth, likely hoping that Madame Restell could convince her to have an abortion. He suggested that she say she was a married woman "whose husband had been lost at sea."[1] If she didn't agree to these conditions, he would not help at all.

Somewhat reluctantly, Mary boarded a train to New York with $14 from Augustus. He apparently promised to send Restell the money for her board.

Here it is worth noting that many midwives, Restell's rival Mrs. Bird among them, allowed pregnant women in similarly complex situations to stay with them and give birth for a fee. That was true even when mothers did not wish to keep those babies. Some babies would be put up for adoption or consigned to the almshouse, where they often died. The woman could then, hopefully, return to her life, with no one in her everyday life any wiser about her pregnancy. Other women would keep the child they gave birth to, and perhaps claim later, as no one had seen them pregnant, that it belonged to a deceased friend or relative, and they had simply taken the child under their wing out of noble obligation or charity.

So Mary Applegate did not come to Madame Restell in order to secure an abortion. She may have been unhappy about her pregnancy, but she fully intended to give birth and keep the baby.

When Mary arrived in New York, she was told that her board had not been paid. After learning her lesson with Mrs. Purdy, Madame Restell was not nearly as flexible or lenient regarding money matters as she had once been. She informed Miss Applegate that if she couldn't pay for board, she would have to stay in a hotel. Mary begged to stay, claiming that she was a stranger in New York and had no idea where to go. Madame Restell allowed her to stay for the night, but said she would have to figure out the money the next day. To everyone's relief, a man then arrived, doubtless sent a bit late by Edwards, to pay $100 for Mary Applegate's boarding fee.

Mary would remain at Madame Restell's for the next month. During that time, Madame Restell talked to her daily. Lest you think this a welcome change from surroundings at Mrs. Bird's, where patients were virtually abandoned to deal with their difficulties on their own, Madame Restell wasn't just making pleasant conversation. In many of her chats she tried to pressure Mary to give her child up for adoption, especially if it was a girl.

Time and again, Mary refused Madame Restell's offer. She was very clear that she wanted to keep her baby. This was true even when

Madame Restell painted a rosy picture of the life Mary could lead as a single woman in New York. She told Mary that "there were plenty of men in the city who would be glad to 'keep' [Mary].... [She] could dress well and live in style."[2] Perhaps, in Madame Restell's mind, the idea of being kept by a rich man (temporary though that arrangement might be) was preferable to working as a seamstress or in a factory to support yourself and a child.

Remember that Madame Restell had been an impoverished single mother herself. It may have been that it was inconceivable to her that an unmarried poor woman would wish to keep a child if *any* other options were available, especially as Mary seemed determined not to take a wealthy lover. There were a great many women boarding with Madame Restell who shared her point of view—they were there for abortions. And there were so many of them that they sometimes slept two to a bed.

Mary Applegate would later recount the stories and backgrounds of these women, who ranged in age from teenagers to midlife. Their reasons for needing an abortion were every bit as varied as those that women have today. One, a widow in reduced circumstances, already had a fifteen-year-old son that she struggled to raise. Another claimed that her husband (and hopefully she) didn't want children. Some were there for the first time, such as a seventeen-year-old factory worker whose wealthy lover had sent her to Madame Restell. Others were repeat clients, including a woman who was visiting Madame Restell for her tenth abortion. That woman was already supporting her mother, brothers, and sisters, a situation that probably made her less than enthusiastic about having another mouth to feed. Many of these women were involved with wealthy men of the town and were of middle or upper class. One "lover" was supposedly a congressman, another was a bank president.

Perhaps the most heartrending account, and certainly of the type that must have motivated Madame Restell to continue providing her services, was that of a young girl whose mother had visited Restell because she could not figure out why her daughter's period had stopped. She wondered if Restell's pills could restore its regularity. Her daughter was demure and pious—she even taught Sunday school—so the mother never imagined that she might have had premarital sex. The *New-York Medical and Surgical Reporter* eventually noted some of the details:

The mother...was told, to her very great surprise, that her daughter was *enceinte* [pregnant], and that an operation would be necessary. The mother doubting the truth of so unexpected a charge,
upon her fair and accomplished daughter, turned and asked if it
was possible that such was the case, and on being answered in the
affirmative, she inquired the name of her seducer. The daughter
replied, that it was their relative—, who had always been so intimate in their family, and made their house his home, whenever he
was in town.[3]

Incest happened in 1846, too. Despite the mother's understandable upset, the idea that a woman might be in this position would not
be entirely shocking to people at the time. There are hundreds of
nineteenth-century newspaper reports dealing with incest. According
to Lynn Sacco, in her book *Unspeakable: Father-Daughter Incest in American History*, "nineteenth century reports most often identified 'incest
fiends' as respectable—even prominent—white men: clergymen, local
officials, men with long and deep ties to the community, and men who
earned or inherited wealth.... [The public] did not react to the reve-
lation of incest with disbelief."[4] Disbelief came later, around the turn
of the twentieth century, when a certain prudishness, as well as censorship of papers discussing any sexual matters, led many to believe that
a respectable man simply could not commit such a heinous act. Sig-
mund Freud, for instance, initially wrote that when his female patients
had been sexually abused by incest as children, the experience often
resulted in long-lasting mental health problems. When his colleagues
said it was impossible that girls from good families could have been
abused in such a manner, he revised his theories to say the women
must have made up such episodes, and that their tendency to fantasize
about it was merely another one of their mental issues—namely, an
Elektra complex.

All of which is to say that, even as this case was disturbing, it would
likely not have been the only case of incest that crossed Madame Restell's doorstep. Fortunately, the daughter's operation was successful.
She left Madame Restell's a week later, no longer pregnant with her
rapist's child.

Meanwhile, on December 11, Mary Applegate went into labor.
She was attended by Madame Restell and Madame Restell's daughter,

Caroline. By now, Caroline was fourteen years old, and Madame Restell had hopes of training her in the family business. The birth went well, and between seven and eight o'clock, Mary laid eyes for the first time on her healthy little girl. Afterward, Restell took the baby away. She brought her back to Mary the next day, and reportedly, two subsequent times. She then informed Mary that the father, Augustus Edwards, had written to her suggesting the child be placed with a nurse.

This practice wasn't uncommon. Historically, while more popular in England than America, many women employed wet nurses to feed and care for their newborns, and that nurse didn't necessarily live at their house. Jane Austen and her siblings, for example, were sent to live with a wet nurse during their infancy. That arrangement had some obvious upsides; not worrying about feeding the child, or the baby screaming at night, gave women more time to recuperate after childbirth, and it also meant that someone else was doing the child's diapers and laundry. Mothers could, theoretically, visit their infants as often as they wished, though this became a less viable option if the wet nurse lived far away.

By Madame Restell's time, the practice was becoming less popular. William Cobbett's 1829 manual *Advice to Young Men* chided men for funding the practice, saying that "all the pretenses about [their wives'] sore breasts and want of strength are in vain." Rather, he claimed, many men wanted to send their infants to board with a wet nurse because of "a desire to be freed quickly from that restraint which the child imposes, and to hasten back, unbridled and undisfigured, to those enjoyments, to have an eagerness for which, or to wish to excite a desire for which, a really delicate woman will shudder at the thought of being suspected."[5] Basically, men sent infants out to board with wet nurses so they could immediately resume having sex with their wives and enjoy their sexy, non-milky breasts.

However, the wet nurse arrangement also had huge disadvantages. For the parents, it meant a lack of bonding time between the mother, father, and baby. It also led to the actual children of wet nurses—the ones for whom the milk was physiologically intended—being neglected in favor of the charges for whom the nurses were being paid. A wet nurse might even send her own child to a baby farm in order to take on a wealthy charge.[6] Wet nurses employed to live at home with wealthy families had pay that ranged from $20 to $50 a month, and according to one newspaper, the *Topeka Lance*, "her expenses are paid, and [she] is fed on the best of everything." However, it meant, in the *Lance*'s words, "the abandonment of their own flesh and blood."[7] Putting their own infants out to board with a baby farmer might cost $10 or $12 a month. And, unlike their mothers, they would not be receiving "the best of everything."

Some baby farms took in as many children as possible for a fee, and they were often dangerous and poorly run. These round-the-clock daycares usually fed the babies cow's milk or pap (made from boiled bread), which were far less nourishing than breast milk. Prior to the use of glass bottles, ill-suited substitutes were also likely to be served in jugs that were difficult to clean, and thus laden with bacteria. That the nurse's child might die was not of concern, at least to the wealthier families. Indeed, it is particularly disturbing to note that it was sometimes seen as a good thing if the wet nurse's child died as it meant all her milk could go to the paying client's child. The idea that this woman might be overwhelmed by grief and sobbing hysterically while nursing a benefactor's infant was, apparently, not a huge deterrent.

In southern states, this practice had particularly grim consequences as slaves were often conscripted to nurse their enslavers' children. If no slave (with a milk supply) was available on a given plantation, a woman might be taken from another one to provide milk for a white child, leaving her natural-born child behind, likely to starve. Some white writers from the period supposed that a special bond developed between such a nurse and the white child—one report from the era claimed, "It is not unusual to hear an elegant lady say, 'Richard always grieves when Quasheehaw is whipped, because she suckled him.'"[8] Unfortunately, it seems the bond was not strong enough to stop the enslaved woman from being physically brutalized. Quasheehaw may have suckled Richard faithfully, and may have given up her infant to do so, but she was still being whipped twenty-five years later.

Sending her child away to a wet nurse may not have been Mary Applegate's preference, but then again, she might have been holding out hope that she and Edwards would reconcile. Based on the little we know about him, Edwards did not seem the paternal type; it's doubtful he would be enthusiastic about helping to change the diapers, or dote on a newborn. Still, it's possible that Mary thought that visiting their daughter at the nurse's home would be a nonintimidating way to ease him into fatherhood.

So, Mary met with the nurse, who said her name was Catherine Rider. She lived in Harlem with her husband, who worked as a mason. Seemingly satisfied that her baby would be in good hands, Mary entrusted the child into her care. Then she stayed with Madame Restell for another sixteen days, recovering from the birth.

By modern standards, this period of rest may seem lengthy. The United States is not generous in giving new mothers time to heal and recuperate, although the need to do so is taken seriously in other countries. In Germany, the postpartum period is known as *Wochenbett*, which translates to "week's bed," and corresponds with a law prohibiting new mothers from working for eight weeks after delivering a child. They receive full pay from work during this period, as well as for six weeks before giving birth. Following a birth—and a period in the hospital, which typically lasts from three to seven days in Germany, or up to fourteen if you had a Caesarean—a midwife covered by the mother's insurance will visit new mothers every day for the first ten days postpartum to help the parents adjust to life with a new baby. In contrast, today, in the United States, insurance is required to cover only two days in the hospital after giving vaginal birth. Most people can't afford to stay longer. We are also the only high-income nation that does not mandate maternity leave, which means that some women (according to one study, 12 percent of them[9]) have to return to work within only a week of delivering a child.

It is perfectly understandable to envy Mary Applegate her bedrest and the notion that she had a nurse to help in these circumstances, but she would not relax for long.

After recuperating, she boarded a train back to Philadelphia to meet with Augustus Edwards, to ask "what he intended to do for the child."[10] Augustus didn't plan to do anything. As far as he was concerned, he'd already *done* everything that was to be expected. Mary asked him if he could give her the money to move to Harlem, so she could be near the baby. He offered $100 to help pay her costs for a year, provided she never contact him again. There was only one problem—and it was a significant one: he claimed he had never written to Madame Restell about a baby nurse.

Panicked, Mary returned to Madame Restell, who claimed that she had no idea how to locate the nurse to whom she'd given the baby, or who even currently had the child under their guardianship. When Edwards arrived at the boardinghouse to try to help find the child—perhaps the only moment in this saga where Edwards seems halfway decent—Madame Restell claimed she had no knowledge of a Mary Applegate at all. Catherine Rider, the wet nurse, meanwhile, was nowhere to be found.

This is some horrifying gaslighting, and people were, correctly, appalled. By February 20, New Yorkers who had heard the story were up in arms. Notices were posted throughout the city calling for people to gather to "compel Madame Restell to deliver up the child taken from the young girl who was confined at her house."[11] The meeting drew over a thousand people. Shouts rang through the air: "Hand her out!" "Where's Mary Applegate's child?"[12] It might very well have become a riot.

In the past, people's dislike of Madame Restell might have been tempered by the fact that she was performing a necessary and much requested public service. Plenty of people abhor the idea of abortion until the minute they or their daughters need one. But now, there was a reason to hate this carriage-riding lady without the risk of making themselves look like hypocrites.

This gathering was, somewhat predictably, called by George Washington Dixon, Madame Restell's longtime adversary. Mounting a hogshead, he suggested, uncharacteristically sensibly, that a group of property owners in the neighborhood should "demand the removal of Madame Restell, on the ground that her presence endangered the property of the neighborhood."[13] It probably did not endanger their property as much as Dixon calling on thousands of very angry people to congregate, but no matter.

Mercifully, despite the cursing and moral outrage, the demonstration remained fairly peaceful. The *Brooklyn Daily Eagle* speculated that the crowd was restrained, either because of "the presence of the Chief of Police with a strong posse, or the knowledge that the object of their maledictions had fled from her den earlier that day."[14] In response, Madame Restell simply went out from her house on Greenwich Street to another on Chatham Street. This was in keeping with her usual evasive pattern. When the police came for her, she lied about her name. When the attacks on her began to mount in the press, she went abroad. When a mob came to her house, she withdrew to a different abode. When she wanted to respond, she did so coolly, in the press, not in the heat of the moment.

Many in the mob seemed to be under the false impression that Madame Restell had somehow kept Mary Applegate's child for herself—which seems extremely unlikely, considering that Madame Restell never expressed any desire for more than one child and was a great believer in the benefits of family limitation. Predictably, the people's cries that she should give back the child were pitifully ineffective. The mob dispersed after a full day of yelling at an empty house.

By February 25, Madame Restell had found time to sit and formulate her response. She wrote an article for the *New-York Tribune* blaming George Dixon for raising the mob, and claiming that, like many others, he had attempted to blackmail her. "Again and again, I have been applied to by his emissaries for money," she asserted, "and as often, they have been refused. As a result, I have been vilified without stint or measure, which, of course, I expected, and of the two, would prefer to his praise."[15] His praise, Madame Restell implied, was easily won for a price. Adding fuel to the fire, she quipped that he had defamed another individual in similar terms to the ones leveled against her—until recently, at which point he had begun writing about how wonderful they were. She suggested that the individual had reached a financial agreement with him.

She also reminded the public that they didn't *like* George Dixon. In this, at least, she could join the people in finding a common enemy. "So satisfied have I been that the public have understood this man's character that I have desisted from the least notice of him," she wrote. "Such a person posts in the dark hour of the night, inflammatory anonymous placards, calling a public meeting at the hour of the day most likely to gather a crowd, gets up on a flour barrel, makes what is termed 'a speech'—then runs to some of the newspapers with the terrific announcement of a 'great mob.'" By writing about the event, the newspapers were culpable of "enabling a person to extort money," or else he might tell his victim that "he'll raise a riot."[16]

In her opinion, the mob gathered by Dixon was merely proof of "the existence of characters, black and fiendish, who hesitate not to use means of violence for the basest purposes."[17]

Accusing protesters of being a violent mob is typically an effective way to draw attention away from whatever they're protesting. In this case, the editors of the *Tribune* agreed that, "if Madame Restell has been guilty let THE LAW deal with and punish her—not a mob."[18]

The problem facing the public in the news was no longer that Madame Restell had, at best, lost a child in her care. The problem was now that mobs were threatening property damage.

The distraction proved effective. The case regarding Mary Applegate's baby was never brought to court. Madame Restell was never even indicted. And in a city where thousands of children were homeless and roamed the streets daily, one more lost infant was not enough to sustain the public's interest for long.

Still, the episode did mark the end of George Washington Dixon's time in New York. It's difficult to say how much of his retreat can be credited to Madame Restell's willingness to call him out in the press, and how much was simply due to new and absorbing interests. In a genuinely bizarre move that seems entirely in keeping with Dixon's persona, by July 1846 he was in Philadelphia. There, he donned a military uniform and declared himself a general who was heading off to the Yucatan. The *Union* had to explain that he had "no commission, and no species of authority from the government of the United States," and that, indeed, his plan to conquer the Yucatan was "abhorrent to the policy of our government."[19] Dixon's mental condition was never fully explored, let alone treated, but the fact that he was a libelous anti-sex blackface performer, who wanted to take over a part of South America while engaging in an act of stolen valor, might temper modern sympathies from those of every political party. By August, he was in New Orleans, still declaring himself a general, and he was promptly arrested for disturbing the peace. In 1848, two men, who apparently were not charmed by his playacting at being a military leader, beat him with his own chapeau bras. He spent his later years running a coffee stand, and he died in a charity hospital in New Orleans. He was immortalized in the *Memphis Daily Appeal* as being "the father of negro minstrelsy." "If a deserved tomb is ever raised to his memory, let it bear the inscription 'born too soon,'" declared one journalist, who apparently had some very incorrect ideas about how popular blackface would be in the future.[20]

That was the end of George Washington Dixon. We at least know what happened to him, strange though it may have been.

But what *really* happened to Mary Applegate's child? There are a few theories. One we could take at face value is Madame Restell's explanation that Mary Applegate was making the story up. But then, Restell was comfortable lying to the police to avoid getting herself in trouble, and Mary had absolutely no reason to do that. Nothing about Mary's behavior or history suggests that she was mentally unstable. Her descriptions of Restell's practice also seem too vivid and consistent with other accounts for her to have not spent significant time in the house. The *New-York Medical and Surgical Reporter* wondered about another sinister possibility: "Could it be, that her seducer had bargained with this wretch who traffics in the lives of her fellow creatures, to starve her innocent child to death?"[21] Maybe. Edwards claimed he'd never written to Madame Restell to even try to dissuade her from letting Mary return with her child, but he seems less than trustworthy. However, if the intent was to kill Mary Applegate's child, there would have been no need to hire a nurse and go through with an elaborate ruse. Doing so would be needlessly complicated when Restell could have very easily put a pillow to the baby's face one night and told Mary the sad news the next morning. An infant suddenly dying in 1846 would not have surprised anyone. It's also speculated, and this seems the most likely answer, that Mary's father paid Madame Restell to abduct the baby.

This account comes from *Restel's* [*sic*] *Secret Life*, by the Reverend Bishop Frederic D. Huntington. While it's the best version of events available, it's a work that should be treated with some skepticism. Not because Bishop Huntington disliked Madame Restell; enemies can paint a well-rounded picture of a person as their dislike generally has some foundation. There are aspects of his book that line up with other accounts. However, large portions of *Restel's Secret Life* are full of so much one-on-one dialogue that it veers toward being elaborate fiction. Barring the possibility that Huntington had hidden himself inside Restell's home, there's no way he could have witnessed private chats between Restell and her husband, let alone those where they supposedly cackled about how much they loved demonic misdeeds. (And lest you become genuinely, neurotically concerned that maybe this was the case, and that Huntington had hidden himself in a closet like

Columbo to listen in on people, you should know he lived in Boston at the time of the Applegate incident.) Nonetheless, in this nineteenth-century bishop's imagining of the scene, he claims that the exchange between Restell and Mary Applegate went as follows:

> "Your father don't want you to have that baby" [said Madame
>   Restell].
>
> "I don't care what my father says," exclaimed the mother, in a
>   fury, "I want my baby!"
>
> "Well, you can't have your baby! I adopted it out to a strange
>   lady!"[22]

This is not even very good fiction. Brusque though Madame Restell could be, it's highly doubtful that she ever shouted that she adopted a baby out to a "strange lady." And, let's be honest, she was a well-read and well-spoken woman with, by all accounts, elegant manners. She wouldn't have made the grammatical error of "don't."

Huntington then has Mary Applegate exclaim that she's going to make the city "too hot to hold you," and descend into Madame Restell's basement, horror-movie style, to search for infant bones. It is a great shame that Huntington did not live long enough to write film noirs because he crafts what is, admittedly, a very snappy scene.

Snappy enough, according to Huntington, to make Mary Applegate approach the bishop some years later. One day, a woman arrived at his door and declared herself to be "one of the principal actors in a portion of that terrible life which…your little book recounts with such vividness." She thought that if she shared the rest of her story with him, and he relayed it, doing so "will help me in my object, which is to find my child." In what is a remarkable stroke of luck for the bishop, should we take him at his word, his fictional account may have inspired Mary to give him as close to an accurate account of these events as we're likely to find. She corrected inaccuracies in his earlier story (for instance, he'd gotten the sex of her baby wrong), but still lay the blame for her loss on her father. According to Huntington, following the birth of her child and her inability to locate it, Mary went to Peekskill to stay with a farmer's family. Seeing his daughter's distress, her father repented and promised to find her baby. Mary claimed, "Father kept his promise faithfully, and did all that money could do

to trace the woman to whom Madame Restell had given up my child."
When he approached Madame Restell in person, she told him that for
a fee of $5,000, she could give him some direction about the baby's
general whereabouts. However, she also cautioned him that she could
not assure he would actually find the child, as, "you see, when proud
parents employ me to save their daughters from disgrace, and to rid
them of the disagreeable consequences of their peccadilloes, I act
faithfully for them."[23] In other words: he had told her to get rid of the
child, and she had done it.

This quote, relayed by Mary, with its clear undertone of "I did what
you paid me to do," sounds much more like Madame Restell than
shouting about strange ladies. So does discussion of their peccadilloes.
And while it's absurd to think that Huntington was privy to private
one-on-one conversations, it's less absurd to think that Mary might have
read his account of her interactions with Madame Restell and, grateful
someone was so interested in her story, chosen to follow up with him.

This may explain why the child went missing. However, it still leaves
the question of who, exactly, raised the child, if it was raised at all.
Mary Applegate never found out, though she spent the rest of her life
searching. Her father reportedly was able to track the child as far as
Cincinnati before he died. Mary supposedly told Bishop Huntington
that her father had left her his money, and that she had used "much of
that... in the thus-far vain search. But, oh, sir, I would gladly give all I
have left, and work hard the rest of my life to once again clasp my child
to my aching heart."[24]

Nearly two hundred years later, I still wish I could solve that mystery
for her.

The notion of childhood as we now understand it is very modern.
Many adopted children during Restell's era were valued as cheap or
even free labor. In the 1850s, children as young as age one could be
contractually bound to a family as a servant until they reached the age
of eighteen.[25] And servitude could encompass a myriad of different
duties.

Given that Mary's daughter was last seen in the Midwest, she might
have been considered useful on a farm. One farmer noted, "Every boy
born into a farm family was worth a thousand dollars."[26] The orphan
trains, founded by Charles Loring Brace in 1854, took advantage of
that very attitude. Orphaned or homeless children were transported

from New York to the Midwest. The express purpose was not to find them parents but to find them work on the farms. Brace remarked, "Farmers come in from twenty-five miles looking for the 'model' boy who will do light work on the farm.... [H]ousekeepers look for girls to train up, mechanics seek boys for their trade."[27] Children as young as three could be put to work hulling berries. All the earnings from their work, naturally, went to the head of the household.

While Brace claimed an interest in "saving" the children, he really wanted to "save" New York from these particular children. He was wary of immigrants, especially Catholics, and apparently believed that if their offspring remained in Manhattan, they would "perhaps be embittered at the wealth, the luxuries they never share": "Then let society beware, when the outcast, vicious, reckless multitude of New York boys, swarming now in every foul alley and low street, come to know their power and use it."[28]

Mary Applegate's child needn't have been sent out of the city for people to use her for their benefit. In a country free of child labor laws, even very young children could be put to work in factories, and many, especially the children of immigrants, were. At least one factory owner declared that some of the work was best done by "little girls from six to twelve years old."[29] Others "bragged about the intricate piecework produced by children's nimble fingers," according to one reporter who has investigated the practice. When the stories started coming out, "some Americans were shocked...to learn that these children were as young as four."[30]

Or did Mary Applegate's baby simply perish? No matter how comfortable some may have been with putting very young children to work in their factories or as servants in their homes, they would have to wait until the children were old enough to follow commands and act with some degree of rationality. Feeding and clothing them, as well as keeping them healthy until that time, would have been a relatively expensive endeavor. Given the poor conditions they were put in and the high infant and child mortality rates, they might die, and then all effort would be wasted. Meanwhile, there was no shortage of homeless children—approximately twenty thousand to thirty thousand of them in New York City alone in 1850—who could begin working *tomorrow*.

Infants without their parents were more likely to die than be adopted in New York, even later in the century. For instance, in 1895,

129 abandoned infants were housed on Randall's Island in New York; 4 of them were then claimed by their parents, and 1 was adopted. The other 124 died. Adoption was difficult to popularize as many "respectable" people believed that a child of an unwed mother would be genetically inferior. Brace of the orphan trains claimed that "certain appetites or habits if indulged abnormally and excessively through two or more generations, come to have an almost irresistible force, and, no doubt, modify the brain so as to constitute an almost insane condition."[31] Basically, the child of a prostitute was predestined to become a prostitute as well, so adopting her was pointless. He thought the same thing about the children of thieves, even if they had no contact with their parents. This kind of fallacious thinking was a precursor to the eugenics movement that would be used to justify mass sterilization in America and abroad.

Despite the odds, Mary Applegate never gave up hope. She claimed (or at least Huntington claimed) that she could not conceive that her child had died. When asked about that possibility, she remarked, "My darling dead? Oh, no! No! She is somewhere. Somewhere in this great wide, wide world and someday I will—I will see her and clasp her to my bosom once again."[32]

Trying to track an infant years later with almost no information and in a time prior to search inventions made the task nearly impossible. Mary died without ever seeing her child again, despite spending her entire life and the bulk of her funds searching for her.

If Madame Restell was overcome by guilt regarding Mary Applegate's struggle, there is no evidence of it. Certainly, she was less publicly bothered by it than by the mob that congregated outside her house. While modern readers surely see this episode as a profoundly dark blot on her character, if she had been asked about it at the time, and decided to give a straight answer, she might have said that she had just been doing her job.

The idea that women should have sole autonomy over their own bodies was still a long way off, and there is still, today, ample enthusiasm for the idea that single mothers should give away their children after birthing them. You can see this attitude with a number of people exclaiming "We will adopt your baby!" as though they are generously doing the birth mother a favor, and not the other way around. Madame Restell could tell herself that she was doing what was best for Mary in the long run. When it became absolutely clear that she was not, she could remind herself that her client was not Mary Applegate. It was Mary Applegate's father.

And while she may have liked Mary, she had her own family to worry about.

Chapter Ten

MADAME RESTELL WAS IN THE RARE POSITION FOR A WOMAN IN 1847 of being the breadwinner for her family. More surprising than the fact that she'd found herself in such a position, though, was the fact that it was going extremely well.

It was reported that Madame Restell "dresses with splendor, takes her daughter to France to complete her education, as it was very proper she should...and drives in her carriage with four superb horses and servants in livery."[1] Her fortune was vast, her carriage still envied, her closet well stocked, and her teenage daughter was in an excellent school. Who could ask for more?

Even Restell's critics admitted that both she—now thirty-five—and her home were beautiful. They were entranced by her pretty eyes; by her droll, mischievous smile; and by "the faultless development of her bosom." One of her detractors wrote that she had "fine proportions, tending to the em bon point [busty], she had a profusion of dark brown hair, which she dresses tastefully...and dressed...with elegance, and often with splendor." Basically, "she would be considered anywhere a showy and attractive woman."[2]

Her place at Greenwich Street was stocked with "gems of art, real and costly," and the furniture, mirror, and fine rugs all bespoke "the taste and wealth of the owner."[3]

And while money supposedly cannot buy happiness, her critics were especially offended that Madame Restell seemed happy. More than that, she seemed *fulfilled*. She felt her work was meaningful. She was, very possibly, the most skilled person at her profession. She was incredibly well paid. One anonymous account by someone identified only as a "Physician of New York" described his impressions of her in 1847:

Madame Restell is, in her own estimation, a philosopher, a philan-
thropist, and in more ways than one, a public benefactor. She has
the most serene and complacent ideas of her importance to society, she really doesn't see how the community could possibly get
along without her. She would tell you, in a very affecting way, no
doubt, of the fears she had allayed, the agonies she had removed,
and the sorrows and misfortunes concealed. In all this she has the
most unbounded confidence. She positively thinks that she is one
of the nicest, best, bravest little women in the world; and she would
be very indignant, if anyone should offer to dispute it.[4]

The author was not an admirer: the subtitle of the work included
An Account of Her Life and Horrible Practices. After the theft of Mary
Applegate's daughter, you might very well agree with the physician,
and not with Madame Restell. But still—Madame Restell would remain
undisturbed.

Lingering somewhat in the background of this satisfied scene was
Charles, Madame Restell's husband. For all the lavish description of
her, he is something of a footnote in the historical record. A typical
description of the husband of one of the wealthiest women in the city
states only that he was a "tall and handsome man of thirty-five...a
printer by trade and an editor by profession."[5]

Did you forget Charles existed? You wouldn't be alone. While
Madame Restell was off getting into legal scrapes, buying carriages,
and quarreling with her rivals, Charles's role was decidedly more
domestic. For the most part, he appeared content to linger in the
shadows and do his bit to support his more ambitious and outspoken
wife. He would later be said to have "a bland, courteous manner...
more like a benevolent Samaritan than a designing adventurer."[6] As
hurtful as it might be to be described as bland, it's true that he was
more subdued than his wife, but that's like saying a fire burning in a
grill is more subdued than a firework. Among the people who actually
met Charles, and didn't merely make up theories about his persona,
he seems to have been perceived as pleasant and good-natured. He
was said to be a man of "robust constitution [who was] extremely moderate and temperate in all his habits."[7] He drank, but not too much;
he appeared to love his stepdaughter and, later, his grandchildren;
he didn't gamble or womanize—by the standards of the time, Charles

was an ideal husband. There wasn't the same backlash to him, despite his profiting from his wife's profession, that there was toward Madame Restell. There was nothing fundamentally offensive about a man riding in a carriage, even if he'd engaged in some scurrilous means to get that carriage. A man making money in America by any means was merely considered ambitious (and might even be admired for it, if you look at modern icons like the protagonists of *The Wolf of Wall Street* or *The Godfather*). Men in America are *supposed* to be ambitious. A woman doing the same was, and still is, perceived as defying her natural supportive and maternal nature.

A ruggedly businesslike wife was not only shocking but positively inconceivable to many at the time. In 1847, Charlotte Brontë noted that women might have the same ambition as men, writing in *Jane Eyre* that "they need exercise for their faculties and a field for their efforts as much as their brothers do; they suffer from too rigid a restraint, too absolute a stagnation, precisely as men would suffer; and it is narrow-minded in their more privileged fellow-creatures to say that they ought to confine themselves to making puddings and knitting stockings, to playing on the piano and embroidering bags."[8]

This was an idea that was seen as *extremely* controversial at the time. The author Lady Elizabeth Eastlake thought that notions about women being as ambitious and skilled as men threatened "an overthrowing of social order" (bear in mind that for all her talk of female ambition, Charlotte Brontë still did not believe that women should be allowed to vote).[9] And, of course, there were still people who were convinced that Charles, largely by virtue of the fact that he was a man, *must be* the puppeteer pulling Madame Restell's strings. How could a woman ever be so successful on her own? Newspapers, whose reporters were doubtless eager for an exciting story, declared that he had started Madame Restell down her path as an abortionist. According to them, "after their marriage, business called Lohman to Europe. He took his wife with him and left her in Paris, while he went to Russia. While in Paris, Mrs. Lohman became acquainted with a Madame Restell.... [F]rom her Mrs. Lohman acquired knowledge of the infamous practices which she has followed here."[10]

Throughout many court trials during this period, there was a running theme that a woman could only sin if she was compelled to do so by a man. A woman who had sex outside of marriage must have been the victim of a vile seducer, and a woman who performed abortions must have been made to do so by her nefarious husband. This was not the case here. The notion that Charles took his wife to Europe to train her as an abortionist is absurd. We know the identity of the pill compounder from whom our Madame Restell almost certainly learned her craft—and it wasn't another Madame Restell. Indeed, there is no mention of any Madame Restell in the papers before the 1830s, when Ann Lohman began advertising under that pseudonym. Moreover, shortly after their marriage, when they were working in relatively humble professions as immigrants in lower New York, neither Charles nor Ann would have had the money or the time to go abroad and associate with such exciting and disreputable characters.

People who actually believed that Madame Restell had trained in Europe and not on the Lower East Side were buying into the mythos she created about herself, a persona that Charles may have helped her create. It seems likely that, as a married couple, they devised it together. But as much as the press might have been entranced by the idea of a woman becoming an abortionist because of her decadent, Russian husband, if anything, Madame Restell was probably the one who introduced Charles to the world of birth control pills and, later, abortion. A more likely account was the one that said, of Charles, "He was formerly a printer, but Madame induced him to abandon that honorable occupation."[11] They were both said to possess an "inordinate greed for money," and at some point they must have realized that working as a printer would never earn them a mansion.[12]

A more interesting, if still debatable, claim regarding Charles's involvement in his wife's business is that he was "a shrewd and cunning fellow" and had "written her advertisements, puffs, handbills, etc."[13] The simple fact is that Madame Restell did not *need* Charles to write her ads, because she was plagiarizing them from Charles's acquaintance Robert Dale Owen. While this is obviously a frustrating shortcut for Madame's fans today, Owen was, at least, an excellent choice from whom to plagiarize when it came to moral philosophy. Owen was a social reformer who spent his life advocating for property rights for women, abolition of slavery, and funding for public schools. As a member of Congress, he may be best remembered for helping establish the Smithsonian Institution.

It's not surprising that Madame Restell was a fan of Owen's work. What is surprising—and disappointing—is that passages supposedly written by her are lifted so directly from his 1831 work *Moral Physiology*, which dealt with birth control.

For instance, Restell's lines of questioning in the *New York Daily Herald* in 1841:

> What! Is female virtue, then, a mere thing of circumstance and occasion? Is there but the difference of opportunity between it and prostitution? Would your wives and your daughters, once absolved from fear, all become prostitutes?[14]

This can be found essentially verbatim on page 29 of Owen's work, where he wrote:

> Is this vaunted chastity but a mere thing of circumstance and occasion? Is there but the difference of opportunity between it and prostitution? Would [men's] wives, their sisters and their daughters, once absolved from the fear of offspring, all become prostitutes?[15]

Owen never publicly referenced this plagiarism. It's possible he simply didn't know about it; although he resided in New York from 1829 to 1833, he was living in Indiana by the 1840s. Intellectuals sharing one another's ideas, and using them in print, also wasn't unheard of. Owen's own book contains bits from Charles Knowlton's work *Fruits of Philosophy*. Since Owen was acquainted with Charles Lohman, he might have been perfectly fine with the Lohmans using passages to advance and advertise their business.

Of course, Restell could only reference so much from Owen. Her philosophical arguments might be found in his book, but her beefs with characters of the day were all her own. It's possible Charles did help with those attack pieces. He was a well-read man and editor. However, Madame Restell had modern ideas similar to those of her husband. They were brought together at what detractors would later describe as "an infidel meeting held at Tammany Hall," though this likely merely meant they both believed in birth control and similar modern notions.[16] Their attraction and marriage hinged upon the fact that they had similar philosophical outlooks and progressive ideas for the time.

The belief that Madame Restell must have been lacking in her ability to write a pithy insult—so lacking that her husband was composing all her missives—might have also been especially prevalent during this era, when it was declared, of women in general, "She composes no Iliad, no Aeneid. The strength of Milton's poetic vision was far beyond her fine and delicate perceptions.... [D]o you think a woman could have developed, in the tender soil of her intellect, the strong idea of a Hamlet or a Macbeth? Such is not a woman's province, nature, power or mission."[17] But then, anyone who listened to Madame Restell mock her interlocutors probably realized she was not someone who was short on words.

Charles was not bland, at least not all the time. He was occupied with his own endeavors. It's just that many of his pursuits were intended to bolster Madame Restell's business. It was written after his death that "his wife judged he had possibilities and so...he quit his [job] for medicine."[18]

Early in the marriage, her pills, which she had learned to compound under the direction of her neighbor, had proved to be enormously popular. And so, while Ann created an identity as "Madame Restell," Charles likewise fashioned one for himself. The *Fort Wayne Journal-Gazette* in Indiana wrote that, "after a little equipping, gained mostly under the direction of his wife, he hung out his shingle as 'Dr. Mauriceau, Specialist.'"[19] Charles opened a shop on Liberty Street, from which he began selling pills. Much like the persona of Madame Restell, he claimed that "his knowledge is acquired in the female hospitals in Europe," though this seems as implausible in his case as in her own.[20] Some reports believed that the pills he offered were Portuguese in origin, likely based on Charles's dubious claim that, "while residing in Paris, I had frequent opportunities of witnessing the astonishing efficacy of the Portuguese Female Pills in obstinate cases of the suppression of the menses."[21] While this may have added a certain international glamour, in all likelihood the pills were composed of precisely the same ingredients that Madame Restell used. In that regard, they were all-American.

Logically speaking, there was plenty of sense to this arrangement. Two "doctors" *were* better than one. Charles's presence opened a door to people who wanted birth control pills but felt that, because of her infamy, Madame Restell was simply too disreputable a woman from whom to purchase them. Beyond her infamy, there were also surely some clients who simply preferred a male doctor. Charles's shop also offered a means to sell their pills when Madame Restell was in jail or on trial, which happened increasingly frequently.

However, if women went to Charles expecting more than birth control pills, they would have been disappointed. Dr. Mauriceau, it was reported, "dealt only with the troubles of men."[22] Despite his claims about his education, he did not actually do any operations or doctoring of any sort. Rather, there was "a private passage which ran from the house in Liberty Street [which] led to the back entrance of the woman's house in Greenwich Street, and was used for the conducting of patients to her presence."[23] That "woman's house" was his wife's. Once these clients were safely shepherded there, Madame Restell could examine them more closely and perform abortions as needed.

As his wife tended to the surgical aspects of the business, Charles wrote. Much of the sentiment that he was an intellectual has to do with the fact that he authored (as Dr. Mauriceau) a book titled *The Married Woman's Private Medical Companion* in 1847. Directed toward "the married female of delicate or nervous temperament...whose health imperatively forbids an increase of family beyond the capacity of her strength," the manual advised women on tracking their periods and identifying early signs of pregnancy, as well as how to best avoid becoming pregnant.[24] It also dealt with how, in the event that a woman *did* become pregnant, "to effect miscarriage...with extreme safety."[25]

The book was vouched for in newspaper advertisements through a series of letters from excited "buyers" who seemed to use a truly stunning number of exclamation marks. Notable entries included everything from "Oh! What I would have given to live the last six years over again! What would my wife have given to be spared the long days and still longer nights prostrate on a bed of sickness!" to "How many suffer from prolapsus uteri (falling of the womb) or from fluor-albus (weakness, debility, etc, etc)! How many are in constant agony for many months preceding confinement! How many have difficult if not dangerous deliveries...!"[26] Either these people were abnormally psyched about vaginal discharge, or the endorsements were perhaps written by Charles himself.

Those who really were that interested in prolapsed uteri might have been discouraged to find that the book was composed as much of philosophy as it was of straightforward advice. Like Madame Restell, Charles was adamant that introducing birth control into society was a moral proposition. *The Married Woman's Private Medical Companion* proclaimed that "until men and women are absolved from the fear of becoming parents, except when they themselves desire it, they ever will form mercenary and demoralizing connections, and seek in dissipation the happiness they might have found in domestic life."[27] Which is to say—if you only marry so you can have sex, or have sex without feeling guilty about it, you're very likely to make an imprudent early marriage and cheat on your spouse later. There's some truth to the idea that maturity yields longer marriages; modern research indicates that 60 percent of marriages that take place between the ages of twenty and twenty-five end in divorce, whereas only 25 percent of those that happen after the age of twenty-five do so.[28]

The Married Woman's Private Medical Companion also advocated for women to learn more about their bodies, referencing how obtaining this knowledge was unlikely to turn them into prostitutes. There was, one gathers, a great deal of concern about women turning into prostitutes during this era, and very little effort to address the actual conditions that made women pursue sex work. It was more likely that economic circumstances would do that, Charles argued, which certainly seemed true of the times. Even now, whether they enter the profession voluntarily or not, it's unlikely that many women are prompted to go into sex work because of an awareness of where their cervix is located.

For what it's worth, there was relevant medical advice in the book as well, although it may seem somewhat obvious to modern readers. For instance, it's not a surprise today that some women are uncomfortable in the third trimester of pregnancy as their abdomens have increased in size, although knowing this in advance can be helpful. That said, while some of the advice seems obvious now, there are also insights that are still relevant; even if technology has improved, the condition itself is still very much the same. Regarding discomfort from the third-trimester abdomen, the book suggests a belt to help support the weight. Pregnancy belts are still widely sold today.

The most interesting parts of the book concerned the specifics on miscarriage or abortion. The *Louisville Daily Courier* noted that a large portion of the book seemed designed for Madame Restell's "express benefit…in furtherance of her hellish schemes."[29] If this was the case, it wasn't overly enthusiastic about doing so. For someone actively profiting from the procedure, Charles's book is very quick to say that abortion "will present an extreme and last resource" and that "the abuse and criminal extension of such a resource is reprehensible."[30] That said, it does provide a recipe that might help women restore their menstrual periods if they had stopped:

- Take prickly ash bark, two ounces
- Wild cherry tree bark, two ounces
- Seneca snake root, one ounce
- Tansy, one ounce
- Gum socotrine aloes, half an ounce
- Devil's bit, two ounces
- Pulverize.
- To every two ounces of powder add a half pint of boiling water, and one quart of Holland gin.[31]

Half a wine glass of this brew was to be drunk three to four times a day. The absolutely massive amount of gin women would be consuming seems as likely to induce a miscarriage as anything else in the recipe.

In addition to that protocol, the book offers some information on what happens during the process of the fetus being expelled and the placenta following. It also discusses providing the patient relief as she bleeds afterward (by applying pounded ice to their genitals, or using a rag soaked in snow) that seem to come from firsthand experience.

Charles likely did not know enough about abortion to write this himself. There is no evidence he ever participated in any surgery; he left that side of the business entirely to Madame Restell. So it seems very possible that she, and other physicians whose work he read, had provided substantial input on these passages. Charles himself says as much, noting, in the book's introduction, "It is not pretended that the concentration of the results of medical research emanates from one author, for be he ever so versed in medical science, he would come far, far short of so herculean a task. It is, therefore, necessarily derived from authors on medical and physiological sciences, of great acquirements and distinguished celebrity."[32]

Very few people gave Charles credit for the book. While the *Courier* reported that *The Married Woman's Private Medical Companion* was supposedly written by him, it was widely believed (at least at the paper) that Madame Restell was the actual author. In spite of the common conviction that women were intellectually inferior, and most were incapable of writing anything substantial, these journalists referred to it as "her book," and wrote that "knowing the desperate character she has obtained under her common sobriquet, she has adopted in this book, the name of A. M. Mauriceau." But even if she masterminded the project, the *Courier* is quick to point out, it is not entirely *her* book. Upon a closer look, the *Courier* asserts, "There are fifty-two pages in the middle of the book devoted to the schemes of Madame Restell.... [They] are taken from Robert Dale Owen's notorious book *Moral Physiology*."[33] This is, in fact, correct; the section in *The Married Woman's Private Medical Companion* dealing with birth control is largely the work of Robert Dale Owen.

This couple simply could not stop plagiarizing Owen.

Others agreed it was not Charles's work, though they doubted who the true author was. "The entire work is said to be plagiarized by a French author," sniffed the *Leavenworth Weekly Times*.[34] Lest you think Robert Dale Owen was a Frenchman with an uncharacteristically British name—he was Scottish. Regrettably, the *Times* declined to mention which author he meant, or, indeed, to provide any clues as to that Frenchman's identity. It's most probable that they're merely referencing Owen here. Passages lifted from *Moral Physiology* detail how much more sophisticated French attitudes were regarding birth control. For instance, "A French lady of the utmost delicacy and respectability will, in common conversation, say as simply—(ay, and as innocently, whatever the self-righteous prude may aver to the contrary)—as she would proffer any common remark about the weather: 'I have three children; my husband and I think that is as many as we can do justice to, and I do not intend to have any more.' "[35] This may have given the paper the impression that a French person of some kind was behind the work.

And if there were not already enough suspected authors, there were some who pointed to Madame Restell's brother. Upon immigrating to New York, Joseph Trow first worked for his sister and then, in the mid-1840s, shifted to working in Charles's shop. There, he "swept the sidewalks, attended to the office, put up the pills." As for the pills, he claimed that he "never knew nor troubled himself as to what the pills were for or what they were made of."[36] It's truly shocking that he was in such a state of ignorance as Joseph went on to sell his own version of *The Married Woman's Private Medical Companion*, which Charles denounced as a "base and shameful fraud!!" According to Charles, Joseph had created a pamphlet with "the same font and type size, exactly the same title page, and exactly the same typographical arrangement, but another name [Joseph Trow] substituted for Dr. Mauriceau."[37]

In spite of all this controversy—and the *Louisville Daily Courier* understandably wondering whether Robert Dale Owen would "feel pained" by "the perversion of his sentiments and reasoning in this book"—*The Married Woman's Private Medical Companion* supposedly sold extremely well, doubtlessly adding to the family's coffers.[38]

Charles really can't be given all the credit for it. That's not to say that Charles should be entirely dismissed or forgotten, though.

In this era, when many men believed that it was in women's nature to be submissive to the men in their lives, the fact that Charles was willing to stand behind his wife and try to advance her labors is noteworthy. He does not appear to have been acting as her manager so much as her supporter. His business directed more people toward her. He was willing to work to double her pill sales. His book was considered to be something that would promote her business.

That's not to say this was a perfect marriage. Both the men in Madame Restell's life—her brother and her husband—were quick to disown her practices in print when it was advantageous to do so. When someone went to trial, it was Madame Restell, neither of them. They may have shared the rewards that came from her profession, but they certainly did not share, or even help alleviate, the blame. There were no moments in Madame Restell's life when Charles gallantly leapt forward to say that he was the one who performed the abortion and should be tried, instead of his wife.

Their relationship would, as the years passed, become deeply flawed, marked by "quarrels about money affairs," and the two would frequently fight only to reconcile.[39]

But Madame Restell did not need a protector, and she did not seem to crave a relationship where she was a quiet, untroubled wife and mother. What she required was someone who was not going to hold her back. Charles let her do something that she did well, and probably enabled her to do it more easily than she would have been able to do it without him. While that may not seem like the most exciting stance in the world, at the time, it would have been *far* from bland.

Chapter Eleven

M ADAME RESTELL HAD CLIENTS TO ATTEND TO. IF THE EPISODE with Mary Applegate showed Madame Restell at her most uncaring, her treatment of Maria Bodine, which came into public view in 1847, showed off her best qualities. Ironically, it would also be the episode that would create the most strife for her.

In August 1847, the mayor of New York received a letter from Dr. Samuel L. Smith, a physician in Orange County, claiming that Madame Restell had operated on a housekeeper named Maria Bodine who was now in grave condition. Her employer, a widower named Joseph Cook, was the one who had impregnated her. After the police met with Maria, they reported that she was "truly a pitiful sight...pale and emaciated."[1]

Madame Restell was promptly indicted for performing an operation that some thought had led to Maria's ill health. When the officer arrived at Restell's house to arrest her, her servant informed him that "it was about time for her to return from her usual morning ride with her husband." When she did return, and noticed her unanticipated guest, she was far from perturbed. She "glided in, dressed in the most fashionable manner." As her husband discussed bail with the officer, Restell said she wanted only to change her clothes from "gay to somber colors."[2] The officer allowed this but kept his foot wedged in the door of her room as she changed; quite sensibly, he was worried she might try to run. On September 11, 1847, she pled not guilty and was remanded to prison to await trial.

The next step should have been securing bail—an easy enough matter for a woman who was now worth the modern equivalent of millions. In most situations, Charles could have handled it himself, but he was now facing legal problems of his own. Owing to his promotion of his book *The Married Woman's Private Medical Companion*, he was arrested a few days later on the charge of selling "obscene publications."[3] The section about applying ice to the private parts of a woman who had just miscarried or had an abortion was seemingly too hot for the more censorious members of the public to handle.

This turn of events doubtless went against the couple's well-laid plans. A separate identity under which to keep the business running was sensible, as, by this point, Madame Restell's legal troubles had become somewhat routine. After her first time in prison, the couple had likely realized that the distribution of pills from Charles's office could help steer customers away from going to one of Madame Restell's competitors instead. But this arrangement hinged on the concept that the couple would not both find themselves in legal trouble at the same time. As it was, Charles Lohman had far less time than he would otherwise have enjoyed to help arrange Madame Restell's bail.

No matter. Two men promptly came forward to provide bail for Restell. The first was Joseph A. Jackson, a pawnbroker and former candidate for assistant alderman (a figure elected to a town council) of the 14th ward. The second was Charles Whitman, a stage proprietor. Sadly, both men were rejected, with Whitman further being deemed incompetent. All they got in return for their trouble was criticism from the press. The *Brooklyn Evening Star* sniffily posited that "these men must have very refined ideas of moral character in suffering their names to be brought before the public in such infamous connection."[4] That might have been the case; there were people who believed that birth control and abortions were moral goods and services. Or they might have owed Madame Restell a favor, or been in debt to her financially, or been paid by her to provide bail, a practice Madame Restell would employ in future cases.

Eventually, Benjamin H. Day provided Madame Restell's $28,000 bail, on September 19. The *Washington Union* claimed that she paid him $1,000 to provide it, and that "$1,000 did not begin to pay him for the flaying he got from the District Attorney, unless he was as hardened as the marble pillars at City Hall."[5]

As founder and publisher of a controversial paper, the *New York Sun*, Day was probably more toughened against public opinion than most people. As with the *Herald*, Madame Restell regularly advertised in the *Sun*, and advertising was something that Day took very seriously.

He once went so far as to claim, "The object of this paper is to lay before the public, at a price within the means of everyone, all the news of the day, and at the same time afford an advantageous medium for advertising."[6]

In order to maximize profits from advertising, the *Sun* also needed to maximize its readership, which resulted in stories that were often very far removed from anything factual. The *Sun* is perhaps best remembered for running a six-issue story by Richard Adams Locke about an intelligent group of winged bat-people who lived on the moon. Today that story is known as the "Great Moon Hoax." It was initially intended as a good piece of satire of some of the speculative descriptions of the moon that were popular during the age. However, much of the public fully believed it to be true, in large part because the newspaper did nothing to indicate it was false. A philanthropic group in England started with the intent of "relieving the wants of the people on the moon and, above all, abolishing slavery if it should be found to exist among the Lunar inhabitants."[7] The writers at the *Sun* thought this was hilarious. When a group of students from Yale who fully believed the hoax visited the *Sun*'s offices to see the original sources used to write the piece, the team at the editorial office assured them the sources were at the printing office. The printing office team told them they had just been returned to the editorial office. In such a manner, the Yale students were kept running futilely through the streets. Except for the *Sun*'s anti-slavery stance, which we'll discuss later, the *Sun*'s writers did not really want to report on news of the day, or on issues like the inner workings of government; they just wanted to tell fun stories. In one lesser-known instance, they dismissed the controversial adjournment of the Twenty-third Congress (during which there was debate over whether members of the old congress could act after midnight) in three words—"congress is adjourned"—following with a lengthier item about the health of an anaconda at a local museum, which, in a hilarious misadventure, had swallowed the very blanket it had been wrapped in to keep it cozy. The museum's owner—*and indeed the world*—was very anxious about the health of this "beautiful serpent."[8]

Think what these writers could have done with an adorably ugly kitten and an Internet connection.

The folks at the *Sun* were gleeful agents of chaos, and if Day thought it might drum up some publicity, he would not hesitate to bail out Madame Restell. But then, Madame Restell wasn't the only one who needed to be bailed out of jail: Joseph Cook was also arrested for his role in impregnating Maria Bodine. His bail was first set at $10,000 and then reduced to $5,000—not as much as Madame Restell's, but still a hefty sum. By September 16, the *Brooklyn Daily Eagle* reported that a John McCann had also been arrested. He was an employee of Mr. Cook's who had helped arrange for the abortion in the first place.

Now, this was hardly the first abortion Madame Restell had performed. So why, then, did this cause legal troubles for so many people when, for instance, those responsible for the kidnapping of Mary Applegate's child faced few (if any) repercussions? Certainly the outcry was due in part to the public's sense that Madame Restell had too long remained unrepentant and, in the eyes of many, unpunished for her crimes. By this time, some people did not even know *why* they disliked her—only that they did. One prospective juror in the Bodine trial, when asked if he had formed an opinion on her guilt or innocence, claimed that he'd woken up that morning and decided "she was guilty." When asked what he thought she was guilty of, he replied, simply: "Bigamy."[9] People always greatly overestimated the amount of time Madame Restell had on her hands.

The more significant legal issue was whether Maria Bodine's baby had quickened by the time of the operation. This moment, marking when the mother begins to feel kicking inside the womb, usually happens somewhere around the twentieth week of pregnancy. Much of the emphasis on quickening dates back hundreds of years before Madame Restell's time. Determining when a fetus had a "soul" was more a matter for religion than for science. In the 1200s, the Italian philosopher Thomas Aquinas believed that a fetus became "ensouled" at the time of the quickening, and that, while an abortion performed before that time might be wrong, it was not murder. The fifteenth-century archbishop of Florence, Saint Antonious, even advocated abortion to save the lives of women, provided they took place before quickening. In 1591, Pope Gregory XIV determined that quickening took place around twenty-four weeks.[10]

Performing an abortion on a woman over five months pregnant had been considered a felony in New York since the 1820s, but new laws from 1845 ensured more severe punishment. Now, Madame Restell would be on trial for manslaughter in the second degree, and face four to seven years in prison. This was not an offense that she could easily bat away with her usual aplomb.

Yet Madame Restell carried on with her signature bravado. She may have changed her wardrobe into somber colors, but she was almost blithe in her lack of concern. She informed reporters that "she [had] assisted judges' daughters, magistrates' nieces, and jurors' favorites and friends, and that they dare not ultimately convict her."[11] As a general rule, women on trial are typically advised to seem mollified and demure and to avoid whispering to reporters, for example, "You think they're gonna arrest me? You dumb idiot, you utter, unsophisticated rube," but, as readers well know by now, Madame Restell was far from typical.

And it wasn't all bluster, either. Madame Restell hired excellent legal representation, in the form of James T. Brady, who was said to be "one of the most brilliant of all the members of the New York bar," and David Graham. She paid each man the hefty daily fee of $100. Arriving in court, she gave the appearance of being sure of a favorable outcome—and, to some people's minds, being completely above the law. When the trial began, the *Buffalo Morning Express* moaned, "This is probably the most thoroughly debased and wicked woman in the whole country and yet I saw her going to court this morning in a superb carriage attended by two servants in livery. In appearance, she is rather a handsome woman, about 35 years of age, and wealthy to the amount of $200,000 [$6.4 million today]."[12]

Perhaps she should have walked to court. Because Maria Bodine, her former patient, had a very different demeanor. The woman who had come to Madame Restell for an abortion in 1846 approached the court "with a feeble, tottering walk," despite being "a young woman, about 26 years of age, of middling size." Those watching her could see that she was "evidently in a rapid decline of health." When Maria was first called to the stand and asked where she was born, she replied "in so low and feeble a tone, and...so indistinctly heard, that the court ordered all persons who wished to withdraw to retire at once, as they would have perfect silence."[13]

Whether Maria Bodine was as feeble as she appeared or simply understood that this attitude made for good optics is irrelevant. Madame Restell looked to all the court to be rich, beautiful, and remorseless. Why, she was practically treating the trial as though it were a waste of her time! Maria, on the other hand, seemed downright broken in the wake of her experiences. She had not wanted to speak about this at all—her doctor, upon discovering she'd had an abortion, had alerted the authorities. Maria was in a state of such unhappiness that she cringed every moment she was before the public. The latter pose evoked much more public sympathy than Restell's confidence. You can divine as much from the two portraits in the back of the widely sold transcript of the trial. Maria Bodine, despite being noticeably ill in all the descriptions of her, looks like a fairy-tale princess in her illustrated depiction. She is wearing a white dress, strolling on the hills, overlooking a literal castle. There is also a portrait of Madame Restell, in which Restell is scowling, wearing a shawl made of the wings of a demon, who is greedily devouring a baby. That's a pretty stark contrast.

The nature of these illustrations do seem to overlook the fact that Maria Bodine was the one who initially sought Restell out, and Restell's winged baby-devouring demon was not descending on women out of nowhere.

All of New York was excited by the trial as it promised to offer not only the salacious details of Maria's seduction, but also a behind-the-curtain view of a second-trimester abortion at Madame Restell's boardinghouse. Though conditions surrounding abortions were not unfamiliar to anyone who knew of Mary Applegate's or Ann Maria Purdy's situation, this was the first time that a trial of Madame Restell's would be reported on by the media in such extraordinary detail.

Initially, Maria seemed to be a witness—and a "victim"—that respectable people felt they could support. Mr. Cook had employed her as his housekeeper in April 1845. They began having sex about a month after she moved in and continued to do so for a year. But, as Maria attempted to make clear from her demeanor, she was no wanton woman. By May 1846, she admitted to the jury, "blushing, and after much hesitation," she had found herself "in the family way."[14] She noticed—and perhaps Charles/Dr. Mauriceau would have been proud—that her menses had stopped and her nipples had darkened; after she began vomiting in the middle of June, she took a train to New York. She stayed with her sister for a few days before going to Madame Restell's. Once there, Madame Restell informed her that an examination to see if she was pregnant would cost $5. If she was pregnant, a surgical abortion would cost $100. However, she suggested that Maria could first try taking some abortive pills. Maria said Madame Restell had told her, "If I were so [pregnant] they would bring me right. If I were not so, they would do me no harm, and no good."[15] Despite the fact that it seems misleading to declare the pills had no negative consequences—they might, at least, make a patient feel quite ill—this procedure seems fairly standard to anyone familiar with Madame Restell's practice.

But then Maria informed Madame Restell that she was six months along in her pregnancy. *And Madame Restell explicitly told her not to have an abortion.* She suggested that Maria Bodine instead board with her until the baby was born. In all likelihood, this proposal was not motivated by concern for the infant—Madame Restell would likely dispose of it in a poorhouse as soon as it was born—but by the fact that six months was too advanced to perform a safe abortion at that time, especially using a piece of whalebone, or, as it was suggested in court, a wire under her finger. To do the operation at that point would jeopardize Maria's health and Madame Restell's reputation. People came to her precisely because her patients didn't die.

Maria claimed that she had been open to the idea of boarding, but her boyfriend wouldn't agree to pay the weekly $5 charge. It's unclear whether Bodine was merely trying to haggle down the price or if Cook really wouldn't pay. Foolish choice. Based only on the economics— assuming Maria was twenty-four weeks pregnant, boarding at $5 per week for the remaining sixteen weeks would have cost $80. Compared to a $100 abortion, Cook would have saved $20. He also wouldn't have been at risk of being arrested. He might have worried that Maria would return with the child, and attempt to blackmail him, but Madame Restell could put that worry to rest for a fee, as she had with Mary Applegate. Besides, unlike Applegate, Maria showed absolutely no desire to keep the baby.

Maria went back to her sister's home but returned a week later, imploring Madame Restell once again to perform an abortion. Madame Restell finally agreed and lowered the price to $75 to better accommodate her. Maria only had $30 on hand, so Madame Restell advised her to contact Mr. McCann, Cook's business associate, for the balance. Maria may have hesitated, but Madame Restell claimed that she'd already met McCann, and when she did, she had made it clear that $75 was her lowest price. Maria stayed with Madame Restell while awaiting McCann's response. Doubtless to Maria's relief he provided the money on July 19, and Maria Bodine prepared herself for the operation.

When it was time, Madame Restell took Maria upstairs and told her to lay down on the floor. Then, Maria related to the court in a whisper, Restell inserted her hand into Maria's vagina to examine her, which took about ten minutes.

The use of her hand merits some note.

Maria said Restell was working without a speculum, an instrument typically used to allow medical practitioners a better view of the cervix. Though some version of a speculum dates back to ancient Rome, the modern version was invented in 1825 by the French midwife Marie-Anne Boivin (credit, unfortunately, is often given to J. Marion Sims, "the father of gynecology"). While speculums were in use during Madame Restell's time—one was even used by a doctor to examine Maria Bodine for venereal disease—they were also treated with skepticism and sometimes considered to be penis substitutes that would make women insatiably aroused. In 1853, the physician Robert Brudenell Carter claimed, "I have, more than once, seen young unmarried women, of the middle class of society, reduced by constant use of the speculum to the mental and moral condition of prostitutes; seeking to give themselves the same indulgence by the practice of solitary vice; and asking every medical practitioner under whose care they fell to institute an examination of the sexual organs."[16] Anyone who has been through a routine gynecological exam and seen a speculum up close can now take a moment to laugh uncontrollably at this theory. Nonetheless, in using her hand, Madame Restell was employing a technique that might have been more palatable to a "respectable" woman.

Madame Restell was seemingly very skilled in her ability to detect abnormalities via touch, because she informed Maria that her womb was differently situated than most, which probably meant she had a tilted uterus. Restell continued to work for another ten minutes—again, likely using a wire to complete the abortion—and, upon finishing, gave Maria some pills that would supposedly cause the contents of her womb to be expelled over the next few days. After that, she put her to bed.

Maria began to bleed two days thereafter. Madame Restell said she doubted Maria would need her that evening, but if she did, she should ring the bell in her room. The next day, Maria was very distressed. Madame Restell checked on her throughout the day and, concerned, slept with her that night to make sure she didn't grow more ill. Around the break of dawn, Maria vomited. Maria recalled that when she began to complete her miscarriage, "[Madame Restell] bade me get out of bed, and she told me to sit down on a stool.... [W]hilst seated there I suffered a violent pain, and Madame Restell inserted her hand in my privates, she said it would make it easier for me.... I heard something fall from my body into the stool or chamber, I told Madame Restell of it, she said be patient, one more pain and I would be through."[17]

Afterward, Maria lay in bed experiencing what Madame Restell called "after-pains." Restell tended to her throughout the rest of the day and stayed with her again that night. When Maria asked if she could see what had been expelled, Madame Restell sensibly refused. Seeing the discarded contents of *any* operation might be troubling, but this is especially so for an operation as morally fraught as an abortion. Madame Restell later explained that she had disposed of the matter.

Maria Bodine remained with Madame Restell from Sunday through Thursday. She was first given crackers and tea so as not to upset her stomach, and then soup and vegetables. On Thursday, Madame Restell found Maria crying. Maria recounted that "she [Restell] asked me what was the matter. I told her I wanted to go home, but I had no money to go with. If I wished to go, she said, she would give me some money to pay my passage and get refreshments."[18]

After supplying travel funds, Madame Restell took Maria to the parlor, where she gave her patient a glass of wine and checked to see that no policemen were currently outside her house. After making Maria promise not to tell anyone about what had occurred, Maria recounted, "she shook hands with me on parting, gave me a kiss, and told me I must never do [this] again." Overall, Maria's experience with the abortionist seems to have been rather nurturing and empathetic; Madame Restell had even told Maria, "You will call me mother."[19] She did not mean that she literally wanted to be referred to as "Mom" by her patients, only that she would provide the care and compassion that a mother might during this trying time. Everyone needs someone who will love them when they're at their worst. There's something very touching about the fact that Madame Restell, who was not normally overly tender, realized that a woman who was making the difficult decision not to become a mother might herself need mothering.

To a modern reader who believes in safe, legal abortion, Madame Restell seems to have behaved about as well as one could in these circumstances. She offered her best-informed medical opinion but deferred to her patient's wishes. She didn't pressure her out of her choice. She offered a discount despite having to perform a very risky and illegal procedure. She provided constant care after the procedure. She even made sure her patient got home safely at the time when she wanted to leave.

Unfortunately, after the abortion, Maria Bodine's health remained poor. By her account, she'd been comparatively healthy before her operation. In court, she complained, "My health is still feeble, I have constant distress in my head, pain, falling of the womb, weakness in my back, burning in my hands, weakness and trembling all over me." Maria did not seem to be doing any better during the trial. Between her whispered responses, fainting while on the stand, and wearing a veil on at least one day of the trial, she absolutely came off as being in frail health. Her counsel even suggested that the questions put to her by the defense were a "sequel to the violence perpetrated upon her." Brady, Madame Restell's lawyer, seemed more skeptical; he conceded that he would pay attention to Maria Bodine's health, but said he was "used to these faintings."[20]

If people are cynical about such behavior, that's understandable. But there are also reasons to believe that Maria was in poor health. She had gone through an extreme medical procedure that she had been advised not to undertake. The operation was performed on a floor. Madame Restell did not so much as wash her hands before plunging them inside a woman to extract and dispose of a six-month-old fetus. An abortion well into the second trimester would be much more arduous for the patient than one performed earlier. There was also no modern medication available to help alleviate pain and possible infection.

However, Maria's poor health may also have been owing to the care she received when she returned to Mr. Cook's home. When she arrived, she told him that she felt poorly. Accordingly, he sent for a doctor, who, according to Maria, "leeched me to my bowels."[21] In addition to that bloodletting, he also cupped her on the back and gave her a powder to ingest that she could not identify. This treatment continued for three months. Maria was also taking laudanum, and while its effects couldn't have been as bad for her as for the toddlers who were being medicated in this era, they probably were not good, especially when coupled with what sounds like a great many other wildly unpleasant post-procedure treatments.

Maria's health did not matter much to Madame Restell's lawyers, who were intent on depicting Maria Bodine as a lying harlot who had all but forced Madame Restell at knifepoint to provide an abortion. Despite saying they would be sensitive to Maria's seemingly frail condition, the lawyers didn't let up on their questioning, demanding to know, for example, if she'd had sexual relations with anyone before Mr. Cook. When Maria declined to answer (and her lawyer pointed out that not many virgins were visiting Madame Restell, so this line of questioning seemed irrelevant), Brady declared her to be a prostitute, concluding, "Her present state of health...is caused by a long course of intemperance, a constant career of prostitution, and is the natural consequence not of Madame Restell, but of habitual and promiscuous intercourse as a harlot—not with Mr. Cook but with every man, every hour, or every five minutes of her life."[22]

Admittedly, this is a generalized statement for all the men of the 1840s, but—no one is having sex "every five minutes." No matter *how* unchaperoned they are. Even just the *concept* is exhausting. It is truly fascinating what men during this period thought could unleash a tidal wave of female lasciviousness—a speculum, a walk with a painter and his girlfriend, any unattended interaction with men. One can only imagine the disappointment of these men to find that women are largely left unattended today, and yet, society has not devolved into an unending orgy, because women still have to buy groceries and go to work and call their moms and generally pursue things that are not ceaseless fornication.

Maria, who was subject to this depiction of her nature after politely declining to answer how many men she had slept with, was obviously uncomfortable. The transcript notes that she "became overpowered with sickness...[and] it was with difficulty she was prevented from sinking to the floor." But this reaction did not deter Restell's intrepid legal team. Brady told the jury to feel no sympathy for Maria Bodine because "she [Maria] is the felon, the instigator, the prompter. The defendant had requested her to wait her time—she would not."[23]

Another frustrating aspect of these trials against Madame Restell is how the women were constantly pitted against one another. A motherly nature, tea and crackers, and gentle reassurance may have been possible in Madame Restell's home. Here, the two women's lawyers were determined to cast one woman as a victim, and the other as a pox on society. To tell the truth: that Bodine had been a woman in a difficult situation, and Restell had done her best to care for her in a professional capacity, was not even considered. Camaraderie between such women was of no interest to the jury, or the public.

For all the humiliation and hardship Maria faced during the course of this trial, remember that she was not the one who originated the case. Maria had only gone to a physician for her ongoing medical ailments. When she did, the doctor had "told her she had had an abortion produced on her, and must tell him all about it, or he would do nothing for her."[24] Then *he* reported it to the authorities. *None* of this was at Maria's insistence; as the district attorney remarked, "the girl was taken, drawn, and an unwilling witness, to testify to her own wrong."

Unfortunately, her situation was not unique. It's not unheard of in modern times, even prior to the overturning of *Roe v. Wade*, the 1973 ruling that protected women's right to abort in America. In 2014, the *New York Times* reported on how a pregnant woman in Louisiana went to her doctor for unexplained vaginal bleeding. It was assumed she'd attempted to self-induce an abortion. She was arrested for second-degree manslaughter and held in jail for a year before it was revealed that she'd suffered a miscarriage.[25] In Texas in 2022, a woman was charged with murder for "intentionally and knowingly causing the death of an individual by self-induced abortion" (though the charges were later dropped).[26] This policy can lead to disastrous health consequences as women may be afraid to go to doctors, not only for abortions, but also when they have had miscarriages—lest they be suspected of abortions. In Nicaragua, where women and girls can face jail time for abortions, they often seek out "unsafe clandestine abortions," according to Human Rights Watch in a 2017 report. Afterward, "often too afraid to seek medical care when complications arise from such abortions, some...delay seeking care and do not disclose to doctors the cause of complications. Medical providers, caught in a conflict between the law and medical ethics, have reported women and girls to police for suspected abortions."[27]

Following the overturning of *Roe v. Wade* in 2022, in *Dobbs v. Jackson Women's Health Organization*, we'll see many more such cases. Maria's trial would be just one example in what would turn out to be a long history of doctors forsaking confidentiality with their patients due to the criminalization of women's reproductive choices in the United States.

Much of the rest of the trial was devoted to testimony about whether Maria had indeed been pregnant and whether quickening had taken place. Though she had obviously been pregnant, the only person who would have been able to say with certainty whether she felt the fetus move was Maria, which was why Madame Restell's lawyers were so eager to undercut her credibility. Even so, that did not stop physicians from being called upon to contemplate the matter. One of them claimed that while most of the time quickening occurred at around four or four and a half months of pregnancy, it could happen as early as ten weeks—a rather extreme assessment, as quickening was meant to imply fetal motion, and most women today do not report feeling fetal movement until sixteen weeks at the earliest.

And then there was the challenge of likeability. Trial decisions in the mid-nineteenth century, and to some extent still today, depend on who the jury finds more likable. Making a witty, unrepentant, female millionaire abortionist relatable to an all-male jury is tricky, especially if these men are of the nineteenth-century mindset, believing that normal women have tiny skulls that only contain love, household skills, and/or hysteria.

Madame Restell's lawyer did not take this approach. Instead, Brady gave a speech casting Madame Restell as a Christ-like figure—yes, you read that correctly—who told her client to "go out and sin no more."[28] There's a logic to this if—and truly, only if—you imagine that women might be persuaded to change their lifestyles immediately after a visit to Madame Restell's. The implication seems to be that Madame Restell, like Christ with the woman caught in adultery, had mercifully saved her patients from public scorn and given them the opportunity to be chaste daughters and mothers in the future. This might have been the case with some clients. But much of Madame Restell's business was built around repeat clientele, such as the woman who was seeing her for her tenth abortion. Barring extraordinary circumstances like Maria Bodine's—in which case her warning was more likely to be about the late timing of her abortion than about simply having an abortion—Madame Restell didn't judge women for needing abortions, or try to talk them out of it. If anything is to be learned from the case of Mary Applegate, it's that Restell was more likely to judge them if they wanted to keep the baby.

It was an easier take for Restell's lawyers to cast Bodine as a sinner than it was to portray Madame Restell as a saint. Brady called a neighbor and asked what was thought of Maria's general character. The neighbor replied that it was "very bad." Furthermore, she found that Maria was "impudent in her manner, [and] rude to [her] and [her] daughter." Apparently, when the woman forbade her daughter to associate with Maria, owing to Maria's perceived promiscuity, Maria snapped that "she was as good as my daughter," implying that woman's daughter was as sexually active as her. It's hard to reconcile this bold young woman with the incredibly feeble person in the courtroom. But while this neighbor felt no sympathy for Maria, she attested that "[Mr. Cook] is a person of respectable character and good standing." That was true despite the fact that he appeared to have gotten his employee pregnant and then pushed for an abortion. It had not occurred to anyone to declare that Mr. Cook might be at fault here. Indeed, the opposite was true. Madame Restell's lawyer claimed, "It shall be our effort neither to injure nor to disparage Mr. Cook—his reputation shall not be jeopardized by any insinuation of ours."[29]

Of course. Because Maria just impregnated herself.

Brady went on to claim that Maria had already acquired some manner of sexually transmitted disease by the time she entered Cook's house, and that they would not "do Mr. Cook so much discredit as to his taste as to suppose that he associated with a female so afflicted." The implication was that Cook must not have been the father, because he would not have slept with a diseased woman. But this seems unlikely, even if it was true that she had an STD. There's little evidence to support the notion that men would not sleep with women who had sexually transmitted diseases; if it were true, it would have vastly decreased the number of cases of venereal diseases during the period.

The disease the defense was referring to in Bodine's case was syphilis. A doctor examined Maria prior to the trial. She had a boil under her armpit, as well as some sores in her vaginal region, and it was known that syphilis sometimes caused lesions to appear in warm parts of the body like the armpit or groin. A physician who had treated Maria in the past said she had told him she had "gonorrhea," and he "attended to her for that." However, he claimed that, although in his personal opinion, he "supposed it to be syphilis," he did not tell her that.[30]

It's appalling by modern standards that he did not share his suspected diagnosis with his patient, but it would have been less surprising at the time. Doctors sometimes didn't tell women they had syphilis, because by doing so they would reveal their husbands' adultery. They did not want to violate the privacy of their male patients. After all, it was the male patients who paid their fee. Upton Sinclair's story *Damaged Goods* discusses how a doctor's reluctance to tell his patient's fiancée that his patient has syphilis leads to the infection of not only the fiancée, but, in time, their baby, and the couple's wet nurse. Syphilis is an STD that can, if left untreated with penicillin, cause several significant health problems. It typically manifests in a boil or sore in the first stage. In the second stage, it can cause fever, fatigue, headaches, and muscle pain. In some cases, following a latent period, it also progresses to a tertiary stage, which can cause dementia, loss of muscle coordination, worsening headaches, loss of vision, problems with joints, numbness, and paralysis. All of this seems in keeping with the symptoms Maria Bodine complained about after the infection. Her reported muscle pain and weakness skewed more closely to syphilis than her self-diagnosis of gonorrhea, which is generally associated with burning pain while urinating and vaginal discharge. The doctor who had examined Maria also claimed that he noted her white vaginal discharge to be "periodical, whereas gonorrhea is continuous."[31]

But, of course, Maria wouldn't know that, because her doctor didn't tell her "his opinion."

There's a reason that the information contained in *The Married Woman's Private Medical Companion* was shocking at the time it was published. Syphilis was considered to be such a foul disease that many people were too ashamed to mention it for any reason. In fact, one of the most surprising parts of the transcript of this trial was that they called it by name at all. The skittishness around describing this STD would only increase in the coming decades. By 1886, during the much-publicized divorce between Lord Colin Campbell and Lady Gertrude Campbell, Gertrude claimed that he had given her a "loathsome disease." When London's *Evening News* reported that the disease was syphilis, the National Vigilance Association charged the paper with "obscene libel," for putting the word in print. When the *Ladies Home Journal* published a piece on STDs, including syphilis, in 1906, it promptly lost seventy-five thousand subscribers. The former readers felt the journal had no right to address such a topic. Given the limited information that was available, it's impressive that Maria was able to diagnosis herself with any STD, even if she thought it was gonorrhea rather than syphilis.

None of this information is intended to shame Maria from beyond the grave. It *is* intended to shame that doctor from beyond the grave, but not Maria. Her diagnosis is interesting only insofar as it is possible that Maria had syphilis for some time. Her doctor believed that "her syphilis was cured, but she feigned other weakness"—perhaps for attention, or for relief from her work.[32] You can't "cure" syphilis without penicillin (or, today, if a patient is allergic to penicillin, macrolide antibiotics), which wouldn't be discovered until 1928. Maria's syphilis wasn't cured. It may have entered a latency period, where she didn't experience symptoms—and in some cases, this period could last for decades—except that Maria was very vocal that she was experiencing a great number of symptoms consistent with syphilis. While a late abortion and doctor's bloodletting surely didn't help, it's more likely that her frailty stemmed from that disease rather than from the treatment she received at the hands of Madame Restell.

Again, she probably did not have enough medical knowledge at her disposal to know that. This may simply have been another case like Ann Maria Purdy's, who thought Madame Restell had given her consumption. Which is to say, Maria Bodine knew, unambiguously, that abortions were "bad," and could have come to the erroneous conclusion that the abortion had caused her illness.

It's probable that Maria contracted the disease prior to being employed by Mr. Cook. Her neighbor testified that Maria had told her she had been pregnant once before. Four years before the incident with Cook, the neighbor claimed, Maria had been "with child by Morris Vernoy who was a barkeeper....I told her she had better get married."[33] Maria did not marry. But nor did she appear to have had a child. She might have miscarried, or she might simply have been sexually active and concerned about a late period.

Other neighbors were called to testify that they thought Maria was a liar, and sexually active, and a person of bad character. Some seemed influenced by personal quarrels with her, such as the shoemaker who was upset that she still owed him 50 cents. The defense was not calling up neighbors who got along *well* with Maria. It could easily be argued that, beyond her apparent bad luck in contracting a venereal disease and misattributing its effects to Madame Restell, all this seemed to indicate little beyond the fact that her neighbors enjoyed gossiping.

Brady concluded his arguments by asking the jury, "What has been the testimony of Maria Bodine? What had been her character or disposition to tell the truth at all?" Surely, he suggested to the men of the jury, they would not like it if such a woman were maligning *their* reputations. Maria couldn't be trusted because, in his estimation, for women, "chastity is the basis of character...and when that departs no reliance can be placed in her that loses it."[34] And yes, this is inconsistent with his notion of Maria abandoning her supposed sinning ways after meeting Madame Restell.

They had only Maria's testimony regarding her abortion to go on, and there was some doubt established as to whether Maria could be trusted. Maybe she had been lying for attention. Maybe she'd never even been pregnant, and just had a vivid imagination!

If the jury believed Maria's testimony, and agreed that she'd been pregnant with a quick child, then Madame Restell was guilty of second-degree manslaughter. If they doubted Maria—at least enough to doubt whether they could trust her statement that the child was quick—then Madame Restell was guilty of a mere misdemeanor.

The district attorney countered by pointing out that "the counsel begins by requiring of me a pure and unsullied female to go on that stand and testify against the prisoner [Restell]. This, I know, you know, we all know, cannot be done.... [I]f this girl, Maria Bodine, had been the worst woman living, if she had been rotten, as it were with disease, and completely abandoned, it is utterly impossible for any human being to invent such a story as has been told by her."[35] She would have to be, the DA assessed, a clairvoyant to recount her time inside Madame Restell's house so closely and with such detail.

As the verdict came closer to being delivered, newspapers were once again calling for Restell's immediate conviction. The *Brooklyn Daily Eagle* shouted that "if the jury who are now trying the case of the child murderess Restell do not convict her...they will deserve to be scouted by every honest man and woman in the land!...If they do not bring a verdict of guilty it will be impossible (it surely seems so) to convict a person of the horrid crime in New York on *any* testimony."[36]

They were not wrong. If Maria Bodine's testimony wasn't enough to convict Madame Restell of manslaughter—whether because the jury members sympathized with her or because they just didn't trust Bodine—then the guilty verdict would be challenging to obtain in future cases. No woman wanting to give testimony against Madame Restell would ever come forward who seemed to meet the jury's criteria for chastity and trustworthiness.

When the day of the verdict came, Madame Restell seemed to suspect that the ruling would not be in her favor. Impeccably dressed in what seemed to have become her go-to court outfit—a black silk gown trimmed with velvet, a white satin bonnet, and a heavy lace veil—she was more tense than usual. Newspapers claimed she appeared anxious and looked "excessively pale."[37] In some descriptions, she virtually trembled.

Still, when the clerk asked why judgment should not be rendered against her, one of her lawyers, Graham, spoke on her behalf, saying, "He will consider her to say that the Court has no right to pass sentence."[38] However much we appreciate the "only God can judge me" bravado at work here, she might have done better to say a few words about remorse, instead of the nineteenth-century equivalent of "double middle fingers to all my haters."

In the end, Madame Restell was found guilty not of manslaughter, but of a misdemeanor, and sentenced to one year in jail. The case proceeded to the Court of Appeals. However, in June 1848, that court elected to uphold the jury's decision. By that time Madame Restell had already served seven months in jail on Blackwell's Island, but the Court, rather cruelly, declared that her sentence would begin from the time their judgment was rendered. The seven months she'd already spent in prison did not count.

Uncharacteristically for a woman who generally presented a formidable demeanor, Madame Restell had been horrified by the verdict. She "broke down when she was taken from the court room by the sheriff."[39] Those judges' daughters and magistrates' nieces had not been enough to save her from the law. In less than a year, she had gone from having it all to the prospect of a year in jail, with none of the joyful daily amenities to which she was accustomed.

Cook, whose actions had prompted all this, was never prosecuted for his involvement. A respectable man could be forgiven the occasional fall from grace.

Poor Maria Bodine would suffer a far unhappier fate. In July 1848, the *Brooklyn Evening Star* reported that she was now very infirm and almost destitute. Because of her damaged reputation, it was unlikely that she could find work; if her syphilis was advancing, she may not have been able to work anyway. It was suspected that some sympathetic individuals gave her money after the trial, but "that has long since been expended," according to one paper.[40] The paper begged some benevolent society to take pity upon her, but there's no evidence that any of them did. There were many women like Maria on the streets of New York. For all that the papers were happy to publicize "Restell's victims," they were not very interested in denouncing a society that failed to come to their aid, particularly once the women were no longer sensational fodder.

Madame Restell, on the other hand, would always be sensational fodder. If anyone thought her time in prison would temper her, they were about to be surprised.

Chapter Twelve

MADAME RESTELL WAS RIGHT TO BE FRIGHTENED AS SHE WAS transported to Blackwell's Island.

This island—since renamed Roosevelt Island—lies in the East River off the main body of Manhattan, and it has a rich history of horrors. In 1839, Charles Dickens wrote, of his visit to the island and the asylum housed there, "Everything had a lounging, listless, madhouse air." When the investigative journalist Nellie Bly went undercover at the same asylum in 1887, she was cautioned by an ambulance driver, "Blackwell Island [is] an insane place, where you'll never get out of."[1] During her time there, she wrote, inmates were subjected to a series of horrifying treatments: they were thrown into ice baths, choked by nurses, and fed food infested with bugs. This may have had much to do with the fact that only 18 cents a day—around $6 today—was allotted for the care of each inmate.

The penitentiary was no better; the same commissioners were in charge of the asylum and the prison. Built in 1832, the penitentiary's turreted design lent it a castle-like quality. But it hardly meant the prisoners could expect to be treated with more dignity; the anarchist politician Johann Most described it as "the true Siberia of America."[2] Stranded on an island, the prisoners were removed from sight and happily forgotten by most of the people residing in the city just across the waterway. If the citizenry of New York heard about the prison at Blackwell's Island at all, it was to reassure them that there was no cause for worry. In 1842, the *New-York Tribune* reported, following an investigation, that there was "no cause for complaint, but [the asylum and prison] are found to be all that can be expected from them, as relates to good order, cleanliness, and comfort of the inmates."[3]

The inmates would have begged to differ.

Some reports about mistreatment started to creep out. In 1838, six years after the penitentiary was founded, newspapers claimed there were concerning things about "the treatment of prisoners at Black-well's Island—that they are cruelly flogged, and so forth."[4] That was true, but it was hardly the worst of it.

At Blackwell's, there were four hundred and ninety six cells that were seven feet long and only three or four feet wide.[5] This was not nearly enough space for a fully grown man or woman—and two peo-ple were expected to fit in each cell and sleep side by side.

In addition to being confined to entirely too cramped quarters, younger prisoners were often taken under older ones' rather disrep-utable wings. Many of the prisoners had been thrown into Blackwell's for matters that today seem very minor or unworthy of incarceration. Take, for instance, the case of John Bowen, who was sentenced to three months at Blackwell's in 1839 because he had stolen one basket. Or the forty-two girls sentenced to the penitentiary in 1863—all minors aged fourteen or younger.

The result, according to the *New York Times*, was that "a boy-thief or a stupid young foreigner, caught in a crime which to him was hardly a sin, without a friend and unable in his own tongue to defend himself, was shut up in a cell, some seven feet by four feet, with an old ruffian schooled in crime.... [H]ere, in constant companionship, he learned the flash words and the old haunts of professional rogues...and then after his three or six months term, he was cast out again in the great City."[6] The Reverend William Glenney French, an Episcopal mission-ary who worked on the island, lamented, "If any man, or set of men, should try to find the best possible plan to educate criminals, they could not find one more effectual to that end than the one in exis-tence in this institution."[7]

There were people who tried to remedy these conditions. A Mrs. Gibbons, who with a group of other ladies tried to provide lodging for young women wishing to "change their habits of life" (in all likelihood, stop working as prostitutes), was refused admission to the prison, as the keepers had neither the energy nor the enthusiasm to try to reform the prisoners. As the *New York Evening Post* lamented in 1849, "Instead of any attempt at reformation being made, the prison is so managed as to become a school of vice."[8]

The conditions also seemed designed to evoke despair. The penitentiary was quite literally shrouded in darkness. There were no windows there, and gaslights were rare. The only accoutrements in these tiny cells were two strips of canvas for the prisoners to lie on, a mug, and a chamber pot. At dawn, they shared a tank to wash in—not only with their cellmates, but with all the prisoners. With only one towel for every fifty prisoners, it's likely the quality of that bath somewhat resembled Nellie Bly's description of the bathrooms at the Blackwell Aslyum: "The patients are washed, one after the other, without a change of water. This is done until the water is really thick, and then it is allowed to run out and the tub is refilled without being washed. The same towels are used on all the women, those with eruptions [boils] as well as those without. The healthy patients fight for a change of water, but they are compelled to submit to the dictates of the lazy, tyrannical nurses."[9]

At the penitentiary, after washing, the prisoners marched to the river to dump their chamber pots. During the day, male prisoners often worked in the quarries, breaking rocks that would ultimately be used for structures such as the seawall around the island. Women generally sewed clothing. Many were either very hungry or very ill as they labored. During the summer, the prisoners were served "unwholesome" meat, which is a nice way of saying they were choking down rotten food.[10] The stench in those frighteningly close quarters must have been overpowering. If those same prisoners talked about their misery—or talked about anything—they were flogged, just as the *Herald* had reported.

Liquor was routinely smuggled in—it must have been the only way to make life at Blackwell's even slightly tolerable. Dr. William Kelly, the physician at the island in 1848, said that "liquor is brought to the prison in buckets of sand, and the prisoners are often drunk." Truly, who could blame them? There were even rumors that a "grogshop" operated on the island, where prisoners were able to obtain moonshine. Dr. Kelly complained, "The nurses, who are also prisoners, drink the spirits ordered for the sick." To be fair, the nurses were probably not having a wonderful time.[11]

Inebriated nurses may have contributed to reports that the infirmary was filthy; wildly overcrowded, with seventy-five people in a room meant for thirty; and filled with people dying of "ship fever" (an antiquated nickname for typhus). Dr. Kelly advised that the majority of prisoners needed only "exercise, good diet, and fresh air." Sadly, he also noted that "these were not permitted by [the keeper] Acker."[12] Many of those on the island weren't even allowed proper clothing; instead, those in the penitentiary took to stealing clothing from those in the asylum. Mordecai Noah, who once fantasized about seeing Madame Restell in a tight prison uniform stretching over her breasts rather than clad in her fine clothing, would have been delighted.

When Madame Restell entered the penitentiary on June 29, 1848, after delaying her sentence as long as possible through a series of appeals, there were many in New York who were positively gleeful anticipating the terrible treatment she was about to receive. Newspapers as far away as Alabama exulted, "The notorious Madame Restell has at last been convicted, and will have to pick oakum at Blackwell's Island for a year."[13] Some doubtless wondered whether she would even survive the ordeal. The terror of the island was sufficiently great that at least one man sentenced for larceny "attempted to kill himself in transit, by opening the arteries of his arm with a case knife."[14] This behavior was even more common on the island itself; the *Brooklyn Daily Eagle* reported two suicides in a week, one by a woman who hung herself in her cell, another a prisoner leaping off a balcony.[15]

Others chose a different way out. Cursing the proximity of Manhattan, which was so close they could hear music from its shores, prisoners routinely attempted to flee the island and swim or sail to their freedom. Criminals would bribe guards or convince their friends to show up with a rowboat. And those attempted escapes happened with truly shocking regularity. In 1867, seventy-nine people, or nearly two a week, escaped the penitentiary.[16] The year Madame Restell was sent to Blackwell's, "eight or ten [prisoners] escaped, three simply swam to shore," in May alone.[17] Considering that there were an estimated 820 prisoners there in 1849, losing ten in a single month isn't great, when the goal was to keep them imprisoned.[18] The conditions that seemed to contribute to the squalor also contributed to a remarkable lack of oversight.

One might expect that arranging an escape would be Madame Restell's first response. Throughout her life, she had refused to accept uncomfortable circumstances. She had made the brutal voyage to America specifically to transcend the limitations of her birthplace. She was willing to take on dangerous work as long as it meant she and her family could live in comfort. And she had more than enough money to bribe everyone she encountered. One of her newspaper editors would probably have sent a lovely rowboat if she had promised to increase her advertising budget while allowing him to cover the story of her escape. Yes, she might have been more famous than the other prisoners, and this might have made her more identifiable after her escape. But this was also an age where you could move to another city and, like General Dixon, change your name (a prospect that would likely work out better if you did not, like Dixon, declare yourself to be a general).

But this was not what Madame Restell chose to do. Instead, she took over the island.

There is really no other way to describe what happened when she landed at Blackwell's. The papers would later recount how "she had not been in the penitentiary very long before it began to be whispered about, and then so openly asserted that official notice had to be taken of it, that she was living sumptuously, without prison restraint, and wholly at her ease."[19] In other words, she was spared the bulk of the misery that afflicted nearly all the other prisoners.

As soon as Madame Restell arrived at the island, the keeper of the penitentiary, Mr. Jacob Acker, informed Mrs. Mary Jacobs, the matron of the women's side, that he would take Restell under his own charge. Mrs. Jacobs was removed from her duties in what was said to be "one of the measures adopted to afford the convict Restell privileges to which she had no claim."[20]

What that meant for Madame Restell was that she would not be sleeping on a slip of canvas. And she certainly would not have a roommate. In 1878, a Sergeant Taft, who had been a carpenter on Blackwell's Island during Madame Restell's imprisonment, recalled that he "received orders to fit up her cell, which was No. 1 in the women's prison. It had been used as a storeroom."[21] Instead of the typical scrap of cloth and chamber pots, her room was outfitted with feather pillows and a feather bed. Her cell also came equipped with a light by which she could read her many books. Reports claimed she was not only "excus[ed] from wearing prison garb," but given a closet in which to hang her dresses.[22] Throughout her time there, she was said to "wear the raiment of a fashionable woman."[23]

Admittedly there is some dispute on this point of attire. Taft claimed that she did wear the prison uniform but that it had been "bleached so that it looked like merino a little way off. Over this she wore a black silk apron, that nearly reached to her feet and all the way round. She wore a black silk hood."[24] Whether she was wearing high fashion or just turning prison uniforms *into* high fashion, she was certainly not clothed like the rest of the inmates.

As for that rancid meat, Madame Restell would have none of it. Her husband began paying people on the island $5, not for liquor to be transported on the boats from the mainland, but to ensure she had fresh peaches to eat. In addition, the fortunate prisoner at one point reported, "Mrs. Acker sends me my meals, I have tea, coffee, milk, sugar, etc. and all things good. The servant comes three times a day to bring my food, and takes away the dirty dishes."[25]

She was not lonely, either. Charles reportedly came to visit every afternoon, in either a very sweet show of devotion or to obtain instructions on running her business in her absence. The nature of their conversation was private, as she used Acker's office to receive him.

Madame Restell rarely saw the other prisoners, for Acker seemed to prefer keeping her apart from them. Those she did meet, she quickly turned into servants. When deposed on the conditions of the prison, she said, "I pay the prisoner who takes care of my cell, and also the one who does my washing, and have given Mrs. Bingham, the prisoner who keeps the hall, a few shillings. They are all very kind to me." Mrs. Bingham, a prisoner arrested for larceny, added that "Madame Restell has a feather bed brought to her every night. I take her bed in and out, and see that other little matters about her cell are attended to."[26]

This seems less like a prison sentence and more and more like a year spent in a very cold, badly lit hotel.

All this deference was a touch absurd, giving the impression that Madame Restell was some kind of well-born lady who could not possibly be tasked with emptying her own chamber pot. Recall that Madame Restell had, not so very long ago, been a maid-of-all-work for a butcher. She was capable of disposing not only of her own waste but also that of others. Perhaps the most ridiculous example of how she did not have to do anything as vulgar as work was that she did not even have to sew while imprisoned. The other female prisoners at Blackwell's were tasked with sewing garments to earn their keep. Madame Restell was allowed to work separately from the rest of them, sewing accessories for herself alone. She seems to have given the impression that she was incapable of the task, though, stating that, despite her best efforts, she just "could not make a garment, as others do."[27]

Remember: *Madame Restell had once been a professional seamstress.* She was so good at sewing that she was able to, at least briefly, support herself and her child in an insanely competitive industry. She had taken over making garments for her husband, a tailor, with essentially no training. She could have probably made a garment with as much skill as anyone else imprisoned at Blackwell's.

But that was not the persona it behooved her to adopt. It was clearly much more advantageous to act like a grande dame within the walls of Blackwell's.

It is a tribute to Madame Restell's reinvention of herself that not only the warden and his wife, but other prisoners as well, seemed to see her as a woman set apart from them. That may have been because they had a positive opinion of her work. It's not impossible that some of the prisoners or their acquaintances had used her services in the past. More likely, though, as far as they knew, this was just the way upscale people were treated in prison. Madame Restell may have been infamous, but she was also a lady, at least in terms of her financial bracket. Therefore, she was obviously not the kind of person who could be expected to cook, clean, or sew for herself. Even Taft remembered her as having "acted in a very lady-like way" throughout her time at Blackwell's.[28] The class divisions that existed outside of Blackwell's penitentiary held fast within its walls.

Madame Restell wasn't the only wealthy person at Blackwell's who received favorable treatment. John Harrison, who had owned a successful gambling house, was sentenced to the men's prison in November 1848. He, too, enjoyed luxuries denied to other prisoners; like Restell, Harrison did not have to work, or at least had to work very little: he was "not employed more than an eighth part of the time, and [had] his food sent from Mr. Acker's table."[29]

Regarding the special status of prisoners like Restell and Harrison, the *Brooklyn Evening Star* groused that "money contrives always to procure favors from the hirelings of justice, if not its ministers."[30]

But no one knows how many bribes were actually taken. Other than Charles's $5 peach allotment endowment, reports did not find any evidence that Acker, or anyone else, had taken sizable sums of money from Madame Restell or her husband. Even if she had offered compensation, the treatment she received seemed to go beyond money. Mr. Acker—and perhaps his wife, considering she was sending all Madame Restell's meals to her—appeared to be genuinely protective of her. When District Attorney John McKeon, Esquire, and the recorder of the city, the Honorable Mr. Scott, investigated Blackwell's Island with a committee, they were initially "refused admission to the part of the prison in which she was confined."[31] But they were insistent, and they were finally allowed to see her. The committee found that Madame Restell was "dressed different than the other prisoners. It was evident she was not placed amongst the mass of prisoners."[32] Specifically, they saw "a silk dress concealed under Madame Restell's hastily donned prison garb."[33] The situation didn't improve from there. The *Herald* reported, "On the presiding judge passing into the room where some other prisoners were confined, she used some insulting language to that officer. On the District Attorney appealing to the deputy keeper that such a matter should not be passed unnoticed, that public officers must be secure from insult by prisoners while engaged in visiting the prisons, and that something should be done to make an example of such conduct... this was stated to Mr. Acker, but nothing was done by that officer whilst we were on the island."[34]

There was a great deal of hand-wringing over the fact that a prisoner was *rude* to an *officer of the law*—writers at the *Biblical Recorder* wondered, presumably while clutching their pearls, "Are public officers, appointed by statute to visit prisons, to be treated with incivility and insult?"[35] Sometimes! Madame Restell never publicly expressed regret for whatever she said, though she may have regretted a momentary break in her ladylike composure. She was never punished for telling off that officer. It's a shame that the precise nature of her insult is lost to history. But perhaps the most interesting aspect of this incident is how it suggests that Acker would rather curry favor with her than with the government officials inspecting the prison.

Madame Restell brushed off this inclination of his, saying that Acker was "kind to all."[36] He wasn't. Acker may have been lax in his oversight, but that's not the same as being kind. People were frequently flogged for talking to one another on the island. He was perhaps a bit in awe of Madame Restell, and kind to her, but he seemed neglectful and sometimes cruel when it came to the rest of the people in his care.

If he was a bit in awe of this millionaire in his keep, his reaction would hardly be different from many people's, then or now.

Wealth and celebrity have always had a mesmerizing effect on Americans. In a country where everyone wants to be rich, many refuse to accept that the rich can be bad. This was not an attitude that would have been wholly unfamiliar in the 1840s to citizens of a city that would, in a matter of decades, become the epicenter of an American "gilded age."

Madame Restell, somewhat disingenuously, always claimed that she had no idea why she received such preferential treatment. She was never punished for receiving it, though. The person who suffered for that offense was Mr. Acker.

The grand jury investigated the management at Blackwell's. Its report was released in January 1849. It found that there was, unsurprisingly, "great mismanagement" at work in the penitentiary.[37] The board of aldermen met on February 12 to determine whether "Jacob Acker, the Present keeper, has violated the ordinances of the Common Council, neglected and refused to perform his duties…and suffered a convict to receive, without any right or excuse, partial and favorable treatment, inconsistent with the general management of prisoners."[38] His best defense was perhaps that he was guilty of nothing beyond "a looseness in the management, which had arisen more from the general system adopted previously, and which descended to him from his predecessors."[39]

Saying that someone is doing something badly, but doing it the way things have always been done, may help explain someone's behavior, but it does not exonerate the responsible party. People can choose to do their work, if not well, at least less badly than their predecessors. Rather predictably, the aldermen decided to dismiss Acker from his management position at the island in a vote of 11 to 3. One of the three dissenters claimed that "he did not find fault with Mr. Acker for allowing a prisoner to sleep on a feather bed." Instead, "he wished that every poor creature incarcerated in the penitentiary might have a feather bed to sleep upon."[40] That dissenter was an Alderman Thomas Carnley and he seems like a sweet angel who would be absolutely torn apart on cable news were he alive today.

There was, surprisingly, an outpouring of sympathy for Acker. Despite what seemed like a record of favoritism and ineptitude, many people did not want to see a man lose his job. The *New York Daily Herald* criticized what it seemed to regard as a bit of "cancel culture" at work, declaring, of those who pushed for Acker's removal, that "according to the practice of these modern day Solons, a public officer can be removed not only from his position, but robbed of that which is dearer to him than his life—his character—by an extra judicial body of inquisitors...assuming to pass judgment in secret inquisition upon the motives and conduct of their fellow man."[41] That seems somewhat hyperbolic. The events that led to Acker's downfall were widely reported. His dismissal was hardly masterminded by a group of shadowy, secretive elites, as the *Herald* seems to imply. It seems likely that, rather than this being an egregious miscarriage of justice, people thought he should be fired because a malnourished mass of prisoners were constantly escaping while Acker was running back and forth to Madame Restell's cell and asking if she needed more sugar for her coffee.

By May 1849, a new keeper at Blackwell's Island had been appointed. The *New York Daily Herald* declared that, from a pool of around forty applicants, "Mr. Joseph Kean [was] thus chosen...the lucky man."[42]

Not so lucky, really.

The people who said that Blackwell's was badly run seemed untroubled by the fact that Kean had been the prison's keeper before in 1844. Perhaps unsurprisingly, after the management shift, nothing substantial changed.

People kept escaping. In 1853, twelve prisoners swam together to freedom. In 1855, a group of five attempted a similar swim, somewhat hindered by the fact that "two of them had shackles on and another was adorned with a chain and ball."[43] (Only one succeeded in his escape in this case, though the others were not said to have been punished.) Far later, in 1912, a prisoner named David D. Lewis attempted something a bit different. A clergyman serving a year at Blackwell's for fraud, he made what the *New York Times* called "a brazen escape attempt, climbing up one of the stone abutments of the Queensboro Bridge and grabbing hold of a cable." Once there, "ignoring police gunfire from the island, he climbed hand over hand to the girders and then to the roadway, where he found two bicycle policemen waiting."[44]

As poorer residents continued to find the penitentiary conditions deplorable, administrative policies continued to show favoritism for wealthier prisoners. William M. "Boss" Tweed, the corrupt New York senator, was sentenced to time at Blackwell's in 1874 for embezzlement. Like Madame Restell, he had a relatively cushy time. He was given a proper bed in his cell, a velvet couch, and books to read. Mae West, who was imprisoned at Blackwell's for obscenity in her Broadway play *Sex*, and for "corrupting the morals of the youth," was said to be allowed to wear silk underwear during her imprisonment. Meanwhile, a picture from the 1930s shows a German shepherd belonging to the head of an Irish gang at Blackwell's—and not only was the gang leader allowed to have his dog with him on the island, but the dog was pictured eating a steak, far better fare than what less influential prisoners received.[45]

The penitentiary finally shut down in 1936 after over a hundred years of much brutality for the poor, and significantly less for the rich. Today, Roosevelt Island is home to apartment buildings and the Franklin D. Roosevelt Four Freedoms Park.

Madame Restell was pardoned by Governor John Young and released from Blackwell's on November 11, 1848. Despite the niceties that prison life afforded her, her health was said to be "materially impaired by her confinement."[46] That's not surprising. Emma Goldman, the anarchist and labor organizer who would be incarcerated at Blackwell's in the 1890s, claimed that conditions on the island brought on an attack of rheumatism. Wealth and fame were not enough to keep a prisoner from freezing during the winter or sweltering in the summer in what was said to be a tomb-like building. A police officer recounting the time later said that Madame Restell "seemed to feel her imprisonment greatly" and that "she said when she quit Blackwell's Island that she should never go back there."[47]

But if she emerged frailer, she didn't let any hint of weakness show. A Milwaukee newspaper announced, "Madame Restell, upon the occasion of her return from prison to the practice of her profession, rode through the streets of a great city escorted by chariot loads of the strumpets she had helped make such."[48] By August 1849, she was once again "living in her splendid mansion."[49]

Chapter Thirteen

W HILE MADAME RESTELL WAS INCARCERATED, SIPPING TEA and nibbling on peaches, the world as she knew it was rapidly changing. Women's suffrage was about to blossom from being just an idea held by a small group of Quakers to a national movement that would touch every corner of America.

Amazingly, this would not be a good thing for Madame Restell.

Social tensions that arose as a result of suffragettes promoting a woman's right to vote would be one of the many factors that undermined Madame Restell's profession. But neither she nor any of the suffragettes could anticipate that just yet.

From July 19–20, 1848, the Women's Rights Convention was held in Seneca Falls, New York. The gathering was organized by a group of women, including Elizabeth Cady Stanton, temperance activists, and abolitionists. Stanton later claimed that the convention had launched the "greatest rebellion the world has ever seen."[1]

You might not have known that rebellion was coming from the crowd gathered that day. Only three hundred people showed up—a rather small attendance for an event now regarded as the beginning of the feminist movement in the United States. One of those attendees was the abolitionist Frederick Douglass, who described the convention in the antislavery newspaper the *North Star* as "the basis of a grand movement for attaining all the civil, social, political, and religious rights of woman."[2] The *National Reformer* agreed, declaring that the Seneca Falls Convention was "one whose influence shall not cease until woman is guaranteed all the rights now enjoyed by the other half of creation—Social, Civil and Political."[3]

It might seem at first like this movement would suit Madame Restell. After all, today, the feminist movement and pro-choice advocacy are largely synonymous. Many feminists don't believe that you can have female liberation without bodily autonomy—at least, insofar as not allowing the government to dictate whether women have to use their bodies to bear a child against their will. However, the suffragettes' perspective on abortion was more complicated, and would not have been at the forefront of their agenda. As criticism toward their movement increased, they'd have to push back against it further in an effort to reassure men that they would not be entirely overthrowing the social order.

Elizabeth Cady Stanton was very clear about the Seneca Falls Convention's purpose:

> We are assembled to protest against a form of government, existing without the consent of the governed—to declare our right to be free as man is free, to be represented in the government which we are taxed to support, to have such disgraceful laws as give man the power to chastise and imprison his wife, to take the wages which she earns, the property which she inherits, and, in case of separation, the children of her love;...and to have them, if possible, forever erased from our statute-books, deeming them as a shame and a disgrace to a Christian republic in the nineteenth century.[4]

Her address is similar to the "Declaration of Sentiments" presented on the convention's first day, which stated, "The history of mankind is a history of repeated injuries and usurpations on the part of man toward women, having in direct of object the establishment of a permanent tyranny over her."[5] As proof, they offered the following evidence:

Women could not vote but had to submit to laws.
If women were married, they were "civilly dead," and their husbands had the right to all their wages and property.[6]
A woman was compelled to obey her husband, even if he demanded something she considered immoral.
In cases of divorce, a man would typically receive guardianship of the children.

Men "monopolized all the means of profitable employment," leaving women few ways to make money, despite having to pay taxes if single.[7]

Pathways to education were closed to women.

Women couldn't hold positions of authority within the church.

Many of these points would have echoed Madame Restell's experiences, such as her difficulties in finding employment upon her arrival to the States, and the intensely irritating idea—and one that seemed to irritate her more with the passage of the years—that her husband was in charge of her fortune and property.

However, at Seneca Falls, neither abortion nor birth control are mentioned as being among the ways men exert control over women. The closest they came to that was saying one of the ways men oppress women is by creating "a different code of morals for men and women, by which moral delinquencies which exclude women from society are not only tolerated but deemed of little account in man."[8] Again, this was absolutely within the realm of Restell's experience. As an example, remember the different treatment borne by Maria Bodine and Joseph Cook. Maria was considered a prostitute because she slept with her employer, but the community seemed to feel that Cook having sex with her was no reflection whatsoever on his fine character.

The founders of the Seneca Falls Convention devised a list of eleven resolutions addressing their "Declaration of Sentiments":

1. Women had the right to pursue their own happiness.
2. Laws that prevented women from "such a station in society as her conscience shall dictate, or which place her in a position inferior to that of man," were contrary to nature.[9]
3. Women and men were made equal by God.
4. Women should be enlightened regarding their inferior position and "may no longer publish their degradation by declaring themselves satisfied with their present position, nor their ignorance, by asserting that they have all the rights they want."[10]
5. If men wanted to claim that women were morally superior, then, logically, women should be speaking and teaching in all religious assemblies.

6. Men and women should be held to the same moral standards by society.

7. "The objection of indelicacy and impropriety, which is so often brought against woman when she addresses a public audience, comes with a very ill-grace from those who encourage, by their attendance, her appearance on the stage, in the concert, or in feats of the circus."[11]

8. Women should have access to a wider sphere of activities than the domestic ones.

9. Women should be allowed to vote.

10. Women and men were equal in their abilities.

11. Women had an obligation to speak in public, write, and teach in order to "promote every righteous cause by every righteous means."[12]

The resolution that women should be able to vote—the declaration most associated with these women—was the most controversial at the convention and was barely approved. Both Stanton and Douglass gave speeches regarding its necessity before it passed. Every other resolution passed unanimously.

While the right to vote might have seemed particularly out of the realm of possibility to many of the attendees, all these resolutions were ambitious. Many are *still* rebellious positions, despite some people's protestations that women have achieved perfect equality today.

And although these were bold statements still worth being mindful of, there was, again, no mention of reproductive choice. This omission does not mean that suffragettes were unaware of the number of abortions being performed or the reasons for them. They were far from ignorant in that regard, and they had very strong opinions on the topic.

But the opinions of these women's movement founders sometimes become muddied by modern-day activists. Elizabeth Cady Stanton and Susan B. Anthony (whom Stanton met in 1851, several years after Seneca Falls, and with whom she founded a newspaper called *The Revolution*) are often credited by antiabortionists as being firmly antiabortion. Lynn Sherr, the author of *Failure Is Impossible: Susan B. Anthony in Her Own Words*, and Ann D. Gordon, the editor of *Selected*

Papers of Elizabeth Cady Stanton and Susan B. Anthony, refute this notion, writing that "turning these very progressive activists into pro-life politicians makes as much sense as imagining the pyramids as ancient Cheerio boxes."[13]

Antiabortion activists often credit an article that ran in *The Revolution*, which, though largely about the reprehensible nature of marital rape, also refers to the emotional and spiritual burden women might feel following an abortion: "No matter what the motive, love of ease, or a desire to save from suffering the unborn innocent, the woman is awfully guilty who commits the deed. It will burden her conscience in life, it will burden her soul in death; but oh! thrice guilty is he who, for selfish gratification, heedless of her prayers, indifferent to her fate, drove her to the desperation which impelled her to the crime."[14] That passage might, indeed, imply a profound distaste for abortion. There's only one problem: Susan B. Anthony almost certainly did not write the article. She signed articles she wrote in *The Revolution* "SBA." This one was signed simply with an "A." In other articles in *The Revolution*, there is reference to a "Mr. A"—and some of those articles disagree with those written by "SBA." These sentiments, therefore, are more likely ones that a man projected onto a woman rather than ones felt by Susan B. Anthony.

As for Stanton, she seemed to have a realist's perspective on abortion. When one suffragette declared, that she did not believe that any child should be brought into the world without love, a newspaper reported that "Mrs. Stanton hoped that the majority of the audience did not understand her to speak in favor of infanticide. She only spoke of [abortion] as a fact. There was as much of it as ever and would be until every woman was the sovereign of her own person."[15]

So it's not surprising that, despite her prominence during this period, there was no mention of Madame Restell at the Seneca Falls Convention. If there was a female physician who excited the early suffragettes, it was Elizabeth Blackwell, a woman who was *extremely* different from Madame Restell in her views and path. Two weeks later, at the Women's Rights Convention in Rochester, Blackwell was held up as an ideal for women to follow. One of the resolutions read aloud at the conference stated "that, in the persevering and independent course of Mrs. Blackwell who recently attended a series of lectures at Geneva, and had now gone to Europe to graduate as a physician, we see a harbinger of a day when women shall stand forth 'redeemed and disenthralled' and perform those important duties which are so truly within her sphere."[16]

However, an argument could be made that such a day had already come. Madame Restell and others were already performing surgery, in the way of abortions, doling out the best versions of birth control they had available, and helping other women to deliver children. "Female physicians" served in much the same capacity as modern OB-GYNs. But then, Madame Restell and others like her had to make up their credentials. Blackwell did not do so.

Furthermore, abortion appalled Dr. Blackwell. She so greatly disapproved of it that she studied medicine in part *because* of Madame Restell. Although the two didn't meet, Blackwell wrote that she knew of Madame Restell as a "noted abortionist, known all over the country. She was a woman of great ability and defended her course in the public papers. She made a large fortune, drove a fine carriage, had a pew in a fashionable church and, though often arrested, was always bailed out by her patrons."[17] Blackwell certainly did not see any appeal in Madame Restell's decadent lifestyle, and she was upset that the appellation "female physician" was a term that referenced abortionists. She is quite clear about how much she despised the practice of abortion:

> The gross perversion and destruction of motherhood by the abortionist filled me with indignation, and awakened active antagonism. That the honorable term "female physician" should be exclusively applied to those women who carried on this shocking trade seemed to me a horror. It was an utter degradation of what might and should become a noble position for women....I finally determined to do what I could do "to redeem the hells" and especially the one form of hell thus forced upon my notice.[18]

In 1849, Elizabeth Blackwell became the first woman to receive a medical degree in the United States. She later helped found the New York Infirmary for Women and Children, which opened a women's medical college in 1867. And while she certainly saw women in difficult situations, where they perhaps could have benefited from an abortion, her opinion of Madame Restell never changed. As her biographer Janice P. Nimura noted, it surely frustrated her to open the *Directory of the City of New-York for 1852–1853* and see herself listed on page 63 as "Elizabeth Blackwell, Physician," only to turn to the Rs and see Madame Restell listed exactly the same way.[19]

Beyond her profession, Madame Restell did not appear to have an interest in women's causes. She worked with her husband and her brother, or, more accurately, they worked for her. She had likely been trained by a man. She plagiarized the philosophy in her ads from a man. In prison, she chatted amiably with the male keeper of the island, not his wife who was preparing her meals. The people she enlisted for help when she needed bail were often male newspaper editors. She regarded her female patients with, at best, maternal pity, and at worst, contempt. After many trials, she was aware that those patients to whom she had once been tender could be pitted against her, and her counsel would have to defame them, making any friendship an impossible proposition. Her relationship with her own daughter would prove contentious. And she saw the women who did exist in her sphere, such as Madame Costello, as rivals—not peers.

It is reasonable to cast Madame Restell as the kind of woman who would quickly and a bit proudly proclaim "All my friends are men."

The women at Seneca Falls also unabashedly framed themselves—and all women—as victims of male oppression. Madame Restell, who had built a flourishing empire thanks to the men who taught her and worked for her, might have been disinclined to see herself in that way. As for the notion that women possessed a moral authority that meant they should be heard in the public sphere, she probably had a clearer view than most that women could embrace exactly the same vices as men. She likely would have found these cause-oriented women tiresome, and at least some of them would have found her appalling.

Moreover, Madame Restell's beliefs may have been at odds with the religious leanings of this particular group of women. Most of the female organizers at Seneca Falls were devout Quakers. Although Madame Restell seemingly enjoyed being admitted into a fashionable church, she did not consider herself especially spiritual. Quakers, on the other hand, were (and still are) intensely so, and believed in the presence of God in each person. They also historically opposed slavery, consumption of alcohol, war, and (perhaps most unacceptable to Madame Restell) fashionable attire. George Fox, the founder of the Quaker movement, advised followers: "Do not delight in apparel.... [K]eep to your plain fashions, that you may judge the world's vanity and spirit, in its vain fashions, and show a constant spirit in the truth and plainness."[20]

Madame Restell thoroughly enjoyed the world's vanity and spirit. George Fox's admonition that people "should adorn themselves as becomes the Gospel, with chaste lives and conversation," would not have resonated with her.[21] If anything, it was a point she heard much more from her detractors than her allies. As for the women speaking at Seneca Falls, it would have been hard to reconcile the beauty of a simple, chaste life with, for instance, the alleged actress who expressed gratitude that Madame Restell made her work and life possible.

All this to say—the feminists of the time were not overly concerned with Madame Restell and abortion. Nor was Madame Restell overly bothered with them.

But if there was not a huge overlap between early feminism and abortion rights, men in the medical profession were determined to create one. Within a few decades, the women who had wanted to work and vote and serve in more powerful positions within the church were cast as baby killers intent on destroying motherhood in America.

Dr. Montrose Pallen, who would argue for criminalizing abortion, had aggressively established the erroneous link between feminism and abortion by 1868, saying, " 'Woman's rights' now are understood to be, that she should be a man, and that her physical organism, which is constituted by Nature to bear and rear offspring, should be left in abeyance, and that her ministrations in the formation of character as mother should be abandoned for the sterner rights of voting and law making." If the suffragette movement continued, he felt it would not be long before women's duties (such as motherhood) were "shirked, neglected *or criminally prevented.*"[22]

Meanwhile, Dr. H. S. Pomeroy, the author of *The Ethics of Marriage*, and a fervent antiabortionist, made the same link. He said, "There are advocates of education who seek to deter woman by false pride, from performing the one duty she is perfectly sure of being able to do better than a man! And there are those who teach that their married sisters may save time and vitality for high and noble pursuits by 'electing' how few children shall be born to them."[23] The "electing" part of that statement is important, as it could read as implying that the suffragettes were in favor of birth control or abortion. There *were* early feminists who felt strongly that women should be able to determine how many children they had. However, in general, what they meant was being able to say no to marriage, or, in cases where women were married, to marital rape (though on that front they'd have to wait some time—America would not have its first law against marital rape until the state of Nebraska made it illegal in 1976).

Marital rape was of particular concern for some suffragettes, including Lucy Stone, who wrote, "It is very little to me to have the right to vote, to own property, etc., if I may not keep my body, and its uses, in my absolute right. Not one wife in a thousand can do that now."[24] Elizabeth Cady Stanton agreed that this was a horrible condition. She felt that, due to the laws of marriage, wherein a husband could have sex with his wife whenever he wished, a woman "consents to live in legalized prostitution!—her whole soul revolting at such gross association!—her flesh shivering at the cold contamination of that embrace, held there by no tie but the iron chain of the law." She concluded that "any law or public sentiment that forces two immortal, high-born souls to live together as husband and wife, unless held there by love, is false to God and humanity."[25]

Even with these clear statements, it's not surprising that men quickly tried to establish a link between feminism and abortion. It's a lot easier to decry feminists by claiming they're destroying the sacred institution of motherhood and murdering children than to argue that marital rape is good and that women *should* be trapped as their husbands' property in loveless marriages.

As the feminist movement accelerated, the attempts from detractors to claim that the association was designed for immoral women increased. In 1867, a Mr. Gould made a speech against women's suffrage at the New York Convention. In it, he wondered what kind of women would go to the polls to vote, surmising that "every prostitute in the city of New York would vote....Madame Restell, in her splendid and gorgeous carriage, coming from the slaughter of innocents would vote.... [B]ut who can get the real women of New York to vote? No sir, you could not drag them there with a long chain, you could not drive them there with a whip of scorpions."[26] Mr. Gould's concerns are suspect on several fronts: For starters, you could probably make anyone go *anywhere* with a whip made out of scorpions. However, at least in Madame Restell's case, she wasn't especially eager to go to the polls. She was far more comfortable simply bribing politicians for favors, vote or no vote.

If this contrived link to abortion rights seems tenuous to us now, it would have posed great concern to women struggling to gain the right to vote then. To win public approval, they needed to be seen as worthy voters, which is to say, not grouped with Madame Restell or prostitutes. In order to have male politicians support suffrage, they needed, moreover, to show that they were not trying to make men's lives worse. They needed to do so in the face of cartoons from anti-suffrage groups that frequently depicted men being abandoned to housework and child-care (the horror!) while their wives went to the polls.

Men did not especially like the idea of being treated the way they'd treated women for centuries. In the *Atlantic*, Charles Clark wrote a nearly seven-thousand-word essay expressing his fear that some women were already choosing not to get married and become mothers, and might take on employment such as teaching instead. He believed that with "the right of suffrage [more of them] would develop false ideals."[27] If Clark realized that women not only teach but run for president today, he'd turn over in his grave.

Telling men that they would have no wives and that their children would lack attentive mothers once women had the right to vote proved to be an effective scare tactic. So, for the suffragettes' movement to succeed, it was beneficial to suffragettes to cast themselves as deeply moral, as traditional women who were wrongly kept from the polls, when men who were, in the words of suffragette Emily J. Harding Andrews, "convicts and lunatics" were allowed to vote.[28] Newly enfranchised women would still be mothers tending the home and hearth, they insisted. Indeed, pro-suffrage cartoons depicted babies marching for the vote for their mothers, and explained that women wanted a vote to make choices about those babies' "food, health, play, homes, schools, and work."[29] Suffrage, they seemed to insist, would only help them be better mothers. In this regard, the suffragettes reinforced the importance of motherhood. If many early feminists tacitly condoned abortion and understood the need for it, it was still easier not to mention the subject. If it had been possible to talk about abortion somewhat candidly in the 1840s, it would have been extremely imprudent two decades later.

And so, while feminists fighting for the vote would, very gradually and with enormous personal sacrifices, gain rights, the arguments that Madame Restell and others made for abortion and birth control would fall by the wayside for many decades.

Chapter Fourteen

M ADAME RESTELL WAS NO SOONER FREED FROM BLACKWELL'S than she resumed her normal operations.

As much as the world had changed over the past year, there were still many things that remained the same. Men had not stopped seducing young women during her imprisonment, and not many people were familiar with the ideas being preached at Seneca Falls. Men were not going to change their behavior because Elizabeth Cady Stanton said they should. Certainly, those exhortations—the notion, for instance, that she should only have sex with a man if she wanted to—would not have been known to Cordelia Grant, who was (at least by modern standards) raped by George R. Shackford.

Shackford, age twenty-nine, was fabulously wealthy. Born in New Hampshire and raised in Mississippi, he had three sisters, but as the only son he stood to inherit his parents' entire estate. He was "connected with the Mississippi boats, one of which he commanded."[1] In his twenties, he married a wealthy woman who died when he was twenty-five, leaving him the bulk of her fortune. So he now had her riches to add to the promise of his own. By the time Shackford met Cordelia, his personal net worth was around $100,000 ($3.5 million today); his own family's estate, which would be his upon the death of his parents, was valued at around $400,000 ($13.5 million today).

Cordelia was a fifteen-year-old schoolgirl from a middle-class family. So there was a substantial power differential, as one might expect between a child and an adult millionaire twice her age. Indeed, that power differential is so vast that, to many modern readers, it probably feels as though a relationship between the two should have been illegal. It wasn't. Up through 1880, the age of consent in America was

153

generally age ten or twelve. And that's still leagues better than it was in some states, such as Delaware—where the age of consent was only seven years old. By 1887, the Women's Christian Temperance Union had begun protesting this standard, advocating to have "the age at which a girl can legally consent to her own ruin be raised to at least eighteen years."[2] This request was initially laughed at, with legislators suggesting joke amendments proposing the "age of consent be raised to eighty-one years, that all girls be required to wear a chastity belt, or to mandate that all women *must* consent to sex after the age of eighteen years."[3] Despite the mockery, standards did change, but it took decades. States amended the age of consent to sixteen or eighteen, or, in Georgia's case, fourteen, by the 1920s.

Which was too late for Cordelia.

Cordelia was initially uninterested in Shackford, whom she first met in 1847 out picnicking with a group of her school friends. He "insisted on paying her attentions, despite her brother-in-law's disinclination to permit them from a stranger, and also of the young lady's effort to be free of him." However, he found Cordelia's sister and convinced her to allow him to visit Cordelia at home with her family. There he repeatedly told Cordelia how much he wanted to marry her. Cordelia listened to his flattery with "all the credulity and curiosity of a trusting [girl of] sixteen."[4] Shackford may have had his charms. The *Brooklyn Daily Eagle* reported that he was "one of the gems in fashionable society. He rolls around in a flash equipage, visits the watering places every summer, occupies an elevated pew in church."[5] And Cordelia was still a child.

Once he felt sure she loved him, he asked her to elope with him. Cordelia didn't like this idea—eloping would mean leaving her family and the protection they offered—but, it was reported, "she listened and listened, and verified the adage that 'she who deliberates is lost.'" He promised that they'd go to his mother's house, and after that they'd be married. One night, the two ran away from Portland, Maine, and boarded a steamer bound for New Orleans, accompanied by Shackford's young son from his prior marriage. On the voyage, the son fell off the boat and drowned. This tragic accident is horrifying in and of itself, but even more disturbing is the fact that Shackford "received the intelligence unmoved, while [Cordelia], to whom the child had become endeared, grieved for him."[6]

This should've been a very red flag.

Cordelia might have surmised from this incident that George Shackford did not particularly like or want children. But for whatever reason, she was not sufficiently put off by his behavior to turn back. Perhaps she felt she could not. She may have been nervous about how her family would respond to her getaway. Or perhaps, at her young age, she did not fully consider that life with a man who shrugs at his child falling over the side of a boat might be less than pleasant.

And it wasn't like her family was desperately trying to bring her home. If anyone was concerned about the age disparity and difference in life experience between the two during their courtship, they were troubled only insofar as she might become unchaste and ruin her future marriage prospects. In fact, Cordelia's family fully believed their daughter was married, because she told them as much. Until 1854, "her parents, friends, relatives, and all who knew her were under the impression that she was the lawful wife of Shackford."[7]

Meanwhile, Shackford told his mother and sisters that Cordelia was merely his protégé, a young woman for whom he was nobly caring. Amazingly, though the couple stayed at his mother's house, Shackford's mother and sister "asked no questions, for, by some means, in his mother's house, Shackford managed to make his will absolute." Shackford's mother and sister may have had a better understanding than Cordelia did of what it means to be with a man who can watch a six-year-old fall over the side of a boat without blinking. They likely refrained from asking questions not because they weren't curious, but because they'd known him long enough to know he was a sociopath. The one upside was that, at his mother's house, Shackford was unable to "gratify his unhallowed propensities without [arousing] suspicion" in the family home.[8] After two months, they left St. Louis, with Shackford telling his mother he was taking Cordelia to school.

Instead, they set up house in New York. It seems, at first, that Cordelia kept trying to convince Shackford to make good on his promise to marry her, and refused to sleep with him until he did. In response, Shackford informed her that he would "turn her into the streets unless she made herself comfortable to his desires."[9] Far from home, and with no money of her own, this must have been a terrifying proposition. And so, she was coerced into becoming his mistress.

In January 1850, not so long after Madame Restell left Blackwell's, Cordelia became pregnant.

Shackford first visited Charles Lohman in order to negotiate an abortion, with Cordelia in tow. He paid Charles $50, lower than the typical $100 Madame Restell charged wealthier clients, but then, the couple rarely turned down clients even when they could not pay their full fee. As he was paying, Madame Restell came into the room, whereupon Shackford announced—somewhat unnecessarily—that Cordelia was his wife.

Madame Restell took the young teen upstairs with her. Cordelia recalled that "Madame Restell told me it was a pity for a married woman like me to lose my children, as I was a pretty woman and would have fine children."[10] Whether Madame Restell took Shackford at his word or was trying to suss out details about what she suspected had happened, the comment must have only made this uncomfortable situation even worse.

The operation commenced. Cordelia recalled that Madame Restell "talked with me on more lively matters." She also instructed her to "keep up good spirits."[11]

Unfortunately, Cordelia would be back in a year. In January 1851, when she again fell pregnant, Shackford insisted that she have another abortion.

By that time, the pair were living together in a boardinghouse at 141 Greenwich Street. Shackford had stopped trying to pass Cordelia off as his wife; he was now telling people she was his niece, and that he had enrolled her in school. He actually did do this. According to Cordelia, at Mrs. Hannah Parker's school, "George told the schoolteacher and the parties where we boarded that I was his ward."[12]

When Cordelia was sent to Madame Restell's house for the second abortion, it was arranged for her to board there for two weeks. Shackford paid Madame Restell $100 for the procedure. Cordelia recalled that, after the operation was performed, Madame Restell told her that "George [Shackford] had said I [Cordelia] could be trusted, and all would be kept [secret]."[13] As ever, this was intended as a warning not to tell anyone she'd had an abortion.

After her recuperation, Shackford and Cordelia departed for a vacation. It was now summer. Cordelia may have begun to think of leaving this man who refused to marry her and pressured her into abortions. But she was back to pretending to be his wife rather than his niece when they went to Cape May, New Jersey. Sadly, this meant that by October 1852 Cordelia was once again pregnant—for the third time in two years—and returned to Madame Restell's.

This time, Cordelia noted that Madame Restell's husband wasn't present. Charles had gone to Europe, perhaps to visit the couple's daughter, who was enrolled in school there. Cordelia found Madame Restell in her shop with her brother. By this time, Madame Restell was well acquainted with Cordelia and couldn't have been surprised when she "told her what I had come for, again."[14]

Following the abortion, Cordelia went to stay with Shackford at a boardinghouse called the Westchester House, where she was ill for the next two weeks. She claimed that after she recovered, she went East to visit some friends for three weeks, after which she returned to the city with Shackford. But, according to Cordelia, at this point she and Shackford did stop having sex. By now, she was twenty-one and had been pregnant five times. She claimed that, "each time and in every case, an abortion has been procured, at the insistence of Shackford" (though only three were performed by Restell).[15]

When Shackford was not arranging for abortions, he kept busy building a fine house for himself. He oversaw the construction of what was said to be "a splendid mansion at Fordham, Westchester."[16] Cordelia may have hoped that now, with this home, they might be married. That was not to be. Shackford told Cordelia she could live there as his housekeeper, which must have seemed to be quite a demotion from either wife or niece. By February 1854, the two were fighting. Cordelia felt that Shackford was planning to abandon her. It is entirely possible he was. Or she might have just been understandably suspicious after suffering through a dysfunctional relationship for seven years. Cordelia wanted $6,000 as a kind of palimony, after which she would leave. Shackford refused.

There were a few legal angles that Cordelia could have chosen to pursue, none of which she was probably aware of. One was a breach of promise suit. Through laws most commonly employed in the nineteenth century, women could sue men who had promised to marry them and then reneged; this avenue was available to men as well, but was, in reality, almost exclusively pursued by women. That avenue was especially relevant if there had been "damages" as a result, such as the loss of the woman's virginity, or having had to undergo multiple abortions (though this would mean admitting she'd had the illegal operations). Cordelia could have also tried to have him punished under the (less often pursued) 1848 Act to Punish Seduction as a Crime, which stated that "any man who shall under promise of marriage seduce and have illicit connection with any unmarried female of previous chaste character shall be guilty of a misdemeanor."[17]

She did not try any of these approaches. Instead, Cordelia went straight to the police and informed them that Shackford had paid Madame Restell to perform multiple abortions.

Shackford was promptly arrested. So was Madame Restell, who, on March 1, 1854, issued a statement declaring that Cordelia's statements were "unqualifiedly false."[18] Charles wrote a response to the charges in the *New York Times* in which he claimed the accusation was a ploy to extort money from him and Restell. Seemingly having learned something about defaming women from the defense at the Bodine trial, he wondered, if Cordelia could do this, "What man in the community is safe?...How easily can the most unprincipled woman prefer [*sic*] a complaint, and prepare any possible affidavit against any person, however respectable? Against a husband, or a father of a family?"[19] Madame Restell added a postscript to Charles's statement noting that "all the charges were utterly false, base and malicious." Even so, she prepared for the case as though the claims were true (which, in all likelihood, they were). Madame Restell once again retained Ambrose Jordan as her lawyer. However, when she showed up in court on March 2, the plaintiff was noticeably absent. The court waited two hours for Cordelia to appear, to no avail. Finally, the magistrate announced that "he had heard that Miss Grant, through the instrumentality of Mr. Shackford...had been induced to leave the city."[20]

The trial could not proceed without Cordelia Grant as a witness, so Madame Restell and Shackford were discharged from warrant and arrest.

As for why she didn't show—it's likely straightforward. Cordelia Grant did want money, though not from Madame Restell. It seems that Shackford finally relented and gave it to her, at which point she promptly left town. The magistrate noted that she had been in the custody of a policeman who claimed that she had received a note the prior morning between 9:00 and 10:00 a.m., dressed, and gone out, though—mysteriously for someone leaving town—all her trunks remained at the house. Her lawyer, a seemingly distressed man named Mr. Busteed, announced, "I do not know whether she has been abducted forcibly.... I have my doubts of her leaving of her own volition; her friends and relatives are not appraised of her whereabouts."[21]

New Yorkers, never ones to accept an obvious explanation where a fantastic one might be found, latched on to the idea of foul play. By March 13, it was reported that "the general impression [in New York] is that she has been forcibly abducted."[22]

Speculation increased, and four days later the *Herald* said that her body had been found on the Brooklyn side of the East River, presumably murdered and drowned. "Several persons acquainted with her identity hastened to Brooklyn to ascertain further particulars."[23] This was extremely exciting for the populace. Maybe Shackford murdered Cordelia to stop her from testifying! Maybe Madame Restell did! However, the excitement was short-lived; soon, it was revealed that the body was not Cordelia's but rather belonged to a twenty-five-year-old woman named Sarah Anne Jacobs, who had been "subject to fits of insanity."[24]

Disturbingly, Shackford seemed marvelously untroubled by the reports about Cordelia's whereabouts. But then, he knew what really happened to her. It soon became clear that Cordelia had met with Shackford and departed New York about an hour later. One can only hope that she got the money she wanted and was able to establish a new, much better life elsewhere, and eventually met someone who treated her with considerably more kindness. At any rate, by March 23, about a week after the excitement prompted by her supposed drowning, the justice of the case received a letter from her postmarked from New Jersey, stating that she had "voluntarily left the state, and abandoned the prosecution." She added that she was deterred from returning to New York "for fear of falling under the influence of others who have deceived and misled."[25]

There were, predictably, some who insisted that the letter was a forgery. The *Washington Telegraph* noted that "the theory that the young woman had gone off on her own accord does not have many disciples."[26] Papers from as far away as Ohio insisted that "Madame Restell and Mr. Shackford will be brought before the court again on a new charge"—the implication being that they were about to be accused of *murder*.[27] Nothing came to pass. However horrible a person George

Shackford was, it seems more likely that he paid Cordelia to go away than that he murdered her and forged a letter from her. More moderate voices agreed that "this is probably the last that will be heard of the affair."[28]

Madame Restell emerged as this episode's villain in the tabloids. The *Washington Telegraph* declared that "if ever lynching was justifiable, it is in such a case [as Cordelia's]."[29]

In actuality, men like George Shackford, as the early suffragettes of Seneca Falls noted, seemed to be the ones doing the corrupting—though the *Washington Telegraph* (apparently possessed of a very bloodthirsty staff) said they wished to see him burned alive in a public execution along with Madame Restell. It's hard to imagine a situation where Cordelia Grant and George Shackford could have ever happily raised a child together; fleeing, perhaps with $6,000 and a rather fragmented education, may have been the best outcome for her.

As for Madame Restell, she was wondering how to make Charles's declaration that they were a respectable family in the *New York Times* a reality. Or at least something that people weren't inclined to think of as being entirely far-fetched.

CHAPTER FIFTEEN

B Y THE EARLY 1850S, MADAME RESTELL HAD DECIDED SHE would be respectable. Her less-than-flattering portrayal as an elegantly dressed demon in the newspapers was finally starting to bother her. As much as she might have rationalized characterizations in the press as free publicity or dismissed them as the rantings of fools, no one enjoys being called a devil all the time. And so, at least for a few years, Madame Restell began to strive for something she could not bully or charm her way into: social respectability.

She was not alone; it was a decade when many New Yorkers were fighting to improve their reputations. Their thriving metropolis housed over 600,000 people by 1855. Much of the population growth had been due to massive immigration, but city officials hoped to make New York more appealing to the wealthy and cosmopolitan as well. Streets were being widened and railroads installed on the West Side, causing rents to double. Beautiful townhomes were replacing decaying boardinghouses in fashionable parts of the city, causing the *New-York Tribune* to enthuse that "from the old word of Decay flutters forth the gorgeous butterfly of wealth and beauty."[1]

There was a new class of people in New York, one chronicled in Charles Astor Bristed's account, *The Upper Ten Thousand*, first published in 1852. It perhaps gives the most distinct description of what the elite looked like in New York in that decade. This book was meant to chronicle the behavior of the American upper classes and reassure Europeans that, no matter what they had heard, America was not entirely a land of "sanguinary duels, Lynch law, [Black] babies boiled for breakfast, swamps and yellow fever; in short, a pleasing and promiscuous mess of things horrible and awful."[2]

Bristed assured his readers that now, in New York, many men were clad in spotless white outfits, their scarfs held together with diamond pins, their moustaches delicately dyed. Such young New York men, the trust-fund kids of their day, were "rejoicing in nothing to do and ten-thousand a year." Meanwhile, there were also young women who kept up with all the Parisian fashions and spoke not only proper British English but multiple other European languages. And, no matter what you might have heard, Bristed declared, it was not true that "all our fashionable ladies are in the daily habit of making assignations at the confectioners."[3] Honestly, the fact that he knew that women were not constantly fornicating at candy shops makes him seem more knowledgeable about women than many of his male peers during this period.

Far from being the uncultured hicks wandering around on foot that Europeans might expect, these "Upper Ten Thousand" were people who had *carriages*. Bristed makes that crystal clear, through repeated, loving descriptions of their many coaches and horses. For young prospective Gothamites in the Upper Ten Thousand, Bristed advised that the first thing to do "is to get a horse, the second, to get a wife."[4]

Perhaps even more important than their carriages, the Upper Ten Thousand were hemmed in by the era's continued obsession with respectability. A stockbroker might be successful, but if he was seedy, he could not belong to Bristed's proposed realm of the "exquisites." Members of this elite group were appalled to see a woman who seemed to bear some resemblance to Restell drive by in her carriage and considered such women vile, desiring no acquaintance with women they would have to deny knowing in public. The condemnations could verge on extreme: one man "committed the great crime of blaspheming the polka [dance], for which Young New York thought him absolutely insane and would gladly have put him into a straight jacket." If that seems like a tedious definition of lunacy, the crème de la crème of New York were also, Bristed admitted, "very slow... I have an idea that fashionable people are stupid all over the world."[5]

Most people did not have $10,000 a year, but wouldn't mind being mistaken for people who did. But it was hard to maintain the illusion of living in a city freshly emerging from its chrysalis when drunkards from the local tavern were still vomiting on your stoop. So, as beautiful townhouses sprung up, desperately poor people were displaced and forced to gather together in ever smaller quarters and do whatever they could for money.

Little could be done about the prevalence of vice in New York. Women still flocked to Madame Restell and others like her, erotica was produced and greedily consumed, and there were still thousands of prostitutes; you could see them on virtually every corner in the city. No one thought it was possible to get rid of all this vice entirely—but there was hope among city officials that people could try to be more discreet. A vestryman of Trinity Church, George Templeton Strong, wrote in 1855 that "what the mayor seeks to abolish is not the terrible evil of prostitution, but simply the scandal and offense of the peripatetic whorearchy.... [H]e is trying to keep vice from proclaiming its allurements in the marketplace."[6] Being able to shield yourself from the poverty and vice pervading New York meant that you had achieved a certain amount of success that eluded, for instance, association with the many immigrants. And if you were not successful enough to shield your offspring in your beautiful townhome from the prostitutes and dirty books and taverns—and essentially no one was—you could at least fake it. This was an era when people became positively pedantic about displaying proper public behavior in America. As for what that behavior exactly was, well, it was ambiguous. In 1851, Donald Mitchell, the editor of the magazine *Lorgnette*, which mocked New York's upper crust, satirized this mania, writing, "There are an almost incalculable number of *respectables* in town, both respectable things, as churches, eating houses, slop shops, and the like; and respectable people, as lawyers, note-shavers, fops, and women. I have been puzzling my brain for a long time trying to figure out what made a particular broker or playhouse respectable." He noted that respectability apparently wasn't just about paying one's bills; he'd found plenty of "men about town—both bankrupts and authors," who never had any money but were seen as pictures of propriety. Velvet collars on coats, with their whiff of Europeanness, on the other hand, were *not* respectable. Mitchell painted a picture of bourgeois families in such a way that it's still recognizable today, 150 years later. Respectable people, he declared, had small libraries of best sellers (*Pilgrim's Progress* and *Arabian Nights*), dressed in subdued clothing, drank tea, had sons that worked in finance, mostly discussed babies and the weather, were Christian, and "discourage[d] hilarity in younger branches of the household," as "dullness may be reckoned eminently respectable."[7]

Though she'd gained a vast fortune by this point, Madame Restell faced a number of obstacles on her route to respectability. For starters, she read too much, dressed too well, and had far too much of a sense of humor. She also performed abortions, which made even attempting it borderline insane.

No matter. During 1853 and 1854, she set out to focus, not only on making money, but on securing a social position where she was at least not despised.

In this regard, she fortunately had one very helpful asset—a lovely daughter.

By 1853, Madame Restell's daughter, Caroline, was in her early twenties and in possession of a "first-class education."[8] After spending some years in her youth assisting Madame Restell—seemingly without too much enthusiasm—she had been sent away from Madame Restell's business to school, and she was not expected to pursue a future in it. Rather, Madame Restell hoped that her daughter might pursue a career in the arts; specifically, that she would publish a book of poems. Caroline, alas, did not seem to show as much interest in poetry as her mother did. It seems likely that being a poet was less Caroline's dream, and more what Madame Restell might have liked to do had economic necessity not made her take another path.

But the more urgent matter—especially since people other than her proud mother did not seem to regard Caroline as a great literary talent—was getting her married.

Launching Caroline into the marriage market would have been a costly endeavor.

Due to her mother's infamous reputation, she was not likely to be invited to the more exclusive balls, which wealthy people sponsored and hosted in their own homes, thereby controlling the guest lists. However, there were also City Assemblies, which featured music and dancing, to which she could buy a ticket. These large-scale events were disdained by some of the very upper echelons of society—at such a party they might have to socialize with the sons and daughters of *any* wealthy merchants who could afford a ticket, God forbid—but they were still an effective way for young people of a certain status to mix and mingle.

Caroline was also blessed with a mother who cared a lot about her wardrobe. Girls seeking matrimony were expected to dress in a way that would catch the eye of prospective suitors. In 1854, *Harper's Magazine* noted that "the lovely ladies who had bowling costumes in the morning, have driving costumes tonight.... [T]he ribbons flutter, the gloves glisten." The fancy dress balls required attention-grabbing costumes—at these events, especially bold young women might even wear breeches, to the shock and dismay of some society matrons. No sooner did invitations go out than "all the tailors, and costumers, and milliners, [were] at work all day and night" making these outfits. At least one theater owner rented out props that had been used in plays to help make the costumes more authentic. Families paid hundreds of dollars for their eligible daughters to wear peasant costumes. Society belle Matilda Barclay's family, for example, spent $300 (today's $10,200) for her to dress up as the bejeweled Persian subject of Thomas Moore's romantic poem *Lalla Rookh* at an 1840 ball; the *Herald* reported that was only a "thin slice" of the $150,000 fortune that would go to the lucky man who wed her.[9]

Engaging in this kind of semi-scandalous frivolity would have been worth it if it meant that Madame Restell and her daughter could, paradoxically, gain respectability.

Despite Madame Restell's notoriety, finding a suitable partner for her daughter did not prove difficult. In addition to being well dressed, Caroline Sommers had inherited her mother's good looks and was known to be "an extremely beautiful looking girl."[10] She was accomplished in the arts and enjoyed appropriate athletic pursuits, such as riding; in fact, she was frequently seen on horseback in the company of her stepfather. The author George Thompson wrote that Caroline was "beautiful almost beyond conception, and lovely and amiable in her disposition as a woman can be, she has many admirers who love her for herself, for even the man dyed in crime could not love a woman so utterly detested as her mother."[11]

Isaac Purdy became Caroline's husband on June 27, 1853.[12] He was twenty-two years old and the eldest of eleven—eight of whom lived to adulthood. Isaac was not too obsessed with respectability himself despite the fact that he'd expressed interest in medicine and had studied at Castleton Medical College in 1850. If his enthusiasm for marrying Caroline, the daughter of an abortionist, did not suggest this, then the fact that Charles was more concerned about Isaac's drinking did. But then, this was an age when many young men drank. It did not, at least in Restell's view, cancel out his numerous other charms. His father, Gabriel, was a successful builder from upstate New York and came from a "famous and prominent family."[13] The respectability of the marriage was only enhanced by the fact that the wedding was officiated by Jacob A. Westervelt, the mayor of New York City.

Certainly, the wedding could have been held at a church, as Restell attended her Episcopalian one regularly. However, having a more private ceremony could also ensure that none of Madame Restell's detractors were present. And so, the wedding, which was later said to be "one of the happiest days in Madame's life," a day where she wept with joy, was held at home.[14]

The wedding would have been more subdued than many today. This was an age where brides and grooms were warned against "any expressions of fondness when in company... [as] sentiment which is beautiful in the family circle is often odious in society."[15] That didn't simply mean "do not make out furiously with your new husband in front of your grandmother." It meant barely acknowledging that you might be in love at all. Husbands and wives were instructed to refer to one another by "Mr." or "Mrs." titles, and certainly not to enthusiastically introduce each other as "my husband" or "my wife."

While weddings themselves might have been small, receptions among the respectable, upper-class set would have been large. *The Upper Ten Thousand* described a typical scenario: "Why, my unsophisticated reader, only two families were asked to the wedding; but all the fashionables of New York, some 700 strong, were asked to the reception." Soon after, Bristed explained, an upscale couple would depart on their honeymoon. In Bristed's words, "Repose is not a natural state to an American man, still less an American woman. They like to be continually on the move."[16]

And Isaac and Caroline were given a very extravagant honeymoon. Madame Restell was so happy with the union that, as a wedding gift, she gave the couple $3,000 (about $92,000 today) to spend on a trip across Europe. They sailed on the SS Baltic—a ship designed to outclass all others in luxury and speed. In 1851 it had won the Blue Ribbon for fastest transatlantic passage, accomplishing the trip from New York to Liverpool in only nine days. Upon the couple's return, Restell purchased a house for them in Tarrytown, New York, where the couple settled down. She picked an excellent location: the New York and Hudson River Railroad had come to Tarrytown in 1849, and the town was quickly becoming a fashionable spot. Restell may have hoped the railroad would allow for easy visits between herself and her only child. Caroline and Isaac lived there until his death in 1864. And, as one later description of her life by the author Denis Tilden Lynch noted, Madame could rejoice that soon she would have a granddaughter, and "All grandmothers are respectable."[17]

With her only child wed and out of the house, Madame Restell now focused on a more pressing concern: her immigration status.

Anti-immigrant sentiment was increasing in the United States. In 1830, New York City had 202,589 residents, of whom 17,773 were foreign born. By 1850, the population was 515,547, and 235,733 of those people were foreign born. Much of this influx was a result of the Irish potato famine. In 1845, a blight began to sweep through Ireland that destroyed up to three-quarters of the potato crop over the next seven years. As British taxes, such as those on corn and bread, made other foods unaffordable, and landowners exported more profitable foods (such as butter or cheese) to Great Britain, many Irish tenant farmers had been subsisting almost entirely on the potatoes they grew. Without the potatoes, they starved.

The situation in Ireland became utterly unendurable. One parish priest wrote that in an Irish village, he had seen evidence of horrible deaths. In one case, a father and son were lying dead together: "Their flesh was torn off their dead bodies by rats, and by each other; flesh was found in their mouths. His wife and child died the week before of hunger.... These are true facts."[18] It's estimated that a million people in Ireland starved during the great famine, and that another million immigrated to America. As the number of immigrants increased—not only from Ireland but, to a lesser extent, from Germany, in the middle of the nineteenth century—so did native-born New Yorkers' prejudice against them. Many saw them as poor people of low moral standing who would bring corrupt influences to New York.

Most of the immigrants were poor, though their poverty resulted in part from the willingness of native-born Americans to exploit them. The *Albany Evening Journal* reported in 1852 on one con frequently run on immigrants. Scammers would charge immigrants an exorbitant

$11 for a train ticket from Albany to Buffalo, if they got a real ticket at all. Other scammers convinced them that the (valid) tickets they had bought were counterfeit, but offered to pay a few cents for them. They could then turn around and sell those tickets to different immigrants for $11. As a result, "the poor man loses not seldom his last cents."[19]

The immigrant situation was especially challenging in New York City: 14,153 immigrants were reported to have arrived at the port across the span of only four days in 1852. When they got there, they found themselves with nowhere to go. The Board of Health closed down immigrant lodging houses in Lower Manhattan because administrators felt they contributed to the spread of disease, but "without providing any substitute for them." As a result, the *New York Daily Times* reported, "there are several large and comfortable apartments lying unoccupied, while hundreds, if not thousands, of poor creatures who just arrived in the country shiver and suffer the live long night or huddle together in groups and take unquiet sleep under stoops... or under piles of lumber."[20] Others decided they'd take up residence in the cellars of Five Points buildings. Edward Martin would later describe these in his book *Secrets of the Great City*, writing that "in night these poor creatures huddle into cellars so damp, foul and pestilential that it seems impossible for human beings to exist in them. The walls are lined with bunks or berths and the woodwork and bedding is alive with vermin.... [M]en women and children crowd into these holes, as many as thirty being found in some of them."[21]

Such figures were viewed with suspicion. In the words of the head of the New York City Health Department, John Griscom, "The disturbers of the peace are from cellars and alleys where they have never been taught to respect themselves, much less others."[22]

In truth, many immigrants came to America hoping to lead perfectly respectable, tea-drinking lives. But labor was in massive supply; jobs were not. Martin estimated that for every position of regular labor, there were five applicants. Deprived of money and lodging, many immigrants were willing to work for horribly low wages—just so they could make a living at all. In turn, factories hired them, rather than native-born counterparts, to save money. Or, as some wealthier, native-born people have been putting it ever since, the immigrants "stole" jobs from "real Americans."

The result of this bubbling xenophobic turmoil was the rise of the Know-Nothing movement, which was more formally known as the

American Party. The Know Nothings were defined by their opposition to immigrants and calls for a return to traditional American values— such as reading the Bible in school, banning all Catholics from office, immediate deportation of all foreign beggars or thieves, and a twenty-one-year naturalization period for immigrants.[23] The Know-Nothing name, often invoked today, was derived not from the fact that their members were poorly informed, though their opponents often said as much. Rather, it was because their meetings were secret. Much like the Ku Klux Klan later, entry into the group involved a great deal of pageantry. Members had to testify that they were of pure Protestant blood and rejected Catholicism, and then memorize a series of hand signals and codes. If asked about the movement, they were supposed to say they "knew nothing." You might, quite reasonably, think the group was composed largely of people who had lost their jobs to immigrants. It was not. The movement had approximately the same number of professionals as other political organizations. Only 9 percent of the members of the East Boston chapter, for instance, were "unskilled laborers." Historian Tyler Gregory Anbinder noted that "Know Nothings were not workers who 'suffered from the most traumatic economic changes of the decade' but rather 'those whose lives were relatively prosperous and whose jobs were relatively secure.' "[24]

Even though it's often cited as the root of conflict, it is not necessarily economic insecurity that causes people to dislike immigrants.

Many people rejected the Know Nothings, whose ethos was described by the *New York Daily Herald* in 1854 as "hostility to adopted citizens—hostility to Catholics—hostility to emigration—hostility to all men holding office who are either Catholic or adopted citizens." The author disputed such bias, claiming those views were "an advertisement of ignorance, which, in this age, should repel, instead of attracting support." Later on in the piece, he wondered, "How long is it, Mr. Know-Nothing, since your father came to this country? . . . He may have been the oldest inhabitant or he may have been the newest, but as he followed after the Indians, he was himself a foreigner. And pray, friend, what right have you, a foreigner's descendent, to persecute those who, like him, choose to settle among us? You ought to be ashamed of yourself!"[25]

Unfortunately, despite the fact that people keep trying this strategy 170 years later, there has never been a moment where shouting

"But we're a nation of immigrants" has changed the minds of those who would like to believe that they have more of a right to America than others, especially when their egos are inflated by the leaders of nationalist-leaning parties.

While many intellectuals and progressives at the time might have despised Know Nothings, their numbers continued to swell, as did their influence. In New York City, it reached an apex with the death of William Poole, aka "Butcher Bill," a leader of the New York Know Nothings. Bill, who was best known for being the leader of the Bowery Boys gang, also wrote anti-immigrant poetry, featuring lines such as "Let not our country in their hands be given / and thus betray the trust received from heaven."[26] Bill's position as head of a gang was by no means disqualifying for membership in the Know Nothings. Rather, it was extremely useful to the party, as it allowed him to call on the gang to terrorize voters they disapproved of at polling places. Bill was killed at the behest of his Irish immigrant rival, John Morrissey, a boxer who worked for Tammany Hall. Before passing, Poole rasped the words, "Goodbye, boys; I die a true American."[27] He was honored by his acolytes in a manner befitting a war hero. Five thousand men marched in his funeral procession, which was truly more of a parade, as it also featured half a dozen brass bands. Poole associations sprang up in New York, Baltimore, and Philadelphia. Meanwhile, "actors in melodramas would literally wrap themselves in the flag" and repeat Poole's final words to wild applause. Much of the press also strongly implied that the people mourning Poole were good, the salt-of-the-earth type. The *New York Times* even said that the spectators' "appearance and demeanor were in the highest degree respectable and decorous."[28]

Little wonder that during this period any politician, in the words of the *Buffalo Daily Republic,* "courting the foreign vote is doomed": "He is at once placed on the Know Nothing wheel and a single turn of that instrument crushes every bone in his body."[29] Plenty of other politicians found it easy to attract voters by decrying the people those voters hated most. By December 1855, forty-three members of Congress were from the Know-Nothing American Party.

No doubt if Madame Restell had predicted the kind of frenzied nationalism that would grip New York during this period, she would have gone by the name of Mrs. Liberty and claimed Nebraskan origins.

Being an immigrant, even one with a supposedly glamorous French (or British) background, was now less charming than it used to be. Any hint of foreignness could be used against even New York's most respectable citizens. Know Nothings charged, for instance, that "George W. Matsell, the acting Chief of Police of the city of New York, is alien born. That he is a subject of the Queen of England. That he has taken no step whatsoever to become a citizen of the United States... and should therefore be removed from his position."[30] After a protracted trial, that charge was finally dismissed in 1856. But Madame Restell would certainly have taken note of the Know Nothings' animosity toward the chief of police long before then. Not only was she acquainted with Matsell, but she was a subject of the Queen of England who had taken no step whatsoever to become a citizen of the United States.

If people were going to critique her, she could at least try to make sure they would do so for her work, and not her immigrant background.

And so, Madame Restell, aka Ann Trow Sommers Lohman, officially took an oath of loyalty to America in April 1854 and became an American citizen. Her daughter, now Mrs. Purdy, vouched for her moral character. Whether because of her daughter's new social status, or Madame Restell's own wealth, this was one instance when no one seemed to question her morality.

Citizenship would ensure that she couldn't be deported. Beyond that, this step honestly did not make much of a difference to many people, including the Know Nothings, who were as hostile to adopted citizens as they were to those who had just arrived on American soil. For all her efforts, in 1856, the *National Police Gazette* declared, "Madame Restell is a German. She was educated as a midwife in Vienna."[31]

Given her accent, it's positively amazing her detractors didn't say she was Irish.

The prejudices of the Know Nothings would linger in the public consciousness enough to create a new attack on her business—the charge that she was filling the country with Irish people. She'd be denounced in newspapers with xenophobic rhetoric declaring, "Restellism is murder with the Roman Catholics. Half a dozen children in every Irish family. Only two in the modern American family. What is the matter? Answer—Restellism. That is why, shortly, the children of the Emerald Isle will be walking through the graveyards of the Puritans."[32]

Latching on to people's fears regarding immigration was an effective way to impugn women who got abortions as unpatriotic. In 1868, the antiabortion author J. T. Cook worried that "the Anglo-Saxon race is rapidly dying out…and the Germans, and Irish, and Swedes…are fast taking the country…by the sheer force of their ever increasing armies of babies." Cook felt the only answer for this was for women to "stop murdering their children, and stop trying to defeat nature in any way, so that our American homes may again become populous with incipient citizens and voters, and incipient mothers of citizens and voters, and so that the American family shall not become an extinct institution in this country."[33]

As immigrants now made up nearly half of New York's population, there was a heightened level of panic that native-born Protestants were becoming outnumbered. This led to passionate antiabortion sentiment, at least insofar as white, middle-class American women were concerned.

And if Madame Restell's measured attempts (via marriage and citizenship) to comport herself as an upstanding citizen during these years had benefited her to some degree, they couldn't, under these circumstances, help her achieve the reputation she desired.

On one notable occasion, she couldn't even buy a dress. When she submitted an order with the Shirt Sewers and Seamstresses Union, she was rejected. She found that the seamstresses had "bundled up her linen, and promptly returned it to her with a polite note from the secretary saying that, although in need of work they should never be poor enough to accept patronage from a woman of her character."[34]

She may have regretted not refreshing her sewing skills at Blackwell's Island.

In 1856, the *National Police Gazette* proclaimed that Madame Restell and her husband had "no company or friends": "When they drive through Broadway, they are shunned like a pair of lepers. They are as isolated in a city of three quarters of a million [people] as they would be on the most desolate spot on God's earth." Being ostracized in this manner may have been especially hard on Charles, who the *National Police Gazette* said had a "downcast, gloomy expression when walking the streets."[35]

As for the Know Nothings, their political influence waned. Abraham Lincoln privately bemoaned their existence, noting, "As a nation, we began by declaring that 'all men are created equal.' We now practically read it 'all men are created equal, except negroes.' When the Know Nothings get control, it will read 'all men are created equals, except negroes, and foreigners, and Catholics.' "[36] By 1856, papers remarked that "when leaders and members of the Know-Nothing lodges were pointed out they were hissed at in the streets, and the very name has become a byword for scorn among the people."[37]

Their last dregs of influence had petered out by the Civil War. The party maintained a focus on opposing immigration, but the nation's interest turned toward abolition. In an attempt to rally up local support, northern Know Nothings claimed that Catholics and immigrants were proslavery, while southern Know Nothings claimed that Catholics and immigrants were all abolitionists.[38] The schism over slavery eventually separated the chapters entirely.

Their ideas and methods, however—the notion that you could court votes by appealing to people's prejudices against outsiders, that immigrants should be treated with disdain and suspicion, and that it would be horrifying if "real" Americans were replaced by minorities—remain woven into the American fabric to this day.

Madame Restell, who had always worked alone, was uninterested in such debates. After her more modest attempts to appear respectable weren't successful, she decided to go all-out and become even more extravagant. "Mere money does not confer respectability," the *National Police Gazette* chided her. Fine, she seemed to reason. In that case she'd just focus on the money. In the years to come, she would build a veritable palace, and it certainly ended up attracting more attention than her solemn adoption of US citizenship had. And, for all the public pressure to remain demure and "respectable" during this period, throwing herself into single-minded empire building may have been the most quintessentially American thing Madame Restell ever did.

Chapter Sixteen

B Y 1856, MADAME RESTELL'S BRIEF SOJOURN INTO RESPECT-
ability had come to an end. She was in the news once again in
two new cases, neither of which cast her as a retiring American matron.

In July 1855, Frederica Medinger, a servant in the last few weeks of
her pregnancy, went to Madame Restell's house to give birth. Before
the baby was born, she asked Madame Restell whether anyone ever
came to her establishment looking to adopt, and Madame Restell
acknowledged that some people did. Following up, a few days before
the birth, Madame Restell informed Frederica that "she had an application from a lady who desired to adopt a child, at which [Frederica]
manifested much joy." Frederica's healthy baby boy was "by the mother's direction given to a third party to be adopted."[1] Hopefully, that
third party intended to care for the child as one of her own.

After Frederica recovered from childbirth, Madame Restell—in an
act of kindness—employed her as her own servant. This would have
been especially generous of her, considering that the recent pregnancy might have caused other families to consider Frederica unem-
ployable. This arrangement continued for a few months, during which
Frederica "never made any complaint in reference to the disposition
she had made of her child, but always expressed satisfaction that the
child had been given away by her." Everything was going well—until
Madame Restell fired her "in consequence of unbecoming conduct
on her part."[2]

Following her dismissal, Frederica's opinion of Madame Restell
changed dramatically. Eight months after her child was born, she went
to the police and informed them that Madame Restell had abducted
her child. She cried that she had no idea that Madame Restell was

174

an abortionist when she went to her house to give birth—although how she seemingly knew enough about Madame Restell to know her address but did *not* know she was an abortionist boggles the mind. After the delivery, she claimed, Madame Restell took the child and did not allow her to see him, though she asked several times. Finally, she lamented, "Madame Restell told her that, by direction of the gentleman who had placed [Frederica] there, [she had] sent the child to Philadelphia."[3]

Frederica claimed that she then went to Philadelphia but could not find the child. At that point, she said, "Madame Restell told her the child was dead and told her to make 'no more fuss about it.'"[4] Admittedly, this last bit does sound like something Madame Restell might say.

When the case went to trial, Frederica failed to prove herself to be the most reliable witness. For instance, when she had asked the child's father for financial assistance, she had claimed she was paying to have their boy boarded with a woman in Brooklyn. A friend of the father's went to the location and did find a woman with an infant. However, that woman eventually confessed that the baby was her own; Frederica had asked her to pretend it belonged to Frederica in order to defraud the former lover.

Madame Restell asserted in her deposition that the case had been brought forward "for the purpose of vexing and annoying her, and to extort money from her."[5] The judge in the case agreed. He dismissed the claim of abduction as groundless and unproven.

But the trial dragged on, with Frederica's attorney reintroducing the complaint for years afterward. The closest she came to victory was in 1857 when one judge declared that "a child cannot be disposed of or alienated like a chattel." Furthermore, he argued, "Those countries in which the father has a general power to dispose of his children have always been considered barbaric." The only exception, he felt, should be a temporary apprenticeship. However, he didn't seem eager to see the child returned to Frederica, either, asserting, "A mother who was willing and even anxious to part with her infant immediately after his birth must be destitute of the affection without which no one is capable of suitably rearing and bringing up a child."[6]

It was a rare judge who was not only antiabortion but also passionately anti-adoption. It's very unclear what he thought *should* happen to this child, as it seems unlikely that he had an apprenticeship in mind for the toddler. He gave Madame Restell ten days to produce the child or give an account as to his whereabouts. She could not. However, her failure to do so brought about no repercussions.

In an age when women were often victimized, the fact that Frederica was so willing to dupe and exploit anyone would have interested Restell even as it vexed her. Today, it might even read as a kind of pluck. But at the time, it made much of society less invested in Frederica's case. People did not gather clamoring for the return of her child as they had Mary Applegate's.

Elizabeth Kaiser, on the other hand, was a very different kind of woman.

In August 1856, twenty-five-year-old Elizabeth Kaiser insisted that Madame Restell had performed an abortion on her at the behest of her employer, a German man named Mr. Schultz, for whom she worked as a housekeeper. Among her other duties, she was there to care for his three children, as he had been recently widowed. While she was in his employ, "he was in the habit of taking her out afternoon carriage riding to places of pleasure and amusement."[7] He told her— and even a few of his friends—that he was going to marry her, and their relationship became sexual. But when she became pregnant, he changed his mind very quickly.

Schultz asked Madame Restell to come to his home to perform the abortion on Miss Kaiser in total secrecy. Madame Restell declined, with *Reynolds's Newspaper* noting, "She refused to operate outside of her house. It was only to first class families that she rendered outside services."[8] She suggested that Schultz bring Elizabeth to her house instead.

Schultz followed these instructions, albeit under false pretenses. He told Elizabeth they were going to visit Madame Restell to confirm that she was pregnant. Madame Restell, he promised, "would inform her whether her surmises were correct, and, if they were, he would marry her at once." When she arrived, Madame Restell examined her and promptly performed an abortion, "without her being aware, until too late to prevent it, of what she was doing."[9] It may seem surprising that the instruments Restell used did not tip Elizabeth off, but this was an age when many women were kept very much in the dark about their own bodies.

Remarkably, this may not have been the worst part of Elizabeth's experience.

After her abortion, she insisted that Mr. Schultz make good on his promise to marry her. He hemmed and hawed and generally gave no indication that he planned on doing this any time soon. So Elizabeth claimed that she would go to the police and say he made her get an abortion. At that, he threatened to shoot himself.

Elizabeth did not carry out her threat, but Schultz no longer felt safe—and subsequently trapped Elizabeth inside his house. He forbade her from having contact with any other women. As for men, he was so terrified that she might wave to one for help that he painted over the windows. Elizabeth was reported to be "lying a helpless invalid, unheeded and uncared for by the wretch who worked this ruin."[10]

Shortly after the incident, Schultz decided he did want to get married—just not to Elizabeth. He wrote to his brother in Germany about his predicament, claiming that he was very well off in America and needed only a wife to complete his happiness. His brother said he would send one of his daughters—read: one of Schultz's nieces—for him to marry. When the girl arrived in New York, Elizabeth was promptly thrown out of the house. It was only later, after she had moved in with some charitable friends, that she relayed her horrible story.

These two cases both appear to have involved many instances where the women's rights to choose outcomes regarding their own health and lives were violated. No one comes out well in these stories.

But at the time, it was good for Madame Restell's business. As *Reynolds's Newspaper* wrote, "Each arrest is nothing less than a blazing advertisement which every paper gives her gratis."[11] Indeed, an observant reader of the paper might take note of the fact that, presumably, for a "first class" amount of money, Madame Restell could come to your house and perform an abortion in the utmost privacy and comfort. Though, at this point, her own lodgings were considered very comfortable: her abode at Chambers Street was valued at $50,000 ($1.6 million today). "The wealth of these abortionists," one reporter wrote, "will give a much more correct idea of the business they drive than any estimate we might make."[12]

Regarding the lawsuits and court cases, Madame Restell was reported to "not trouble herself very much about the matter. She has

long been in the business and knows how to get out of such difficulties."[13] She'd done what she could to be seen as a respectable American,
it hadn't worked, and she'd decided to at least affect an indifference
toward public opinion.

Though she was constantly flogged in the press for her activities,
no one doubted that her activities had made her very rich—and this
inspired other hopefuls who wanted to cash in on the American
Dream. The papers never ceased talking about how "her city residence
is palatial, her country villa recherché."[14]

So, while Madame Restell may still have been the best-known abortionist in New York (if not America), others were vying for those same
clients. The days when Madame Restell had only two serious competitors, Madame Costello and Mrs. Bird, were long past. Abortionists
were springing up with such regularity that she could no longer know
them all by name, though she could read about them frequently in
the papers. It was reported by the *New York Police Gazette* that a "Mrs.
Crocker now drives a trade surpassed by none of her class in the city [of
New York]—not even Madame Restell."[15] Given the profound dearth
of information about this Mrs. Crocker compared to Madame Restell,
it's doubtful this was true. Unless she was just very good at operating in
secret, save this one mention.

Few of this new group were skilled, let alone as skilled as Madame
Restell. A sixty-four-year-old Mrs. Mastin of Franklin Street had "long
deceived giddy young girls by advertising herself as a fortuneteller."[16]
That profession already opened her up to criticism at a time when fortune tellers and tarot readers were not considered fun bachelorette-
party novelties, but "low, debased, miserable types of their sex, neither
affecting learning nor morality."[17] In any case, Mrs. Mastin decided to
try her hand at a more lucrative side career as an abortionist. After
selling a girl some ineffective pills, she attempted to operate on her
using a gum elastic catheter. Tragically, the girl she operated on died.
Mrs. Mastin was accused of second-degree manslaughter and submitted a guilty plea, miserably declaring that she had "had no intention
of harming the girl."[18] It was perhaps lucky that she was incarcerated
so early on; at the time she was arrested, there were another three
would-be patients in her waiting room.

In 1857, a woman named Mrs. Lawson went to Madame Restell
for help aborting her fetus. Madame Restell told her that she couldn't

perform the operation for less than $200—it appears her asking price had increased—even though "Mrs. Lawson thought she was not able to pay so much."[19] Instead, she went to a wigmaker named Elijah Hunt who agreed to do it for $25. He killed her.

It's easy to look down on cut-rate abortionists, but it's worth remembering that Madame Restell was also once a lower-class person with no training who thought herself able to determine how to perform abortions effectively. For all that can be discerned from public records, her patients all survived, but at least at the beginning of her career, that might have been due as much to luck as skill.

Undeterred by deadly cases, fledgling abortionists were starting new businesses across the country. The Philadelphia correspondent of the *New-York Tribune* wrote how "your [New York] hardened abortionists are imitated by volunteer disciples among us."[20] A male and female abortionist in Philadelphia were brought to court in 1858 after having allegedly buried a dead patient's body in the woods. Unlike Mrs. Mastin or Mr. Hunt, the couple was bringing in a tremendous sum from their profession, and had clientele that included the daughter of a bank president. That said, they were also apparently burying women in the woods (though they were released for want of evidence), so their refined clientele alone didn't necessarily connote great skill.

Madame Restell's old rival Madame Costello was also still in business, though she no longer went by the name Costello. She had dropped the European pseudonym in favor of operating under her far more American-sounding married name, Mrs. W. H. Maxwell. Her address, 34 Lispenard Street, remained the same. Never quite as successful as Madame Restell, she had adopted a new pro-America stratagem that must have delighted the Know Nothings. Whereas in 1843 she had boasted of being "educated at the Medical Faculty in Paris," her ads in 1856 claimed that she "wishes the ladies to understand that she is a regular, educated physician, a Graduate of this city."[21] When her reportedly Scottish-born husband died, Mrs. Maxwell/Costello wrote a letter to the editor of the *New York Daily Herald* stating, "If there was one thing more than another on which Col. Maxwell prided himself it was being a native born American."[22] In fact, she declared, he was so American that he was a member of one of the oldest families in the country. This may have been true, but it's just as possible that her husband was Scottish, and she was just leaning very hard into the nativism that was in vogue.

Also operating during this time was a physician named Dr. Thiers. The man was said to be such a mighty figure in the abortion business as to "cast Madame Restell entirely in the shade."[23] His advertisements, however, seemed to follow in her precise footsteps. He promised a "French Panacea...an invaluable scientific medicinal combination for female debility, constitutional derangement, and periodic irregularities."[24] When warrants were issued for his arrest in 1855, Thiers managed to slip away before the trial began. But by 1859 he had reemerged and was once again selling abortive pills and performing abortions on West Twenty-Fourth Street. Although he continued to practice until 1867, it's hard to pretend he ever eclipsed Madame Restell in reputation (or notoriety). The notion that he was a colossus in the field may have had more to do with the mere fact that he was a male abortionist rather than, for instance, a wigmaker who performed abortions on the side. The fact that men were starting to practice a field of medicine that had traditionally been largely left to "female physicians" was a testament to its riches and potential.

For all we know, Madame Restell paid Dr. Thiers little mind. His tactics were aboveboard, and while she didn't relish competition, she accepted it as a fact of life.

By 1857, she was more concerned about Dempster Moore, a particularly devious fellow who, rather than merely adopting some of her methods, had begun selling pills under her name. He claimed, in the *Syracuse Daily Courier,* that he was "the sole wholesale agent of Madame Charlotte Restelle [*sic*] whose address is not and never was 162 Chambers Street": "I still sell these wonderful pills wholesale and retail at my store, No. 16, North Salina Street, Syracuse," he added.[25]

As it turned out, he was *not* an agent of Madame Restell—whose first name was not Charlotte, and whose last name was not spelled with an "e" on the end. Upon discovering these fictitious ads, the real Madame Restell was shocked and denounced him.

Moore was almost certainly attempting to dupe the public. But instead of disappearing after being exposed, he claimed that Madame Restell's statements decrying him were merely a work "concocted and written by a brace of scamps residing in Syracuse." Surely, whoever these scamps were "have also manufactured a bogus Madame C Restell and located her in Chambers Street."[26] He asserted that if papers continued to say that he was not an agent of Madame Restell, he would sue them for libel.

Madame Restell was flabbergasted. "Any merchant or businessman in Syracuse or elsewhere," she said, "can ascertain by writing to any acquaintance in New York whether the person known as Madame Restell is located at 162 Chambers Street." Why, she seemed to wonder, were these credulous residents of Syracuse *letting* themselves get conned? She was so well known, she remarked, that "the public, generally," could tell anyone interested her address.[27]

One aspect of having such a charlatan claiming to sell her wares that surely bothered Madame Restell was that *he was charging more money than her* in the pill market. Moore sold pills for $3 a box, even though Madame Restell angrily pointed out that "the price is one dollar, the same as for upwards of fifteen years." Certainly, part of her upset stemmed from the fact that she hadn't raised her prices. However, her outrage was rooted in something much, much deeper. She declared, "I will not permit either Dempster Moore of Syracuse, or any person or persons to appropriate the trials and persecutions I have endured, as a basis for any speculation out of the public by representing himself or themselves as my agent."[28] If Madame Restell was going to endure jail sentences, blackmail, and routinely being defamed in the press, she'd be damned if she was going to let someone else make money off it. And $2 more per box than her, at that.

Madame Restell did everything she could to get newspapers to stop running Dempster Moore's fraudulent advertisements. She wrote in a letter directed to the editor of the *Syracuse Daily Courier*. "I am not about to threaten you with (or begin for effect) a pretended libel suit. It is sufficient to me to know that you, as gentlemen, will not prostitute your columns for an unwarrantable and inexcusable purpose." While the mention of a libel suit was probably meant primarily to remind the paper's editors that she *could* institute a libel suit, she did make a very reasonable case, stating that "it is a gross wrong to the public, to you, and to myself for persons to assume as being my agents and to represent themselves as selling 'Madame Restell's Pills.' "[29]

Madame Restell's husband, Charles, also stepped in on her behalf. On May 21, he swore an affidavit against Moore claiming that Moore's advertisements were "entirely false, untrue and devoid of foundation."

J. B. Nones, a notary public, swore that he knew both Charles Lohman and Madame Restell, and added that there was no other Madame Restell. As for the idea that Dempster Moore himself might bring a libel suit against newspapers—or, in Madame Restell's words, "browbeat and intimidate the public press"—she promised $500 to any one charitable institution in Syracuse if Moore were to actually come forward with such a suit, and another $1,000 if that suit were not thrown out of court immediately.[30]

That was the last anyone heard of Dempster Moore, but his disreputable rise and very existence were reminders of the lucrative potential of the birth control industry. And if fraudsters like Dempster realized that, real doctors were not far behind.

Chapter Seventeen

I N 1859, MIDWIVES AND ABORTIONISTS WERE THRIVING. THE population growth in urban centers had brought about a need for their services. Doctors could not say the same.

Doctors were not a group held in the high esteem they are today. In the 1850s, the *Cincinnati Medical Observer* wrote, "It has become fashionable to speak of the medical profession as a body of jealous, quarrelsome men, whose chief delight is in the annoyance and ridicule of each other."[1]

If you're wondering *why* doctors weren't held in good esteem, it was likely due in part to the fact that the bar for becoming a physician during this time was, compared to modern standards, set very low. Throughout the eighteenth century, physicians were primarily trained by apprenticeship. A young aspiring physician would work for one already established, first running menial errands, then assisting him with his tasks, and, eventually, when the mentor judged him ready, performing medical duties on his own. This is how Madame Restell likely had learned her profession. Wealthier young men would go to Europe, where they "walked the hospitals" (though in many cases this meant that they just walked around looking at patients) and listened to lectures given by the doctors employed at those hospitals. Given that this involved crossing the Atlantic, studying abroad was not an option available to the common man. But, in the nineteenth century, the United States thought that it could offer something equivalent— albeit without the rather significant portion of the experience that came from actually studying patients in a hospital.

And so the nineteenth century saw a rise of commercial medical schools in the United States. These medical schools were run for profit, with the instructors accepting as many students as possible in order to increase the amount of money coming in. Between 1810 and 1840, twenty-six such schools sprang up in America. Between 1840 and 1876, forty-seven more did. At these schools, in the words of Abraham Flexner, an advocate for medical education reform who made a study of such schools, "nothing was really essential but professors... a hall could be cheaply rented....Occasional dissections in time supplied a skeleton—in whole or in part—and a box of odd bones. Other equipment there was practically none." Students who enrolled in these schools in October could expect to graduate by spring. Classes, with the exception of a few demonstrations involving that box of bones, consisted entirely of lectures. And if you didn't make all of them, no need to worry; in Flexner's words, "The man who had settled his tuition bill was practically assured of his degree, whether he had attended lectures or not."[2] Essentially, you could graduate and go to work as a doctor without ever seeing a sick person up close.

Pretty predictably, this was not a system that churned out very effective doctors.

As the *Orleans County Gazette* noted, "There is great reason to believe that many who have gone through the regular routine of study are mere quacks after all, and many more mix up but a little scientific practice with a good deal of quackery."[3]

But, despite criticism, young men would continue to flock to such schools at a time when they promised prosperity in the big city. According to Flexner, "A clerk at a country store...gets an alluring brochure [from a medical school] which paints the life of a physician as an easy road to wealth."[4] This sudden surplus of doctors—and the Flexner report noted that towns were filled with four times as many doctors as they needed—would be disappointed to find that the standard fee for seeing a physician was about $2.[5] This was a great deal more than women in factories were making, but the earnings of an average doctor in 1860 would establish him as only "lower middle class."[6] Many doctors during the period took on second jobs, like being a postmaster, to supplement their incomes.[7]

"Female physicians" like Madame Restell, however, were flourishing. Abortions in the 1850s usually cost between $25 and $50.[8] Madame Restell and others like her had patients galore and were quickly becoming wealthy, even budgeting for costs that came with choosing to pursue an illegal profession. When the Boston abortionist William Clark was put on trial for causing a woman's death in 1851 (the body was said to "exhibit signs of great violence"), he was able to easily pay his $8,000 bail and return to his office. In the Philadelphia case in 1858, the female abortionist on trial appeared "elegantly dressed, rustling in silks and bedecked in laces."[9] When Sarah Sawyer, the "Restell of Boston," went on trial in 1873, she wore a dress that was estimated to cost $1,500.

No one stood out more as a symbol of the wealth accrued by abortionists than Madame Restell. "She is rich," declared one newspaper in 1860. "She owns blocks and acres of lots and stocks of all kind. Her income from books and others is $21,000 per annum. She has three grandchildren who will inherit about $400,000 when Madame Restell turns up her toes."[10]

At the time, the president of the United States made $25,000 a year, which meant that Madame Restell was quickly gaining on him.

One doctor from the period asked, "In view of the unparalleled success that attends the financial operations of such quacks, what inducement is offered to the young, educated physician?"[11]

How many of these physicians were truly "educated" is debatable. But it's clear that a surplus of so-called doctors were setting up shop, owing to the profusion of medical schools, and that most of the graduates were not earning nearly as much as they had hoped to.

The fact that a portion of the profession was dominated by women making more money than they did rankled the male doctors' egos. But it also showed that there was an untapped market for treating female patients—and money to be made in the field. As the doctor Joseph B. DeLee wrote fifty years later, in 1916, arguing in favor of obstetrics as a bona fine field of medicine, "As long as the medical profession tolerates that brand of infamy, the midwife, the public will not be brought to realize that there is high art in obstetrics and that it must pay as well for *it* as for surgery. I will not admit that this is a sordid impulse." He thought it was important for the public to understand the OB-GYN's skill.[12]

The problem was that, having left women's reproductive health issues and childbirth largely to women for centuries, doctors found they were not very good at treating them.

DeLee even conceded that "more women die during confinement in the hands of doctors than among midwives."[13] This admission, in

1916, was even truer in the 1850s. One woman in two hundred died in childbirth when tended by a midwife. The maternal mortality rate was ten to twenty times greater if a doctor delivered the baby.[14]

But then doctors set out to lay their profession's claim on women's health. Eliminating the competition would prove to be challenging, especially when midwives and female abortionists were often a good deal more skilled than their male contemporaries, and a great many women preferred them.

One doctor, though admittedly not an American one, wanted to change that. When the Hungarian doctor Ignaz Semmelweis began working in the maternity ward at the Vienna General Hospital, there were two clinics, the first staffed by doctors and medical students, and the second by midwives. Semmelweis noted that somewhere between 13 percent and 18 percent of the patients at the first clinic died. Meanwhile, the midwives had only a 2 percent mortality rate among their patients.[15] Luckily for his patients, Semmelweis discovered that by washing his own hands with bleach before touching patients, the mortality rate dropped 90 percent. That difference was largely due to the fact that, in the hospital where he worked, male doctors would go from autopsying cadavers straight to placing their unwashed hands into women's birth canals. Women were then much more likely to die of sepsis, or, as it was then known, "childbed fever." Women knew it was riskier to be treated by a doctor. They called childbed fever "the doctor's plague."[16]

By the middle of the nineteenth century, childbearing women came to regard doctors as idiots who would do more to harm their health than help it. "The disrespect displayed toward the personnel of the first clinic [doctors] made me so miserable that life seemed worthless," wrote Semmelweis. For women, the only upside to being admitted to the hospital's first clinic for childbirth was being able to recuperate there *after* giving birth. The hospital would only admit women who intended to give birth in the hospital, which led to considerable sub-terfuge. Some women preferred to literally give birth in the street out-side the clinic, alone, and then go into the hospital once they'd had their baby, to rest up. Upper-class women might choose to "be deliv-ered by midwives in the city and then be taken quickly by coach to the clinic[,] where they claimed that the birth had occurred unexpectedly while they were on their way."[17] This situation was obviously less than ideal, but it was slow to change, even after Semmelweis implemented the handwashing policy in his own practice.

The maternal mortality numbers by patients whose doctors had washed their hands was very low; indeed, it dropped to be on par with those who'd been delivered by midwives. And this policy could have gone on to save countless lives had it been adopted widely. Semmelweis did not anticipate, however, how much his fellow doctors, confident in their knowledge, would hate being told they had to change.

When other doctors first heard Semmelweis's idea, they dismissed it almost entirely. There were many arguments at the time as to why Semmelweis's theory couldn't be right, but they all boiled down to the fact that men in positions of authority hated being even slightly discredited far more than they hated women dying. The obstetrician Charles Meigs wrote in 1854 that doctors didn't need to wash their hands because doctors were gentlemen, and "a gentleman's hands are clean."[18] Gentlemen must also have been pretty nearsighted, because why they did not glance down and note that their hands were, literally, covered with cadaver blood is a mystery.

Semmelweis's ideas were later confirmed with the rise of germ theory, which posited that pathogens invisible to the naked eye could transfer from one host to another and cause disease. Unfortunately, the theory would not be accepted by the American medical community until three decades later. That was too late for Semmelweis, who responded to the medical blowback by furiously telling his bosses that, in refusing to take his advice, they were killing mothers. He was right! Despite the fact that he was absolutely correct, he was fired. He later died in a mental asylum at the age of forty-seven.

There's a nice statue of him in Albany, New York, now, though it's doubtful that knowledge of that honor would have comforted him or any of the mothers who needed his expertise at the time.

Part of the resistance to Semmelweis's idea lay with doctors' skittishness around treating female patients in general to begin with. This was especially true at American medical schools, where examining a pregnant woman was strictly forbidden in class. Study of the female reproductive system was done "through the use of diagrams and mannequins made of buckskin." Armed with this knowledge, when doctors graduated and found they had to examine an actual pregnant patient, they did so with her fully clothed and "the doctor carefully averting his eyes."[19]

Midwives had a pretty significant advantage, insofar as many of them had actually been pregnant themselves, or were, at least, in possession of a pelvis. They also knew what a pregnant body looked like without clothing on.

So doctors in the 1850s couldn't say they were better than, or even equal to, midwives in terms of their skills. The fact that male doctors thought they should take over a field in which midwives excelled and of which they had virtually no knowledge would seem bizarre were there not so much money to be made. As such, it seems sadly predictable.

Having no advantage in expertise, their best bet to establish dominance in the realm of obstetrics was to cast midwives as immoral witches. One way they could do that was by stressing that midwives performed abortions, and that abortions, and the people who did them, were deadly, monstrous, and never necessary.

This would seem to be something of a challenging prospect in an age where, as Walt Whitman wrote in 1858, it was "no uncommon thing for medical attendants to be as coolly and unconcernedly asked to produce an abortion as a dentist would be to draw a tooth."[20] But that was before the American Medical Association began its "physician's crusade against abortion."

The AMA had been formed in 1847 with the intent to "promote the art and science of medicine and the betterment of public health." It did so by calling for stricter regulations regarding medicines sold. The organization initially had no opinion on the subject of abortion. It only began taking a formal stance on the issue—coming out against it—in 1857, at the behest of the doctor Horatio Storer, a twenty-seven-year-old Harvard-educated gynecologist who joined the AMA the year prior. Storer was fervently antiabortion. He believed that as soon as a woman was impregnated, the embryo was an independent person. In his words, "Before the egg has left a woman's ovary, before impregnation has been effected, it may perhaps be considered as a part and parcel of herself, but not afterwards. When it has reached the womb, that nest provided for the little one by kindly nature, it has assumed a separate and independent existence."[21]

The notion of a separate and independent existence was more than Storer would admit to women, over whom he felt justified in exerting enormous control. His idea that the fetus was a person and the woman's uterus a mere resting spot for it is one still employed by antiabortion advocates today, complete with pictures of a fetus floating in a pink cloud blissfully devoid of context. The fact that the fetus is so entwined with a woman's body that birthing it regularly caused her to die was not something Storer was overly concerned with, though his fellow physicians did notice his theory's implications. In 1857, Dr. Charles Edward Buckingham wrote that Storer "seems to have thrown out of consideration the life of the mother."[22]

It's little wonder these fetuses Storer and his cohorts referred to were always described as "the potential male" or "the future young man."[23]

Beyond his conviction in fetal personhood, Storer's sentiments also had to do with his fears about the replacement of the white race in America. He wondered, regarding the western states, "Shall they be filled with our children or by those of aliens? This is the question that our own women must answer; upon their loins depends the future destiny of the nation."[24] Soon after he joined, the AMA formed a Committee on Criminal Abortion that Storer chaired. It pushed for stricter laws punishing abortion throughout the country. Though the members of the AMA may not have shared all Storer's convictions, many of the doctors were doubtless aware that discrediting midwives and insisting that men were the only ones qualified to oversee women's reproductive health would open up a new and welcome source of income for them.

Storer and the AMA were aware that their campaign would take some work. After all, much though people would rant against Madame Restell in the press, they also liked having her around when they needed her.

Around this time, physicians started employing every tactic they could—no matter how outlandish—to convince women that abortions were an abomination on many levels.

Storer, in what can only be considered a really big swing to the fences, claimed that even *thinking* about having an abortion could kill you. "The thought of the crime," he explained, "coming upon the mind at a time when the physical system is weak and prostrated is sufficient to occasion death." As if the threat of death wasn't absurd enough, Storer also wanted women to know that just thinking about it was "undoubtedly able, where not affecting life, to produce insanity."[25]

And if one of these women actually had an abortion? Then she would *definitely* go mad. Dr. John Gray of the New York State Asylum in Utica, noting that "[abortion's] terrible prevalence has steadily increased," relayed, "I have for many years received and treated patients whose insanity was directly traceable to this crime."[26] Dr. Hiram Pomeroy further warned that "no one escapes, for sooner or later Nature will extract a grievous penalty for every violation of her laws."[27]

The mental health concerns here are particularly interesting. The psychological ramifications of abortion have been studied over time, especially because antiabortionists are still apt to argue that the operation negatively impacts women's mental health. However, modern-day studies have not found this to be true. A 2018 study found, for example, that "having an abortion does not increase a woman's risk for depression, anxiety or post-traumatic stress disorder."[28] In June 2022 the American Psychological Institute reported that, "More than 50 years of international psychological research shows that having an abortion is not linked to mental health problems."[29]

What does cause modern women psychological distress—and we might imagine this also applied to women of the past—is being denied access to the care they need. According to a 2016 study, women who are denied an abortion are more likely to report "anxiety symptoms, lower self-esteem, and lower life satisfaction" shortly after they are denied care.[30] Long before this study, the same thought played a role in the US Supreme Court's 1973 opinion on *Roe v. Wade,* which stated that "maternity, or additional offspring, may force upon the woman a distressful life and future. Psychological harm may be imminent."[31]

The mid-1800s was not a great time for women or their mental health on any level, but there were still doctors who realized that tying abortion to insanity was something of a stretch. When a Dr. Barrett presented a paper in 1867 arguing that abortion could "be an active cause in the production of insanity," the other doctors present at the conference did not all agree. According to the *Detroit Free Press,* "Dr. Stebbins remarked that his personal experience had proved the contrary....Dr. Brodie and Klein made some remarks to substantially the same effect." The paper also noted that "only a few statistics were at the Doctor [Barrett's] disposal."[32]

But even mild dissent among members of the medical community didn't make its way to members of the general public, who were being fed antiabortion rhetoric by the spoonful by Storer and his cohorts.

And the arguments were as much centered on a woman's physical health as they were on her mental health. Massively popular antiabortion works, including Storer's *Why Not? A Book for Every Woman,* captivated the public. In it, Storer stated that "in no case should abortion be permitted, or allowed to be permitted, by the advice or approval of a single physician.... Ill health is no excuse for there is hardly a conceivable case where the invalidism could either not be relieved in some other mode, or whereby an abortion it would not be made worse."[33] Childbirth, he assured women, was much safer than abortion.

There is no question that abortions performed during this period could result in death. But, at the time, one physician argued that death occurred in one abortion out of a thousand performed by a skilled physician.[34] That's not good, but if he was correct, it's a better rate than the five deaths out of a thousand that were estimated to result from childbirth at the hands of even the relatively competent midwives.

If, as estimated in the late 1850s, one in five pregnancies terminated in abortion, people quite certainly knew someone who had undergone such a procedure.[35]

As Dr. Thomas Blatchford wrote to Storer, abortion had been a much more "rare and secret occurrence" when he was "a young practitioner"; forty years later, the topic had entered the public discussion simply because its very occurrence in everyday life had become so "frequent and bold." In medical journals from the period, it was as likely to see a profile of a "physician's wife" or "the wife of a wealthy banker" who'd had an abortion as it was to see one of a woman from a lower-class background.[36] When one pastor's wife died, a doctor reported that he was told, quite calmly, that the cause of her death had been "a hemorrhage," but, he added, it was "pretty well known it was the result of an abortion." That prompted the doctor to remark, with some anger, that "in that community abortion was so lightly thought of that even intelligent and influential people who were friendly to the minister were willing to believe his wife died from its effects."[37]

Despite Madame Restell's notoriety and the growth of the birth control industry as a whole, respectable people were now supposed to be stunned that anyone was having an abortion. Certainly they were not supposed to say that people they *knew* had had one. Silencing people—and ensuring thereby that no one knows precisely how common such a procedure is, and how normally life might go on afterward (though not, clearly, for that pastor's wife)—goes a long way in making abortion seem shameful.

Having established the procedure as a source of shame and scandal, doctors went a step further. They made it clear that there was only one reason a woman would choose to have such an operation at all: vanity. Vanity and selfishness. Aborted fetuses, the 1860s antiabortionist crusader J. T. Cook claimed, "premature martyrs to woman's vanity, woman's selfishness, and woman's inhumanity, have gone up to the great white throne with no earthly record of their sacrifice, save the painted, fleeting and fading beauty of vain and fashionable mothers!"[38] Storer agreed, opining that, sadly, women who had abortions were "under that strange and masterful thralldom of fashion."[39]

This take on abortions was as old as the procedure itself. The second-century philosopher Favorinus reportedly condemned women "who strive by evil devices to cause abortion of the fetus itself which they have conceived, in order that their beauty may not be spoiled by the weight of the burden they bear and by the labour of parturition."[40] Soranus, a physician of the same time period, said that although he performed them, he and his fellow physicians did not "prescribe [abortions] when a person wishes to destroy the embryo because of adultery or out of concern for youthful beauty; but only to prevent subsequent danger in childbirth."[41] This attitude continued to be prevalent among people who were against abortion for centuries. In 2017, Pope Francis lamented that in Buenos Aires he'd encountered "a woman, a good woman, very, very beautiful and who bragged about her beauty, [who] commented as if it were natural: 'Yeah, I had to have an abortion because my figure is so important.'"[42]

There's little evidence to suggest that this is the impetus that men through the ages have imagined. The frequent claim that vanity is the main reason for having an abortion is little more than a tactic to make people who seek out abortions seem frivolous. It is far, far easier to say that women get abortions because they're irresponsible and self-involved than to address (and perhaps try to remedy) the social causes that, for many women, necessitate abortion. A 2004 study of over one thousand women found that the most common reason women cited for having abortions was that "having a child would interfere with [her] education, work, or ability to care for dependents." The second most common reason was that they "could not afford a baby now."[43] "Worried about beauty diminishing" was not cited at all.

The reasons modern women give for needing abortions do not seem radically different from the reasons of many women in the 1850s.

Even the patrons of an upscale abortionist like Madame Restell were not generally worried about gaining an extra thirty pounds during pregnancy. Instead, as many trial transcripts show, they were often the mistresses of wealthy men whom society would unhesitatingly cast aside and render destitute had they decided to bear and raise their children. But while Madame Restell's patients in the early 1800s had often been seen as helpless, virginal victims of their male seducers, now antiabortion doctors painted women seeking abortions as rich, villainous socialites. Such theoretical women were far less popular and easier to discredit than the women who actually sought abortions.

Because, while people might have sympathized with women like Cordelia Grant, there was great public antipathy toward the kind of self-involved women that Storer and his contemporaries described. Women's lives had changed during these decades, though not largely because of abortion. The agrarian life some older people remembered and younger people may have romanticized was very different from the city life of the mid-1800s, where women could dance the night away at balls and attend—horror of horrors—suffragette rallies.

The antiabortionists were primarily concerned that when women had more opportunity to socialize, they had more opportunity to misbehave. They did not have to sit at the farm with only their husband and children for company; rather, in the city, with the free time accorded to women of means, they could mingle with a number of friends and acquaintances on a daily basis. In doing so, they might even become eager to vote, or elope, or wish to enter a profession, or otherwise take on identities other than that of the obedient wife and mother whom some men, such as Storer, preferred. In large part, the quarrel with abortions had to do with the fact that these operations might lead to privileged women "overlooking the duties imposed on [them] by the marriage contract."[44] That would be especially upsetting to people like Storer who believed that white, bourgeois wombs had to be used as a national resource to populate the Midwest.

Strangely, even as antiabortion crusaders tried to villainize such city women as evil and frivolous, they also tried to tailor their antiabortion rhetoric to appeal to their evil or frivolous sensibilities. For women concerned about their looks, doctors assured that abortion would make them repulsive. One particularly dramatic physician even went so far as to claim that proof of the operation would be "physically stamped on the face divine, forever effacing its light and beauty, and be forevermore a tell-tale witness against so Unchristian and unnatural a mother."[45]

Gaining traction, Storer persisted in his campaign. Ever the misogynist, he did not believe women were mentally capable of making decisions about whether to have an abortion in the first place. He contended that if the decision were left up to them, they would probably just continue to get abortions whenever they felt they needed them. "If each woman were allowed to judge for herself in this matter, her decision upon the abstract question would be too sure to be warped by personal considerations, and those of the moment. Woman's mind is prone to depression and temporary actual derangement under the stimulus of uterine excitation."[46]

Storer's conviction that all women were borderline insane begs the question, was he, in reality, just driving those around him crazy? It seems hard to imagine a woman so saintly that she could interact with him and not want to yell at him on a regular basis.

Incidentally, the cure Storer devised for "female insanity"? Removing women's ovaries. As horrific as it may seem now, many doctors adhered to this faulty "logic"; by 1906, according to a modern account, "doctors had performed an estimated 150,000 ovariotomies on American women under the guise of protecting their emotional stability and mental health."[47] Without her ovaries, a woman would be unable to have children at all. Men like Storer would be able to make such a decision for her.

Women, physicians seemed to concur, simply could not be trusted with their own bodies, let alone other women's bodies. Hugh Hodge, a professor of obstetrics at the University of Pennsylvania from 1834 to 1863, explained that rather than the women bearing them, "physicians, medical men, must be regarded as the guardians of the rights of infants."[48]

Storer's campaign succeeded. His report on abortion would be accepted by the AMA in 1860, and its findings would define the organization's official policy for over a hundred years, until 1967. The

AMA would subsequently push for more antiabortion laws, and forty different statutes would be written into state laws from 1860 to 1880.

Thus doctors' efforts to paint abortion as a repellent procedure performed by nefarious midwives was successful. By 1907, according to a report on midwives by the nurse Elisabeth Crowell, to many, "the two terms 'midwife' and 'abortionist' [were] synonymous."[49] By 1916, Dr. Joseph B. DeLee (who, remember, wanted a great deal of money for the same treatments midwives had long done) was declaring, "The midwife is a relic of barbarism. In civilized countries the midwife is wrong, has always been wrong."[50] In light of this public opinion put forth by men of science, many midwives were driven out of business, to the delight of their male competitors.

And yet, despite every effort made to convince women of their immorality, it did not stop women who wanted abortions from having them.

What Storer did not seem to anticipate was that women would not cheerily agree with his opinions. Eliminating midwives, or at least declaring them barbaric, did not stop women from needing abortions. Michele Goodwin, author of *Policing the Womb*, noted that "for Storer, it was a problem that women [were] not 'deterred by [gynecologists'] refusal [to perform abortion] from going elsewhere for aid, or from inducing abortion upon themselves.'" Storer sighed. "In very many instances, from our own experience, has a lady of acknowledged respectability, who had herself suffered abortion, induced it upon several of her friends: thus perhaps endeavoring to persuade an uneasy conscience, that, by making an act common, it becomes right."[51] Abortions have been considered many things over the centuries, but rarely have they been dubbed a fun bonding activity. It was more likely that women were resorting to the help of their friends rather than professionals because they felt a strong need for secrecy, and because the availability of women skilled in performing the operation was being deliberately diminished. With their legal options eradicated, women turned to self-induced abortions. In 1888, one doctor found, to his surprise, that when he visited a "young unmarried woman of excellent family" for what her parents thought were unusually heavy periods, "his diagnosis and her confession to him reveal[ed]...the effects of self-accomplished abortions."[52]

The obstetrician Moses Montrose Pallen noted in 1869 that even well-to-do women were engaging in self-abortion:

Ashamed or afraid to apply to the charlatan, who sustains his existence by the price of blood, dreading, it may be, publicity, she reck-
lessly and boldly adopts measures, however severe and dangerous,
for the accomplishment of her unnatural, her guilty purpose....
[S]he will swallow the most nauseous, irritating and poisonous
drugs, and, in some instances, will actually arm herself with the surgeon's instruments, and operate upon her own body, that she may
be delivered of an embryo, for which she has no desire, and whose
birth and appearance she dreads.[53]

Medical men could only ascribe this to a certain level of insanity on
the part of women. In 1859, the physician Walter Channing remarked
that "women for whom this office of foeticide, unborn-child-killing, is
committed, are strong-minded, and the natural is strengthened by the
recently-established uterine function. It becomes irritable, morbidly
sensitive[,] and what is resolved upon is done."[54]

The notion that women would not always cheerfully consent to be
mothers was, to these medical men, proof that they must be mad.

Madame Restell often thought she knew better than her patients.
But she did not harbor the illusion that they should be content to
be merely kindly nests for future generations, regardless of their circumstances. Nor did she see her patients as deranged lunatics, or
shameless narcissists. In this regard, she had a considerable edge over
the male physicians of the period. Women—those makers of kindly
nests—continued to flock to her.

Chapter Eighteen

As the 1860s commenced, Madame Restell was faced with the question of what to do with the great sums of money she was making. She was already traveling back and forth to Europe regularly. She had generously lavished gifts—clothing, gloves, and jewelry—on her daughter and now her grandchildren, for whom she was known to "entertain the warmest affection."[1] She also indulged herself with fine clothes and jewelry; in less than a decade, the papers would describe her as "one of the principal diamond owners in New York," with a brooch costing $15,000 (approximately $280,000 today) in value.[2] She had bought houses for every one of her relatives back in England. For one brother who'd chosen to move to the American West, she'd bought a farm.[3]

And yet, Madame Restell still continued to operate out her office and home in Chambers Street, not so far from where she'd begun. Now flush with cash, it was time to build an extravagant mansion uptown.

She already had the land: a plot at the corner of Fifty-Second Street and Fifth Avenue that she'd purchased in 1857, the same year Horatio Storer was compiling his report on the evils of abortion. While people who visit Manhattan today will think of that area as prime midtown real estate, at the time it was firmly on the outskirts of New York City, so far north that the roads were not fully paved. The houses of anyone stylish, or even respectable, came to an abrupt stop at least twenty blocks south. In *The Age of Innocence*, published in 1920 but set in the 1870s, author Edith Wharton wrote about the character Mrs. Manson Mingott (inspired by her great aunt, Mary Mason Jones), who famously built a house in the same area as Madame Restell, still far before it was fashionable:

She was sure that presently the hoardings, the quarries, the one-story saloons, the wooden green-houses in ragged gardens, and the rocks from which goats surveyed the scene, would vanish before the advance of residences as stately as her own—perhaps (for she was an impartial woman) even statelier; and that the cobble-stones over which the old clattering omnibuses bumped would be replaced by smooth asphalt, such as people reported having seen in Paris.[4]

After the opening of Central Park in 1858, fashionable New Yorkers craving a bit of greenery and space were drawn up north from their homes in Stuyvesant Square. By the end the century, the streets along Fifth Avenue from the Fifties through the Seventies would be known as "Millionaire Row."

Madame Restell can't be credited with the kind of faith possessed by Mrs. Manson Mingott. She was not a person who anticipated the future; she was one who acted based on her needs of the present. In fact, she likely would never have even purchased the land, or built her house there, had it not been for the construction of St. Patrick's Cathedral, and, more importantly, Madame Restell's personal squabble with the archbishop of New York.

In 1850, Archbishop John Joseph Hughes announced his plan to replace the old St. Patrick's on the Lower East Side with a new, magnificent edifice befitting the city's growing Catholic population uptown, on Fifth Avenue and Fifty-First Street. He also intended to build a residence for himself on a plot of land across from the church.

Had they shared even the smallest philosophical similarities, John Hughes and Madame Restell might have gotten along well, as both were somewhat combative, ambitious immigrants who had found success in America. Hughes, who was nicknamed "Dagger John," was said by one reporter from the period to be "more a Roman gladiator than a devout follower of the meek founder of Christianity."[5] Hughes had been born in 1797 to an Irish Catholic cabbage farmer, and his family had faced tremendous discrimination, as did all Catholics in Ireland under English rule. When his sister died, the family wasn't even allowed to have a Catholic priest preside over her burial. The Hughes family immigrated to America in 1816 in the hopes of finding a nation where, according to the future archbishop, "no stigma of inferiority would be impressed on my brow, simply because I professed one creed or another." Once his family settled in America, he applied to study for the priesthood at Mount Saint Mary's College in Maryland.[6] His application was denied, so he asked to work there as a gardener. That they agreed to. He was admitted to the school after all (while studying, he continued to take care of the garden). He then rose rapidly through the ranks of the clergy, overseeing, among other things, the construction of St. John's Orphan Asylum. By 1850, at the age of fifty-three, he was ordained the archbishop of New York.

Never forgetting his roots, Hughes advocated tirelessly for Irish immigrants. One of his most notable challenges came in attempting to ensure that public schools didn't discriminate against Irish Catholic students. That was a formidable challenge at a time when schools taught that "the emigration from Ireland to America of annually increasing numbers, extremely needy, and in many cases drunken and depraved, has become a subject for all our grave and fearful reflection."[7] Though he was initially unable to raise public funding for Catholic schools, undeterred, he fought to build over a hundred privately funded Catholic schools in his diocese, where children could learn to be proud of their heritage and religion, or, at least, not learn that they were genetically drunken and depraved.

All this pro-Catholic activism enraged the Protestant nativists, who, at one point, attempted to burn Hughes's house to the ground. The fact that they did not cause him to retreat, even slightly, from his advocacy for the Irish meant that the Irish population of New York adored him. In 1850, one paper excitedly anticipated that he would soon become a cardinal, and, "It is but one step from Cardinal to Pope, and it would not be the strangest thing in the world if a New Yorker should occupy the Papal chair." Certainly, the paper proclaimed, "John would make the best Pope they have had for two centuries."[8]

Spoiler: he did not become the pope, and the idea of a pope from the United States is, as of this writing, still so far-fetched as to inspire HBO dramas.

But Hughes was, at least, going to enjoy a beautiful, unburnt home next to the cathedral, the construction of which he carefully oversaw. He imagined it would offer him a fitting place of respite after his years of work and devotion. And this peaceful prophecy would have come to pass, except that he was foolish enough to tangle with Madame Restell.

Shortly after obtaining the land for the new cathedral, the archbishop "openly denounced [Madame Restell] from the altar of the old cathedral."[9]

What Hughes said specifically is—deeply infuriatingly—lost to history, but the condemnation in and of itself was hardly surprising. Hughes was an avid newspaper reader; his biographer noted that his newspaper reading "was a stimulant for his appetite for controversy." And Madame Restell was, to Hughes's mind, a prominent easy target; in addition to being an abortionist, she appeared to be sinful in a slew of ways. Hughes would have especially hated her philosophical ruminations about limiting family size, and how children could be detrimental for families, which ran with her ads in the press at a time when he was trying to improve life for many of the poorest children in the city. These concepts were the kind he raged against when he talked about newspapers "making their pages eloquent by a stupid imitation of Tom Paine and Voltaire."[10]

One of his specific concerns, as someone ministering to a large population of Irish immigrants, was the licentious nature of society, and the fact that there were supposedly thousands of Irish prostitutes in New York City whose occupation many saw as enabled by Restell. Many of Hughes's sermons exhorted the "ladies of New York" to choose chastity—and he worked with charitable organizations that taught immigrant women how to cook and clean, and that aided them in finding employment as servants (though whether this secured their chastity is another matter entirely).

Whatever criticisms Hughes offered eventually made their way to Madame Restell in the pews of her Episcopal church. While normally she would have been content to dismantle her adversaries in the press, this time she seemingly had the means and desire to take it one step further.

And so, Madame Restell decided to bring the battleground to her—and bought the plot on which he intended to build his house. There, she would build a house of her own, a house so ostentatious that parishioners at St. Patrick's would be forced to look at it every time they went to church. The land purchase would also serve to tell the archbishop who had the real power in New York City. It no longer had anything to do with organizational affiliation, or even respectability. No—it had to do with money.

When Hughes placed his bid on the plot of land across from where St. Patrick's would be built, he was shocked to find that "Madame Restell had doubled his offer."[11] Judge Wednell, representing Hughes, then bid against Restell, who placed her ensuing bid through her husband, "the latter running the price up to a figure too high for the former and thus securing the prize."[12]

Besides Hughes, Madame Restell was the only other bidder for the prized plot. Some accounts claimed that her bid was made anonymously, as otherwise people appalled by her might have tried harder to outbid her. But then, others might have found that difficult to do. In 1857, New York, like the rest of the United States, was in the midst of a financial panic. The collapse of the Ohio Life Insurance and Trust Company, a banking institution, had triggered the collapse of numerous other banks, and, subsequently, of manufacturers and merchants throughout the nation. There are myriad reasons for the Ohio company's collapse: overinvestment in railroads; overreliance upon foreign imports, coupled with the fact that Europeans no longer needed as many agricultural exports from America after the cessation of the Crimean War, which subsequently ran up debts abroad; and speculation in stocks. That said, according to the *Merchant's Magazine and Commercial Review*, "the more immediate cause of the panic, and which tended to aggravate the evils more than tenfold, is the operation of the electro telegraph."[13] People across America could now immediately hear about the financial failure of the Ohio Life Insurance and Trust Company, as soon as it happened, which caused a run on the banks. Fearing that their own financial institution might be next, they were frantic to withdraw their money. This left the banks, devoid of cash, to collapse. No banks meant no loans, which meant the collapse of businesses, which meant no jobs, all of which added up to a huge mess.

You know what wasn't affected at all? The number of people who needed abortions.

If you were a man who didn't want your mistress having a child during times of economic prosperity, you definitely didn't want her to have one when your business was about to go under. Birth rates generally decline in times of economic uncertainty. That has to do with fewer couples having sex—people don't generally find the possibility of losing their job to be a lust-inducing aphrodisiac—but it also stems from an increased use of contraception and more abortions.

And so, while the rest of the country pinched pennies, Madame Restell bought the land across from what would be St. Patrick's Cathedral for a total of $36,500 ($1,160,402 today). Spending a million dollars on a plot of undeveloped land in a largely unpopulated part of town to snub someone was absolutely her style.

At the time, it was agreed that what the Lohmans paid for the lot was "far beyond its value."[14] Yet they could have made a profit almost immediately. Madame Restell's purchase threatened the financial future of St. Patrick's Cathedral. Archbishop Hughes had initially projected that the church construction would cost $750,000, but proposed it might be offset, as "we own another block of the same dimensions on the eastern side of Madison Avenue, it is our intention to lease that block for private dwellings of a choice character, and thus make provision for the support of the cathedral in all future times."[15]

Good luck finding buyers for those private dwellings of choice character right next to one of the most infamous and controversial mink-clad, carriage-riding characters of the city.

When Madame Restell announced her intention to build on her newly purchased plot, "the neighbors were horrified, and offered to buy her off for $150,000 [$4,768,775 today]."[16] However, Madame Restell, unlike the church, could not be outbid. She claimed "[that] she had bought the place for a home, and that she intended to end her days there." Moreover, she said, she was "a regular physician, and as much entitled to practice her profession as Dr. Carnochan or Dr. Dixon."[17] And, unfazed, she did proceed to build her home, which, as the *Chicago Tribune* related, was locally nicknamed "Madame Restell's Asylum for Lost Children."[18] Her house would stand alone on the block, "to the great pecuniary detriment of the owners of the adjacent property," who realized they could not easily sell their lots of land.[19]

And if it was to be the only house on the block, then Madame Restell was determined to make it a truly exceptional one. If the place on Chambers Street had been an office first and a home second, this new building would function primarily as a showcase for her tremendous wealth.

The construction of the mansion itself was estimated to cost $165,000. Upon its completion, it stood three stories high, with a basement, and was twice the width of the other homes in the area. The architect, Robert Mook, decided to create an elegant masterpiece in the style of the Italian Renaissance, as Madame Restell had given the twenty-seven-year-old architect carte blanche to build the kind of home that would be a calling card for him. Mook garnered so much praise for the building that he was later hired by other uptown settlers, such as the aforementioned Mary Mason Jones, for whom he designed a row of marble homes. Today, his best-known building is likely 64 Perry Street, the fictional home of *Sex and the City*'s Carrie Bradshaw, a fact that likely would have positively tickled Madame Restell.

Mook was more than willing to fulfill the brief that the house must be magnificent. The portico was supported by Corinthian columns, and the building was said to have windows that seemed like "gracefully shaded eyes" (and were literally shaded by flying buttresses).[20] A metal railing across the front, doubtless intended to keep the kind of mobs that had confronted Madame Restell in the past at bay, spanned 100 to 150 feet.

Along Fifty-Second Street, Madame Restell built stables for her five carriages and seven horses (though, typically, her carriage was drawn by one pure white horse and one jet black one). The stalls themselves were "mahogany, ornamented with German silver."[21] The whips used on the horses were kept in a glass case fit for Snow White. And that was, for all intents and purposes, just her garage.

Inside, the foyer was laid with mosaic tiles, with the columns painted to match the designs of the mosaic. The drawing room was spacious for the age—eighteen by eighteen feet—with folding doors made of mahogany and rosewood. On the first floor, the marble-clad rooms flaunted floors inlaid with oak, while the ceilings were dotted with medallions. That floor boasted three dining rooms, each adorned with gold and bronze finishings. In those dining rooms, it was said that there was an "enormous French mirror in mosaic gilding at every pane."[22]

This may feel like a very ostentatious style to modern readers. At some point in her European travels, Madame Restell had been inspired by Versailles, as would be the Astors, who built a Fifth Avenue mansion in that same neighborhood some decades later. But it is—admittedly— far from the masterpiece of white, unadorned (read: *incredibly bland*) minimalism that many people favor today. Even at the time of its construction, there were reporters eager to find the house tasteless. One such reporter described it as a "tall, tawdry looking house": "The curtains are daubs of color, and everything about it indicates vulgarity and prosperity. Those who have been inside say that gilt and gaudiness are visible from cellar to garret."[23] But the fact that he's relying on "those who have been inside" for confirmation does indicate that he was never invited in, so his opinion should be taken with a grain of salt.

Others thought that Madame Restell's taste was somewhat subdued, at least in some regards. Reporters noted that they missed some of the decorative flourishes, such as carved trefoils and quatrefoils, that might have been seen in similarly expensive houses. They thought it was clear that Madame Restell's house had been deliberately built in a "more modern, and, in some respects less ornate style."[24]

But the ground floor was far from all that the house had to offer. Behind another set of columns was an elegantly carved staircase that would bring guests to the second, somewhat more intimate, story. There, the bedrooms were hung with lace curtains and had frescoes of flowers painted on the ceilings. Every one of those bedrooms had a boudoir for dressing, which was considered quite a luxury at the time. One bedroom in particular stood out, even amid the opulence of the home. In it, the walls had been covered in blue satin, and the bed was adorned with gold. It was said that this guest room was intended for Madame Restell's daughter.

But it wasn't only family members whose comfort Madame Restell considered. Even the servants' quarters were carefully designed and furnished. Unlike the spartan rooms Madame Restell had once occupied in her youth, the servants in her employ could enjoy rooms that were paneled in mahogany with a colorful Brussels carpet. This was at a time when, if a servant's room in New York was furnished with anything beyond a bed and a chamber pot, it was with family hand-me-downs so threadbare as to be nearly useless. The notion that an employer cared about a servant's comfort, as well as the servant's utility to the employer, would have been meaningful to the staff. The care taken on the servants' quarters also speaks to the fact that, while Madame Restell built this house to indicate how far she'd come, she had not forgotten her origins.

Beyond the symbolism it conveyed to the outside world, the construction of the house also indicated that, for perhaps the first time, Madame Restell was ready to have some fun. Her life, until this point, had been almost singularly devoted to her work. Other than traveling to Europe, her amusements seemed to consist of "reading" and "going for carriage rides"—and she was quite often using that carriage to travel to clients' homes, so all of her outings weren't scenic rides through the park. Before settling into her new abode, Madame Restell made sure the house was outfitted with a dancing hall, a billiards room, and not one but two gorgeous pianos, despite there being no indication that Madame Restell danced, played billiards, or was especially interested in music.

If the place was designed to impress—tasteful or not—and provide a comfortable home for Madame Restell and her loved ones, it succeeded. Some found the building so beautiful that their commentary made little mention of her profession at all. One paper remarked, "The general merit of the building is an almost absolute combination of beauty, simplicity, and boldness; and to stand at a distance and gaze up at the vista of Fifty Second Street, it is almost impossible to repress an apostrophe of admiring rhapsody." It resembled "a palace like that of Prince Prospero in Poe's tale *The Masque of the Red Death* [more] than a dwelling of the 19th century, erected on Fifth Avenue, for the more ordinary purpose of a city residence."[25]

But not everyone was so easily distracted from its owner's controversial source of funding. "Call it what you will," conceded the *Cincinnati Gazette*, "it is a very handsome structure, and a sad comment upon the success of crime."[26]

Others were given the false impression that Madame Restell intended to retire. One journalist alleged, "Whether Madame Restell intends to follow her profession in her new residence, our reporter is not definitely informed, but from the utter absence of the usual decorations and paraphernalia of the demimonde such as cupids, Venuses and the like, there is no probability that she will."[27] As it turned out, Madame Restell did have statues in her home—figures of prominent leaders such as George Washington and Benjamin Franklin, the famous abortion recipe provider. And that wasn't the only thing the reporter got wrong.

When walking by the house, passersby would see, sitting at the basement level, a heavily plated sign reading "Office." Although far more spacious than the one at Chambers Street, this office was not as gilded or elaborately furnished as the rest of the home. Visitors descended three steps and waited inside what was said to be a "plain but handsome hallway."[28] There, they'd pull a silk cord with a bell attached, which would be answered by Madame Restell or one of her servants. The waiting room itself was dimly lit—unsurprisingly, as it was in a basement—but appointed with comfortable couches. There was also a Bible in the room, displayed in a glass case. It was rumored that she once told a friend, "When my customers come to me, they're generally nervous with their danger, and they need something to inspire them with complete confidence. There's nothing like a Bible for that."[29]

The existence of that office meant that, while people admired the home as an architectural marvel, there were still many who considered it to be built on babies' bones. The lawyer Richard O'Gorman went so far as to say that "the mortar was mixed with human blood."[30] Bishop Huntington declared that the marble tablets "remind[ed] [one] of tomb-stones."[31] There was also a particularly vicious rumor that there was a furnace in that basement which burned the corpses of murdered children.

In reality, the basement was a fairly standard doctor's office, where Madame Restell continued to dole out contraceptive pills and abortions to patients exactly as she had been for years prior. After all, as she herself had stated, she was as much a doctor as anyone, and no one had a right to tell her to stop her practice—even if a policeman was stationed outside her door to try to catch her in illegal acts.

But if Madame Restell spent much of her time tending to her patients in the basement, she also had the sky at her disposal. On the highest story of her home was the pièce de résistance. There, if you were the kind of friend permitted into her most private sanctum, you would see a skylight, which rested upon four columns. People claimed that when light streamed in, it was like walking through the clouds. In an age before airplanes, where tenements blotted out the sky in so much of Manhattan, to experience this joy must have felt like being a god on Mount Olympus. After years of hard work, Madame Restell had finally carved out a bit of heaven for herself.

Much to the church's dismay.

CHAPTER NINETEEN

WHILE RESTELL'S MAGNIFICENT HOME WAS BEING ERECTED, the rest of the United States was dissolving into turmoil.

The Civil War, so long brewing, had finally erupted by 1861. After the first shots were fired at Fort Sumter in Charleston, South Carolina, one paper said, "The greatest calamity that can befall any nation has fallen on us": "If the most powerful nation on earth, or all the nations combined had assailed us, it would not have been so deplorable an evil as this of civil war. United we might have defied the world in arms, but now the hand of brother is raised against brother, and the land is convulsed by intestine feuds."[1]

It's misleading to imagine that all the northerners who enlisted did so out of a righteous desire to free the enslaved people in the southern states. Only 2 percent of northerners were abolitionists.[2] The mayor of New York, Fernando Wood, felt that New York should secede from the Union so it would not have to fight against the South, with which New York had strong financial ties. It's estimated that 40 percent of the revenue from the cotton trade in the United States went to New Yorkers via their financial firms and the insurance and shipping industries. People in the city may not have had slaves, but they benefited from slavery. Unsurprisingly, forty thousand New Yorkers—one-twentieth of the city's population—signed a petition begging for compromise with the South in 1860, a year before the Civil War began.[3] The *Herald* fatalistically proclaimed that abolition meant "you will have to compete with the labor of four million emancipated negroes."[4]

Pretty delightfully, the *New York Sun*, the paper in which Restell had long advertised, which was besotted by animals and tales of batmen on the moon, had the distinction of being on the right side of history when it came to slavery. As comically preposterous as some of its stories were, the *Sun* was also known to be an outspokenly abolitionist paper. The writers, particularly George Wisner, who would become a co-owner of the paper, were so dedicated to the cause that publisher Benjamin H. Day, who favored a gradual end to slavery, complained about what he regarded as too many antislavery articles in his paper. In retrospect, "too many" on that topic was probably the right amount; the paper was campaigning for freedom for enslaved people twenty-eight years before emancipation began.

The fact that the *Sun* also ran Restell's advertisements is interesting to note, as some modern Americans, such as former Department of Education secretary Betsy DeVos, have been known to liken the attempt to end abortion to the attempt to end slavery. DeVos remarked that President Abraham Lincoln "contended with the 'pro-choice' arguments of his day....Lincoln was right about the slavery 'choice' then, and he would be right about the life 'choice' today."[5] The fact that there are many problems with likening a publicly Black person laboring for a white person's benefit to a zygote sustained by the labor of another person aside, this presupposes that abortion was not an issue being regularly discussed in Lincoln's own day. That's obviously untrue. And while Lincoln did not speak to that issue, people's attitudes toward slavery at the time aren't consistent with the notion that people who were antislavery would also be antiabortion. People like those in charge of the *Sun*, a newspaper opposed to slavery, were quite accepting of abortionists, or at least fine with providing them a public forum to hawk their services. Meanwhile, Samuel Jenks Smith, who was positively itching to defend the "holy institution" of slavery, was passionately antiabortion. The papers that were most fervently opposed to Madame Restell's activities—such as the *Richmond Dispatch*, which claimed that she was "a demon who is permitted to corrupt and kill innocent girls, body and soul, and who has never suffered the penalty for her fiendish depravity"—segued effortlessly into articles denouncing the "insane abolition fanaticism which has taken such strong hold of the British mind," and claiming that "Northern abolition is made up of fanaticism, envy, hatred and uncharitableness."[6]

Sadly, many northerners might have agreed with them.

A more general sense of northern patriotism surfaced following the attack on Fort Sumter. In Washington, the *New York Times* reported after the announcement of the war, "the wildest scene of excitement ensued. Among the Union men here there was general rejoicing that an issue was made at last, while no advocates of Southern rights were to be found."[7] When it was announced at the Brooklyn Academy of Music that the Union forces had prevailed, and the "Stars and Stripes" still waved over Fort Sumter, "but one feeling seemed to pervade the audience, that of rejoicing."[8]

The sentiment touched even the *New York Herald*, which would become known for its Civil War coverage. That was surprising, as its editor, James Gordon Bennett, was deeply racist. He claimed, for instance, that "niggers and thick lips from Timbuctoo cannot expect to compete long with pure Anglo-Saxon blood."[9] His biographers agree that his general politics were "racist, pro-slavery and anti-abolitionist." Nonetheless, the *Herald* backed the North during the Civil War following the attack on Fort Sumter. This prompted one critic of Bennett's to note, "The conversion of the New York Herald is complete.... [Bennett] is a discreditable ally for the North, but when you see a rat leaving the enemy's ship for your own, you overlook the offensiveness of the vermin for the sake of what the movement indicates."[10] The shift may have had something to do with the fact that, following the attack, a mob stormed the *Herald* offices and refused to leave until an American flag was hung out the window. Bennett's personal opinions did not change, but he could see which way the wind was blowing.

There was the general initial sense in New York that the Union would certainly emerge victorious and that, in the meantime, men might become heroes. In July 1861, when a regiment that had been at war for three months returned to New York City, banners were flying from nearly every window: "The city was kept alive with tales of war, the rejoicings of the returned soldiers and their friends, and general jubilancy until the crowing of the cock," said the *New York Times*.[11] Predictably, within that rejoicing, there was a fair amount of sex— often with men who were going away to war and not coming back. New York would provide more soldiers to fight for the Union than any other city. However, the general upbeat spirit with which people approached the first days of the war soon began to fade as the war dragged on.

In the Draft Riots of 1863, New Yorkers, many white, turned violently against Black people. The riots broke out in Lower Manhattan, where lower-class people resented the fact that, for $300, upper-class men could buy their way out of the draft, as well as the fact that Black people, who were not citizens, were exempt. These unhappy draftees did not attack upper-class men, however; they attacked Black people. As the *New York Times* reported, "It seemed to be an understood thing throughout the city that the Negroes should be attacked wherever found." After five days, when the Draft Riots came to an end, the *Times* wrote, "Hundreds [of Blacks] have been killed in the public streets with atrocities such as we have never seen before in a civilized country.... [H]undreds of them have had their houses sacked and burned, and their little property all forcibly taken from them; thousands of them have fled from the city in abject terror; and nearly all of them have been thrown out of employment."[12] The burning included a Black orphanage. Lynching was common, and for days, the bodies of Black men, women, and children could be found hanging from New York's lampposts. Irish people, feeling no kinship with their persecuted brethren, made up most of the mob's participants.

The people who felt abortion was wrong because it might mean Protestants could be "replaced" by Irish Catholics in America were still afraid of being replaced. It was just that now their terror turned toward being replaced by free Black people. In 1867, the *Brooklyn Daily Eagle* published an excerpt from a book suggesting that all Blacks should be deported to South America, though the author was "both willing and anxious to see the negroes, like the indians and all other dingy-hued races gradually exterminated from the face of the whole earth."[13]

While it was a dark time for the country, conditions were still good for Madame Restell's business. Women who had flings with departing soldiers in the heat of the moment would be calling on her a few months later. Even so, the war's effects were felt by Madame Restell's family. Isaac Purdy, Caroline's husband, enlisted in August 1862 and became a private in Company G, 7th Regiment of the New York Heavy Artillery. He planned to serve for three years, or the duration of the war. God help him, he probably thought he was going to be a hero.

Madame Restell wasn't overly sorry to see him go. The marriage, which she had hoped would bring her daughter security and respectability, had fallen short. Isaac Purdy had the same propensity for drinking that had affected Madame Restell's own first husband.

Drinking a great deal in this age wasn't uncommon. An exhibition hosted by the National Archives in 2015 noted that in the mid-1800s the average American drank approximately 7.1 gallons of absolute alcohol per year. Today, it's only 2.3 gallons.[14] Back then, the British naval officer Frederick Marryat noticed all that drinking when he visited America:

> I am sure the Americans can *fix* nothing, without a drink. If you meet, you drink; if you part, you drink; if you make acquaintance, you drink; if you close a bargain, you drink; they quarrel in their drink, and they make it up with a drink. They drink, because it is hot; they drink, because it is cold. If successful in elections, they drink and rejoice; if not, they drink and swear;—they begin to drink early in the morning, they leave off late at night; they commence it early in life, and they continue it, until they soon drop into the grave.

He also noted that in his travels in America, if he had drunk as often as American people asked him to, he "should have been in the same state as many of them were—that is, not really sober for three or four weeks at a time."[15]

And drinking wasn't a class-specific indulgence, either; it appealed as much to well-born gentlemen as to lower-class ones. While factory workers went to a tavern before work, gentlemen would enjoy an alcoholic equivalent of a coffee break at 11:00 in the morning.

You might wonder why they did not just drink water. The simple answer is: it wasn't that simple.

The Croton Aqueduct, which would provide water both to New York City and to Isaac Purdy's native Tarrytown, didn't open until 1842. Until Isaac was age eleven, the water from New York wells was so filthy that, when one man was asked whether it was safe to drink, he replied, "I cannot pretend to say, as I never tasted water there that was not mixed with some kind of liquor."[16] When the aqueduct opened, people were still reluctant to drink from that source. On July 4, 1844, the mayor, James Harper, set up a basin for locals to convince people that the water was safe. But if you'd grown up drinking whiskey rather than water, well, you might continue on as you always had because you were addicted.

Poor Isaac never had a chance.

If this intemperance was a habit in daily life, it was even more pronounced in the military. Dating back to colonial times, life in the military revolved around alcohol; military officials were even elected in taverns, where they were then expected to treat everyone to alcoholic refreshment. One newly minted colonel declared, "I can't make a speech worth a damn, but what I lack in brains, I will make up for in rum."[17] The navy continued to dole out daily half-pint rum rations to sailors until 1862. One of the many reasons the North emerged victorious during the Civil War was that Congress raised funds to pay for military expenses by taxing bourbon at 20 cents per gallon.

But Isaac Purdy was drinking so wildly that he was court-martialed for being drunk on duty. Specifically, he had been assigned to guard a group of southern prisoners. Instead, he took them into town, where they went on a drinking binge. The notion of a bitter war where brother was pitted against brother extended, in Isaac's mind, only until the minute he was bored and needed some drinking buddies. Still, Isaac wasn't discharged. Young men defecting after they realized the grim reality of life in the army was a bigger concern than men partying with the enemy. Rather, he continued to serve until the Battle of Petersburg, where his commander said he was "captured by rebels" on June 16, 1864.[18]

Unfortunately, Isaac wasn't destined to be treated the same way he had handled his prisoners. He was instead taken to Camp Sumter in Andersonville, Georgia. If war is hell, then prisoner-of-war camps tend to be one of its deepest and most depraved circles. Camp Sumter was no exception. Originally built to house 10,000 prisoners, it eventually housed 45,000 incarcerated men. The overcrowded conditions quickly became unsanitary. Sergeant Samuel Corthell, Company C, 4th Massachusetts Cavalry, claimed, "The camp was covered with vermin all over. You could not sit down anywhere. You might go and pick the lice all off of you and sit down for a half a moment and get up and you would be covered with them. In between these two hills it was very swampy, all black mud, and where the filth was emptied it was all alive; there was a reglar buzz there all the time, and it was covered with large white maggots."[19]

If that wasn't sufficiently horrifying, the camp was overseen by Henry Wirz, a man given to fits of what a prisoner called "spasmodic rage." Prior to the war, Wirz had overseen a large plantation, and he treated the prisoners the same way he had treated enslaved people. He set dogs on prisoners who tried to escape. He consigned them to deadly punishments with some glee: when prisoners noted that a man he'd trapped in stocks during a rainstorm was drowning, he quipped, "Let the damned Yankee drown."[20] Following the war, 150 people from the camp, including guards and doctors, testified that his treatment of the prisoners had violated the rules of war. He was subsequently hanged as a war criminal. "There are deeds, crimes that may be forgiven," the author Walt Whitman wrote of Wirz, "but this is not among them. It steeps its perpetrators in blackest, escapeless, endless damnation."[21]

Oh, and if you were wondering—is there a statue commemorating this lovely man anywhere? Of course there is. The Daughters of the Confederacy erected one in Andersonville in 1909.

Suffice to say, Camp Sumter was not what New Yorkers imagined when they celebrated the beginning of the war. In addition to the tortures doled out, prisoners were left to drink from a river black with sewage. Rations were distributed so sparingly that the prisoners became skeletally thin. There were no permanent shelters, so prisoners had to huddle under tents constructed of whatever they could assemble. Some dug holes in the ground in which to sleep. They weren't given clothing, so they either went naked or remained in their uniforms until those fell like rags from their bodies. Illness swept through the camp. By the war's end, 13,000 prisoners had died at Camp Sumter, Isaac among them. He passed away in November 1864, roughly five months before the Civil War came to an end.

And he wasn't the only member of the family lost during those years. In addition to her husband, Caroline had also lost two of her four children.

The death of her granddaughters completely devastated Madame Restell. She had delivered them herself at the 162 Chambers Street location. She commissioned an Italian sculptor to build a tomb to commemorate Frances Ann, who had passed away in 1859 at the age of two, and Florence Annie, who had died in 1863 at the age of three. Rumor had it (and this is according to Rev. Huntington's extremely colorful account, so again, take it with a grain of salt) that when the sculptor arrived, he found that Madame Restell had placed the dead child under a blanket in a crib, and instructed the man to carve what he saw in marble. After he engaged in some hemming and hawing about how this was not his typical process, Madame Restell told him, "It's got to be done the way I want it."[22] The tomb was eventually erected in Tarrytown, where it stands today, in roughly the form Madame Restell desired. Even Huntington, normally Madame Restell's most staunch critic, praised it:

> It is very odd and beautiful, and is enclosed within heavy slabs of the finest French plate glass, as clear as crystal. On one side is:

> *Hush, tread lightly, our child is sleeping;*
> *Her life on earth is o'er*
> *Vacant hearts at home are weeping*
> *She sleeps to wake no more.*[23]

The loss of Frances and Florence made Madame Restell cling even tighter to her two remaining grandchildren. Her oldest granddaughter, Caroline, often known as Carrie, was already ten years old when Isaac died. The younger child, Charles, was only four. Isaac had left his widow a paltry pension from the military for $8 a month, with an additional $2 for each child. Madame Restell invited her daughter to move in with her, and Caroline, grieving her losses, accepted.

For a while, it was a happy reunion. Caroline was a welcome addition on the afternoon carriage rides Madame Restell took through Central Park. Charles and his namesake grandson made good use of the billiards table in the mansion. And while Madame Restell's daughter had never taken special interest in her mother's work since departing for school, her granddaughter, Carrie, was now able to assist her.

The whole arrangement might have been wonderful, except that Caroline was lonely for the companionship that neither her mother nor her children could provide. She had, until recently, been married—albeit, not in what appears to have been an ideal marriage. Perhaps more importantly, in her youth she had been told that much of her worth came from being married. It's not surprising that she would hope to secure a new husband for herself.

Before long, she met a twenty-nine-year-old policeman named William Booth Farrell, who worked at the Chambers Street precinct, near Madame Restell's original location. Caroline and William quickly struck up a romance. Even at age thirty-three and with two children, Caroline was still beautiful. Gentle and poetic, there was plenty to draw suitors to her. Unfortunately, Farrell seemed more entranced by the idea that he might "expect great things" financially from a marriage to Madame Restell's daughter than he was with Caroline herself.[24] Like many in a city where money had become increasingly important, he thought he might be able to advance his position if he married the only daughter of one of the wealthiest women in New York.

Madame Restell likely was not horrified by the idea that someone might marry her daughter for money. In less than a decade, "dollar princesses"—American heiresses who married financially down-on-their-luck aristocrats—would abound. There's an irony in fighting a revolutionary war so that, a hundred years later, American daughters could financially support cash-poor British dukes, but that did not seem to trouble mothers of the era. In America, many could say they were rich, but how many could say they spent summers at their daughter's castle? There was even a song about these kinds of courtships:

> The almighty dollar will buy, you bet
> A superior class of coronet
> That's why I've come from over the way
> From New York City in USA.[25]

These matches, while they elevated the woman's status, were often far from romantic. Consuelo Vanderbilt, the New York heiress, famously consented to marry the dour Duke of Marlborough only after her socially ambitious mother locked her in her room for months to coerce her. Consuelo later claimed that she spent her days gazing longingly at a pond where one of the couple's butlers had committed suicide.

Madame Restell doted too much on her offspring to have forced Caroline into such a marriage. But if her daughter had made a pragmatic marriage based on money and status, well, she would have thoroughly enjoyed being the mother to a duchess. She might even have thought it appropriate, especially at a time when she was being referred to in newspapers as far away as Milwaukee as a member of "the medical aristocracy."[26]

But to use your position to marry a policeman? The kind of man Madame Restell had to bribe or avoid? And an *Irish* policeman at that, opening herself and her family to the kind of nationalist criticism she had also hoped to avoid? It was too much to tolerate.

Nevertheless, on October 14, 1867, Caroline married Farrell. No mayor officiated this time. Instead, the modest ceremony was conducted by the Reverend Fitzgerald of Trinity Church. Two witnesses, Richard Berrian van Varyck and Andrew Craig, were present. Caroline's mother did not attend.

Caroline wouldn't be the first woman to marry someone who upset her parents. Still, she likely didn't anticipate precisely how much the marriage would trouble her mother. As soon as Madame Restell was made aware of the wedding, she "expressed the most bitter indignation, and practically disowned her daughter."[27]

This was not what William Farrell had hoped for. For a time, he soldiered on without his mother-in-law's support. He continued to work on the police force and was even promoted to sergeant. However, eventually, his drinking became uncontrollable. He was let go from the police force and had difficulty finding other work. "For a long time, [Farrell] led a shiftless life obtaining odd jobs occasionally," the *New York Times* later reported.[28] He worked as an attendant at buildings, but never seemed capable of holding onto any job for long.

Madame Restell may have been furious at what she saw as her daughter's poor choice (and it may be fair to say that marrying a shiftless alcoholic who was only interested in your family's money *is* a poor choice), but she continued to "entertain the warmest affection to her grandchildren" and "freely lavished her ill-gotten gains" on them.[29] Both of them adored her in turn and were soon referring to her as "mother." Before long, Madame Restell asked if they could live with her, and their parents agreed. Future visits with Caroline and her children were fraught. Later, Carrie would recall a New Year's Day where some country cousins visited, and Madame Restell gave them presents. Largely to ensure that Carrie did not feel left out, she also gave Carrie a box of gloves. Caroline promptly burst into tears. Carrie imagined it was "because she did not get a present also."[30]

Unfortunately, it probably was not that simple.

Caroline was not doing well.

Around the time she entrusted her children into her mother's custody, Caroline, who had lived with two alcoholic husbands, began drinking heavily herself. Alcoholism in women was less common than it was in men during this period; women were discouraged from drinking, save perhaps a few spirits after an arduous journey or the occasional celebratory toast. While plenty of medicinal tonics women took were heavily laced with alcohol, drinking was considered unseemly for a respectable lady. That said, social concern probably goes out the window if, in a short number of years, a woman loses two children and a husband. Sadly, alcoholism's frequent outcome was the same for women and men. In 1871, Caroline was committed to the penitentiary for "habitual drunkenness."[31]

Madame Restell at last took pity on her daughter and Farrell. Her daughter was struggling and not likely to survive, let alone thrive, without her support. The couple lived downtown at Houston and Varick, and "the grocers, bankers, and butchers in that vicinity became accustomed to receiving their pay in postage stamps which came from the Restell mansion."[32] She finally obtained for her son-in-law a position as a watchman at Grand Central Depot and rented the couple a house on Forty-Seventh Street. She never allowed them to move back into the mansion, although her grandchildren continued to live with her. Her home would be for herself, her husband, and Carrie and Charles alone.

Her efforts to ensure Caroline the life of a genteel lady—sending her abroad, educating her in a private school, and attempting to help her marry respectably—had ultimately been for naught. She would not repeat this effort with her grandchildren. Rather than attempting to isolate her grandchildren from her work, she shared it with them, and so they grew up molded in her image. Both were blessed with good looks, and both, in their own ways, followed in their grandmother's footsteps.

Charles loved the mansion. He took note of his grandmother's foresight, eventually erecting a home in an area she suspected would go up in value. As he grew older, he watched the buildings spring up along the formerly desolate blocks in the Fifties. As soon as he was old enough, he became "assiduous in managing [Madame Restell's] houses and other real properties, collecting rents, paying taxes, etc."[33]

In time, he'd move to Bayport, New York, where he became "one of its best-known residents and largest property owners." He eventually got involved in real estate development, erecting the bulk of properties along one avenue, as well as single-family cottages. All the while, he himself occupied "one of the most handsome residences on Main Street."[34]

Meanwhile, Carrie, in time, would become Madame Restell's apprentice, helping with her work and patients. She would later be named the executor of her grandmother's estate—a mixed blessing that meant she'd be in court for years debating payouts to various lawyers and relatives who felt short-changed. When she came of age, she married a young medical student named William Shannon. Though her grandmother may have appreciated his choice of profession, William was the son of a prominent southern judge, and Madame Restell had no affection for anyone involved in law *or* order. As such, she was said to find this marriage "almost as repugnant as that of Mr. and Mrs. Farrell." At least by that point, "her demeanor towards her family was mild and conciliatory."[35]

Madame Restell may have still been frustrated that none of her female offspring would be an unmarried, independently wealthy poetess (which, admittedly, sounds like it might be a fun thing to be). But she understood—and accepted—her granddaughter's headstrong nature.

In many ways, Carrie represented a young Madame Restell, gorgeous and brazen. When visiting her mother's humble home during her teen years, she was typically "blazing in diamonds, driving in the splendid equipage of her grandmother."[36] But even though she carried herself in style, Carrie was fortunate to find herself part of a new generation, one that didn't fetishize respectability the way it did glamour. The gilded age was dawning.

Chapter Twenty

IF CARRIE'S YOUTH WAS DIFFERENT FROM HER MOTHER'S, IT IS IN part because New York after the Civil War was not the same city it was prior to the war. By April 9, 1865, the southern general Robert E. Lee had surrendered, although skirmishes in Texas meant that President Andrew Johnson wouldn't officially announce that the war was over until August 1866. The North had emerged victorious, the Union was intact, and as the South lay in ruins, New York, with its ports to which the world's trade could flow, could establish itself as the center of commerce. The unofficial motto in the city in those years seemed to be "Get money, honestly if you can, but get money."[1]

Money and sex.

As immigrants and those displaced by the war flooded into the city, prostitution experienced massive growth. The number of brothels in the city climbed to six hundred, hosting an estimated twenty thousand prostitutes. No more were they confined to the tawdrier parts of the city; girls were stationed at cigar stores who would happily offer gentlemen sex in the back room.

Newspapers during this decade lamented a new generation of "sons who are educated to believe all this splendor constitutes the best of life, and that fast horses and champagne are emblematic of high life. Daughters brought up by a silly, ridiculous mother, who glories in her curtains and her carpets, her carriage and her parties."[2]

This description may have fit Charles and Carrie, save that Madame Restell was not silly, or ridiculous. She also hadn't had a party.

But by 1865, Madame Restell was ready to open her house to festivities. The papers claimed that in doing so she would be "throwing her marble impudence into the face of New York fashionable society."[3]

A perplexing turn of phrase, perhaps, but Madame Restell was essentially flinging herself like a Grecian bust into a group of snobby, prudish New Yorkers.

The public anticipated that as soon as Madame Restell's house was complete, she would attempt to establish herself as "a leader of the ton [fashionable society]." "Then," wrote a reporter, "we shall hear of magnificent receptions given by the wealthy Madame to the cream of our up-town circles, and social affairs on Fifth Avenue will progress swimmingly under her patronage." As for how this would be possible, the same writers shook their heads and admitted that "money [in New York] is more than morals."[4]

That's debatable. But the moral outlook was certainly in flux.

A new level of sophisticated cynicism about religion had arisen following the conclusion of the Civil War. That cynicism probably had much to do with a war where the desire to march to "fiery gospel writ in burnished rows of steel" had led to the death of thousands of young men. The arguments about God supporting either one side of the war or the other faded quickly in light of the horrific, daily realities of bloodshed and brutality. Among the defeated southern soldiers, there were those who struggled. One, in Louisiana, wrote, "I fear the subjugation of the South will make an infidel of me. I cannot see how a just God can allow people who have battled so heroically for their rights to be overthrown."[5] The short answer to how God could allow that is that maybe God hated slavery? But the more atheistic response is that the North was in a vastly superior position in terms of technology and infrastructure—cue Rhett Butler shouting, "There's not a cannon factory in the whole south" (not quite accurately, there was one cannon factory in Richmond)—but it's never quite so simple as that.

Despite the victory in the North, religious disillusionment also extended to the Union soldiers. "It is hard, very hard for one to retain his religious sentiments and feelings in this Soldier life," wrote a New Jersey surgeon. "Everything seems to tend in a different direction. There seems to be no thought of God, of their souls, etc. among the soldiers."[6] When told that God led soldiers to victory in battle, the men laughed and asked if God was going to be promoted.

It might seem that skepticism toward religion would lessen with the cessation of the war, but it did not. Civil War historian Allen C. Guelzo noted that "American religion...became one of the Civil War's major casualties." After the war's conclusion, the *New York Daily Herald* published a speech by Wendell Phillips, the beloved abolitionist, discussing what he felt to be the failings of organized religion. Received to thunderous applause, he stated that "[the church] only helped anti-slavery when forced to do so by the events at Gettysburg, Vicksburg, and other points." Phillips was correct that prominent theologians, including Robert Lewis Dabney, the Confederate chaplain, had used the Bible to defend slavery, asserting that "the relation between Master and Slave is perfectly lawful and right," and that slavery was a punishment from God in "the peculiar moral degradation of a part of the human race."[7] Phillips continued, saying that the church was in a terrible state because it was a "capital-punishment, pro-slavery, woman-under-the-bed society." Moreover, he felt that "if Jesus should come and try to preach in the streets of Boston and try to create a feeling among the masses, he would be in jail in less than a week."[8]

If Madame Restell had found Archbishop John Hughes irritating a decade ago, she now found many more people who shared her sentiments, and Hughes's denunciations about her from the pulpit carried significantly less weight than they had before the war. In America, the pendulum is always swinging between enlightenment and puritanism, and never rests entirely to one side. The slight swing toward a degree of religious skepticism worked to Madame Restell's benefit, though probably not as much as some thought it would.

By the spring of 1865, her house was finished. Reporters announced that Madame Restell was poised to "give magnificent parties, which will be attended by the 'dem foines' of the city, and reported by the 'Jenkinses' of the press, and paraded in Bennett's *Herald* and *Playbill* as the most magnificent entertainment ever given by the elite!"[9] (The term "the Jenkinses" referred to flowery society reporters who were perhaps a bit too enamored with their subjects.)

The idea that someone who had shown minimal interest in anything but working and making money would immediately establish herself as the most magnificent hostess in the city is a large leap, to put it lightly. Especially when she didn't come from family money, and her chosen profession—not to mention her public reputation—was so controversial. It was only possible because the "elite" in New York City at that time, and those who qualified for it, were evolving concepts.

By the late 1860s, being part of the elite required more than just having fine transportation and the proper moral outlook. Now, you had to be fun. And being fun meant throwing wonderful parties. The decades to come would see some of the city's most memorable fetes. One gala, hosted by Mrs. Stuyvesant Fish, the wife of a railroad tycoon, was given in honor of Prince del Drago of Corsica—who turned out to be a monkey. Another dinner, featuring the finest meats, was held for bejeweled collar-wearing dogs, arriving with their owners. Industrialist tycoon C. K. G. Billings even hosted a dinner party on horseback, where guests guzzled champagne and caviar as they raced around a ballroom converted to accommodate horses for the evening.

It all sounds vulgar, and tasteless, and really, really fun. Madame Restell would likely have loved seeing all the hijinks that would ensue later in the century. Luckily for her, the shift in favor of frivolity and excess was already happening in the late 1860s. By that time, Mrs. Astor's cousin Samuel Ward McAllister, the social chronicler, had moved to New York. Once there, he quickly began declaring who was and who was not high society. The high society set fell into two categories: the nobs and the swells. The nobs were the de facto nobility of New York, members of that Knickerbockracy who could trace their wealthy lineage back to the Dutch that settled New York when it was New Amsterdam. They were white, and Protestant, and respectable.

The swells, on the other hand, were new money, but they had a *lot* of money. Not "I own a carriage money," but "I own multiple mansions, all with their own stables money." They might, like Andrew Carnegie or the Vanderbilts, have gotten rich thanks to the railroads—something the old school Astors considered very vulgar. Many of them had moved to New York from the Midwest, or, like McAllister himself, from the South after the Civil War left that region in tatters. Many more would rise up from the streets of New York and become wealthy by obtaining political power. Lots of the swells were seedier, and more ruthless, and just plain less pleasant than their nob counterparts. But they weren't boring.

Madame Restell would never become a true leader of the ton. The nobs who had seen their land lose value because of the construction of her house never forgave her. Others, whose daughters had abortions at her hands, were afraid to interact with her in public on the off-chance people would suspect as much. The elites who had the luxury of being seen as respectable wouldn't be caught dead attending Madame Restell's receptions. "The aristocracy are not able as yet to reconcile themselves to the proximity of so notorious a character, even though matching the best of them in splendor of externals," explained one paper.[10] But there were plenty of swells to be found, and Madame Restell hadn't built a ballroom and put that billiards table in her house for nothing.

Near the end of May 1865, newspapers declared she planned to open her home in a manner "surpassing all the most splendid 'crushes' of the aristocracy." It was widely understood by the public that, while certain people might not come, "her vast wealth will, of course, ensure for her a reception of considerable éclat among the 'fair women and brave men' with whom Fifth Avenue abounds. Cards will be issued, and a reception of no ordinary magnificence will take place."[11]

There's certainly a cinematic version of this story where Madame Restell throws a party and no one comes, and she is subsequently left to sob in her ballroom and wonder what her wealth was for. However, since this is real life (as opposed to a salacious British drama), and people enjoy parties hosted by millionaires in extravagant houses, pretty much everyone she invited showed up. Invitations to her festivities were happily accepted by railroad magnates, executives, lawyers, physicians, and even "a few magistrates and legislators—the names charitably omitted by the [party's] chronicler."[12]

At the very least, many of those attendees probably came because they wanted to see her house. Everyone knew about it, although some who had watched it being erected didn't know who owned it. There was speculation that it was built for General Robert E. Lee, though why a southern general wholly associated with Virginia would want to live in the up-and-coming portion of New York following a Civil War loss was anyone's guess. A paper as far away as Milwaukee reported that some believed it belonged to "a foreign count, or possibly a prince of the royal blood."[13] This was wrong, but still more logical than the General Lee notion.

When the guests arrived at Madame Restell's housewarming party, they received a welcome fit for aristocrats. There were servants, clad in black, who circulated throughout the house with refreshments on trays. In the dining room, meats and delicacies were in buffet order. The precise nature of what was served was not recorded, but in the

1860s, based on the menu at the Manhattan Club (where the Manhattan cocktail was later invented), guests probably would have dined on dishes such as pheasant, oysters, sweetbreads, pâté de foie gras—honestly, many of the same meats that can be found at fine restaurants today. It's likely that Madame Restell served all of these. Another room was set aside for smokers. There, men—and very daring women—could enjoy the fine cigars Madame Restell had placed atop étagères. Those who were not content to simply puff away filled their pockets with them like party favors. Madame Restell's friends were, as always, overwhelmingly men, but there were enough women in attendance to allow for dancing in the ballroom.

Madame Restell presided over the entire affair with the poise and regality of a queen. It was reported that "she was attired in a Paris creation of silver brocade, and on her black tresses, slightly streaked with gray…was a crown of diamonds. The same precious stones glittered in her bracelets and on her fingers. A dog-collar of brilliants adorned her neck. Clusters of blue-white gems dragged heavily on the lobes of her ears." "Through the house made bright as day by hundreds of gaslights," the party reporter added, "one walked on soft, smooth carpets of the best manufactures of Europe. They alone were worth a fortune."[14] It would be hard for anyone to condemn Madame Restell's business while reveling in the luxury it made possible.

In any person's life, there is a high point that is obvious only in retrospect. This may well have been Madame Restell's. She was said to look especially happy as she went out for her afternoon ride the next day, still glistening head to toe in her diamonds.

And this was far from the only party Madame Restell ever hosted. Her annual New Year's Eve fetes were said to be especially crowded, and just as luxurious as the first event. As the events progressed, the guest lists continued to evolve. Despite being a popular host, it's unlikely that Madame Restell ever felt, as some suspected, that she would "meet the Astors and the Belmonts on terms of social equality."[15] But the politically powerful figures emerging from Tammany Hall? Those she thought she could manage.

William Magear Tweed—commonly known as "Boss" Tweed for his role as the head of Tammany Hall, the group that controlled the Democratic political machine in New York—was far from old money. His grandfather hailed from Scotland, though Tweed grew up on the

Lower East Side of Manhattan. He trained to be a chairmaker and briefly worked as a carpenter before he joined the Big Six Fire Company in New York. There his extremely violent temperament—and willingness to go after his rivals with an axe—was notable even among the firefighters of the time. However, it did not stop him from advancing, and he was made Big Six's foreman. The Democratic Party took note of him. With its support, he quickly became a school commissioner and, after two runs, alderman of the 7th ward. There he was beloved by his Irish constituency, to whom he all but guaranteed jobs. The age where courting the Irish vote would crush a politician had thankfully waned. It was in part because of the Irish turning out to vote for him in droves that Tweed was made the "Boss" of Tammany Hall, the executive committee of New York City's Democratic Party. In that role, he was allowed to dole out political appointments to friends as he saw fit, which he did—with the expectation that they'd pay him back however they could. He was also able to decide who to hire for taxpayer-funded projects. He took control of the city treasury by 1870, and he and his cronies drew from its coffers liberally. Certainly, plenty of the elite in New York were offended by the fact that many of their construction projects now required a kickback to Tweed—a man who paraded through the city with a ten-carat diamond glinting from the stickpin in his tie—but at least, they reasoned, he kept the Irish occupied.

The *Brooklyn Union* bemoaned how, in supporting Tweed and his cronies, "wealthy citizens...allowed themselves to be used to serve the purposes of corrupt men." They further intoned, "If Madame Restell could vote, she'd be found voting with the rest of them."[16]

Of course, she could not vote. In 1867, an argument against giving women the vote in papers as far away as Ohio was precisely that "Madam Restell and all the New York prostitutes would go to the polls."[17] That's a touch ironic in a time when someone as corrupt as Tweed could not only vote, but become an elected official and effectively run all of New York. If Madame Restell had strong political feelings toward one party or another, no one knew them. Denis Tilden Lynch, a biographer of Tweed, claimed that Restell "played no favorites but contributed to all campaign funds." She tended to donate discreetly, in the form of gifts. Supposedly "she sent out presents to her friends in office at Christmas time—always in the shape of new gold pieces."[18] She sent so many trinkets to Tweed's office that he had to warn the treasurer not to accept anything from her, lest his Irish, Catholic supporters think he was acquainted with the famed abortionist. This must have been difficult for Tweed, a man who loved baubles so much that one of his biographers noted, "The Tweed family seemed to be a Christmas tree of diamonds."[19]

Madame Restell was determined to get to know Tweed. Surely, she might have thought his political or judicial connections could help her. But perhaps, too, she saw herself in him—another figure from the Lower East Side who'd clawed his way to prominence and wealth using some not strictly legal means. It was said that she "offered a handsome sum to any of her circle who could induce this lion of politics to attend one of her dances."[20] The eager friend who accepted this offer was Henry W. Genet. Genet was a state senator and said to be Tweed's right-hand man. If Madame Restell wanted glamorous acquaintances, Genet fit the bill: He was known as "Prince Hal" for his wealth and his willingness to spend that wealth lavishly. His fortune was, at the time Madame Restell knew him, estimated to be half a million dollars. He bought a mansion on 5th Avenue and 126th Street—dubbed "Prince Hal's Castle"—for $125,000, and kept excellent horses, carriages, and a private stable on the grounds. His obituary later said that "his dinners and breakfasts were famous, and his exploits at the horse track were the sensation of the day. Fifty-thousand-dollar bets were often offered by him."[21] It was said, too, that "his power was dependent on his wealth, and his wealth seemed inexhaustible. Hundreds hung about him to catch the gold he showered."[22]

When the invitation was proffered, though, "Tweed stared for a moment at Genet and, without a word, turned on his heel and left the room to Senator Genet."[23] Tweed's position of moral hauteur in this instance is particularly surprising as Madame Restell's bribes were probably the only ones he did not accept.

Despite his standoffishness toward her and her parties, Tweed never tried to put an end to Madame Restell's establishment. Appeals were made, but it was stated by his biographer that "Madame knew too much. Tweed did not want to bring down her wrath upon his friends."[24] If Genet was close enough that Madame Restell could send him with invitations on her behalf, there were countless others in his cohort who probably employed her services.

The fact that she could never befriend Tweed aside, these would be a very pleasant few years for Madame Restell, ones where she could drift along on a river of champagne, happily clad in sparkling diamonds.

But, as is often the case, it was only a matter of time until the magnificent life she'd built for herself began to crumble—as the pendulum of respectability started to swing back.

Chapter Twenty-One

N O PARTY LASTS FOREVER.
Though Madame Restell did have a few fairly pleasant, uneventful years sipping champagne with notable swells.

One of the only real threats to her reputation during the years between the end of the Civil War and the early 1870s came in 1866, from within her home. It occurred when a former servant, after being fired by Madame Restell for theft, claimed that babies were being burned in the mansion's basement furnace. Since the woman making this accusation presumably had no real estate aspirations and could not launch a bidding war, Madame Restell resorted to the press. She informed the *New York Times* that "some prominence has been given to a case of petty larceny hereby merely because I was the complainant," and she would accordingly "state in your columns the facts as they are." She wrote that the woman making the accusation, Elizabeth Finley, had worked in her house as a cook for eight months. Eliza's husband had been employed as a coachman, and their child had been allowed to live with them at the mansion. Madame Restell continued, "When Eliza, from indisposition was incapable of performing her work for several weeks, I continued paying her wages, and paid another person to do her work, and members of the family procured her delicacies during her indisposition."[1]

Around this same time, however, Madame Restell noticed that bed linens, towels, handkerchiefs, tablecloths, and other small items had gone missing. When Eliza returned to work two months later, things were missing *again*. Initially, Madame Restell contended, she wasn't going to take any steps against Eliza—she didn't really care about missing towels all that much—but because of some "outrageous conduct" (which possibly means Eliza attempted to blackmail her), she eventually reported Eliza's thefts to the police.[2]

Notably, throughout her life Madame Restell had almost bewilderingly few publicized problems with her servants, who surely could have sold stories about her and her home to the press if they had wanted to do so. This is a testament to the fact that she probably treated and paid them well. Eliza was found guilty of theft at trial, and the court "severely reprimanded [her] and told [her]...that she was treated kindly and paid regularly."[3]

Eliza, now deprived of her many towels, promptly told everyone that Madame Restell had a fetal inferno in her basement.

Gruesome though it may seem, the problem with having such a furnace was that, if she was burning aborted bodies, she was doing so "without the license usually accorded to bone dust people and fat boilers."[4] So, in January 1867, the Sanitary Department of the New York City Board of Health announced that it would search her home for such a furnace. By February, a furnace was reported, although it was hardly a surprise to find one, as every home as large and well appointed as Madame Restell's would have contained a furnace for heat. And yes, it is also possible that Madame Restell used the furnace to burn effluvia. In her statement at the time, she did not so much dispute the use of the furnace as claim that Eliza had reason to spread unkind rumors.

This contentious incident aside, the years, overall, were kind to the aging abortionist. Even the newspapers seemed to temper their hatred and accept that, whether they liked her or not, she was a fixture in the city. In 1868, an otherwise critical article admitted, "It is said she gives liberally to people who are poor and in distress," noting that she had "sheltered many a poor girl from the pursuit of libertines and... restored not a few to the homes from which, in moments of weakness and passion, they had strayed."[5]

Sure, a policeman was stationed outside Restell's home to dissuade potential customers, but even this was treated with a bit of an eyeroll. The papers noted that being given that post was "a good thing—for the policeman," owing to the many bribes he'd be sure to receive.[6]

Madame Restell was able to live a life of "queenly splendor."[7] It was said during these years that "she seem[ed] to enjoy herself and grow fleshy as if she had the approval of a good conscience and lived a life of innocence and good deeds."[8]

While people might have been treating Madame Restell with less fury than usual, some were already taking steps to limit abortion. In 1869, a law was passed by the New York State Legislature that made abortion a misdemeanor regardless of how far the pregnancy had progressed. This eliminated the idea of quickening, effectively acknowledging the embryo's personhood from the moment of conception; it also made it a crime for anyone to buy medications to induce an abortion, even if they were not pregnant. Intent in procuring such medication no longer mattered. Coincidentally or not, this was the same year the Catholic Church declared that abortion at any stage—not merely after ensoulment—was homicide.

And then, only two years later, there was Dr. Jacob Rosenzweig. He, too, performed abortions, but, sadly, despite claiming he had abilities and facilities "the same as Madame Restell and the others," he performed them poorly.[9] After immigrating from Poland, he had begun his career in America as a saloon owner in Philadelphia before realizing—as so many did—that a career as a doctor would be much more lucrative. He then "purchased, for the sum of $40, a diploma from a Philadelphia College and, thus armed, he went to New York and set up as a Doctor."[10]

It was Alice Bowlsby's misfortune to turn to this "doctor" for help in 1871. Alice was considered to be an extremely upstanding young woman. She was twenty-two years old, still unmarried, and a member of the Market Street Methodist Church in Paterson, New Jersey, where she regularly attended Bible study classes. Her father, like many men during this era, was an alcoholic. Her mother, for the sake of her three daughters, had separated from him and started earning a living as a dressmaker. Alice was close to her mom and assisted in the business, until, in August 1871, five months pregnant, she was unable to hide her condition much longer. On August 23, she traveled to New York City from Paterson, wearing a white dress with a blue sash and a locket bearing the picture of her mother, to receive an abortion from Dr. Rosenzweig. She paid $50 before the procedure and promised $25 more afterward. He operated that day—it supposedly took only ten minutes—and by Friday, two days after her abortion, Alice had died of peritonitis.

As always, in an age before doctors used proper equipment or observed sterilization practices and had adequate training, complications and death were not uncommon. But Dr. Rosenzweig panicked. Rather than reporting her death and offering up some plausible excuse, he first went to an undertaker and asked if he could bury a "servant girl, who was poor, in the cheapest cemetery without a burial permit." After the man informed him that this was not possible, Rosenzweig stuffed her naked body inside a trunk. He then conscripted a woman whom he had operated upon in the past to call a carman to take Alice's body to the Hudson Railroad Depot. There, he had the woman buy a ticket to Chicago and leave the trunk to be loaded onto the train. Surprisingly for a doctor, though perhaps not during this time, Rosenzweig apparently overlooked the fact that dead bodies smell bad. Noticeably, unmistakably bad. Soon, the trunk had assumed a "repulsive odor exuding from it," which prompted railroad officials to break it open, whereupon they found poor Alice's mangled corpse.[11]

Once the body was discovered and identified by dental records, everyone connected to Alice was devastated. Her twenty-five-year-old lover, Walter L. Conklin—tall, good-looking, charming, and regarded as "one of the most promising and respectable of Paterson's young men"—committed suicide. He did seem more horrified by the shame of being involved in such an event than by the fact that his girlfriend had had an abortion and died. He left a neatly written note proclaiming, "I have long had a morbid idea of the worthlessness of life, and now to be obliged to testify in this affair and cause unpleasantness to my family is more than my life is worth. Goodbye, dear father, mother, brother, and sister. Forgive me."[12] Meanwhile, Alice's mother went into convulsions after hearing about her beloved daughter's death. The papers declared that she was driven insane with grief.

Here was a crime where "three, and perhaps four lives have been sacrificed."[13] The public was, understandably, outraged, and Dr. Rosenzweig was soon identified by the carman who had picked up the trunk. When the police asked him if he knew a girl named Alice Bowlsby, he went white and exclaimed, "Hell!," before attempting to coolly play it off, saying, "Oh, yes, I have heard of her but I never knew her."[14] This haphazard nonchalance was somewhat undercut by the fact that a handkerchief reading "A. A. Bowlsby" was discovered by police at his house, as well as Alice's blue scarf.[15]

At the trial, everyone testified that Rosenzweig had killed Alice and tried to dispose of her body. In spite of that, the jury bizarrely recommended the judge be merciful in sentencing. People had a lot of sympathy for this enterprising man. The judge refused, stating, "Ordinarily I would mind the recommendation of the jury, but in this case I must ignore it, for you deserve no mercy."[16] Rosenzweig was sentenced to a seven-year-long stint in Sing Sing prison. Before he went, he was told that prisoners worked so hard there that they sometimes died under the strain. Surprised, he threw up his hands and protested, "Look at my fingers! I have never worked a day in my life."[17] He wondered if it might be possible for him to receive better treatment in prison.

Everyone was horrified. Little wonder it was said that in 1871 that New York was "going through one of its moral spasms."[18]

It wasn't enough for the media that Dr. Rosenzweig had been convicted of manslaughter. The papers declared that "if he were the only person in New York engaged in this horrible business it would be sufficiently horrible, but when we know he is but one member in a trade almost as numerous as the respectable practitioners of medicine, there is a responsibility on society which cannot be evaded."[19] Of course, not all abortionists were stuffing their victims into trunks and trying to ship them out of state; Rosenzweig was an anomaly. And, to be sure, the controversial aura of the profession didn't help matters either. If a man had died on a dentist's table, and a dentist had tried to dispose of his body, for example, there would not have been a public outcry to ban dentistry.

But then, unlike dentists, abortionists tended to work as lone wolves and never really thought of themselves as a collective. They had been far too focused on protecting their business interests and making as much money as possible individually—and accordingly, competing with one another—to come together as a group to advocate for their profession. Though they had accumulated many customers and even a few friends, no one was willing to take to the streets to defend them or their work.

By 1871, many other groups of professionals had realized that they could become more powerful and financially secure if they banded together than if they continued pursuing their interests separately. The American Medical Association (which stood to benefit by the eradication of female abortionists) had been operational since 1847. But there were a number of female-focused groups as well, including the National Woman Suffrage Association that fought for women's right to vote. The Women's Christian Temperance Union—which eventually helped launch the failed experiment that was Prohibition in the United States through one of its social reform platforms—formed in 1874 and quickly picked up steam. Usually, when people united for a common cause, they got things done.

Instead of learning from the experiences of their peers, however, abortionists mostly spent their time sniping at one another in the press, just as Restell and Costello had done.

When they weren't bickering, they were wrapped up in their own legal anxieties. After Rosenzweig's conviction, it was reported that "the abortionists are greatly frightened and some of them have fled [New York]."[20] Rosenzweig wasn't the only one being arrested around this time. Other physicians, including a Dr. Perry and Madame Van Buskirk, were also arrested for performing illegal operations, and were subsequently refused bail. When Rosenzweig's daughter came to jail to bring him food as he was awaiting trial, she was arrested and placed in a cell herself because the police suspected she might be involved in his practice.

The notoriety and scandal surrounding the Rosenzweig case and others like it aroused great curiosity in the general public, partly because people desperately wanted to know more about the procedure itself. Where there's demand, supply will follow—which is how some particularly dramatic investigations of undercover reporting got started.

In July 1871, prior to Alice's murder, a reporter named Augustus St. Clair had attempted to grill Dr. Rosenzweig, who was then using the pseudonym Dr. Archer. Instructed by his editor to find out all he could about the abortion business, the reporter had taken a woman with him to various doctors under the guise of needing an abortion. Dr. Archer agreed to perform the abortion for $200, claiming that he was just as well equipped, if not better equipped, than Madame Restell. Presciently, the reporter asked what Dr. Rosenzweig would do if the woman died. Rosenzweig claimed, "The lady can be disposed of without trouble. I can get...burial certificates without trouble."[21] Reader, he could not.

When the reporter kept pressing for more details, Rosenzweig became suspicious. He was right to be wary. He was wrong to shout, "You are an [expletive], and a liar! You are an [expletive] spy and I will split your head for you, you [expletive]...I'll kill you," and then lunge at the reporter, thus leading the reporter to jauntily quip, "I had not expected such a denouement."[22] The reporter then claimed he *drew a gun on Rosenzweig* and ran out the door.

After Rosenzweig's arrest, this newspaper article predictably drew a great deal of interest, especially as St. Clair claimed that he'd seen a girl who perfectly matched Alice Bowlsby's description in the abortionist's office. In all likelihood, he didn't; he had visited Rosenzweig in July, after all, not August. Still, not so long ago, a newspaper had claimed that bat-people lived on the moon: a reporter spotting Alice in the flesh was at least closer to the realm of possibility.

St. Clair also visited Madame Restell and her husband, though he did not have to draw a gun on them. When he called on Charles—"Dr. Mauriceau"—at his office at 129 Liberty Street, and asked if the doctor could relieve a woman of her pregnancy without danger, Charles smiled calmly. He assured the reporter that he had helped in "thousands of cases—have them all the time and never have any trouble at all." Madame Restell herself was hardly more guarded. When a reporter—not the same one—came to her door, he was greeted by "a handsome young woman": Madame Restell's granddaughter, Carrie. When St. Clair eventually sat down with Madame Restell and asked whether she could terminate a pregnancy, she replied, "There will be no difficulty about that. Of course, such affairs are expensive, you know. The charge will be—." At that moment precisely, Carrie, who had seemingly been paying more attention to the news than her grandmother, intervened. After Carrie and her grandmother conferred for a few minutes, Madame Restell backtracked and told the journalist, "I can sell you some pills but really we do no other business. We have had so much trouble about these matters that we don't take any more risks. In all the six years we have lived in this house there has never been a stranger who slept under the roof—none in fact but our own family."[23]

Not so long ago, Madame Restell had considered the newspapers a platform she could dominate through advertising and bold op-ed pieces. However, the climate in recent years had noticeably changed, such that her only recourse was to deny, although to little avail. Her new statements were so clearly false that newspapers felt obliged to tell their readers that "other parties who have been there had a different experience."[24]

For years, Madame Restell had worked to establish herself as the most famous abortionist in America. Now, she had finally achieved her goal—and the timing couldn't have been worse. She was probably wise to deny her actions, unlike some of her contemporaries. When a competitor named Madame Grindle was approached by St. Clair, she exclaimed, "Poor unfortunate women! How little the world knows to appreciate their trials. We think it our mission to take them and save them—and noble work it is, too."[25] Unfortunately for both her and her business, Madame Grindle was pretty out of touch with the common public sentiment of 1871.

Established reporters weren't abortionists' only concern. There were also outright swindlers *pretending* to be reporters to blackmail them. Harry Haskins, a con artist, was arrested in September 1871 after trying to blackmail Madame Restell and her husband. Luckily, she seemed to suspect he was not a reporter, but she still paid him off for $25. When Haskins tried the same ruse on Charles, he found the man uncharacteristically a bit braver than his wife, for Charles refused to give him anything and "defied all the newspapers combined to inure his business."[26] And he didn't only try to extort abortionists like Madame Restell and her husband. Haskins had once conned the president of the United States out of $50 by pretending to be a police officer and claiming he had brought two burglars to justice. It's unclear why the president would give him $50—maybe just because he thought he was a cool guy?—but either Haskins was a truly excellent con artist or Ulysses S. Grant was overly generous.

But cons were far from the only concern occupying Madame Restell's mind at the time. Public sentiment against abortion, spurred on by newspapers, was growing, along with the conviction that *something must be done* about it. As far away as Galveston, Texas, it was reported that in New York City people and the press were "demanding a general cleaning out of [abortionist] establishments by the police. It is believed the indignation of the public will result in securing some action in this direction." The American Medical Association did all it could to stoke this frenzy, promising to stamp out from the medical profession those (often female) "monsters of iniquity" who were "as hideous a view of moral deformity as the evil spirit could present."[27]

With antiabortion arguments in full swing, no one proposed regulating abortion—a highly in-demand service—in order to reduce mortality and ensure that those performing the procedure were properly trained. This could have gone a long way in preventing tragedies like the untimely death of Alice Bowlsby. Outside the medical profession, some people suggested reducing the number of abortions by treating unwed mothers better, noting, "Of course we can save the lives of a great many illegitimate children by destroying the sense of shame which attaches to the bearing of an illegitimate child." Yes! Great idea. But then, they were worried that dignifying single mothers might create a world without proper shame, and "whether the result will be worth the price we must pay for it is a question which the advanced reformers have not stopped to consider. Mrs. Woodhull [a stockbroker, a newspaper editor, and the first woman to run for president] believes she could prevent infanticide by abolishing marriage."[28]

That wasn't true, though she did advocate for free love and believe in "an inalienable, constitutional and natural right to love whom I may, to love as long or as short a period as I can....And I have the further right to demand a free and unrestricted exercise of that right."[29] As a result of these prescient words, which seemed to anticipate both the sexual revolution and the battle for LGBTQ rights, her contemporaries labeled her "Mrs. Satan."

Victoria Woodhull and Madame Restell were sometimes linked in the press, largely because they were two women who did not feel that a woman's ambition needed to begin and end with motherhood (or, in the estimation of people at the time, were both demons sent straight from hell). When it was announced that Woodhull intended to run for president, a newspaper angrily declared, "The next step to be taken is to nominate Madame Restell the abortionist for Vice-President. She is a millionaire, and of course this covers all imperfections in an *enlightened* age like this."[30] They didn't actually have *that* much in common when it came to their thoughts on reproductive rights. Woodhull was opposed to abortion unless it saved the life of the mother. Still, she was open to discussion about abortion, and in December 1871, she wrote that "the columns of the *Weekly* [Woodhull's newspaper] are open to the communications of even a Madame Restell to advocate the beneficence of her institution, of which so many of my self-constituted judges have occasion to make use, and of which, if they were to tell the truth, as they felt it, they would be obliged to say it has been a blessing to them."[31]

Madame Restell, perhaps to her detriment, never took Woodhull up on her offer.

In light of the terrifying prospect that some women might retain their dignity after having children out of wedlock, people decided it would probably be better to err on the side of shaming women more rather than less. "It is probable that American mothers have no very distinct idea of the enormity of the crime which they commit in the slaughter of unborn infants, and, clinging to old fallacies about the period when life begins, do not understand that they are guilty of murder whenever, at any stage of pregnancy, they rid themselves of the sacred burden which heaven has laid upon the sex," declared the *New-York Tribune.* "Is there no voice to tell them of the awful guilt they are laying upon their souls, and the terrible consequences they are bringing upon the country!"[32]

Ah, yes. The consequences they were bringing upon the country by not having enough white Protestant babies. Historically, people who have treated minorities abominably have hated the idea of becoming a minority themselves. There was much emphasis on the fact that white women having abortions were undermining America as a whole, as "the Anglo-American race is actually dying out."[33] A pastor explained that abortion was evil precisely *because* it was causing "race deterioration in America."[34]

There was also a notion that abortion was prevalent because American culture wasn't European enough (by which people meant white and rich European and not, for instance, Irish). A Washington, DC, journal claimed that "the fount and origin of the crime [is] the freedom of intercourse between the sexes which distinguishes in such a marked manner the social laws of America from those of Europe." If only this man had picked up a copy of *Les Liaisons Dangereuses,* which would have reminded him that the French—famous Europeans!— were so perennially associated with extramarital sex that Madame Restell pretended to be a French person so as to lend herself and her business a sophisticated frisson. The *New-York Tribune* at least refuted this by pointing out that in Europe, "sins against the marriage law are most common."[35]

Taking to the law, some thought the best way to "drive all the Rosenzweigs out of existence" was by amending the Constitution itself, creating legislation that would force women to bear their pregnancies to term.[36] By 1872, the New York Legislature had passed a law by which abortionists found guilty of practicing such procedures could be punished by up to twenty years in jail—and people still did not feel that went far enough.

Thus began an era where, as the judge in Rosenzweig's case stated, "the authorities, one and all, shall put forth every effort and shall strain every nerve, until these professional abortionists, these traffickers in human life, shall be exterminated."[37]

Charles seemed genuinely shocked by the vehemence of the press. In response to the criticism of his wife's (and his) profession, he wrote frenzied letters to the *New York Times* claiming that the publishers had "bitter, malignant, unrelenting and the most venomous and mean enemies.... [T]he slightest thread put into their hands to injure you would be seized with greedy avidity.... Everyone has a right to defend himself or herself from virulent, false and malicious attacks with such weapons as they are driven to use."[38] He was theoretically ready to release the names of those who had patronized his services, as well as those provided by his wife, but he'd never run the risk of doing so when it would destroy their business. Discretion and patient confidentiality in their line of work were vital. As such, the editors dared him to go ahead. He stayed mum. At a time when more savvy abortionists were trying to avoid attention, Charles's instinct to publicly air his grievance was misplaced. The fact that this letter came from Charles rather than Madame Restell—who had historically loved sharing her sentiments in print—suggests that she understood the severity of people's feelings better than he did.

As for the influential friends Restell might have imagined could protect her, they were long gone. Tweed and virtually all his cronies were swept out of power in November 1871 after the *New York Times* ran a meticulously researched exposé on corruption. Tweed died in jail after stealing millions of dollars from New York taxpayers, without ever having danced in Madame Restell's opulent ballroom. Madame Restell's old pal "Prince Hal" Genet, too, ended his life as a scandalous figure. He was arrested in 1873 for, among other financial offenses, stealing materials intended for the Harlem Court House to help build his mansion. He was to appear on trial for two indictments of grand larceny, but "visions of a zebra uniform and hard labor arose before his mind and he fairly wilted."[39] He escaped by racing across his house's rooftop and leaping into a waiting carriage, fleeing the country for Europe.

Any help these men could have offered was now a thing of the past.

Reformers, who could not be bribed by Madame Restell's customary gold watches, were now in charge, and they were eager to turn the city into something much tidier and more puritan.

And the best known among them would be Madame Restell's greatest nemesis, Anthony Comstock.

CHAPTER TWENTY-TWO

ANTHONY COMSTOCK'S FAITH HAD NOT BEEN SHAKEN BY THE
Civil War or the decadent delights of New York City. He very
much believed in both Satan and God, and wanted to purify the earth
of sinful temptation. The former head of the New York Society for
the Suppression of Vice is described nowadays as a "moral hysteric."[1]
However, in his time, and certainly in his own mind, he was regarded
as a crusader for virtue—in his own words, "a weeder in the garden
of the Lord."[2] He wished to curb the publication of any material that
could possibly be regarded as obscene, which included information
for women on how to exert reproductive control over their bodies.
Women like Madame Restell, who not only shared birth control information with women one on one but also doled it out in the press, had
to be brought to justice.

These post-Rosenzweig years would belong to him.

Anthony Comstock came from a devout background. Born in New
Canaan, Connecticut, in 1844, he grew up on a farm where his father
read the Bible to the family daily and promoted a deeply conservative
worldview. Women, in Anthony Comstock's estimation, should be religious, obedient to their husbands, and willing to bear and rear children without complaint, no matter their circumstances. They should,
in short, take after his own mother. Polly Comstock imparted a fiercely
religious upbringing, full of Bible stories with an emphasis on refusing sensual temptation. A later opponent of Comstock's, who dealt in
contraceptive syringes, once quipped, "If Comstock's mother had had
a syringe and known how to use it, what a world of woe it would have
saved us!"—Anthony might never have been born, and that would have
been *great*.[3] Sick burn. But in a bit of sad irony, Comstock's mother had

actually died hemorrhaging after bearing her tenth child. Anthony was only ten years old, and thereafter he felt adrift and alone, bereft of "the loveliest mother that ever lived."[4] Had she been given access to reproductive control, she might have lived past Anthony's tenth year, and he might have grown up with a sunnier worldview.

By the time he was a teenager, Anthony had discovered masturbation. Like most human beings, he enjoyed it, for which he felt profound guilt, declaring, "I deplore my sinful, weak nature so much."[5] This was not without cause. At the time, it was believed that masturbation led to insanity, illness, and—worst of all—hairy palms. But when most people heard that (false) information, they either decided to stop masturbating or continue masturbating, warnings be damned. Anthony Comstock, however, would take the unusual course of attempting to create a world where there would be nothing left that tempted him to masturbate. Later in his life, a professor at a southern college wrote to Comstock that he estimated that "ninety percent of our young men are victims of self-abuse [masturbators]." Comstock did not consider this reassuring. Readers today might think if 90 percent of people do something, it is, at least, not freakish. Comstock felt otherwise. He thought the statistic meant that "lives that might shine as stars in the firmament are shrouded with a veil of darkness, with horrors to the victim's mind which no pen can describe." Distressed, he mused, "Is not this awful curse to the young enough to command a remedy?"[6]

It's unclear what exactly Comstock was thinking about when he masturbated. Most of the erotic prints of the era consist of bejeweled naked women lying on sofas. They don't really constitute "a horror that no pen can describe," a description that feels more applicable to, for instance, Cthulhu.

His preoccupation with sin did not endear Comstock to young men his age. Nor did the fact that, during his time as a soldier in the Civil War, he chose not to drink his whiskey ration. Rather than pass it to a soldier who might enjoy it, he dumped it on the ground while lecturing his compatriots about the evils of drink. They responded by trashing his bunk—literally filling it with their garbage. "Seems to be a feeling of hatred [towards me] among some of the boys," Anthony noted in his diary. After his return from the war, a family friend suggested he go to New York City and make a name for himself there. He replied that would be difficult as he had "no money and no friends."[7]

But that was about to change.

Comstock moved to New York and by 1868 had obtained work as a dry-goods clerk at a shop on Warren Street. There, a fellow clerk showed him an obscene book, claiming it had given him an STI. There is much scholarly debate about whether this clerk was poorly informed and genuinely believed that he contracted an STI from reading a dirty book, or was trying to cover up his visits to prostitutes. No one has suggested that the fellow might have been playing a joke on Anthony, which, considering how his peers had historically treated him, seems like a fair possibility. Anthony did not see any joke. Indeed, he was horrified, so much so that he tracked down the publisher, Charles Conroy, who was illegally selling other, similar books from his shop. The Obscene Literature Bill of 1868 forbade the production of such works, but this ruling was not frequently enforced. Anthony bought a book, submitted it to the police, and led them back to the store to arrest Conroy. Afterward, "newspapers picked up the story of the valiant dry goods salesman." When a reporter suggested that Comstock might want to check out another street where pornography was often sold, he bought more pornography and had *those* purveyors arrested. Once again, the deeds of this abject narc merited "glowing coverage."[8]

Comstock proceeded to call upon the police with great enthusiasm, reporting numerous figures for crimes either real or imagined. In 1870, he reported two men for "attempted burglary," although one of the men in question explained that he was using a key to enter the home of a girl he had a date with; by Comstock's estimation, that was likely as bad as burglary, if not worse.[9] In 1871, Comstock charged a saloon keeper with "keeping open and retailing beer and liquor on the Sabbath" (surprising none of his army buddies, Comstock had been a member of the "Sons of Temperance" organization since 1868).[10] Throughout the following year, he would attempt to jail about twenty men, including a producer of condoms, the owner of a book printing establishment, and the owners of a large bindery.

Many considered Comstock to be an intolerable busybody. Writers for the *Brooklyn Daily Eagle* claimed in 1872 that they never referred to him: "for same reason we don't refer to last year's flies—he is entirely unimportant."[11] But, far more commonly, he was praised for "pursuing...criminals like a relentless fate" and "bringing...harpies to justice."[12] As far away as Cincinnati, Comstock was praised as "a young Hercules, doing battle with the many headed monster lasciviousness, whose slimy folds envelop society in every direction."[13]

For a man who, not so long ago, had had his bed trashed by his peers for his nebbish worldview, being considered a Hercules was a thrilling reversal. Finally, he was garnering his long-awaited praise from the public. Ministers offered accolades, and reporters in 1872 assured him—this man who had only a few years prior considered himself to have no friends—that he was "not now alone, nor unsupported by those who [would] gladly share in the burden of [his] war."[14] Incentivized, Comstock was determined to rid the world of sin.

But while Comstock now had friends, or at least admirers, he did not have much money to back up his efforts. He had journeyed to New York with only five dollars in his pocket, and he continued to spend much of his salary buying pornographic products that he would then use to expose criminality. While this is, in many ways, hilarious, it was also a hindrance. When Comstock tried to have one surgeon arrested for publishing explicit books, the surgeon committed suicide. He asked the surgeon's widow for the plates her late husband had used to print the books so he could destroy them. The grieving widow in turn demanded $650, which Anthony did not have. For the past year, he'd been laboring "at his own cost, in seizing obscene literature and bringing those engaged in the trade to trial and penitentiary."[15] Constant vigilantism isn't cheap.

And so, Comstock wrote to the YMCA for help. Comstock had been a member of the YMCA since his move to New York. Believing that men were more susceptible to vice in urban areas, the organization was formed to offer a sanctuary to religious young men who did not want to give in to these temptations. This respite was accompanied with more than a soupçon of misogyny directed toward modern, urban women. A pamphlet published in 1865 lamented that, in the country, "female society uses its power to cheer, refine and elevate, seldom to debase and ruin."[16] Not so in the city, where young men could easily engage the services of a prostitute or simply have an affair with a willing woman. Anthony could hardly have agreed more that this was a most unfortunate turn of events.

When Morris Jesup, the president of the YMCA, and Comstock met, they were almost immediately simpatico. Jesup would later recall that he made up his mind that "what little I could do to aid in fighting this sin, I would do that."[17] He not only agreed to help Comstock financially but made him the secretary of the YMCA's recently formed New York Society for the Suppression of Vice. This elite committee was supported by Jesup and by other extremely prosperous men, including the financier John Pierpont Morgan, Samuel Colgate (who founded the toothpaste company), and the publisher Alfred S. Barnes. These men vowed to offer the "heartiest support and cheer to the poor young man who started the conflict against the corruptors of our youth."[18]

The benefits of supporting Comstock and the YMCA for men like Barnes were cynically obvious. If you are a successful publisher, it is in your best interest to run other publishers out of business. If you can do it while claiming it's out of concern for the youth, so much the better. For other businessmen, such as Morgan and Colgate, the YMCA and its committees seemed capable of improving the behavior of their massive workforces.

By 1873, Comstock was in Washington, attempting to convince legislators to pass the the Act for the Suppression of Trade in, and Circulation of, Obscene Literature and Articles of Immoral Use. This would later come to be known as the "Comstock Act" which banned sending "obscene, lewd, or lascivious" publications through the mail. Unlike past laws, this one considered any information about contraception or abortion, as well as instruments or pills that might prevent or eliminate a pregnancy, to be "obscene."[19]

Essentially, not only would it forbid distributing birth control or performing abortions, it would also forbid even talking about them.

Lest you think this legal effort might distract from his prurient concerns, during his time in Washington Comstock attended a reception at the White House where the women wore what he considered low-cut dresses. This prompted him to rage, "How can we respect them? They disgrace our land but consider themselves ladies." Afterward he found he passed a difficult night in a hotel bed where he was "tempted to sin against God."[20] Have no doubt, Comstock would have restricted female attire to shapeless robes if he had found a way to do so legally.

After being debated for less than a day, the Comstock Act passed at 2:00 a.m. on March 3, 1873, and Comstock was appointed a special agent in the United States Post Office, charged with enforcing the law by examining the mail. "In a special charter," as the historian Elizabeth

Hovey has noted, "the New York state legislature granted to the NYSSV [New York Society for the Suppression of Vice] the assistance of all police organizations in the state in order to 'suppress the trade' in all obscene matters."[21] Half of all the fines collected would go straight to the NYSSV. Comstock could now direct a significant segment of the police to do his bidding rather than merely appealing to them for help. By the following year, he had personally arrested fifty-five people who had distributed (in his estimation) obscene materials through the mail. He also sustained a knife to the face by one pornographer who felt *very* strongly about freedom of speech. Comstock loved this scar, "a gash from the temple to the chin."[22] What better proof that he was a Herculean warrior and no longer the feeble young man who'd once been so despised?

If you were wondering whether Anthony Comstock was still ridiculed for being a dweeb who found everything terrifying in its lewdness, the answer is yes, of course he was. The humor magazine *Puck* published one of the better-known cartoons about him, featuring a woman exclaiming, "O, dear me, what shall I do? My shoestring has come untied, and there's that dreadful Anthony Comstock just behind me!"[23] A particularly cheeky piece by Robert Minor depicts Comstock dragging a woman before a judge and exclaiming, "Your honor, this woman gave birth to a naked child!"[24]

The fact that he was a perpetual joke in sophisticated circles did not make Comstock less terrifying in his influence. The mockery of male intellectuals and artists was nothing compared to the support he gained, financial and otherwise, from people who longed for a more religiously conservative version of the United States. He was dangerous in the manner of all fanatics who believe in blotting out everything that "corrupts the minds and morals of our women and children" without ever consulting women, children, or anyone else whose lives might be altered by their policies.[25]

Chapter Twenty-Three

A FTER THE PASSAGE OF THE COMSTOCK ACT, MADAME REST-
ell's practice was still operational, but she had paid special
attention to the new laws, and was trying, as much as was possible for
her, to be discreet. Her newspaper advertisements diminished substantially. Where once she wrote paragraphs about the effects of bearing
too many children, by 1874 her new wording in the *Herald* stated only
her address and that she had been a "physician since 1840."[1] Uncon-
vinced by her uncharacteristic demureness, some in the press started
suggesting that she be thrown into a French jail.

Meanwhile, the land she owned next to her home, which she had
purchased over a decade earlier in her attempt to outdo Archbishop
John Joseph Hughes, remained largely empty.

These lots were not impossible to sell. In 1871, the Lohmans sold
off one lot at what is now 3 East Fifty-Second Street to Oliver H. P.
Archer. Mr. Archer was a millionaire, largely thanks to his work with
the Erie Railroad Company and his real estate holdings. He likely
knew Madame Restell socially. But new money aside, and much as he
might have enjoyed her company, he was not going to live next to the
Lohmans at a time when public vehemence against abortionists had
reached a fever pitch. Instead, he used the lot to build a three-story
stable. The upper floors were occupied by his coachman and "ostler"
(the horse handler). He wasn't the only one to go in that direction; in
fact, "by 1880 the block was dominated by stables."[2]

This trend frustrated Madame Restell, and not only because it
meant she had new competition for the best stable. She could make
more money if people were building houses upon the land she was

selling. However, it was simply unthinkable for people who could afford to build a brand-new mansion to have Madame Restell as a neighbor. For, as much as notable men might have smoked cigars in her house, "good women, when they passed her residence, were wont to turn their faces away that they might not see it."[3]

And so, in 1875, Madame Restell came up with a revolutionary idea to make use of the empty lots.

She would construct an apartment building.

In spite of the opprobrium that surrounded her, papers noted that "her business prospered so well she was now putting up a French flat building adjoining her residence."[4]

A "French flat" appears to be a pretentious name for an apartment building, but this wasn't a dig at Restell's aspirations. At the time, the term "apartment building" simply wasn't in use yet. Upscale apartment buildings barely existed in the 1870s, even in New York City. Of course, there were tenement buildings downtown, where families of immigrants crammed into underheated rooms, but that wasn't the kind of residence Madame Restell had in mind. She wanted to expand her horizons (and perhaps improve upon her reputation) by introducing a French concept (dating back to the seventeenth century) to the Big Apple in the most ostentatious way possible.

The first apartment building in New York City is thought to have been the Stuyvesant, which was built on Eighteenth Street and Irving in 1870; Madame Restell's apartment complex, constructed in 1875, is widely considered to have been the second. She planned to outdo the Stuyvesant in terms of luxuries and style, which wasn't necessarily an unsurmountable undertaking, as the Stuyvesant had been criticized for looking "rambling and incoherent," and her lot was in the more stylish neighborhood.[5] What would prove more challenging was that Madame Restell was intent upon managing this project by herself, separate even from her husband.

Originally, Charles was the one who had taken out a mortgage for the lots on Fifth Avenue. Now, Madame Restell was eager to ensure that she alone, not her husband, had claim to the apartment building. So, without his knowledge, she bought out the mortgage. She was determined to build the flats entirely with her own money, and, in doing so, she "advanced $147,000 in cash, and took out a mortgage in her own name in that amount."[6]

Her refinancing put something of a strain on her relationship with Charles. They were known to be on contentious terms by that point in their marriage over financial disputes much like this one.

Restell and her husband now lived in separate apartments and were not as close as they might have been. Still, their granddaughter would later recall that she "had never seen any exhibition of unhappiness between [Restell and] Dr. Lohman," so their cooled ardor to one another didn't have overly obvious negative impacts on their family dynamic.[7]

Madame Restell's focus was now on the apartment building, which she would call the Osbourne.

The name was a popular one for buildings during this period. While it's a common English name, it had nothing to do with Restell's background. Most likely, it was intended to bring to mind Osbourne House, Queen Victoria's favorite residence, which was considered the height of fashion. It would be a bit like living in an apartment building called the Buckingham or the Palace today.

Attempting to make the building fit for New York royalty, she retained the services of Duggin and Crossman, an architectural firm. Charles Duggin and James Crossman were generally considered to be "the great leaders of fashion in house building...architects, as they prefer to be styled—really artist builders."[8] Their work could be seen all along Fifth Avenue and the streets up in the Fifties; Duggin, in particular, had designed a house on almost every block. Those buildings may have been artful and ornate, but they were, in most regards, still very traditional brownstones in terms of the actual structure. However, they offered some quirky details, such as more elaborate window moldings or unusual quoins, notable traits that helped their work stand out just enough to be stylish without ever becoming so unique as to seem "incoherent." In hiring Duggin and Crossman, Madame Restell showed that she was in tune with the latest fashions and trends, but she was also ensuring that the apartment she was building would look just like the other houses on the street. Her main goal was to rent out apartments to people who were tight on funds, but worried that others might consider them poor or lower class if they lived in an apartment. A casual passerby could easily assume that any tenant walking in the front doors owned the whole house.

Madame Restell also placed pots of flowers leading up to the building. At a time when one of the downsides of apartment buildings was that there were no yards or gardens, this thoughtfully placed greenery must have seemed a homey and comforting touch.

The building's interior was as charming as the exterior. Each of the first five floors of the six-story building housed two apartments. The sixth floor was far from being a penthouse—it contained the "washroom, ironing-room and drying closets…and the extra rooms suitable for servants or storage, as required."[9] This arrangement was common, a design choice that explains why, today, those who buy the highest floor in an old New York building, sight unseen, may be disappointed. In the 1870s, elevators were still largely unreliable, and no one wanted to be stranded on the very top floor. As such, the top floor could be dark and cramped, reserved for activities such as drying clothing, as there would be no outside line to hang out the wash.

Madame Restell knew the elevator issue, and those she installed at the Osbourne—one for baggage and one for passengers—were of the highest quality she could find. The elevators also made the building much more appealing than the Stuyvesant, where people had to walk up stairs to reach their apartments. The passenger elevator at the Osbourne was kept "in constant motion from an early hour in the morning until a late hour at night."[10] Still, in keeping with general skepticism regarding the elevator's reliability, merited or not, rent was more expensive on the first floors of the Osbourne, starting out at $210 per month, than on the upper floors, where it dwindled down to $150.[11] This would mean a range from $5,400 to $3,800 today, so the rent was still substantial, especially during a time when—within a decade—you could find a decent apartment in New York for $400 to $1,000 a year.

Justifying the high price, the *Journal of Carpentry and Building* explained, in an article so fawning in its admiration of the Osbourne that it's surprising Restell did not write it herself, that rent was higher at the Osbourne because it was "very stylish."[12] Buyers, it added, received a great deal for their money. Each apartment had nine rooms, without taking into account the bathroom, the butler's pantry, and the larder. The first two rooms—a library and a parlor—could have the adjoining doors opened to allow for a larger space for entertaining. Each of the three bedrooms contained a closet, out of an assumption that any buyers would have an impressive wardrobe. Bewilderingly to modern sensibilities, the apartments only contained one small (6 by 9.6 feet) bathroom for the entire unit, and the dining room separated it from one of the bedrooms, meaning that tenants would have to sprint through a room full of chairs should they need the toilet in the middle of the night. But then, New York City's public sewer system had only been constructed in 1849. Older people who moved into the Osbourne might have grown up using a chamber pot or an outhouse. So for them, even one bathroom with indoor plumbing could seem luxurious.

The Osbourne employed a janitor, who would service the building and take on various duties. Such tasks might include making small repairs, collecting packages, and providing all the apartments with coal, which, at least at the Osbourne, was kept in the basement. He was also in charge of taking out the garbage and ashes, though buildings at the time were generally equipped with an ash chute, where those from a fireplace or kitchen could be dumped. And the janitor wasn't the only serviceman on the grounds; a man in a uniform—who would come to be known as a doorman—would always be there at the entrance, waiting to open the door for visitors. These men were employed by Madame Restell herself, not the individual families, which was seen as one of the perks of living in an apartment. In the years to come, as apartment buildings became more common, reporters would credit their popularity to, among other things, the difficulty of finding good help. Young people especially were less likely to hire a household staff, as they were said to prefer to "occupy private apartments and are supplied outside by caterers with their food."[13]

By 1880, four years after the Osbourne opened its doors, other apartment buildings boasted "a restaurant upon the lower floor, with a general dining-room attached, to which families may repair for their meals, or from which meals may be ordered served in the rooms."[14] In imagining a world where families wouldn't have a live-in chef, builders of apartments began to anticipate the growing independence fostered by the twentieth century, when city dwellers would be ordering take-out, going out for a quick bite, or even cooking for themselves at home.

The Osbourne's architects did assume that there would still be a servant or two in each household, whether or not they would be cooking. Each unit correspondingly contained two additional smaller bedrooms next to the kitchen. The position of the kitchen was considered especially clever, as it was "placed so that it is impossible for the fumes from cooking to reach those portions of the building occupied by the families, a great desideratum in apartment houses."[15] It's unfortunate that this consideration has been entirely forgotten by twenty-first-century designers of open floor plans, who apparently think that everyone in a living space wants to marinate in the smell of cooked fish, not merely through dinner, but for the entire evening and next day.

The servants' rooms were located next to a back stairway, which allowed servants to run errands without disturbing the family at the front of the apartment. In traditional Madame Restell style, these rooms were also larger than expected—9 by 11 feet and 9 by 9.5 feet, as compared to the more traditional 6 by 10 feet. Do the extra square feet matter? They do if you are having trouble finding good help; in that case, more spacious accommodations were a plus.

Apartment living appealed to a generation of young people who had not migrated to New York City but grown up within it. These natives were far too accustomed to the city to ever consider living on a farm or traveling west. And as they started making money from their jobs, or received their inheritances, they were well enough off to afford an apartment in a stylish part of the city, but not well enough off to purchase a whole house there. As they were intimately familiar with the city, they'd rather live in a smaller place in a chic part of town than buy a house in a dowdier neighborhood. "The purely family life," the *Real Estate Record* quipped, "is voted a bore. Our young men and young women wish to see and be seen, and society means not a few choice friends but many people of kindred tastes and habits."[16] For this ambitious and social set of young people, apartment living was perfect.

The *Real Estate Record* suspected, in 1879, that apartments would stop being so popular when better public transit opened access to more land and allowed people to travel more easily to and from work. Then, the *Record* mused, it would be curious to see if "all Americans would prefer their own home, vine and fig tree to living in a huge establishment."[17] In other words, it anticipated the rise of suburbs.

In building the Osborne, Madame Restell showed remarkable prescience, entering the blossoming real estate market at the very beginning of what would become a massive trend. Within four years, the *Real Estate Record* noted, the number of "French flats" in New York was now "overdone,"[18] and it hoped the craze for them was nearing an end. Unfortunately for the *Record*, the rest of New York was decidedly not on the same page.

Not only did Madame Restell anticipate the popularity of apartment living, she had also crafted a superb building. By 1880, the *Journal of Carpentry and Building* was referring to the Osbourne as "one of the most stylish and best-appointed apartment houses in the city" and "the extreme of elegance and comfort."[19] Madame Restell was beyond thrilled. Reporters were quick to note, "The Osbourne as it was named was soon filled." They weren't entirely inclined to credit Madame Restell for her architect's choice of sensible layouts and amenities and instead attributed its appeal as being solely due to the fact that "the neighborhood was very fashionable, and the tenants tried to ignore the proximity of the unsavory madame." Madame Restell had, rightly, "estimated that a number of genteel families would live where a single family would not; they would think that by dividing the moral responsibility it would cease to affect any of them."[20] The glamour would only last so long. Madame Restell would have to eventually lower rents.

Still, Madame Restell's early tenants included some very interesting people. The most notable was George Ripley, the utopian socialist who in 1841 had founded the secular commune Brook Farm, a community seemingly at odds with his eventual choice to live in an apartment in a bustling city. The Farm, in rural Massachusetts, allowed each member, male and female, to do work of their choosing and share the farm's profits equally, in the hope that this would leave them ample time to pursue creative endeavors. Brook Farm attracted some well-known members, including the novelist Nathaniel Hawthorne. The novelist later wrote about a thinly fictionalized version of Brook Farm in *The Blithedale Romance*, where the protagonist found, among other things, that if you spend all day working on a farm, you are far too tired to write poetry at night. When he left the commune, Hawthorne rejoiced that his soul was no longer "buried beneath a dung heap."[21] Brook Farm came to an end in 1847 after one of its buildings caught fire and the commune was rendered bankrupt.

Maybe that's why living in an apartment later seemed preferable to Ripley.

Despite Madame Restell's significant efforts to establish the Osbourne as her own project, Charles received credit for the building after their deaths. The *Hartford Courant* lauded his foresight for building the apartment building, and in doing so, proving himself to be "one of the shrewdest operators in New York," and one who "never made a losing speculation in real estate."[22] No matter how ardently Madame Restell had tried to make the Osbourne her triumphant second act, her husband lapped up the accolades. In an age when women could barely own property, what—the public imagined—could women possibly know about real estate? Women were supposed to be decorating and tidying homes, not investing in them.

The difficulty for a woman to successfully break into a new industry and gain acclaim for her accomplishments—even for a woman as wealthy as Madame Restell—also underscores how much was being lost to women as men took control of the obstetric profession during these decades. The women who had made their living, and their fortunes, as midwives could not simply "go out and get a new career" as the laws and restrictions tightened around them. Even if one succeeded brilliantly in a new field, the general public would not applaud or even acknowledge it.

The apartment era might have harkened a new age in living accommodations, but not new attitudes about the roles of men and women in society.

Chapter Twenty-Four

I T IS DIFFICULT TO BEGRUDGE CHARLES LOHMAN THE CREDIT
for being a real estate genius when he had such a brief time left
to enjoy the acclaim. By January 1876, he was dead. Madame Restell
was, somehow predictably, accused by the public of murdering him.
Or, more specifically, poisoning him.

Granted, the two hadn't exactly been on the best terms. Shortly
before his death she'd told friends that she was "living unhappily with
her husband."[1] After their falling out over the Osbourne, she was
worried about keeping her government bonds separate from their
joint finances. But after three decades of partnership, the idea that
Madame Restell was responsible for her husband's death still seemed
a bit far-fetched.

The "evidence" for this accusation came from a young man who
had visited Charles in his sickbed, via a Chicago newspaper, the *Inter
Ocean*:

> The doctor lay on his bed but did not seem to be particularly ill. He
> had been unwell for some time past, but no grave apprehensions
> as to the result were entertained by anybody who knew of his con-
> dition. This young man had been visiting him every day. On this
> occasion Dr. Lohman raised himself in bed and said, "Hand me
> that medicine bottle from the bureau, will you!" The visitor looked
> round and, seeing no bottle, replied, "What bottle? There is none
> here." "Why, it was there a few minutes ago," the invalid exclaimed.
> "Who could have taken it?" In a fit of angry impatience, he rang the
> bell. Mme. Restell appeared in answer to the summons, holding a
> medicine bottle in her hand, and looking, this eye-witness states,

with emphatic particularity, strangely excited. "What the devil did you take my medicine away for?" he exclaimed impetuously. "Well, I thought it was getting empty," she replied. "And I had better replenish it." "Why it was more than half full before, it didn't need any replenishing at all." She only replied, "Well, I thought I had better fill it up," and with that she deposited the bottle which was now quite full on the bureau. That very night, Lohman died, though when the visitor left him, late in the afternoon, he seemed as well as usual, and by no means appeared as though he was about to die.[2]

The report essentially insinuated that Madame Restell slipped her husband poison. There are a few reasons this accusation was absurd. One was that she would have no reason to want to do so, especially in the midst of a career where, to our knowledge, she had never poisoned *anyone*, despite there being people it would absolutely have benefited her to poison. Quite frankly, if she'd been inclined to poison a family member, it wouldn't have been the man who had helped her raise her daughter and grandchildren, it would have been her despised son-in-law. Another reason was that if she was going to poison anyone, she'd most likely be clever enough not to do it in front of another person.

Nonetheless, given the money that Madame Restell was set to inherit in the event of her husband's passing, this death—and a potential poisoning—was considered a serious matter. Some citizens wished to bring the rumor before the state attorney general, hoping that he would investigate further, but Madame and Charles's grandchildren, Carrie and Charles, took a break from riding their "two superb turnouts through the park" to discuss the matter with the attorney general and quickly shut it down.[3]

Dr. Jones, the physician who had been treating Charles for the last six months of his life, testified that Charles died of cystitis that had probably led to kidney or renal failure. His prostate gland was enlarged, he'd been ill for months, and during that time he had undergone, by the doctor's recollection, "two or three operations." When autopsied, "there was no feature in his illness or his death which could in the slightest degree suggest the possibility of his having died from causes other than those [above] mentioned."[4]

As Charles was a lifelong atheist, there were no last rites performed over his deathbed, and he was buried without ceremony. His corpse was interred at night so as not to attract attention. It was said that Charles's corpse had been accompanied to the Tarrytown cemetery only by Joseph Trow, Madame Restell's brother, who had been Charles's "friend while living."[5] However, while Charles may have spurned ceremony, Madame Restell was sufficiently sentimental to see to it that he was buried next to her two departed grandchildren.

The papers insisted that these steps were taken because she was trying to keep people from exhuming the body to reveal *poison*. The *Chicago Inter Ocean* reported that it had been heard on "good authority" that Charles had relatives back in Eastern Europe, so his money might go to them rather than Madame Restell. If they existed, they never came forward.[6]

If there is any sadness in this, it is that Charles died after a mostly supportive life spent largely in the background of his successful spouse. But then, that is the kind of life that history has told countless women they are lucky to experience.

Meanwhile, her husband was not the only man leaving her life. Her brother, Joseph Trow, had long been Charles's devoted friend and business partner, and he'd spent most of his life churning out the "preventative powders" they sold. However, Joseph was no longer on good terms with his sister. In 1873, he had gotten married, and, "as Madame Restell did not like the lady of his choice, they quarreled and broke up their business arrangements."[7] She informed her friend G. P. Howe that "there was no necessity for him to marry, he will always be provided for here."[8] Madame Restell did not seem to like *anyone's* choice of spouse, be it her daughter's or her brother's. Yet, in what feels like a moment of real pettiness, Joseph Trow took on the name Dr. Mauriceau after Charles's death and began advertising his wares under it. Madame Restell responded by taking out ads describing herself as Dr. Mauriceau's widow. She ceased to pay Trow income from some bonds that he claimed she had given him "in reward for thirty years of faithful service."[9] She didn't deny that he'd been assisting her for thirty years, but she did, absolutely, refuse to give him any more money.

Now sixty-four, Madame Restell's trusted circle was quickly tightening. Her husband and helpmeet was dead, and she was estranged from the man who was not only her brother, but one of her most devoted assistants. She was not close to her daughter, nor to her son-in-law. Whatever friends she had were largely run away by press so brutal that it supposed she was capable of mariticide. With the exception of her grandchildren, who were fiercely loyal to her, she was without allies or accomplices.

This situation could not have come at a worse time for her as the press was bleating that "such beings as Restell are ministers of the gospel of Satan, tempters of the weak and erring, incarnate fiends doing the work of the Destroyer."[10]

Such descriptions couldn't fail to catch the attention of Anthony Comstock.

CHAPTER TWENTY-FIVE

B Y 1877, ANTHONY COMSTOCK HAD MADE GREAT HEADWAY IN stopping the publication and distribution of pornography in New York. The New York Society for the Suppression of Vice even became concerned that there wasn't much they could do to make front-page news, which they needed to convince their backers to pay the society's $10,000 annual budget.[1]

That was precisely the time when Madame Restell entered Comstock's orbit.

Here was a woman Comstock unequivocally despised. He regarded her as a "murderess" who destroyed "safeguards set by God and nature." He felt that any woman riding by her mansion, "unless lost to all self-respect, must shudder as she passes this monument of infamy." He also noted that the mansion had a long line of carriages outside it. "For years," he claimed, "this iniquitous business was winked at by the police while hundreds of thousands of dollars were garnered by an ignorant woman."[2]

Now that he had the law on his side, it was time to pursue Madame Restell. Meanwhile, his target sat in her mansion, as alone as she had been since she had come to America.

And so—Anthony Comstock and Madame Restell came to meet when he knocked on her doorstep that frigid night in the winter of 1878, disingenuously inquiring if Madame Restell lived at that address and if she might be able to help him. The approach he took, preying on her sympathy and acting as so many men must have, as though they were shaking with fear regarding their visit, was far more effective than the boisterous tone adopted by undercover reporters who confidently burst into abortionists' offices.

The most curious aspect of the accounts is that Madame Restell did not recognize the infamous Anthony Comstock at first. She was an avid reader of New York's newspapers, and Anthony Comstock was in all of them. He had a hugely distinctive scar. That said, Restell might well have thought that Anthony Comstock had earnestly come to her for help. He wouldn't be the first moralist who changed his opinion on abortion when someone he knew needed one. And if he had, who knew what favors she could extract from him later? In retrospect, it's a shame her granddaughter Carrie was not there to advise her.

When Comstock returned on February 11 with the police, Madame Restell did her best to remain calm. She would not give this nebbish man the satisfaction of feeling that he'd gotten the best of her. Besides, if she seemed frightened, that would frighten the patients in her house, and they were already so nervous that they were covering their faces under veils before arriving.

Still, there was something to her insistence that she arrive at the courthouse not with the policemen but "in my own carriage."[3]

As she demanded this, Madame Restell surely knew that this might be the last time she could venture forth in her famously elegant carriage, now drawn by two gray horses and driven by a purple-clad coachman. The same was true of her request to "take oysters." The world, Madame Restell could not have failed to notice, had changed in the past few years. The policemen may have been deferential as always. She still had the authority that came with wealth. But if she went to jail this time, she likely knew she could not rely on a regular supply of peaches.

Chapter Twenty-Six

⬥⬥⬥

A s soon as a well-fed Madame Restell arrived in front of a judge, she demanded to be excused on her own recognizance. She explained that "she had several ladies from good families under her charge, that they needed her personal care, and that her enforced absence would place them in great danger." In addition, she "alleged she had patients at their own homes who, if neglected, as they would be if she were denied liberty, would run great risk."[1]

Until this moment, nothing had ever stopped Madame Restell from her work. Not public shaming, not incarceration, not the death of her husband, and, thus far, not even Comstock and his ridiculous laws. Yet, this time, upon word of her arrest, many of her clients were frightened. Abortion, under Comstock, had gone from being a minor offense to a literally unspeakable crime. A later account claimed that "persons who had been the woman's clients flew together in agitated groups. Men and women trembled at the peril of exposure."[2]

Madame Restell held firm. She consulted with her lawyer, a former district attorney related to Isaac Purdy named Ambrose Purdy, but, privately, she felt she had nothing to fear from Comstock. What he had done seemed to be, quite clearly, entrapment. A lawyer could easily argue that Comstock had pressured her into counseling him. It was even reported "on good authority that she was charged with no indictable offense."[3] If anything, she seemed mildly irritated, as though this business was yet another waste of her valuable time.

At court before Judge Kilbreth, Anthony Comstock described, with typical bombast, how he'd gone about catching Madame Restell in the act. Pulling his whiskers, he stated, "I have been twitted with the taunt that I am afraid to tackle Restell, and I concluded it was best to do so."[4]

He seemed very pleased with his courage in asking a sixty-six-year-old woman for medical help for his lady friend and then descending upon her home with an entire police force as his entourage.

After Comstock's statement, the judge asked Madame Restell for her perspective. She simply stared at Comstock—this pink-cheeked Babbitty bloviator—and then "she suggested there was probably no use in her talking."[5] She was not going to try to gain sympathy from these men, especially one who alternately worked himself into states of lust and fury over seeing a mere drawing of a naked woman. If she was going to communicate, it was going to be with money. It had served her well in the past, and this was, after all, still New York, where money was supposed to count more than morals.

She asked the judge how much her bail was going to be.

"Well," Kilbreth replied, "the penalty is $5,000 for each offense, and I should not feel warranted in putting bail at a less figure. Say, $10,000."

"All right, here it is," she answered, reaching into her purse to withdraw $10,000 of government bonds.[6] She had arrived with $20,000, just in case. In retrospect, she probably should have acted as though procuring funds was more difficult, and not an amount to be paid with the mild annoyance of a modern person paying a speeding ticket.

Judge Kilbreth then decided that he would prefer real estate security. While Madame Restell pointed out that she could pay the money in bonds right now and skip having someone else with real estate holdings bail her out, he doubled down on the idea, claiming, "I don't propose to be the custodian of $10,000 for anybody."[7]

Eager to be out of the court's grasp, Madame Restell sent a message to her grandson, Charles, now twenty years old, to find someone who both owned real estate and could offer her bail. He tried, but, to his dismay, "one man was out, another was hampered by his partnership, another had real estate in Kings County [Brooklyn]."[8] The latter ought to have been satisfactory, but Kilbreth then specified that it needed to be real estate in Manhattan, not Brooklyn. The *Sun* noted that he seemed determined to treat Madame Restell as though she were "a common pickpocket without a bond to her name."[9]

Charles, devastated, visited his grandmother in jail at The Tombs. As he recounted his failure, she reassured him that he was still her sweet baby, something reporters found absurd, as "the grandson is a man grown, competent to look out for himself."[10] If Madame Restell had a soft spot, it would always be for her grandchildren.

Unfortunately, however, this meant that Madame Restell remained in prison. She didn't love it, of course, but neither did she seem terribly bothered. The *Sun* reported that "Mrs. Foster, the Matron of the City Prison, made Madame Restell as comfortable as she could." Her cell was reasonably well furnished. It held a lovely bed with fresh pillows and quilts, and she had novels to read. For someone who worked as unceasingly as Madame Restell, a time to catch up on some books might have been a relief, at least at first. She was said to have "slept like a top and enjoyed her breakfast."[11]

A reporter who visited found her untroubled and pleasant. Not only did she look beautiful—he claimed "time had delt with her very gently, her hair being black and thick, her eye full and sharp"—she was wearing diamond earrings and dressed in black silk. She was "calm and mild as a morning in June, betraying no emotion whatsoever, save now and then a gleam of indignation at 'Comstock's Trick' and regret that her granddaughter should be alone for so long."[12]

With the mention of her granddaughter, people assumed that Madame Restell was taking care of a young child. They were surprised to find that her granddaughter, Carrie, was "a very graceful woman of about twenty-five, with clear complexion, fair hair, light eyes and unusual self-possession. She showed none of the agitation of the older woman, whom she called 'mother.'"[13] As for Carrie being lonely, although she still lived in Madame Restell's mansion, she was far from alone. She lived there with her husband, William Shannon, who was also a close friend of Charles's. During Madame Restell's arrest, Carrie would be running the office for her imprisoned grandmother, meaning that Madame Restell's concerns had much more to do with Carrie's business acumen than her solitude. But then, given that Carrie could spot an undercover reporter while Madame Restell could not identify Comstock, Carrie may have been better suited to run the office than her grandmother in this decade.

When a reporter asked Madame Restell why she thought Comstock was pursuing her, she sighed with resignation and explained that she didn't think he had much against her personally. She had never even met him before. It was merely that "he's in this nasty detective business, you know. There are a number of little doctors who are in the same business as him. They think if they can get me in trouble and out of the way, they can make a fortune.... [T]hey are envious because I have a fine house in such a splendid location."[14]

This supposition that others were envious was probably correct. Lots of doctors *did* think that if they could run female practitioners out of business they could make a fortune. But Comstock was a true believer regarding Madame Restell's evil nature. He was adamant that no one had pressured or bribed him, especially not—as some people uncharitably claimed—her estranged brother, Joseph. When asked if anyone had "backed" him in this escapade, Comstock insisted, "Literally no one. I know Restell says there is, but that's bosh. I have done it on my own responsibility."[15]

Madame Restell assumed Comstock wouldn't have hunted her down without a financial incentive, because *she would never have done that herself.* She didn't enjoy trials or lawyers. She'd have regarded his efforts as a lot of work to do for free. But Comstock was perfectly capable of acting on wounded pride and indignation at the claims that he was scared to pursue Madame Restell. Hunting her down was not work for him; it was a pleasure, if not a life calling. He loved trials and lawyers and bursting into places of employment accompanied by the police. He was also savvy enough to know that headlines provided sensational publicity and secured more donations for his society. So the financial incentive was there after all.

But while Comstock may have been having an excellent time, Madame Restell was growing tired of the lawyers and onlookers, who she claimed "buzzed about me like flies."[16] Increasingly impatient, she sent her lawyer, who was more experienced than her grandson, out on the next foray to find someone to bail her out of jail. He found men who would oblige under the promise of anonymity. "I can find plenty of men willing to go bail for Madame Restell, but I can't find one who will allow himself to be published as her bondsman for fear they will be compromised by association with her," he said. He appealed to the judge, "Can't you exclude the press? Can't you prevent the reporters from getting and publishing the name of Restell's bondsman?"[17]

The judge, rather smugly, refused. If anyone wanted to offer $10,000 to indicate that this woman was a respectable citizen, unlikely to flee any consequences dealt by the court, the judge contended, they should be proud to be associated with her in the newspapers. Potential bondsmen disagreed. One man, when begged by Madame Restell's lawyer to act as a "good Samaritan," spoke for many when he replied, "Good Samaritan be blowed! I have got a wife and a family of girls and I'll be hanged if I'm in the papers as a bondsman for an abortionist."[18]

This may have been the first time in Madame Restell's life that she needed to have people on her side morally as well as financially.

And so she was forced to linger in The Tombs. In her cell, when not talking over her concerns with reporters, she was happy to "make herself at home with the newspapers and a cup of tea."[19] Jail also afforded her the time to refine her strategy. She promised to "call a great number of druggists to prove that her wares [were] identical with those sold all over this city." She would argue "that Comstock did not procure the articles with the intent to violate any law, and that, therefore, she [was] not guilty of any offense."[20] To reporters she declared that the so-called instruments to perform abortion that Comstock had found were basic corkscrews, and that the powders she gave people were harmless. She may have also had a more underhanded plan. Comstock later claimed that he had an affidavit to show that "witnesses had been hired by Restell to defame him by false testimony in order to break down his testimony."[21]

But she still had to find bondsmen.

It would take three days to do so. The "gentlemen who consented to face public opinion and become her bondsmen" were James Gonoude, who owned two houses, on 80th Street and 2nd Avenue, and Jacob Schwartz, a German baker who owned four lots and buildings, on 113th Street and 3rd Avenue. Schwartz "did not seem to fear the reporters"; Gonoude's consent was more conditional. After going before the judge and swearing that the deeds to his properties were on record and he was free of debt and mortgages, he implored the reporters, "Can't you, to oblige a fellow who has the best of will towards you all, print my name with a mistake or two in it...so that folks won't know it's me?"[22] Whether or not he thought the journalists would take his request seriously, no papers significantly changed his name.

At last, Madame Restell departed the jail, "accompanied by her grandson, a handsome young man who has patiently and laboriously struggled for his grandmother's release, being the first one in court every day and the last to leave."[23] People may have felt negatively about Madame Restell, but the press's surprisingly universal reaction toward her grandchildren was that they were gorgeous, and really cool, and just loved their grandma. So, just exactly the kind of grandchildren anyone might hope to have.

Madame Restell returned to court the next day, February 15, to testify. She and her lawyer, Ambrose Purdy, were initially happy to hear that Comstock was out of town and that the hearing would be postponed until February 23. But then they heard that James Gonoude had backed out of providing bail. This was not, as some might expect, because his friends or family were upset when they saw his (correctly spelled) name in the papers. Instead, as Madame Restell's lawyer admitted, it was that "he wasn't paid enough." Gonoude now denied that he'd ever met Madame Restell. According to the papers, he was simply a man "trying to turn an honest penny."[24] He had agreed to be a bondsman at the urging of a man named Mr. Thompson, whom Madame Restell's lawyer had sent out with $500 to secure bail. Thompson, however, had decided to pocket the money rather than give it to Gonoude. John Lovetts, a saloon owner with "an air of solvency that was not unbecoming," agreed to step up to the plate after Madame Restell promised him $300.[25] But then, "upon sober second thought" he backed out.

Jacob Schwartz proved more reliable. He felt Madame Restell was not "quite as bad as some of the people in the world." He remained her bondsman because he thought she deserved a chance, noting, "I want her to have a fair show."[26] Once again, she was allowed to leave, escorted by Charles.

On February 23, Comstock, with great pageantry, offered his testimony and displayed the pills and syringe that Madame Restell had provided to him. This testimony, however exaggerated, may have been overshadowed by the media's gushing reports of Madame Restell's attire. Her sealskin cape had already been the envy of other prisoners in The Tombs. This day, she wore the black silk she favored for courtroom appearances, though she'd accessorized it with "a velvet hat trimmed with deep crimson" and a crimson-lined cape for the occasion.[27] These "scarlet woman" touches were notably jauntier than the Whistler's Mother bonnet she had worn in past trials.

Samuel Colgate, Anthony Comstock's mentor, sat beside him on the bench, as did a number of lawyers. If a few years ago Comstock had been a relatively unimportant clerk, Colgate's presence made it clear to everyone that this was no longer the case. Comstock had scaled New York's social pyramid at a rapid pace, promising those atop it respectability.

Comstock's account of his visits to Madame Restell's home went on for five days. Afterward, Purdy, Restell's lawyer, moved that the entire case be dismissed, as there was insufficient evidence that a crime had been committed at all. When Madame Restell finally spoke on March 1, she answered basic questions about her name and residence in a "monotonous voice" that made it clear she was thoroughly unimpressed with the whole ordeal. When asked whether she was guilty or not guilty, she replied, "I have nothing to say."[28] Again, it probably would have been helpful if she had tried to look even a little bit nervous at the trial rather than like she was on the verge of telling the judge to go to hell at any given moment.

Before his departure, Purdy submitted a writ claiming that Madame Restell was being illegally detained. Judge Kilbreth was unimpressed and curtly declared, "It has been shown that there is reason to suspect her of a crime. On these grounds, I commit her to The Tombs."[29]

"I appeal to you as a Gentleman," begged Purdy. "Do not take her to The Tombs."[30]

Ultimately, Madame Restell was taken to the New York State Supreme Court and detained there until her hearing. Though the courtroom around her was abuzz with people excited to see her, the *Herald* reported that Madame Restell herself was frosty and "paid very little heed to the scrutinizing glances of the curious throng."[31] She remained subdued as her counsel continued to plead for leniency, and it was agreed that arguments would be heard before the State Supreme Court on March 5. As she left the courthouse, relieved to be out of jail, Madame Restell asked only that the name of the hotel at which she was staying be kept secret, as she didn't want to see anyone.

When she returned to court, she brought with her not only her grandson but also her daughter and granddaughter. The women both wore veils, and Madame Restell was "elegantly dressed, as usual." Likely anxious for the ordeal to be over, she was said to keep up "unceasing conversation" with her family before the trial commenced.[32]

From the start, Purdy made the argument that since Comstock had not purchased the abortive powders with the intention to commit wrongdoing, there could be no crime. The only way to prove that the powder Madame Restell had provided was dangerous would have been to give it to a pregnant woman, which, of course, he didn't. Why, the powders Madame Restell had sold Comstock had not even been analyzed by "a competent chemist!"[33] Very possibly, they contained no ingredients at all that might be harmful to a woman or a fetus.

The prosecution retorted that this hearing was merely to see if there was enough evidence to hold Madame Restell for trial. To that end, the prosecutor recited the instructions that came with the abortion-inducing powders Madame Restell had sold to Comstock. Shocked, Mr. Purdy exclaimed, "I object to such language being uttered in the court!"[34]

If you couldn't even read a description of abortive medicine at a trial about abortion, it truly was Comstock's world now.

Purdy persisted, acknowledging that, yes, Madame Restell might be a well-known abortionist, but "it is wrong that her past life be gone into."[35] Judge Lawrence, who was now presiding, however, was not convinced. On March 7, the judge announced that Madame Restell's trial would move forward as planned, meaning that the matter of bail had to be settled *yet again.* John Lovett supplied $5,000, and, mercifully, this time the court accepted the remaining $5,000 from Madame Restell.

Now safely home and surrounded by her family, Madame Restell made the curious decision to fire her lawyer. Purdy's defense had been passionate and wholehearted, and he had defended his client as best he could in the face of a difficult judge and negative coverage. Still, after receiving a bill for $2,600 from him, a price that made her mutter that "everybody had combined to defraud her," Madame Restell discharged her counsel.[36]

On March 9, she sought out the assistance of the lawyer Orlando T. Stewart. If firing Purdy was odd, hiring Stewart—a former judge, who considered abortion to be a social evil—was an even stranger choice.

Perhaps she was impressed by his credentials. He later said that at their first meeting, Madame Restell, a woman who was known for her sangfroid, "immediately almost threw herself upon her knees with her arms stretched out on the table and, her hands clasped appealingly, begged me, 'Oh, don't refuse me! Take my case. I am able to pay you well and willing to pay liberally!'"[37] After reviewing the evidence, Stewart assured her that he saw nothing indictable in the case. He told her he wasn't even sure it would make it to trial, but that he would be very willing to defend her. Seemingly he did not believe abortion was *such* an evil prospect that he would not defend a well-known abortionist, provided she paid liberally.

Madame Restell had seemingly undergone a complete 180-degree change of attitude. Just a few weeks ago, she had been calmly enjoying prison life and having discussions with reporters from her jail cell. Whereas once she'd been calm and sleeping notably well in prison, now she was flinging herself prostrate on the ground and begging. Even Stewart, who might have been receptive to the idea that Madame Restell had become guilt stricken late in life, found this transformation to be excessive. He remembered that she had been in legal trouble in the past, and "thought that she might, from that experience, and her life, have taken the matter a little more philosophically."[38]

Rather dramatically, Madame Restell promised Stewart that she had not performed abortions for the past twelve years. She also claimed that she didn't even give her clients medicine, only harmless sugar pills, thereby conning them. This was very different than how she'd behaved with lawyers in the past. For instance, she had been friends with G. P. Howe, a well-known lawyer, for thirty years. He had visited her office, a generally private space, and she had seemed unconcerned when she told him, "You know how I get my money."[39] This assertion made to Stewart conflicted with her earlier statements about having young women recuperating in the house who needed her care. It also conflicted with the absolute flood of business streaming through her doors at all hours. And it certainly conflicted with the prior investigations into her pills, which had been found to contain ingredients that would cause a miscarriage. Despite her best efforts, Stewart did not believe a word Madame Restell said. He told her to "go home and take down your sign, and if you have any recipes for pills or medicines, burn them. If you have any instruments for this evil purpose, destroy them."[40]

And that wasn't all she was expected to get rid of. Stewart also deemed her beloved carriage too flashy and instructed her to exchange it for a less expensive coupe. This last edict finally shook Madame Restell out of her hysteria. She told Stewart her coachman had worked for her for eighteen years, and she had no intention of firing him. He compromised by deciding that she could hire a coupe and let her coachman drive that vehicle, while leaving her beautiful carriage in the stable.

Given her desperation to retain his services and earn her freedom once and for all, you would think that Madame Restell must have had great faith in Stewart's ability. She did not. She telegrammed him daily to come to her house at odd hours and, once there, repeatedly informed him that he was going to lose her trial. Insulted, he kept trying to tell her that, actually, he was going to win! She did not care, and just kept telling him they were doomed. Again and again, he also assured her that her will would not be disputed, a topic that held a morbid fascination for her.

The trial officially began on Saturday, March 29. Disregarding Stewart's advice, when she rolled up to court, it was in her "splendid equipage" of a beautiful carriage with her grandson, who, the *Sun* reported, "has the air of a dashing youth about town, by her side on the satin cushions."[41] She was reportedly still elegantly dressed, but she walked more slowly than before, hoping that the halting gait might remind those in attendance of her advanced years. Stewart filed a petition of not guilty, still hopeful that he could quash the indictment. The case was then adjourned until Monday. If the indictment proceeded, Madame Restell's trial would begin the following Thursday.

That Monday morning—April Fool's Day—the court was packed to the brim with people hoping to catch a glimpse of the notorious woman. But as the clock ticked and ticked, she did not arrive. Whispers began to spread through the courtroom, growing in intensity. Finally, Mr. Stewart burst into the room. He announced to a shocked courtroom that the so-called "wickedest woman in New York" was dead.

Chapter Twenty-Seven

PPARENTLY, SHE HAD KILLED HERSELF SOMETIME THAT morning.

At 7:00 a.m., Madame Restell's chambermaid, Maggie McGrath, rose to have her breakfast. As she walked downstairs, she noticed that Madame Restell's bathroom door was open. She knew "it was not Madame Restell's practice to bathe in the morning," but she didn't think it overly strange. After all, her employer had been having difficulties sleeping lately and was under a great deal of stress. It was only at 8:00 a.m., when Maggie returned to assist Madame Restell, that she was surprised to see that the bathroom door was still open. Madame Restell clearly had not moved. Maggie knocked on the door, but no answer came. She entered tentatively. The bath itself was behind a screen, but Maggie thought she saw a smear of blood on the protruding portion of the tub. When she finally looked behind the screen, she was horrified to find a nude, bloated body in the tub, the water still warm. The hands were crossed on the chest for modesty, and perhaps to showcase the three diamond rings encircling waterlogged fingers. Of the entire sight, Maggie's eyes were instantly drawn to the body's neck, which was gruesomely slashed. A huge carving knife lay at the bottom of the tub, while Madame Restell's costly robe and nightgown lay on the chair next to it. Horrified, Maggie ran "screaming from the room."[1]

There was some initial speculation of foul play in the death of New York's most infamous physician. After all, plenty of wealthy people in New York wouldn't have wanted their names to come out at trial, and Madame Restell's upcoming testimony undoubtedly posed a threat to their anonymity. Others wrote it off as a hoax. After all, it was April Fool's Day, and this seemed like the kind of macabre joke Madame

Restell might play. Before long, however, the coroner officially ruled the cause of death to be suicide, and all the wild theories were dispelled. It was reported that he "conjectured that she opened the faucets, and then seated herself in the bottom of the tub, cut her throat, and, while the blood was flowing, settled herself backwards into the position in which she was discovered."[2]

A reception was held in Madame Restell's honor. Her body was reported to look curiously beautiful and at peace at last, preserved in an ice chest with the pall drawn slightly back to reveal her face. The *Sun* claimed that it was a face that looked "surprisingly youthful for one so far advanced in years" and that it "had a kindly look, an expression you would hardly expect in the countenance of a woman so stained with crime."[3]

Whatever Madame Restell's concerns had been, they were long gone now.

For the past few weeks, Madame Restell had ostensibly been overcome with anxiety about the possibility of a return to jail. If she *was* convicted, it was likely that she would have only been sentenced to two years. However, in this new reformer-era climate, she couldn't rely on the stay being as cushy as it had been on Blackwell's Island, though the policemen who had arrested her and the matron at the city prison had certainly been very accommodating. Her earlier strategy—to tell the court that Anthony Comstock had found nothing in her house that he couldn't find in a drugstore—must have seemed insufficient against the censure of a moralistic public. And what was the point in staying alive if her twilight years were to be spent in a frigid room rather than under her blue silk canopy?

William Shannon, Carrie's husband, told reporters that his grandmother-in-law "had seemed very much depressed all day Sunday, walking from room to room, wringing her hands, and asking why she should be persecuted, when she had never done anybody any harm in her life." After attending an evening church service, William and Carrie had returned to the residence and chatted with Madame Restell. According to William, her last words were "Oh, how I dread two o'clock!"[4]

Some people assumed this meant she had died by suicide at two in the morning, though it must have actually been closer to dawn when, no longer willing to face the coming day, she had slit her throat with her ivory-handled knife.

The *New York Times* noted that Madame Restell had been "driven to desperation at last by the public opinion she had so long defied." Carrie agreed and told the newspaper she had heard her grandmother say, "If I could only get sick and die. I wish I were dead, it would end all."[5]

At the same time, Orlando Stewart informed the papers that Madame Restell had grown irrational in her final days. The day before her trial, he noted, she had "suddenly become monomaniacal" on the subject of her inevitable arrest and, even before that, had "constantly talked about it." This increasing doubt bewildered him as he had been confident that he could win the case, but Madame Restell had remained stubbornly convinced that she would lose and had descended into a state of sheer panic. Stewart could only deduce that "while laboring under this aberration she took her own life."[6] After visiting the home, seeing the body, and speaking with the family, he raced off—in Madame Restell's carriage, no less, a detail that would have undoubtedly infuriated her no end—to inform everyone of his client's passing.

Comstock, ever empathetic and forgiving, was not surprised by the course of events. Just as Madame Restell could not figure out why Comstock would pursue her if no one was paying him money to do so, he could not understand how an abortionist could not be suicidal with guilt. He declared that, in a fit of conscience, Restell had "passed the sentence of death upon herself, and with her own hand executed the decree."[7] Others agreed with him for decades to come. Clifford Browder, one of Madame Restell's biographers, suggested that her behavior was so erratic that it could only be attributed to "a disintegrating mind."[8]

Not everyone was convinced that she'd lost it, though. One paper noted that she "had probably summed up that she had done pretty well for a British kitchen maid and that the fight wasn't worth the candle."[9] She might have believed she was near enough to death and, as many had pointed out in the past weeks, her grandchildren were perfectly competent adults. They would be fine, and she would provide for them well.

Madame Restell had signed her will, witnessed by William Shannon, on April 28, 1877, almost a year before her death. She left behind a fortune to her daughter and grandchildren estimated between $600,000 and $1.5 million.[10] Madame Restell's daughter, Caroline, was provided with $3,000 a year for the rest of her life, provided her husband did not control any of the money. Caroline's life would sadly not be a long one. Dissipated from drink, she died of a stroke in 1881, only three years after her mother's death.

The house and all other property were divided equally between her grandchildren, Carrie and Charles. Charles received the horses and carriage in which he had so faithfully accompanied his grandmother. All Madame Restell's jewelry, dresses, and furs went to her grand-daughter, as did a Steinway piano that Carrie loved playing. Last on the list of items bequeathed to Carrie were the family Bible and the stand on which it was mounted. Madame Restell never believed in the book, but it had become a much-used comfort in her office waiting room. In many ways, leaving the book to Carrie was like openly leaving her with a reliable tool of her professional trade.

Still estranged from his sibling at the time of her passing, Joseph Trow received nothing. He later sued Carrie over this, lost, and continued manufacturing pills until his death.

Madame Restell's family was not the only one touched by her suicide. Other women followed in her footsteps, fearful of a future where abortion was so forbidden. Less than a week later, a Pennsylvania paper reported that a woman by the name of Virginia Coland had also cut her throat with a razor, because "after Madame Restell's suicide, she had been despondent."[11]

In light of her demise, some people even started to regard Comstock as less than the noble Hercules he'd been considered in the past.

On April 7, the Reverend Charles McCarthy gave a speech shaming Comstock for his treatment of Madame Restell at the University Building in Union Square. He sympathized with Madame Restell, a woman he somewhat surprisingly praised as an excellent wife and mother (though, considering the difficulties she'd often had with her husband and daughter, it might've made more sense to label her an excellent businessperson). As for her business, Rev. McCarthy felt that, in performing abortions, she was not doing anything most doctors didn't. He personally knew others who performed abortions and noticed that "in high social circles [it was] advocated as a proper method for evading the duties and anxieties of maternity." Given that abortion was seen as acceptable and accessible for the wealthy, he declared, "The fraud and falsehood by which she was made amenable to a law that is universally violated by the medical profession of this city cannot be too strongly condemned." Furthermore, he lamented, Madame Restell had been "hunted down by miserable subterfuge, by cunning and heartless fabrication, by open and mean lying, and by specious arguments which were craftily devised to work on her better nature."[12]

Much of America agreed that Comstock had overstepped when it came to attacking Madame Restell and others he deemed sinful. By October, a judge found that some of the people Comstock prosecuted were legally innocent, as they'd been "induced by a sort of constable [Comstock himself]." He had, after all, lied to people about his need for help. Under such circumstances, even the most unoffending citizen might, out of sympathy, be induced to commit a crime. The doctrine was proclaimed "very sensible," and if this had been better understood back in April, the *New York World* noted, "it would have rendered Madame Restell's suicide unnecessary, if it was due to fear of conviction."[13]

Comstock and his cronies were not in the least troubled by the criticism directed toward them. After all, Madame Restell was not the first person Comstock had driven to suicide; he bragged, in a very morbid flex, that at least fifteen people had killed themselves because of contact with him. For the time being, he was pleased with himself. He declared that Madame Restell's demise had been "a bloody ending to a bloody life."[14] It had allowed him to launch his name (and his cause) in the national headlines; Madame Restell's was the arrest by which later reporters would say, "This intrusive Comstock lept to a sudden famousity."[15]

And he didn't stop at Madame Restell. Soon after her death, Comstock pursued another birth control entrepreneur, Sara B. Chase, whom papers deemed "the successor to Madame Restell."[16] People may not have liked Comstock's methods, and they questioned whether "our taste in art and literature [must] come under the scrutiny of a censor," but many were still excited to see women arrested after violating what they perceived to be the proper social order.[17] Even when there was some question about whether Sara was being wrongly pursued, papers felt she should recognize Anthony Comstock's "zeal as legitimate and encourage him in it."[18] Which is to say—if Sara was guilty, it was good that Comstock was pursuing her. If she was innocent, then she would not be troubled by being pursued, and would applaud Comstock for being such a good fellow.

This is a lot of politeness to be expected to extend to someone trying to jail you.

Whether they liked Comstock or not, people saw Madame Restell's death as setting women back on their proper path. Papers reported on an "ugly social feature"—there were 89,000 wives in Massachusetts who were childless, of which a full 68,888 were native (white, Christian) Americans. "What kind of nation," they wondered, "can be expected to grow up under influences that foster such an evil as is known by the name Restellism?"[19]

Many people wished to remind women that their place was not in the world of business, nor was it campaigning for the vote. Madame Restell was proof that women who did business were evil. Instead, a woman's place should always be at home, breeding and tending to children. Only a day after Madame Restell's death, the *Brooklyn Daily Eagle* wrote, "It is the cry of the advanced and progressive woman that every profession is closed to them.... Is it to be wondered at? Are honest practitioners to be blamed for refusing to consort with doctoresses when chances are that, to even a limited extent, these women follow the calling of Madame Restell?" Somehow, bad men existing in occupations did not mean *no* men should be allowed to practice those occupations. If Rosenzweig also existed, and this did not prevent men from engaging in every profession, the *Eagle* did not notice. Rather, the paper mused, it would be wonderful if Anthony Comstock could bring about "the extirpation of the whole sisterhood" of female doctors and women demanding entry to the professional sphere.[20]

In truth, though, he may not have even brought about the extirpation of Madame Restell.

CHAPTER TWENTY-EIGHT

REFUSING TO BELIEVE THAT THE INFAMOUS ABORTIONIST WAS gone, plenty of people felt strongly that Madame Restell had faked her own death. Her old friend Henry "Prince Hal" Genet had eluded the law and escaped to Europe, after all: it was said that Madame Restell did the same.

A Detective Brittain told the *Boston Globe*, "How ridiculous it seems for a woman who knew medicine and surgery thoroughly to kill herself in such a brutal manner. It is hardly in accord with what I have seen of her character. It would be a marvelous thing if she had succeeded in deceiving everybody and escaping."[1] In a decade where many people had come to believe that abortionists were horrible—if not direct emissaries from Satan—people like Brittain still held authorities in such high regard that they had a glimmer of extremely American respect for anyone who outsmarted them. Even when they *themselves* were the authority.

No sooner was the death announced than people started discussing how likely it was that Madame Restell had somehow escaped. According to the *Boston Globe*, "Opinion was soon divided into two classes, those whose faith in the original suicide theory could not be shaken, and those who believed Madame had out-witted justice and escaped scot free." The writers at the *Globe* believed that she was "tossing on the [ocean] billows and not under the turf at Tarrytown," where her corpse had supposedly been buried, alongside those of her former husband and deceased grandchildren.[2]

We know that she at least considered this plan, because her son-in-law, William Farrell, leaked to the press that she had concocted a plan to flee the country. The two had long remained on acrimonious terms, in spite of Restell's financial help, so it's not exactly surprising that he gave an interview saying that "it had been her intention to leave the city," going first to Poughkeepsie and then hopping over the border to Canada. From there, Farrell said, she would take a ship to England, where she "would pass the rest of her life in quietness and peace as she had sufficient means to maintain herself in absolute luxury."[3] He then hastily clarified that she didn't *actually* follow through on this plan, but that was perhaps due to the realization that it would reflect badly on him not to have alerted the authorities in advance.

The suspicions seemed to rattle Anthony Comstock, who'd been so happy to see Restell dead. As rumors of her survival surfaced, he said he believed that Madame Restell might have been "putting up some job" to evade justice. He said he'd always "feared some trickery" and that "the indecent haste with which the body was to go underground...and the manner by which her relatives allowed the body to be buried without any reverence or any ceremony are very suspicious." He couldn't say for certain whether she had committed suicide, and the circumstances had, in his words, "put me all at sea again."[4]

But in terms of Comstock's own interests, it wasn't really important whether she had committed suicide. If she had just been run out of town, his job was effectively done. He could count her death or exile as a victory, one that had reportedly brought him to "brilliant notice," and then move on to his next opponent in the name of civil society.[5]

Theories that notorious individuals like Madame Restell had avoided or even tricked death weren't out of the ordinary at the time—and judging by all the people who think JFK's "real" killer has somehow managed to evade law enforcement for over half a century, it's still pretty common. Following the death of President Lincoln's assassin, John Wilkes Booth, the *Chicago Tribune* remarked that "many simpletons are still willing to bet Lincoln's murderer is yet alive, and that someone else's bones rest in a grave in Baltimore." The same was true regarding the Harvard professor John White Webster, who had been convicted of the murder of a man he was in debt to—even though Webster was publicly hanged. As the *Tribune* noted, "Thousands of people believed firmly that [Webster] was not swung off at all, but that a dummy was hanged in his stead, and that the real murderer escaped to Norway."[6] That said, during this time there *were* individuals who escaped justice and fled to Europe, including Restell's friend Henry Genet.

The greatest evidence to counteract the theory that Madame Restell had fled was that people had seen the corpse.

If she had planned to flee, she would have known that securing a substitute corpse would present a problem. She might have thought of burning her house to the ground. If it went down in a blaze, people would simply imagine that her body was lost in the rubble. That would explain why she began, out of nowhere, talking to a reporter from the *Philadelphia Times* about how she had a great fear of fire. This was not a fear she had ever mentioned before, and nothing about the design of her home evidenced it. However, as she sat in the justice's private room following her arrest, she told the reporter, "I never go to bed without a great dread of fire.... [I]t may be silly but I am morally certain that sooner or later the house and all there is in it will be burned to the ground." She also explained, "I am an old woman and want to take my comfort where I may. If not for this constant fear of fire, I would be happy as a bird."[7]

There was one notable problem with this notion—her grandchildren liked the house. They lived in that house. The house was the bulk of their inheritance. They would eventually end up selling it for over $1 million in 1903, enough to allow them to live in great style for the rest of their lives. As for Madame Restell, she, too, loved that house. It was the embodiment of her success. It was not only "a triumph of architectural beauty," but, standing across from St. Patrick's Cathedral, it was also a middle finger to the establishment that wanted to pretend her profession didn't exist.[8] The house would stay.

There was a body. But, as the *Brooklyn Daily Eagle* noted, for Madame Restell to procure a body from the undertaker, "cut its throat, and place it in a bathtub would be no very terrible performance for a woman who took chances furnishing the undertaker with a fee every day of the year, and as an alternative to lifelong imprisonment would be a device of comparative excellence."[9]

Restell's heirs claimed the body in the tub was hers, but then, they would have had an interest in helping their beloved grandmother escape. As for Maggie, the maid who had first found Madame Restell's body, it is possible she was so startled she did not look at it closely. Or perhaps Madame Restell's generosity to her servants paid off in this instance. Newspaper reporters had been in the house and observed the body in person. But they had not been very familiar with Madame Restell while she was alive. They might have been better able to identify her carriage, which they'd seen streaking through the park, than her body. The corpse had been largely covered, and even at their best, corpses tend to look different from live people—let alone if they've been submerged in water for hours. The initial published description of the corpse merely reported that it was a dark-haired woman who looked "surprisingly youthful."[10] As for the people who were supposed to confirm the identity of the body, the coroner himself said that "he could not positively swear the body he saw in the bathtub was Madame Restell's."[11] Neither could the deputy coroner.

A group of the coroner's jurymen were assembled to judge whether the body was truly hers, and even they seemed somewhat skeptical. The foreman, who had in the past seen Madame Restell in person, when she had tried to buy some real estate from him, testified that the corpse didn't look much like Madame Restell. He claimed, "I am not positive the remains were those of Mrs. Lohman.... [T]he face of the corpse looked shorter than hers, as she had in life rather long features, and again, the forehead looked fuller than her's." This was more comprehensive than another juryman, who shrugged, "The coroner told us it was [her body], and that is all I know about it."[12] With the exception of the foreman, none of the jurymen had ever encountered her in life.

Substituting a different body for Madame Restell's own would have been trickier than the *Brooklyn Daily Eagle* might have imagined, but hardly impossible. A well-placed bribe at the morgue would probably have granted the family access to one. Even the skeptical *Chicago Tribune* noted that the weakest point in the argument that Madame Restell could not have escaped was when people claimed, "She could not have done so because it would have involved the corrupt collusion of so many officials."[13] Madame Restell and her family had been bribing officials for years. This time, she only needed one corpse.

It was entirely possible that William could have retrieved the corpse from the morgue during the period of the evening when he told reporters he was out of the house. Neighbors claimed that they saw "a couple of large trunks" taken from the house the evening before Madame Restell's death.[14] As readers will remember from the Rosenzweig case, old trunks can be handy when you want to hide a dead body.

The deputy coroner thought this scenario was unlikely, saying, "It is not probable the body could have been taken through the house without some members of the family knowing about it."[15]

But what if they helped?

Madame Restell's grandchildren adored her and were highly aware of her occupation and the underworld surrounding it. They helped her with her business. They sat by her devotedly in court. In all likelihood, they would have unhesitatingly schlepped a body to the bathtub before giving speeches to the police about how their grandmother had been extremely suicidal, was definitely dead, and most *certainly* was not hiding out in Europe.

The body—whoever's it was—was buried as quickly as possible in Tarrytown. Madame Restell had discussed the limitations of a coroner's jurisdiction with a detective prior to her death. "Tell me," she inquired of the detective, "if I ask you a certain question, will you solemnly promise me never to reveal that I asked you the question?" He immediately promised her as much, in spite of the fact that he later gave an interview to a reporter where he detailed exactly what she had asked. Once assured, she said, "I want you to tell me if the Coroner of New York has the power to make a post-mortem examination or hold an inquest out of the city?" The detective informed her, "Of course not, his powers are confined to New York."[16]

It turns out this was a lie! But Madame Restell's grandchildren didn't know that. By April 12, they had told people that if they had any doubt about their grandmother's suicide, the body should be exhumed from its resting place in Tarrytown. So the coroner did just that. The body was found to "not greatly resemble the features of [Madame Restell]," though the article makes it clear that decomposition does change the appearance of a corpse. During the proceedings, her lawyer, Orlando Stewart, "looked upon the corpse for a moment and turned away," but then "described a ring he had often seen her wear." The ring found on the corpse was considered "conclusive proof of identity."[17]

Because apparently no one could even *imagine* putting a ring on a corpse to disguise its identity.

Funny story about the three rings found on the corpse—they were the only jewelry anywhere in the vicinity of the body or the house. It was reported that the rest of Madame Restell's "most valuable wearing apparel and finest jewelry were nowhere to be found."[18] Which was definitely suspicious for a woman who prided herself on her appearance and her rich accessories throughout her life. If she'd fled to Europe, she'd have wanted her diamonds.

During this extended inquiry, none of Madame Restell's descendants seemed troubled. In fact, they appeared notably composed. At the reading of the will, it shocked onlookers that "the ladies were gayly attired and the presence of light bonnets and fashionable appendages shows no outward sign of grief at the bereavement."

But then, if she wasn't dead, they wouldn't have felt much need to break out mourning attire.

Those who believed Madame Restell was hiding away in Europe would've been especially interested in Carrie's and Charles's subsequent trips to Europe following her death. In 1888, a full decade after Madame Restell's suicide, it was reported that every year they "depart[ed] on a mysterious trip" for two or three months.[19] It's entirely possible they were just keeping in touch with relatives there or going on vacation. But the theory was that they went to visit Madame Restell—not back in England, but in France.

Whether or not this was true, many people seemed to want to believe that it was. In 1879, an Egyptian astrologer by the name of Charles Malogole was asked "if he [had done] business for the late Madame Restell." He replied, "I did business for Mme. Restell, but not the late Mme. Restell because that woman is not dead....She is now pursuing her avocation in Paris. She had good reasons for leaving the city, and it was part of the programme that she was reported dead." Then again, Malogole may not have been the most reliable witness, because he also claimed that "Lucretia Borgia told me herself that she and Queen Elizabeth had appointed a committee to receive Mme. Restell [in Hell] and that she would be appointed ruler over the thousands of souls whom she had sent to the shades of darkness."[20] Also, apparently Lucretia Borgia looked stunning, and he was very sad when she left him.

More legitimate sources, who did not make Hell sound like a cool place peopled by an enthusiastic welcoming committee of powerful women, continued to report on Madame Restell's possible reappearances as well. In 1889, eleven years after the supposed suicide, the *Buffalo Evening News* announced, "They have rediscovered Madame Restell, of infamous memory, in a neighborhood in Paris." The

Viscountess Veniski, a lady who had been known in New York society before going to Europe, calmly admitted that "she met Restell in Paris recently."[21] A physician, who wished to remain unnamed, claimed likewise that he "had seen and attended her in both cities [New York and Paris]."[22]

Madame Restell may have died by suicide in that bathtub, Comstock's pursuit having overwhelmed her. Or she might have died later, peacefully sipping champagne in Paris and covered head to toe in her diamonds. But her age was over. The time when a woman could run ads in a newspaper suggesting family limitation and think that people would respond calmly was a thing of the past. Abortionists of the future would not flaunt themselves in their carriages. They'd try desperately to remain under the radar. Yes, Madame Restell's time was at an end. But America's long and contentious battle over abortion was only beginning.

ÉPILOGUE

U PON MADAME RESTELL'S DEATH, THE SATIRICAL MAGAZINE
Puck ran a comical illustration depicting what Fifth Avenue
might look like in five years. In Restell's absence, it imagined, the
street would be filled with children and heavily pregnant women push-
ing baby carriages.

That proved to be less than prophetic.

Comstock had made abortion shameful for women, but he'd done
nothing to change the circumstances that caused women to have them.
So, they kept having them, though they often attempted to inflict such
procedures on themselves rather than seeking the help of physicians.
Without readily available information on the topic, they often had
scant idea of how to go about this. They knew only that they would do
anything not to be pregnant.

An 1898 estimate by the Michigan Board of Health found that, in
spite of Comstock's efforts, one-third of the pregnancies in the state
were terminated via abortion.[1] By 1916, the New York branch of the
Metropolitan Health and Life Insurance Company had revealed that
"one quarter of its claims [for life insurance] were puerperium [post-
partum] related," and of those claims, one-quarter were from women
attempting to abort without the aid of trained professionals.[2] A Stanford University study from 1921 estimated that one in every 1.7 to 2.3

283

pregnancies ended in abortion. Banning abortion did not stop the procedure and, in some cases, it seems to have increased the rate at which women had them.[3]

Turning back Comstock's dangerous edicts would take decades. It's difficult to pin a reversal to any specific individual, but some say it began in 1912, when Margaret Sanger, an obstetric nurse, tended to a woman in terribly poor health following the birth of her third child. "Wagging a jovial finger at the sufferer [the doctor presiding] warned her that if she persisted in having babies, she would die of it the next time." When the mother asked the doctor how to keep from having children as her husband was seemingly not going to stop having sex with her, "the man of medicine shrugged his shoulders" and left without saying another word.[4] Comstock's laws forbade any discussion of family planning, meaning that women could not even have conversations with their doctors about the options available to them. Sanger saw the patient again the following year as she gave birth to her fourth child. Tragically, the woman died as a result of this childbirth, just as the doctor had predicted.

Sanger dedicated the rest of her life to becoming Comstock's fiercest adversary. Shortly after the death of this patient, she started to write a column in a socialist newspaper titled "What Every Girl Should Know." Comstock promptly had the column shut down after it published the words "syphilis" and "gonorrhea." This prompted a retort by the editors in the same newspaper: "What Every Girl Should Know—Nothing; by Order of the U.S. Post Office."[5] Undeterred, Sanger launched her own newspaper, *The Woman Rebel* (motto: "No Gods, No Masters"), prompting Comstock to threaten her with a forty-five-year jail sentence. She ignored these warnings and never prepared a defense, mainly because she was too busy writing a book on family limitation. Her husband, however, was eventually jailed for unknowingly giving one of her pamphlets regarding birth control to one of Comstock's undercover agents. In 1916, Margaret Sanger opened the first birth control clinic in Brownsville, Brooklyn, only to be arrested and sent to jail for a month nine days later.

Her legal battle wouldn't be for nothing, though. As a result of *New York v. Sanger* in 1918, a judge ruled that physicians could give married patients contraceptive information if they did so for "the cure and prevention of disease."[6]

In 1936, due to Sanger's continued legal efforts, the Comstock Laws were revised in such a way as to allow doctors to prescribe contraceptives and distribute them across state lines.

It would take until the passage of *Roe v. Wade* in 1973, which protected women's right to have an abortion without government interference, for abortion providers, and the women who had abortions, to emerge from the shadows.

And now, here we are, fifty years later, going back to the shadows again. *Roe* has been overturned, which means individual states can now choose whether they will allow abortions. As I type this, in July 2022, nine states have already banned abortion. The next move for antiabortion activists is likely to push for a nationwide ban. This May, the *Washington Post* reported that Marjorie Dannenfelser, president of the antiabortion group Susan B. Anthony List, had discussed how to approach a nationwide ban with ten possible 2024 presidential contenders from the Republican Party. They had "assured her they would be supportive of a national ban and would be eager to make that policy a centerpiece of a presidential campaign."[7]

This may upset you, but it should not surprise you. The same sentiments that motivated Comstockery are alive and well today, and have been for a while. History may not exactly repeat, but the exact same attitudes do surface hundreds of years later dressed in modern clothing. Once again, some people in America seem gripped by the fear that there will not be enough American (read: white) babies. You can see that fear in the May 2022 manifesto of the Buffalo supermarket mass shooter, who claimed, "If there's one thing I want you to get from these writings, it's White birth rates must change. Every day the White population becomes fewer in number." This isn't just a position held by the fringe; a *New York Times* investigation found that in more than four hundred shows on Fox News, commentator Tucker Carlson had amplified the idea of a great replacement in which a "cabal of elites want to force demographic change through immigration."[8]

Similarly, there's a focus on banning books under the guise of protecting children, just as Comstock wished to. In 2022, Pen America described the right-wing effort to ban books pertaining to race and LGBTQ issues in schools as being "unparalleled in its intensity."[9] In 2021, 1,586 bans were implemented in eighty-six school districts across twenty-six states.

Just as was the case in the late 1800s, women attempted to make some strides toward equality, this time with the #MeToo movement in 2017, and that, too, was met with backlash. Now, specials like the documentary *The End of Men*, which Carlson produced, stoke fears that men are losing power in America. One man, Roy Den Hollander, attempted to kill a woman, whom he called a "lazy and incompetent Latina judge," because he believed that "manhood is in serious jeopardy in America." (The intended victim was New Jersey District Court Judge Esther Salas; Hollander accidentally killed her son instead.)[10] In 2022, the US Secret Service released a report warning that misogynistic extremism was on the rise, but it's nothing many women haven't already been experiencing in their daily lives.[11]

There are quite a lot of people who would like to see women back in the kitchen, barefoot and pregnant. Whether women like it or not.

In America, the unspoken conservative position, now or 150 years ago, has been that a "good" woman is one who is virginal but flawlessly attractive enough to get a man to marry her, after which she should keep his house, satisfy all his sexual desires, bear and raise his children, and never complain for any reason. If you are a woman, and you don't criticize this outlook—if you loudly agree that these requirements are reasonable—there's still no guarantee that conservative men will be nice to you. But if you do complain, you can be sure they'll call you a bitch or a slut or a dog or, like Restell, the "wickedest woman in New York."

Just as they always have. It is exhausting, just as it has always been.

And so, a great many people stay politely silent as their rights slip away.

To point out that repealing women's access to birth control is perhaps not motivated by a beneficent spirit on the part of Republican lawmakers feels a bit fruitless. Still, it remains easier to protect theoretical children—by forcing women to do something they do not wish to do at risk to their own health—than to protect actual children. The government can force a person to give birth, but its interest and responsibility ends there. It is a wonderful way for certain politicians to seem caring without actually having to *do* anything.

It does not mean, for instance, that they have to feed those children; after all, one hundred ninety-two Republicans voted against a bill to ease the baby formula shortage in 2022. For many children, life does not improve once they are no longer consuming formula. Texas, for instance, where abortion is forbidden after six weeks' gestation, has more food insecure children than any other state, as of 2020.[12]

And forbidding abortion certainly does not mean you have to do anything to stop women from wanting abortions. That woman of Madame Restell's time who suggested that women would not turn to sex work if factories paid better had a point. Women might be less likely to have abortions if they were better paid—because they would feel more able to care for a child—but that would require raising the minimum wage. They might think it would be easier to have a child if the United States was not the only industrialized country without a paid family leave policy.[13] But that might negatively impact businesses. Women might be less concerned about giving birth if the United States did not rank worst in the developed world in terms of maternal mortality.[14] But that would require addressing flaws in our health-care system, which, among other challenges, leaves a great many people uninsured and without proper care.

Even if all these criteria were met, there would still be women who would want abortions, and who should have every right to have them if they wish. Anything else undermines the courage that choosing to give birth entails.

Motherhood in and of itself is an act of bravery, even if you choose it with pure joy. And this is where history starts to get very personal for me.

I wanted my daughter more than I have ever wanted anything in my life. I had medical challenges that made it difficult for me to have a baby, so I did multiple rounds of in vitro fertilization (IVF). Infertility does brutally drive home the fact that, happy and hopeful as you might be about a fertilized embryo, it is not yet a baby. And much though they might like to accuse women who have abortions of murdering babies, insofar as it comes to anything as concrete as economics, Republicans generally understand this, too. You can't get life insurance for a fetus because, as the US Insurance Agents website explains, "Life insurance, by its very nature, cannot be purchased for a life that does not yet exist."[15]

When I was pregnant, I was thrilled to be so. I doubt you will ever find anyone happier about experiencing morning sickness than I was.

And, while I was optimistic, I was also very worried about complications that I knew might arise. I kept thinking of an article in the *Guardian* where a woman was told that her fetus had not developed in a way that was compatible with life. She asked her doctor, "What can a baby like mine do? Sleep all the time?" I could see myself in her place. I would be doing just the same kind of mental gymnastics to try to figure out any way I could still care for such a child. Her doctor informed her, "Babies like yours are not generally comfortable enough to sleep." She had an abortion in her third trimester to spare a child a brief life of agony. Being in that position is one of the worst things I can imagine, and I pray that woman has found some measure of peace.[16]

Then I recalled former president Donald Trump denouncing late-term abortions as doctors "rip[ping] the baby out of the womb of the mother just prior to the birth of the baby"—as the *Guardian* also reminded its readers—as if people were having such abortions for fun, and not for absolutely heartbreaking reasons like the one that woman described.[17] So when I was finally ready to give birth—to have a *baby*—I was ecstatic and deeply relieved.

I was a week past my due date, so I was induced. For anyone unfamiliar, that's a procedure whereby pregnant women go to the hospital at an appointed time and are given Pitocin, a hormone that causes the uterus to contract and labor to begin. It's often suggested that women have an epidural when being induced, as Pitocin can cause especially strong contractions.

For whatever reason, in my case, the epidural didn't work as it was intended to. This was no one's fault; epidurals have a failure rate of about 10 percent. However, if you are induced and have an epidural, you cannot move around or do any of the exercises that supposedly lessen some of the pain of contractions. You're in a hospital bed hooked up to, among other glamorous things, a catheter. The pain was such that I started vomiting, and I continued vomiting on a regular basis for the next twenty-six hours. And when I vomited, I was pleased, because it was a momentary distraction from the fact that my body felt like it was being torn apart from the inside. I often see women screaming comically on televised depictions of birth and marvel that anyone has the strength to scream. I could not do more than whimper and clutch my husband's hand.

When my daughter finally made her entrance (to David Bowie's "Oh! You Pretty Things" playing in the background, because she has flawless timing), I hemorrhaged. My husband told me later it looked as though someone had overturned a jug of milk, but all the milk was blood. The room filled very quickly with doctors discussing how much blood I'd lost. The number they kept estimating was two liters. That did not seem like so very much to me; after all, I've carried two-liter soda bottles without any trouble. That was before I learned that the average person has about five liters of blood.

I lost close to three.

I had a minute to tell my husband and daughter that I loved them before I was wheeled into the operating room. There, as various nurses encouraged me to try to remain conscious, doctors worked on my "ratty placenta." I was not at my most alert through this, but I remember one nurse holding my hand the entire time. Later, I told my aunt, also a nurse, how much I appreciated that. I thought it was so kind that there was someone whose job just consisted of providing that sort of comfort. "Yeah," my aunt explained, "they do that when they're worried you might go into hemorrhagic shock."

At the time, lying on the table, I kept thinking that if this had happened to me in any other era, I would have died. I did not think about how hemorrhaging is still "worldwide, the leading cause of maternal death."[18]

I was, also in the course of this, a well-off white woman at a wonderful hospital. Black and non-white women in the United States have almost three times the risk of death from hemorrhaging than white women do.[19] I didn't die. I was fortunate. I had excellent doctors.

Some time later, after I'd been monitored, I was moved to a private room where my husband and I could discuss how beautiful our baby was at length. Every so often a nurse would come in, look at my chart, and remark, "Oh, you've had a bad day."

It was the best day of my life. It was the day I met my daughter. I *chose* to go through that, and for her, I'd do it again a hundred times.

If I had not chosen this, however—if this experience had been assigned to me against my will by a faceless bureaucracy—it would have been nothing less than pure torture.

A case could be made that forcing someone to undergo losing about half the blood in their body is worth it if it saves a life, but there are a great many bodily sacrifices that save lives. Donating a kidney to someone in need would, for example, absolutely save a sentient, fully developed life. Consenting to donate your organs after death saves lives, at no inconvenience to you. My life was saved because people donate blood.

The government can't force you to do any of those things, nor should it be able to.

But in much of America, the land of the free, you *can* be forced to give birth.

Cis-gendered men are not generally expected to sacrifice their bodies to sustain others' lives in the way women are. The closest example I can think of is the draft, which was abolished in 1973. As nice as it is to see a sign reminding me that the pint of blood I donate can save up to three lives, I do not go about informing those who choose not to give blood that they have murdered three people.

I cannot deny that some aspects of my pro-choice view are shaped by my experience giving birth. I can imagine some people saying that I'm being dramatic, that birth isn't that bad, certainly not bad enough to merit considering abortion. Some people do have much easier deliveries than I did, and that is wonderful for them. But I actually don't consider my birth experience to have been that bad. I did not, like many of my friends, have postpartum depression afterward; if anything, I've found my first year with my child almost overwhelmingly wonderful. I did not experience, more frighteningly, postpartum psychosis. I didn't have a fourth-degree tear. I didn't have to have a hysterectomy. I did not suffer through undiagnosed preeclampsia (something Lucy Knisley details wonderfully in her memoir *Kid Gloves*). I did not have postpartum eclampsia, or seizures. I did not have a pregnancy-related stroke. Nor did I have a pregnancy-related heart attack.

And, above all else, I did not die.

I did not die.

Not everyone can say that. Hundreds of women die from pregnancy-related causes in the United States each year. And now, in a country where *Roe* has been repealed, all manner of new terrors await pregnant women. Despite anti-choicer's gib claims to the contrary, there are numerous cases where abortions are necessary to save the mother's life. One could look to the case of Savita Halappanavar who, in 2017, died of sepsis because she could not access an abortion.[20] Exceptions for the life of the mother have already left doctors attempting to decide when, precisely, the life of the mother is sufficiently threatened. In Texas, where a 2021 law prohibited abortion as soon as a fetal heartbeat could be detected, a woman who experienced a premature rupture of membranes at eighteen weeks of pregnancy, in 2022, found herself at a crossroads. The fetus would not survive. She was susceptible to a uterine infection called *chorioamnionitis*, among other risks, some of them life threatening. "There's very little amniotic fluid left," a doctor told her. But because the fetus still had a heartbeat, she was also told that she could not abort until it was clear that her life was in danger.

She went home to wait. She began passing blood. She had cramps. She began to vomit. She was told that those symptoms weren't sufficiently serious and she needed to wait until her vaginal discharge was "smell[ing] foul, really bad. Enough to make her retch." When it finally did, she brought her discharge in a plastic bag to the hospital, afraid the doctors would not believe her. All of this was happening as she was also grieving the loss of a wanted pregnancy. The doctors finally induced, but the woman in this case remarked, "It's just really unimaginable to be in a position of having to think: How close to death am I before somebody is going to take action and help me?"[21]

For anyone aware of these possibilities, being pregnant in the United States must be frightening in ways it simply was not for me in 2021.

Sometimes I look at photos of teenage boys confidently holding their signs at anti-choice rallies. I look at them and wonder whether, if they had to spin a wheel where a bodily punishment, ranging from "bad cramps" to "death," was randomly assigned to them upon the eve of their (wanted or unwanted) child's delivery, any one of them would still feel so enthusiastic about forcing people to give birth. It's a theoretical argument, of course. But their arguments about theoretical babies end with us literally bleeding on operating tables.

As for the notion that if women were simply *chaste* they'd have no problems—every generation's fertile people sleep around for fun. Always. Even in eighteenth-century New England. And well before that, too.

It's easy to say that people who do not wish to become pregnant should simply use birth control. Many do. A majority—slightly over half—of women in need of abortions report using birth control the month they became pregnant. Birth control is not perfect. Given that Clarence Thomas indicated that the US Supreme Court should reconsider *Griswold v. Connecticut*—the 1965 case that allowed unmarried people access to birth control—people have also been concerned about whether it will remain available to them. A bill called the Right to Contraception Act recently passed in the House of Representatives protecting the right to access birth control. It did so with 8 votes from Republicans, but 195 Republicans voted against it. It is unlikely to gain the support from Republicans that it needs to pass in the Senate.

Many people in the past and present do not like the idea that women choose to have sex for pleasure, just as men do.

Already we have seen the gleeful misogyny that accompanied the repeal of *Roe*. On Twitter, an anti-choice advocate wrote, "If you're scared for your daughter's future, maybe focus on raising her to not be a slut."[22] The comment so far has more than twenty-seven thousand likes.

Meanwhile, less than one month after *Roe* was repealed, a ten-year-old rape victim had to cross from Ohio to Indiana to get an abortion. In Ohio, abortion is now banned at six weeks. That's around two weeks after a missed period, before many women know they are pregnant. The state has no exceptions for cases of rape, incest, or fatal fetal anomalies.[23] The doctor who helped her soon will not be able to help others as Indiana is poised to restrict abortion, too. If anti-choice activists achieve their aim of a nationwide ban, girls like this will have no one in the country to help them.

Some Republicans, such as Representative Jim Jordan of Ohio, responded that this story was "another lie" while the editorial board of the *Wall Street Journal* sneered that it was "An Abortion Story Too Good to Confirm."[24]

A day after the *WSJ* story ran, a man was charged with raping a ten-year-old girl in Ohio who then traveled to Indiana for an abortion. Which is to say, the story was true.

For a party quite capable of catastrophizing about slews of women casually aborting moments before birth, it sometimes seems like, when it comes to believing that ten-year-old girls are raped, or women die in childbirth, right-wingers are incapable of believing that bad things happen. In truth, they happen every single day. They always have.

So, I think about what my daughter will be like when she's ten. I think about what I was like when I was ten. I still slept with a stuffed animal. I think about that little girl in Indiana listening to people jeer that she is either a liar or a slut because sluts are the only people who need abortions.

I am so terribly sad for my country.

Americans are entering a new age of Comstockery, where, if women do not want to be mothers, they will be made to be. Madame Restell will not be there to assist women. In fact, in areas where abortion is restricted, it's almost certain that a great many *less* effective people will offer their services. And just as Horatio Storer found that women will do dangerous things to induce their own abortions, so will we. Imagining that everyone will know about mifepristone and misoprostol, or have access to them, is a fantasy.

If this frightens you—if it fills you with dread, as it does for me, that your daughters will grow up with fewer rights than their mothers and grandmothers had, and that the use of their bodies will be dictated by legislators who have never met them—then, please, remind them of history.

By and large, Americans don't like learning history. They like learning propaganda. They enjoy stories that are exclusively about how America is great and always has been. Do not let your children believe in a fictitious, rosy version of the past where every woman was happily a mother. Tell them the true history of this country, where abortion has always been commonly practiced.

And tell them your *own* history.

My greatest fear is not that abortion rights will be taken away in America. That is horrible. But that is already a reality for many people and has been for some time. It's that we will stop being angry about it. I am frightened that my daughter will grow up thinking her position as a second-class citizen, whose health and goals are less important to people in power than her capacity to breed, is normal and right. That she will think that this is just how things are.

It isn't. Around the world, in countries from Mexico to Benin, the work of pro-choice advocates has made abortion more accessible and safer. The European Parliament has voted to denounce the overturning of *Roe v. Wade.* Around the world, women are gaining greater control over their bodies.

Though not in America.

So, tell the next generation that there was a time when we owned our bodies. Tell them they still deserve to, and that, whatever the age, it is not the state's right to tell anyone otherwise. Tell them the history of people like Madame Restell, and the history of her patients, and how common abortion has always been. But more than that, tell them the history you lived.

Let them know where we came from.

And perhaps, in time, they'll fight their way back there.

Acknowledgments

WRITING A BOOK IS ONE OF THOSE THINGS THAT, LIKE RAISING a child, takes a village. The village that helped on *Madame Restell* was an amazing one.

First and foremost, thanks to my editor Carrie Napolitano, who believed in this project from the very beginning and fought so hard for it.

The same applies to my agent, Anna Sproul-Latimer, who helped me refine my vague idea that "someone should write a book about how abortion has always been common" into this specific book.

Everyone at the Research Services department of the New York Public Library—particularly Maurice Klapwald—is better at finding information than Google will ever be, and deserves undying respect.

Copy editor Katherine Streckfus, indexer Sherri Linsenbach, production editor Sean Moreau, proofreaders Erica Lawerence and Lori Lewis, thank you so much for polishing this manuscript into the best possible version of itself.

The entire team at Hachette, truly, has been so kind and thoughtful in their approach. Hopefully this will be the first book of many with you!

The fact-checking team—Beth Fulmer, Robert Van Rens, and Morgan Baskin—were all rigorous and smart, and capable of reading this manuscript with wonderfully clear eyes. Your efforts have saved me many sleepless nights of second-guessing myself, and any nonfiction writer would be lucky to have such a team.

In retrospect, my notion that I would simply write this book while my newborn slept was delusional. I'm grateful to the many people who babysat my actual child while I worked on this. Kay, Martha, Abby, Bella, Mrs. Kibblesmith, and, of course, my mom, you are wonderful human beings.

Speaking of my mom—thanks to my parents for their support and enthusiasm regarding this project, and so many others over the years.

And Daniel. Jesus Christ, what would I do without you? The fact that you are a wonderful partner, a creative genius, and you keep me laughing in spite of the news cycle is a triumph. My life is better in every way because of you. Thank you for being the best husband, the best father, the best human, and, maybe most importantly, my best friend.

Thank you to all the pro-choice doctors out there who still, as George Tiller did, "trust women." Your strength every day is an inspiration.

And for my daughter. You are the closest thing I have ever seen to perfection. Each day with you is a gift, and everything I do will be for you, always.

NOTES

PROLOGUE

1. "Madame Restell," *New York Daily Herald*, February 24, 1878.
2. Edward Van Every, *Sins of New York as "Exposed" by the Police Gazette* (New York: Frederick A. Stokes, 1930), pt. 1, chap. 7.
3. "An Astrologer from Egypt," *Cincinnati Enquirer*, August 2, 1878.
4. "The Wages of Sin," *Brooklyn Daily Eagle*, February 24, 1878.
5. "Madame Restell," *New York Daily Herald*, February 24, 1878.
6. "Madame Restell," *New York Daily Herald*, February 24, 1878.
7. "Madame Restell," *New York Daily Herald*, February 24, 1878.
8. "Madame Restell," *New York Daily Herald*, February 24, 1878.
9. "Unveiling Vice," *Cincinnati Enquirer*, February 12, 1878.
10. "The Woman Restell," *Brooklyn Daily Eagle*, April 2, 1878.
11. "Unveiling Vice."
12. "Suppressing Vice—a Raid on Madame Restell," *Saint Paul (MN) Globe*, February 16, 1878.
13. "Unveiling Vice."

CHAPTER ONE

1. Sarah Morris and Natalie Grueninger, *In the Footsteps of Anne Boleyn* (Gloucestershire: Amberley, 2009), 142.
2. R. R. Gordon, *The Little Book of Little Walks Around Little Villages in the Cotswolds*, book 2, *Painswick Valley*, edition 01 (self-pub., Smashwords, 2014).
3. Timothy Mowl, "In the Realm of the Great God Pan," *Country Life*, October 17, 1996.
4. Jack Larkin, "The Secret Life of a Developing Country (Ours)," *American Heritage* 39, no. 6 (September/October 1988).

5. Richard Godbeer, *Sexual Revolution in Early America, Gender Relations in the American Experience* (Baltimore: Johns Hopkins University Press, 2004), 129.

6. Richard Godbeer, *Sexual Revolution in Early America, Gender Relations in the American Experience* (Baltimore: Johns Hopkins University Press, 2004), 129.

7. Larkin, "Secret Life."

8. "Trends in Premarital Sex in the United States, 1954–2003," *Lawrence B. Finer Public Health Rep.* 122, no. 1 (Jan–Feb 2008): 73–78.

9. Nancy F. Cott, "Passionlessness: An Interpretation of Victorian Sexual Ideology, 1790–1850," *Signs* 4, no. 2 (Winter 1978): 219–236.

10. Gloucestershire Archives; Gloucester, Gloucestershire; Gloucestershire Church of England Parish Registers; Reference Numbers: P244 in 1/8.

11. "Madame Restell," *Brooklyn Union*, April 1, 1878.

12. Jonathan Swift, "Directions to Servants," in *The Works of Jonathan Swift* (London: Henry Washbourne, 1841), 366.

13. Anonymous, *My Secret Life*, vol. 2 (Amsterdam: 1888), 15.

14. Eliza Haywood, *A Present for a Servant-Maid: Or, the Sure Means of Gaining Love and Esteem* (Dublin: George Faulkner, 1744), 46.

15. "Madame Restell," *Brooklyn Union*, April 1, 1878.

16. "Madame Restell," *Brooklyn Union*, April 1, 1878.

17. "Madame Restell's Suicide," *New York Sun*, April 2, 1878.

18. "Madame Restell's Suicide."

CHAPTER TWO

1. *Quebec Gazette*, June 2, 1834, quoted in "Emigration and Immigrant Life—Subject Cards O–Z," Clark Historical Library, Central Michigan University, www.cmich.edu/research/clarke-historical-library/explore-collection/explore-online/michigan-material/beaver-island-history-helen-collar-papers/beaver-island-history/emigration-immigrant-life/subject-cards—emigration-and-immigrant-life-o-z.

2. George W. Potter, *To the Golden Door: The Story of the Irish in Ireland and America* (Boston: Little, Brown, 1960), 150, quoted in "Emigration and Immigrant Life—Subject Cards O–Z," Clark Historical Library.

3. John Simkin, "Journey to America," Spartacus Educational, September 1997 (updated January 2020), https://spartacus-educational.com/USAEjourney.htm.

4. Frances Trollope, "An Englishwoman in New York, 1831," reprinted in *City Journal*, Spring 1995, www.city-journal.org/html/englishwoman-new-york-1831-11931.html.

5. Helen L. Sumner, "The Historical Development of Women's Work in the United States," *Proceedings of the Academy of Political Science in the City of New York* 1, no. 1, The Economic Position of Women (October 1910): 17.

6. "Percentage of American Labor Force in Agriculture," from *Digital History*, website maintained by Steven Mintz, Sara McNeil, and John Lienhard, www.digitalhistory.uh.edu/disp_textbook.cfm?smtID=11&psid=3837, accessed January 20, 2020.

7. "Susan," "Letters from Susan," *Lowell Offering* 4, no. 11 (September 1844): 257–259, at *Mill Girls in Nineteenth-Century Print*, American Antiquarian Society, https://americanantiquarian.org/millgirls/items/show/42.

8. "Care of Rooms in Boarding-Houses," in *The New England Offering*, vol. 2 (Lowell, MA: Harriet Farley, 1849), 100.

9. Edith Abbott, "History of the Employment of Women in the American Cotton Mills: III," *Journal of Political Economy* 17, no. 1 (January 1909): 23.

10. Thomas Dublin, *The Transformation of Work and Community in Lowell, Massachusetts, 1826–1860* (New York: Columbia University Press, 1979), 55.

11. Thomas Dublin, *Women at Work: The Transformation of Work and Community in Lowell* (New York: Columbia University Press, 1946), 56.

12. Sumner, "Historical Development of Women's Work."

13. "f. niha," "The Collect Pond," *History of Health in New York* (blog), Baruch College, City University of New York, May 18, 2019, https://blogs.baruch.cuny.edu/histmed3450/?p=170.

14. Davy Crockett, *Life of Col. David Crockett* (Philadelphia: G. G. Evans, 1859), 190.

15. Julie Miller, *Abandoned: Foundlings in Nineteenth Century New York City* (New York: NYU Press, 2008), 29.

16. *Brooklyn Daily Eagle*, November 28, 1849.

17. Physician of New York, *Madame Restell: An Account of Her Life and Horrible Practices* (New York: Charles Smith, 1847).

18. Miller, *Abandoned*, 104.

19. Hon. W. P. Letchworth, "The Removal of Children from Almshouses in the State of New York," 1894.

20. "New York as a Nursing-Mother to Her Foundlings," *Harper's Weekly*, February 26, 1859, from "On This Day," *New York Times*.

21. *Buffalo Commercial*, January 18, 1850.

22. John Duer, Benjamin Franklin Butler, John Canfield Spencer, Simeon Eben Baldwin, Ebenezer Baldwin, and James Hillhouse, *The Revised Statutes of the State of New-York, Passed During the Years One Thousand Eight Hundred and Twenty-Seven, and One Thousand Eight Hundred and Twenty-Eight: To Which Are Added, Certain Former Acts Which Have Not Been Revised* (Albany, NY: Packard and Van Benthuysen, 1829), 653.

23. Herbert Asbury, *The Gangs of New York: An Informal History of the Underworld* (New York: Alfred A. Knopf, 1927), 25.

24. Peter Adams, *The Bowery Boys: Street Corner Radicals and the Politics of Rebellion* (Santa Barbara, CA: ABC-CLIO, 2005), xiv.

25. "Godfrey's Cordial," *New York Evening Post*, March 15, 1833.

26. "Opium Eating in New York," *Brooklyn Evening Star*, May 29, 1857.

27. *Philadelphia Inquirer*, December 25, 1860.

28. "Distressing Accident," *New-York Tribune*, April 6, 1844.

29. Sumner, "Historical Development of Women's Work," 16.

30. Amy Dru Stanley, *Bondage to Contract: Wage Labor, Marriage, and the Market in the Age of Slave Emancipation* (Cambridge: Cambridge University Press, 1998), 238.

31. *Supplement to the New-York Daily Tribune*, March 21, 1846.

32. Charles Sutton, *The New York Tombs: Its Secrets and Its Mysteries*, ed. James B. Mix and Samuel A. Mackeever (San Francisco: A. Roman and Company, 1874), chap. 10.

33. *New York Daily Herald*, April 12, 1836.

34. Patricia Cline Cohen, *Murder of Helen Jewett* (New York: Vintage, 2010), 17.

35. James Miller, *Prostitution Considered in Relation to Its Cause and Cure* (Edinburgh: Southerland and Knox, 1859), 12.

36. "The History of Prostitution," *Buffalo Morning Express*, November 13, 1858.

37. *New York Mercury*, July 18, 1832.

38. *Buffalo Morning Express* and *Illustrated Buffalo Express*, November 13, 1858.

39. W. T. Stead, "The Maiden Tribute of Modern Babylon (The Report of the Pall Mall Gazette's Secret Commission)," *Pall Mall Gazette*, July 6, 1885.

40. Anya Jabour, "Women's Work and Sex Work in Nineteenth-Century America," PBS, February 22, 2016, www.pbs.org/mercy-street/blogs/mercy-street-revealed /womens-work-and-sex-work-in-nineteenth-century-america2.

41. Timothy J. Gilfoyle, *City of Eros: New York City, Prostitution, and the Commercialization of Sex, 1790–1920* (New York: W. W. Norton, 1992), 39.

42. Sumner, "Historical Development of Women's Work."

CHAPTER THREE

1. "The Celebrated Chamomile Pills of Dr. William Evans," *Gettysburg (VA) Compiler*, January 2, 1838.

2. *Newbern (NC) Spectator*, October 25, 1839.

3. "Ann Lohman's Life," *New York Sun*, April 2, 1878.

4. "Madame Restell's Suicide," *New York Times*, April 2, 1878.

5. Charles Savona-Ventura, *Ancient Egyptian Medicine* (self-pub., Lulu.com, 2017; originally published as a series of articles in *Synapse, Hera, Treasures of Malta*, and *Malta Medical Journal*), 8.

6. Vicki Oransky Wittenstein, *Reproductive Rights: Who Decides?* (Minneapolis: Twenty-First Century Books, 2016), 12.

7. John M. Riddle, *Contraception and Abortion from the Ancient World to the Renaissance* (Cambridge, MA: Harvard University Press, 1999), 69.

8. *Oath of Hippocrates*, in *Harvard Classics: Scientific Papers*, vol. 38, ed. Charles W. Eliot (Boston: P. F. Collier and Son, 1910).

9. Sarah B. Pomeroy, ed., *Women's History and Ancient History* (Chapel Hill: University of North Carolina Press, 1991), 80.

10. Pomeroy, *Women's History and Ancient History*, 80

11. Lynnette E. Leidy, "Possible Role of the Pessary in the Etiology of Toxic Shock Syndrome," *Medical Anthropology Quarterly*, n.s., 8, no. 2 (June 1994): 198–208.

12. Riddle, *Contraception and Abortion*, 78.

13. Gina Kolata, "In Ancient Times, Flowers and Fennel for Family Planning," *New York Times*, March 8, 1994, www.nytimes.com/1994/03/08/science/in -ancient-times-flowers-and-fennel-for-family-planning.html.

14. Sarah Handley-Cousins, "Abortion in the 19th Century," National Museum of Civil War Medicine, February 9, 2016, www.civilwarmed.org/abortion1.

15. *New York Daily Herald*, January 16, 1843.

16. *Muscatine (IA) Weekly*, October 22, 1875.

17. Clifford Browder, *The Wickedest Woman in New York: Madame Restell, the Abortionist* (Hamden, CT: Archon Books, 1988), 15.

18. Molly Farrell, "Ben Franklin Put an Abortion Recipe in His Math Textbook," *Slate*, May 5, 2022, https://slate.com/news-and-politics/2022/05/ben-franklin -american-instructor-textbook-abortion-recipe.html.

19. Thomas Shapter, "Report of the Trial of a Medical Practitioner, on a Charge of Intent to Produce Abortion," in *Provincial Medical and Surgical Journal*, ed. Robert J. N. Streeten (London: John Churchill, 1844), 19.

20. *Brooklyn Daily Evening Star*, March 24, 1841.

21. *Brooklyn Daily Evening Star*, March 24, 1841.

22. Molly Redden, "Please I Am Out of Options: Inside the Murky World of DIY Abortions," *Guardian*, November 21, 2016.

23. "Mother, Cousins Charged with Forcing Teen to Drink Turpentine for Abortion," WTVM, September 26, 2006, www.wtvm.com/story/5462044/mother -cousins-charged-with-forcing-teen-to-drink-turpentine-for-abortion.

24. "Tansy," RXList, September 17, 2019, www.rxlist.com/tansy/supplements.htm.

25. *New York Daily Herald*, August 13, 1839.

26. Lucy Ferris, "Facing My Second Unwanted Pregnancy," *New York Times Magazine*, June 10, 2012, 58.

27. *Chicago Inter Ocean*, May 8, 1880.

28. *Fort Wayne (IN) Journal-Gazette*, June 9, 1918.

29. *Hull Packet* (East Yorkshire), April 19, 1878.

30. *New Orleans Times-Picayune*, April 6, 1878.

31. *New York Daily Herald*, December 25, 1839.

CHAPTER FOUR

1. Marvin Olasky, *The Press and Abortion, 1838–1988* (Hillsdale, NJ: Laurence Erblaum Associates, 1988), 8.

2. Olasky, *The Press and Abortion*, 9.

3. *Philadelphia Public Ledger*, November 12, 1839.

4. *York (PA) Gazette*, December 26, 1837.

5. *New York Daily Herald*, December 7, 1837.

6. *New York Daily Herald*, February 10, 1840.

7. *New York Daily Herald*, April 13, 1840.

8. *New York Daily Herald*, April 13, 1840.

9. *New York Daily Herald*, December 25, 1839.

10. *Philadelphia Public Ledger*, April 28, 1840.

11. *Boston Post*, February 4, 1843.

12. *The Age and Lancaster and Chester County (PA) Weekly Gazette*, March 27, 1841.

13. *Philadelphia Public Ledger*, April 28, 1840.

14. *New York Daily Herald*, December 25, 1840.

15. *New York Daily Herald*, February 24, 1840.

16. *The Age and Lancaster and Chester County (PA) Weekly Gazette*, March 27, 1841.

17. *The Polyanthos* (New York), May 9, 1841.

18. *New York Daily Herald*, October 27, 1843.

CHAPTER FIVE

1. *New York Daily Herald*, June 24, 1839.

2. *New York Daily Herald*, August 21, 1839.

3. *Philadelphia Public Ledger*, November 16, 1839.

4. "Vaginal Hysterectomy and Criminal Abortion," *London and Edinburgh Monthly Journal of Medical Science* 4 (1844): 987.

5. Jen Gunter, "Anatomy of a Coat Hanger Abortion," July 13, 2013, https://drjengunter.com/2013/07/13/anatomy-of-a-coat-hanger-abortion.

6. "Another New Move in Philosophy—a Beautiful Female Physician," *New York Daily Herald*, June 21, 1839.

7. Russell M. Jones, "American Doctors and the Parisian Medical World, 1830–1840," *Bulletin of the History of Medicine* 47, no. 1 (January/February 1973): 40, 51.

8. William McCormac, "The Development of Surgery," *Science*, n.s., 12, no. 294 (August 17, 1900): 261.

9. Lindsey Fitzharris, *The Butchering Art: Joseph Lister's Quest to Transform the Grisly World of Victorian Medicine* (New York: *Scientific American*/Farrar, Straus and Giroux, 2017), 11.

10. Fitzharris, *The Butchering Art*, 8, 11.

11. Fitzharris, *Butchering Art*, 9.

12. *New York Daily Herald*, April 23, 1838.

CHAPTER SIX

1. "Another Move in Philosophy—a Beautiful Female Physician," *New York Daily Herald*, June 21, 1839.

2. Cyril Elgood, *Medical History of Persia and the Eastern Caliphate from the Earliest Times Until the Year A.D. 1932* (Cambridge: Cambridge University Press, 1951), 7.

3. Katherine Roeder, *Wide Awake in Slumberland: Fantasy, Mass Culture, and Modernism in the Art of Winsor McCay* (Jackson: University Press of Mississippi, 2013), 3.

4. *New York Daily Herald*, quoted in Stephanie Buck, "The Salacious Murder of This New York City Prostitute Changed the American Media Landscape: Two Centuries After Helen Jewett, We've Got TMZ," Timeline, April 28, 2017, https://timeline.com/helen-jewett-murder-7acc3cc812c.

5. Louis M. Starr, "James Gordon Bennett, Beneficent Rascal," *American Heritage* 6, no. 2 (February 1955).

6. *Charleston (SC) Daily Courier*, September 18, 1835.

7. Harriet Anne Jacobs, *Incidents in the Life of a Slave Girl, Written by Herself* (Chapel Hill: Academic Affairs Library, University of North Carolina, 1998 [1861]), chap. 9, reprinted at "A Slave Is Tortured," PBS, www.pbs.org/wgbh/aia/part3/3h1516t.html.

8. Samuel Jenks Smith, *Charleston (SC) Daily Courier*, September 18, 1835.

9. Samuel Jenks Smith, "Sunday Morning News," *New York Evening Post*, May 5, 1835.

10. *New York Sunday Morning News*, July 7, 1839.

11. *Morning Herald*, New York, New York, July 15, 1839.

12. *Morning Herald*, New York, New York, July 15, 1839.

13. "More of the Doctors," *New York Daily Herald*, July 17, 1839.

14. *New York Daily Herald*, August 21, 1839.

15. *New York Daily Herald*, August 21, 1839.

16. *New York Daily Herald*, September 24, 1839.

17. *New York Daily Herald*, September 24, 1839.

18. "The Late Samuel Jenks Smith," *Ladies Home Companion* 13 (1840): 100.

19. George Washington Dixon, "Our Position," *The Polyanthos* (New York), January 17, 1841.

20. *United States Gazette* (Philadelphia), June 22, 1836.

21. Dale Cockrell, *Demons of Disorder: Early Blackface Minstrels and Their World* (Cambridge University Press, 1999), 104.

22. Cockrell, *Demons of Disorder*, 106.

23. "The Buffalo in a Hobble Again," *Baltimore Sun*, January 4, 1839.

24. Cockrell, *Demons of Disorder*, 115.

25. *Lancaster (PA) Examiner*, May 23, 1839.

26. Dixon, "Our Position."

27. *Lancaster (PA) Intelligencer*, May 7, 1839, via *New York Despatch*.

28. Cockrell, *Demons of Disorder*, 115.

29. *Boston Post*, September 14, 1841.

30. George Washington Dixon, "Keep It Before the Public," *The Polyanthos* (New York), February 16, 1841.

31. Dixon, "Keep It Before the Public."

32. *Trial of Madame Restell, Alias Ann Lohman, for Abortion and Causing the Death of Mrs. Purdy, Being a Full Account of All the Proceedings of the Trial, Together with the Suppressed Evidence and Editorial Remarks* (Bethesda, MD: National Library of Medicine, 1841), 7.

33. "Contraceptive Use in the United States," Guttmacher Institute, April 2020, www.guttmacher.org/fact-sheet/contraceptive-use-united-states.

34. *New York Evening Post*, March 18, 1841.

35. Madame Restell, "Madame Restell's Reply to Mr. John D. Keese (Druggist), and Other Gentlemen of the Grand Jury," *New York Daily Herald*, March 19, 1841.

36. Restell, "Madame Restell's Reply."

37. Restell, "Madame Restell's Reply."

38. Valerie Lee, *Granny Midwives and Black Women Writers* (New York: Routledge, 1996), 25.

CHAPTER SEVEN

1. "Madame Restell in Prison on a Charge of Manslaughter," *New York Evening Post*, March 24, 1841.

2. *Brooklyn Daily Evening Star*, March 24, 1841.

3. *Brooklyn Daily Evening Star*, March 24, 1841.

4. *New-York Tribune*, July 20, 1841.

5. "Madame Restell in Prison."

6. *Brooklyn Daily Evening Star*, March 24, 1841.

7. *New-York Tribune*, August 24, 1842.

8. *New-York Tribune*, July 20, 1841.

9. *Brooklyn Daily Evening Star*, March 24, 1841.

10. *Trial of Madame Restell, Alias Ann Lohman, for Abortion and Causing the Death of Mrs. Purdy, Being a Full Account of All the Proceedings of the Trial, Together with the Suppressed Evidence and Editorial Remarks* (Bethesda, MD: National Library of Medicine, 1941), https://collections.nlm.nih.gov/ext/mhl/101521473/PDF/101521473 .pdf, 19.

11. *New York Evening Post*, February 1, 1840.

12. Janice Hopkins Tanne, "Abortion Does Not Raise Risk of Breast Cancer, US Study Finds," *British Medical Journal* 333, no. 7600 (May 5, 2007).

13. *Brooklyn Daily Evening Star*, March 24, 1841.

14. "Madame Restell," *New-York Tribune*, May 1, 1841.

15. Chelsea Rose Marcius, "NYC's Most Notorious Jail: A Look Back at the Tombs," *New York Daily News*, October 17, 2020.

16. Peter Libbey, "New York's Tribute to the Tombs Angel, Lost, Found, and Now Restored," *New York Times*, June 16, 2019.

17. *New York Herald*, New York, NY, Aug 21, 1839.

18. *Trial of Madame Restell*, 20.

19. *Advocate of Moral Reform* (New York), April 15, 1841, quoted in Clifford Browder, *The Wickedest Woman in New York: Madame Restell, the Abortionist* (Hamden, CT: Archon Books, 1988), 39.

20. *Boston Post*, May 17, 1841.

21. *Buffalo Courier*, March 20, 1851.

22. *Trial of Madame Restell*, 8.

23. *Trial of Madame Restell*, 5.

24. *Trial of Madame Restell*, 12.

25. *Trial of Madame Restell*, 12.

26. *Trial of Madame Restell*, 10.

27. *Trial of Madame Restell*, 10.

28. *Trial of Madame Restell*, 18.

29. *Trial of Madame Restell*, 18.

30. *Trial of Madame Restell*, 18.

31. "City Intelligence," *New-York Tribune*, July 21, 1841.

32. *New-York Tribune*, July 21, 1841.

33. *Trial of Madame Restell*, 20.

34. *Trial of Madame Restell*, 20.

35. *Brooklyn Evening Star*, July 21, 1841.

36. *New York Sun*, New York, New York, June 21, 1841, via Marvin Olasky, "Advertising Abortion in the 1830s and '40s," *Journalism History* 13, no. 2 (1986).

37. *New York Daily Herald*, via *Charleston (SC) Mercury*, March 31, 1841.

38. *New-York Tribune*, August 24, 1842.

39. *New York Evening Post*, March 4, 1842.

40. *New-York Tribune*, August 24, 1842.

41. *New-York Tribune*, August 24, 1842.

42. *New-York Tribune*, August 24, 1842.

43. *New-York Tribune*, August 24, 1842.

CHAPTER EIGHT

1. Mordecai Noah, *Buffalo Courier*, November 8, 1844.

2. *The Polyanthos* (New York), April 11, 1841.

3. *New York Daily Herald*, via *Charleston (SC) Mercury*, March 31, 1841.

4. *Buffalo Courier*, November 24, 1842.

5. *Brooklyn Evening Star*, January 17, 1844.

6. *Brooklyn Evening Star*, August 15, 1843.

7. *Brooklyn Evening Star*, January 17, 1844.

8. *Brooklyn Evening Star*, March 26, 1844.

9. *New-York Tribune*, March 26, 1844.

10. Jennifer Daniel and Ford Fessenden, "An Animated History of New York's Love-Hate Relationship with Commuting," *New York Times*, December 29, 2014.

11. Sylvie Douglis, "The Carriage Tax," Planet Money, NPR, December 6, 2019.

12. *New York Daily Herald*, February 28, 1844.

13. *New York Daily Herald*, March 10, 1846.

14. *New York Daily Herald*, March 17, 1846.

15. *Buffalo Commercial*, April 18, 1844.

16. *Whig Standard* (Washington, DC), April 18, 1844.

17. *Buffalo Commercial*, April 18, 1844.

18. *Buffalo Commercial*, April 18, 1844.

19. *New York Daily Herald*, April 17, 1844.

20. *New York Daily Herald*, April 17, 1844.

21. *New York Daily Herald*, April 17, 1844.

22. *New York Daily Herald*, September 14, 1844.

23. Andrea Tone, ed., *Controlling Reproduction: An American History* (Rowman & Littlefield Publishers, 1996), 100.

24. James C. Mohr, *Abortion in America: The Origins and Evolution of National Policy* (New York: Oxford University Press, 1978), 76–77.

25. *New-York Tribune*, May 11, 1844.

26. *New York Daily Herald*, July 8, 1845.

27. Christopher Claxton, *History and Description of the Steam-Ship Great Britain, Built at Bristol for the Great Western Steam-Ship Company: To Which Are Added, Remarks on the Comparative Merits of Iron and Wood as Materials for Ship-Building* (New York: J. S. Homans, 1845), 23.

28. *New York Evening Post*, September 3, 1845.

29. *New York Daily Herald*, October 4, 1845.

CHAPTER NINE

1. *New York Daily Herald*, February 6, 1846.

2. *New York Daily Herald*, February 6, 1846.

3. "Madame Restell, and Some of Her Dupes," in *New-York Medical and Surgical Reporter* 1, no. 10 (February 21, 1846): 161.

4. Lynn Sacco, *Unspeakable: Father-Daughter Incest in American History* (Baltimore: Johns Hopkins University Press, 2009), 2.

5. William Cobbett, *Advice to Young Men and, Incidentally, to Young Women, in the Middle and Higher Ranks of Life, in a Series of Letters* (self-pub., 1829), 233.

6. Sherri Broder, "Child Care or Child Neglect? Baby Farming in Late-Nineteenth-Century Philadelphia," *Gender and Society* 2, no. 2 (June 1988): 133.

7. *Topeka Lance*, September 15, 1888.

8. John Davis, *Travels of Four Years and a Half in the United States of America During 1798, 1799, 1800, 1801, and 1802* (London: R. Edwards, 1909 [1803]), quoted in

Andrea Freeman, "Unmothering Black Women: Formula Feeding as an Incident of Slavery," *Hastings Law Journal* 69, no. 1545 (August 2018): 1558.

9. Sharon Lerner, "The Real War on Families: Why the U.S. Needs Paid Leave Now," *In These Times Magazine*, August 18, 2015.

10. *New York Daily Herald*, February 6, 1846.

11. *(Natchez) Mississippi Free Trader*, March 12, 1846.

12. *Nashville Tennessean*, April 5, 1878.

13. *New York Daily Herald*, February 24, 1846.

14. *Brooklyn Daily Eagle*, February 24, 1846.

15. *New-York Tribune*, February 25, 1846.

16. *New-York Tribune*, February 25, 1846.

17. *New-York Tribune*, February 25, 1846.

18. *New-York Tribune*, February 25, 1846.

19. *Baltimore Daily Commercial*, July 8, 1846.

20. *Memphis Daily Appeal*, November 12, 1882.

21. "Madame Restell, and Some of Her Dupes," 160.

22. F. D. Huntington, *Restel's Secret Life: A True History of Her from Birth to Her Awful Death by Her Own Wicked Hands* (Philadelphia: Old Franklin Publishing House, 1897), 26.

23. Huntington, *Restel's Secret Life*, 26, 30, 33.

24. Huntington, *Restel's Secret Life*, 33.

25. Sunny Jane Morton and Judy G. Russell, "How to Research Orphaned and Adopted Children in Your Genealogy," *Family Tree Magazine*, December 2016, www.familytreemagazine.com/birth-families/adoption/researching-orphan-children-genealogy.

26. Michael Schuman, "History of Child Labor in the United States—Part 1: Little Children Working," *Monthly Labor Review*, US Bureau of Labor Statistics, January 2017, www.bls.gov/opub/mlr/2017/article/history-of-child-labor-in-the-united-states-part-1.htm.

27. Barbara Bisantz Raymond, *The Baby Thief: The Untold Story of Georgia Tann* (New York: Carroll and Graf, 2007), 73.

28. Richard Wexler, "The Real Lesson of the Orphan Trains," *Orlando Sentinel*, October 5, 1997.

29. Schuman, "History of Child Labor in the United States."

30. Raymond, *Baby Thief*, 75.

31. Raymond, *Baby Thief*, 68, 72.

32. Huntington, *Restel's Secret Life*, 31.

CHAPTER TEN

1. Physician of New York, *Madame Restell: An Account of Her Life and Horrible Practices* (New York: Charles V. Smith, 1847), 13.

2. Physician of New York, *Madame Restell*, 4.

3. Physician of New York, *Madame Restell*, 18.

4. Physician of New York, *Madame Restell*, 19.

5. Physician of New York, *Madame Restell*, 22.

6. *Leavenworth (KS) Weekly Times*, August 31, 1871.

7. *Chicago Inter Ocean*, May 8, 1880.

8. Charlotte Brontë, *Jane Eyre* (New York: Charleton, 1864 [1847]), 114.

9. Sally Shuttleworth, "Jane Eyre and the 19th Century Woman," British Library, www.britishlibrary.cn/en/articles/jane-eyre-and-the-19th-century-woman, accessed May 15, 2021.

10. *(Natchez) Mississippi Free Trader*, April 8, 1841.

11. *Leavenworth (KS) Weekly Times*, August 31, 1871.

12. *Chicago Inter Ocean*, May 8, 1880.

13. *(Natchez) Mississippi Free Trader*, April 8, 1841.

14. *New York Daily Herald*, March 19, 1841.

15. Robert Dale Owen, *Moral Physiology, or, a Brief and Plain Treatise on the Population Question* (New York: Wright and Owen, 1831), 29.

16. *Evansville (IN) Daily Journal*, June 4, 1850.

17. "Introduction," *Pediatrics* 71, no. 4 (April 1983): 679–680, https://pediatrics.aappublications.org/content/71/4/679.

18. *Fort Wayne Journal Gazette*, June 9, 1918.

19. *Fort Wayne (IN) Journal-Gazette*, June 9, 1918.

20. *Natchez (MS) Weekly Courier*, March 31, 1847.

21. A. M. Mauriceau, *The Married Woman's Private Medical Companion* (New York, 1847), 16.

22. *Fort Wayne (IN) Journal-Gazette*, June 9, 1918.

23. *Brooklyn Evening Star*, September 15, 1847.

24. *Natchez (MS) Weekly Courier*, March 31, 1847.

25. Mauriceau, *Married Woman's Private Medical Companion*, 5.

26. *Enterprise and Vermonter*, November 12, 1851.

27. Mauriceau, *Married Woman's Private Medical Companion*, 124.

28. "Divorce Statistics: Over 115 Studies, Facts and Rates for 2020," Wilson and Finkbeiner, www.wf-lawyers.com/divorce-statistics-and-facts, accessed April 12, 2021.

29. *Louisville (KY) Daily Courier*, September 27, 1847.

30. Mauriceau, *Married Woman's Private Medical Companion*, 181.

31. Mauriceau, *Married Woman's Private Medical Companion*, 15.

32. Mauriceau, *Married Woman's Private Medical Companion*, iv.

33. *Louisville (KY) Daily Courier*, September 27, 1847.

34. *Leavenworth (KS) Weekly Times*, August 31, 1871.

35. Mauriceau, *Married Woman's Private Medical Companion*, 120; Owen, *Moral Physiology*, 24.

36. "Law Reports: Mme. Restell's Estate," *New York Times*, December 10, 1878.

37. *Lancaster (PA) Intelligencer*, August 2, 1853.

38. *Louisville (KY) Daily Courier*, September 27, 1847.

39. *Chicago Inter Ocean*, May 8, 1880.

CHAPTER ELEVEN

1. "Madame Restell," *New York Times*, September 3, 1871.

2. "Madame Restell," *New York Times*, September 3, 1871.

3. *New York Evening Post*, September 16, 1847.

4. *Brooklyn Evening Star*, September 15, 1847.

5. *Louisville (KY) Daily Courier*, September 27, 1847.

6. Frank M. O'Brien, "The Story of the *Sun*," *Munsey's Magazine* 60 (1917): 586.

7. István Kornél Vida, "The Great Moon Hoax of 1835," *Hungarian Journal of English and American Studies* 18 (2012): 436.

8. O'Brien, "Story of the *Sun*," 599.

9. *New York Daily Herald*, October 22, 1847.

10. Patsy McGarry, "Catholic Church Teaching on Abortion Dates from 1869," *Irish Times*, July 1, 2013.

11. *Louisville (KY) Daily Courier*, September 27, 1847.

12. *Buffalo Morning Express*, October 27, 1847.

13. Madame Restell, New York State, Court of General Sessions, New York County, *Wonderful Trial of Caroline Lohman, Alias Restell, with Speeches of Counsel, Charge of Court, and Verdict of Jury, Reported in Full for the National Police Gazette* (New York: Burgess, Stringer, 1847), 5.

14. Restell et al., *Wonderful Trial of Caroline Lohman*, 5.

15. Restell et al., *Wonderful Trial of Caroline Lohman*, 6.

16. Robert Brudenell Carter, "On the Pathology and Treatment of Hysteria," *British and Foreign Medico-Chirurgical Review* 11, no. 22 (1853): 70.

17. Restell et al., *Wonderful Trial of Caroline Lohman*, 5.

18. Restell et al., *Wonderful Trial of Caroline Lohman*, 8.

19. Restell et al., *Wonderful Trial of Caroline Lohman*, 7–8.

20. Restell et al., *Wonderful Trial of Caroline Lohman*, 7–8.

21. Restell et al., *Wonderful Trial of Caroline Lohman*, 10.

22. Restell et al., *Wonderful Trial of Caroline Lohman*, 9.

23. Restell et al., *Wonderful Trial of Caroline Lohman*, 9.

24. Restell et al., *Wonderful Trial of Caroline Lohman*, 30.

25. Lynn M. Paltrow and Jeanne Flavin, "Pregnant and No Civil Rights," *New York Times*, November 7, 2014.

26. Yeganeh Torbati and Caroline Kitchener, "Texas Woman Charged with Murder After Abortion," *Washington Post*, April 9, 2022.

27. "Nicaragua: Abortion Ban Threatens Health and Lives," Human Rights Watch, July 31, 2017, www.hrw.org/news/2017/07/31/nicaragua-abortion-ban -threatens-health-and-lives.

28. Restell et al., *Wonderful Trial of Caroline Lohman*, 22.

29. Restell et al., *Wonderful Trial of Caroline Lohman*, 21–23.

30. Restell et al., *Wonderful Trial of Caroline Lohman*, 27.

31. Restell et al., *Wonderful Trial of Caroline Lohman*, 27.

32. Restell et al., *Wonderful Trial of Caroline Lohman*, 27.

33. Restell et al., *Wonderful Trial of Caroline Lohman*, 24.

34. Restell et al., *Wonderful Trial of Caroline Lohman*, 33–34.

35. Restell et al., *Wonderful Trial of Caroline Lohman*, 35.

36. *Brooklyn Daily Eagle*, October 27, 1847.

37. Restell et al., *Wonderful Trial of Caroline Lohman*, 38.

38. Restell et al., *Wonderful Trial of Caroline Lohman*, 38.

39. "Stories of the Time: A Strange Life," *Hartford (CT) Courant*, April 3, 1872.

40. *Brooklyn Evening Star*, July 3, 1848.

CHAPTER TWELVE

1. Stacy Horn, *Damnation Island: Poor, Sick, Mad and Criminal in 19th-Century New York* (Chapel Hill, NC: Algonquin Books, 2018), 7, 79.

2. Horn, *Damnation Island*, 196.

3. *New-York Tribune*, October 21, 1842.

4. *New York Daily Herald*, August 23, 1838.

5. Stacy Horn, "The Cursed Island Before Rikers: Learning from the Story of Blackwell's Island," *New York Daily News*, May 12, 2018.

6. *New York Times*, June 21, 1854.

7. Horn, *Damnation Island*, 195.

8. *New York Evening Post*, January 10, 1849.

9. Nellie Bly, *Ten Days in a Madhouse* (New York: Ian L. Munro, 1877), chap. 14.

10. *New York Evening Post*, January 10, 1849.

11. *New York Evening Post*, January 10, 1849; *New Orleans Crescent*, January 22, 1849.

12. *New York Evening Post*, January 10, 1849.

13. *(Greensboro) Alabama Beacon*, July 22, 1848.

14. *Mobile (AL) Daily Advertiser*, November 21, 1845.

15. *Brooklyn Daily Eagle*, May 17, 1850.

16. Horn, *Damnation Island*, 197.

17. *New York Evening Post*, January 10, 1849.

18. *Fall River (MA) Monitor*, August 4, 1849.

19. *Nashville Tennessean*, April 5, 1878.

20. *New York Daily Herald*, January 23, 1849.

21. *Hartford (CT) Courant*, April 3, 1878.

22. *Brooklyn Evening Star*, January 10, 1849.

23. *New Orleans Times-Picayune*, April 6, 1878.

24. *Hartford (CT) Courant*, April 3, 1878.

25. *New York Evening Post*, January 10, 1849.

26. *New York Evening Post*, January 10, 1849.

27. *New York Evening Post*, January 10, 1849.

28. *Hartford (CT) Courant*, April 3, 1878.

29. *New York Evening Post*, January 10, 1849.

30. *Brooklyn Evening Star*, January 10, 1849.

31. *New Orleans Times-Picayune*, April 6, 1878.

32. *New York Daily Herald*, November 23, 1848.

33. *New Orleans Times-Picayune*, April 6, 1878.

34. *New York Daily Herald*, November 23, 1848.

35. *The (Raleigh, NC) Biblical Recorder*, December 9, 1848.

36. *New York Evening Post*, January 10, 1849.

37. *New York Daily Herald*, January 8, 1849.

38. *New York Daily Herald*, February 14, 1849.

39. *New York Daily Herald*, January 8, 1849.

40. *New York Daily Herald*, February 14, 1849.

41. *New York Daily Herald*, February 18, 1849.

42. *New York Daily Herald*, May 20, 1849.

43. *Buffalo Morning Express and Illustrated Buffalo Express*, May 15, 1855.

44. Christopher Gray, "Doing Time on the River," *New York Times*, February 9, 2012.

45. Judith Berdy, "The Rocky History of Roosevelt Island," *Politico*, June 13, 2015, www.politico.com/magazine/story/2015/06/hillary-clinton-roosevelt-island-history-118970.

46. *Buffalo Courier*, July 4, 1849.

47. *Hartford (CT) Courant*, April 3, 1878.

48. *Milwaukee Daily Free Democrat*, July 22, 1853.

49. *Pittsburgh Daily Post*, August 14, 1849.

CHAPTER THIRTEEN

1. Judith Wellman, "The Seneca Falls Women's Rights Convention: A Study of Social Networks," *Journal of Women's History* 3, no. 1 (1991): 9–37.

2. Lauren Gambino, "Hillary Clinton's Rise Earns Place of Honor in Birthplace of US Women's Suffrage," *Guardian*, June 18, 2016.

3. "Women's Rights Convention," *National Reformer*, August 3, 1848.

4. Elizabeth Cady Stanton, "Address Delivered at Seneca Falls," July 19, 1848, Teaching American History, https://teachingamericanhistory.org/library/document/address-delivered-at-seneca-falls.

5. *New York Daily Herald*, July 30, 1848.

6. *New York Daily Herald*, July 30, 1848.

7. *New York Daily Herald*, July 30, 1848.

8. *New York Daily Herald*, July 30, 1848.

9. "Declaration of Sentiments," in *History of Woman Suffrage*, vol. 1, *1848–1861*, ed. Elizabeth Cady Stanton, Susan B. Anthony, Matilda Joslyn Gage, and Ida Husted Harper (New York: Fowler and Wells, 1881).

10. Stanton et al., "Declaration of Sentiments."

11. Stanton et al., "Declaration of Sentiments."

12. Stanton et al., "Declaration of Sentiments."

13. Lynn Sherr and Ann D. Gordon, "No, Susan B. Anthony and Elizabeth Cady Stanton Were Not Antiabortionists," *Time*, November 10, 2015, https://time.com/4106547/susan-b-anthony-elizabeth-cady-stanton-abortion.

14. *The Revolution*, July 8, 1869.

15. Sherr and Gordon, "No, Susan B. Anthony and Elizabeth Cady Stanton Were Not Antiabortionists."

16. *The Liberator*, September 15, 1848.

17. Elizabeth Blackwell, *Pioneer Work in Opening the Medical Profession to Women: Autobiographical Sketches* (New York: Longmans, Green, 1895), 29.

18. Blackwell, *Pioneer Work*, 30.

19. Janice P. Nimura, *The Doctors Blackwell: How Two Pioneering Women Brought Medicine to Women and Women to Medicine* (New York: W. W. Norton, 2021), 138.

20. *Friends' Library: Comprising Journals, Doctrinal Treatises, and Other Writings of the Religious Society of Friends* (Philadelphia: Printed by Joseph Rakestraw, for the editors, 1837), 132.

21. *Friends' Library*, 132.

22. Reva Siegel, "Reasoning from the Body: A Historical Perspective on Abortion Regulation and Questions of Equal Protection," *Stanford Law Review* 44, no. 261 (1992): 304 (emphasis added).

23. Siegel, "Reasoning from the Body," 304.

24. Laura L. O'Toole and Jessica R. Schiffman, eds., *Gender Violence: Interdisciplinary Perspectives* (New York: NYU Press, 1997), 110.

25. Stanton et al., *History of Woman Suffrage*, 1:719, 496.

26. "Female Suffrage—the Kind of Women Who Would Go to the Polls," *Stockton (CA) Daily Evening Herald*, September 4, 1867.

27. Charles Worcester Clark, "Woman Suffrage, Pro and Con," *Atlantic Monthly*, March 1890.

28. Emily J. Harding Andrews, "Convicts Lunatics and Women! Have No Vote for Parliament She: Is It Time I Got Out of This Place—Where Shall I Find the KEY?," Artists' Suffrage League, 1890.

29. Rose O'Neill, "Give Mother the Vote: We Need It," 1915, courtesy of the New-York Historical Society and the Rose O'Neill Foundation.

CHAPTER FOURTEEN

1. *Evansville (IN) Daily Journal*, March 16, 1854.

2. Women's Christian Temperance Union, "Petition," *Union Signal*, January 13, 1887.

3. Jane E. Larson, "'Even a Worm Will Turn at Last': Rape Reform in Late Nineteenth-Century America," *Yale Journal of Law and the Humanities* 9, no. 1 (1997): 39.

4. *Evansville (IN) Daily Journal*, March 16, 1854.

5. *Brooklyn Daily Eagle*, February 15, 1854.

6. *Evansville (IN) Daily Journal*, March 16, 1854.

7. *Buffalo Daily Republic*, February 16, 1854.

8. *Evansville (IN) Daily Journal*, March 16, 1854.

9. *Evansville (IN) Daily Journal*, March 16, 1854.

10. *Buffalo Daily Republic*, February 16, 1854.

11. *Buffalo Daily Republic*, February 16, 1854.

12. *Buffalo Daily Republic*, February 16, 1854.

13. *Buffalo Daily Republic*, February 16, 1854.

14. *Buffalo Daily Republic*, February 16, 1854.

15. *New York Times*, February 14, 1854.

16. *Richmond (VA) Dispatch*, February 16, 1854.

17. Marilynn Wood Hill, *Their Sisters' Keepers: Prostitution in New York City, 1830–1870* (Berkeley: University of California Press, 1993), 142.

18. *Weekly Wisconsin* (Milwaukee), March 1, 1854.

19. *New York Times*, February 15, 1854.

20. *St. Louis Globe-Democrat*, March 8, 1854.

21. *Richmond (VA) Dispatch*, March 11, 1854.

22. *Washington (DC) Evening Star*, March 13, 1854.

23. *New York Daily Herald*, March 17, 1854.

24. *Richmond (VA) Dispatch*, March 21, 1854.

25. *New York Daily Herald*, March 23, 1854.

26. *Washington (AR) Telegraph*, April 5, 1854.

27. *Zanesville (OH) Courier*, April 18, 1854.

28. *Natchez (MS) Daily Courier*, March 15, 1854.

29. *Washington (AR) Telegraph*, March 22, 1854.

CHAPTER FIFTEEN

1. Edwin G. Burrows and Mike Wallace, *Gotham: A History of New York to 1898* (Oxford: Oxford University Press, 1998), 655.

2. Charles Astor Bristed, *The Upper Ten Thousand: Sketches of American Society* (London, John Parker and Sons, 1852; Miami: HardPress, 2017), loc. 26, Kindle.

3. Bristed, *Upper Ten Thousand*, loc. 121, 337, Kindle.

4. Bristed, *Upper Ten Thousand*, loc. 360, Kindle.

5. Bristed, *Upper Ten Thousand*, loc. 3241, Kindle.

6. Charles Lockwood, "The Annual Battle on Sin," *San Francisco Examiner*, April 29, 1973.

7. Donald Grant Mitchell, *The Lorgnette: or, Studies of the Town. By an Opera Goer* (New York: Printed for Stringer and Townsend, 1851), 90, 96.

8. *Chicago Tribune*, April 4, 1878.

9. Eric Homberger, *Mrs. Astor's New York: Money and Social Power in a Gilded Age* (New Haven, CT: Yale University Press, 2004), 128, 139, 142.

10. *Baltimore Sun*, June 20, 1848.

11. Eric Homberger, *Scenes from the Life of a City* (New Haven, CT: Yale University Press, 1994), 117.

12. "New York, New York City Births, 1846–1909," FamilySearch, https://family search.org, Isaac L Purdy, entry for Charles R. Purdy, August 15, 1858, citing Manhattan, reference vol. 5, p. 394, New York Municipal Archives, FHL microfilm 1,315,312.

13. "Quack's Fortune in Court Fight," *Brooklyn Times Union*, April 1, 1918.

14. Denis Tilden Lynch, *"Boss" Tweed: The Story of a Grim Generation* (New Brunswick, NJ: Transaction Publishers, 2002 [1927]), 180.

15. Committee of Three, *Beadle's Dime Book of Practical Etiquette for Ladies and Gentlemen* (New York: Irwin P. Beadle, 1859), 50.

16. Bristed, *Upper Ten Thousand*, loc. 536, 547, Kindle.

17. Lynch, *"Boss" Tweed*, 183.

18. Cormac Ó Gráda, "The Next World and the New World: Relief, Migration, and the Great Irish Famine," *Journal of Economic History* 79, no. 2 (June 2019): 319–355.

19. *Albany (NY) Evening Journal*, June 24, 1852.

20. *New York Times*, September 28, 1852.

21. James D. McCabe, *The Secrets of the Great City* (New York: Jones Brothers, 1868), 245.

22. Peter Adams, *The Bowery Boys: Street Corner Radicals and the Politics of Rebellion* (Santa Barbara, CA: ABC-CLIO, 2005), xv.

23. Lorraine Boissoneault, "How the 19th-Century Know Nothing Party Reshaped American Politics," *Smithsonian Magazine*, January 26, 2017.

24. Tyler Gregory Anbinder, *Nativism and Slavery* (Oxford: Oxford University Press, 1992), 34.

25. "The Know Nothings," *New York Daily Herald*, June 4, 1854.

26. Elliott J. Gorn, "'Good-Bye Boys, I Die a True American': Homicide, Nativism, and Working-Class Culture in Antebellum New York City," *Journal of American History* 74, no. 2 (1987): 392.

27. Herbert Asbury, *The Gangs of New York: An Informal History of the Underworld* (New York: Alfred A. Knopf, 1927), 90.

28. Gorn, "'Good-Bye Boys,'" 392, 398.

29. *Buffalo Daily Republic*, August 17, 1854.

30. *New York Daily Herald*, March 24, 1856.

31. *Weekly Wisconsin* (Milwaukee), October 15, 1856.

32. *The Revolution*, May 7, 1868.

33. Nicola Beisel and Tamara Kay, "Abortion, Race, and Gender in Nineteenth-Century America," *American Sociological Review* 69, no. 4 (August 2004): 508.

34. *Buffalo Courier*, March 24, 1855.

35. *Weekly Wisconsin* (Milwaukee), October 15, 1856.

36. Abraham Lincoln, letter to Joshua F. Speed, August 24, 1855, from National Park Service, www.nps.gov/liho/learn/historyculture/knownothingparty.htm.

37. *Plymouth (IN) Democrat*, October 9, 1856.

38. Robert N. Farrell, "No Foreign Despots on Southern Soil: The American Party in Alabama and South Carolina, 1850–1857" (master's thesis, University of Southern Mississippi, 2017), 283.

CHAPTER SIXTEEN

1. *New York Times*, December 17, 1856.

2. *New York Times*, December 17, 1856.

3. *Brooklyn Daily Eagle*, August 20, 1856.

4. *Brooklyn Daily Eagle*, August 20, 1856.

5. *New York Times*, December 17, 1856.

6. *New-York Tribune*, April 22, 1858.

7. *Reynolds's Newspaper* (London), September 7, 1856.

8. *Reynolds's Newspaper* (London), September 7, 1856.

9. *Louisville (KY) Daily Courier*, August 5, 1856.

10. *Reynolds's Newspaper* (London), September 7, 1856.

11. *Reynolds's Newspaper* (London), September 7, 1856.

12. *Weekly Wisconsin* (Milwaukee), October 15, 1856.

13. *Reynolds's Newspaper* (London), September 7, 1856.

14. *Louisville (KY) Courier-Journal*, September 17, 1863.

15. *Reynolds's Newspaper* (London), September 7, 1856.

16. *Buffalo Evening Post*, March 29, 1859.

17. *Louisville (KY) Courier-Journal*, September 17, 1863.

18. *Buffalo Evening Post*, March 29, 1859.

19. *New-York Tribune*, January 23, 1857.

20. *Princeton (IN) Clarion-Leader*, July 3, 1858.

21. *New York Daily Herald*, November 11, 1843; *New York Times*, November 25, 1856.

22. *New York Daily Herald*, January 30, 1856.

23. *Buffalo Morning Express and Illustrated Buffalo Express*, September 26, 1855.

24. *New York Times*, November 19, 1860.

25. *Syracuse Daily Courier and Union*, May 18, 1857.

26. *Syracuse Daily Courier and Union*, May 18, 1857.

27. *Syracuse Daily Courier and Union*, May 28, 1857.

28. *Syracuse Daily Courier and Union*, May 28, 1857.

29. *Syracuse Daily Courier and Union*, May 28, 1857.

30. *Syracuse Daily Courier and Union*, June 8, 1857.

CHAPTER SEVENTEEN

1. Ryan Johnson, "A Movement for Change: Horatio Robinson Storer and Physicians' Crusade Against Abortion," *James Madison Undergraduate Research Journal* 4, no. 1 (2017): 14.

2. Abraham Flexner, *Medical Education in the United States and Canada* (New York: Carnegie Foundation, 1910), 6, 7.

3. *Orleans County (VT) Gazette*, February 28, 1852.

4. Flexner, *Medical Education*, xv.

5. "Where the Money Went…in 1860," October 12, 2016, *Portable Press* (blog), www.portablepress.com/blog/2016/10/where-the-money-wentin-1860.

6. Adrian E. Feldhusen, "The History of Midwifery and Childbirth in America: A Time Line," *Midwifery Today*, 2000, www.midwiferytoday.com/web-article /history-midwifery-childbirth-america-time-line.

7. Claire Prechtel-Kluskens, "Researching the Career of a 19th Century Physician," *Prologue Magazine* 36, no. 2 (Summer 2004).

8. James C. Mohr, *Abortion in America: The Origins and Evolution of National Policy* (Oxford: Oxford University Press, 1978), 108.

9. "Medical Intelligence," *Boston Medical and Surgical Journal* 44 (1851): 288; *Evansville (IN) Daily Journal*, July 2, 1858.

10. *Chicago Tribune*, February 25, 1860.

11. *Boston Medical and Surgical Journal* 44 (1851): 84.

12. Joseph B. DeLee, "Progress Towards Ideal Obstetrics," *American Journal of Obstetrics and Diseases of Women and Children* 73 (1916): 410.

13. DeLee, "Progress Towards Ideal Obstetrics," 410.

14. Howard Markel, "In 1850, Ignaz Semmelweis Saved Lives with Three Words: Wash Your Hands," *PBS NewsHour*, May 15, 2015, www.pbs.org/newshour/health /ignaz-semmelweis-doctor-prescribed-hand-washing.

15. M. Best and D. Neuhauser, "Ignaz Semmelweis and the Birth of Infection Control," *BMJ Quality and Safety* 13, no. 3 (2004): 233–234.

16. Markel, "In 1850, Ignaz Semmelweis Saved Lives."

17. Ignaz Semmelweis, *The Etiology, Concept, and Prophylaxis of Childbed Fever*, trans. Codell Carter (Madison: University of Wisconsin Press, 1983 [1861]), 95, 100.

18. Charles D. Meigs, *On the Nature, Signs, and Treatment of Childbed Fevers, in a Series of Letters Addressed to the Students of His Class* (Philadelphia: Blanchard and Lea, 1854), 104.

19. Eric Homberger, *Scenes from the Life of a City: Corruption and Conscience in Old New York* (New Haven, CT: Yale University Press, 1994), 92.

20. Homberger, *Scenes from the Life*, 95.

21. Horatio Robinson Storer, *Why Not? A Book for Every Woman* (Boston: Lee and Shepard, 1866), 30.

22. Charles Edward Buckingham, "Report upon Criminal Abortions," *Boston Medical and Surgical Journal* 56, no. 17 (May 28, 1857): 346.

23. Carroll Smith-Rosenberg, *Disorderly Conduct: Visions of Gender in Victorian America* (New York: Oxford University Press, 1985), 242.

24. Storer, *Why Not? A Book for Every Woman*, 85.

25. Nicola Beisel and Tamara Kay, "Abortion, Race, and Gender in Nineteenth-Century America," *American Sociological Review* 69, no. 4 (August 2004): 506.

26. New York Lunatic Asylum, *Twenty-Fourth Annual Report of the Managers of the New York State Lunatic Asylum for the Year 1866*, State of New York, Transmitted to the Legislature February 5, 1867 (Albany, NY: Van Benthuysen and Sons, Legislative Printers, 1867), 33.

27. H. S. Pomeroy, *The Ethics of Marriage* (New York: Funk and Wagnalls, 1888), xiv.

28. Julia R. Steinberg, Thomas M. Laursen, Nancy E. Adler, Christiane Gasse, Esben Agerbo, and Trine Munk-Olsen, "Examining the Association of Antidepressant Prescriptions with First Abortion and First Childbirth," *JAMA Psychiatry* 75, no. 8 (2018): 828–834.

29. Zara Abrams, "The Facts About Abortion and Mental Health," *American Psychological Association* 53 (June 23, 2022).

30. Andrew M. Seaman, "Women Denied Abortions Face Higher Risk for Mental Health Problems," Reuters, December 14, 2016, www.reuters.com/article /us-health-abortions-mental/women-denied-abortions-face-higher-risk-for -mental-health-problems-idUSKBN1432ZT.

31. *Roe v. Wade*, 410 U.S. 113, 153 (1973). See also Michelle Goodwin, *Policing the Womb: Invisible Women and the Criminalization of Motherhood* (Cambridge: Cambridge University Press, 2020), 63.

32. *Detroit Free Press*, February 7, 1867.

33. Storer, *Why Not? A Book for Every Woman*, 71.

34. Beisel and Kay, "Abortion, Race, and Gender," 506.

35. Andrea Tone, *Controlling Reproduction: An American History* (Lanham, MD: Rowman and Littlefield, 1996).

36. Johnson, "Movement for Change," 19.

37. Pomeroy, *Ethics of Marriage*, 82–83.

38. Beisel and Kay, "Abortion, Race, and Gender," 506.

39. Horatio Robinson Storer, *Is It I? A Book for Every Man* (Boston: Lee and Shepard, 1868; Digital Text Publishing Company, 2009), loc. 918, Kindle.

40. John C. Rolfe, *The Attic Nights of Aulus Gellius, with an English Translation* (Cambridge, MA: Harvard University Press; London: William Heinemann, 1927), 355.

41. Soranus, *Soranus' Gynecology*, trans. Owsei Temkin (Baltimore: Johns Hopkins University Press, 1956 [c. 2nd century CE]).

42. Ruth Graham, "Ugh, the Pope Told a Story About a Woman Who Had an Abortion to Preserve Her Figure," *Slate*, January 12, 2017, https://slate .com/human-interest/2017/01/the-pope-told-a-story-about-a-woman-who -had-an-abortion-to-preserve-her-figure.html.

43. Lawrence B. Finer, Lori F. Frohwirth, Lindsay A. Dauphinee, Susheela Singh, and Ann M. Moore, "Reasons U.S. Women Have Abortions: Quantitative and Qualitative Perspectives," *Perspectives on Sexual and Reproductive Health* 37, no. 3 (September 2005): 110.

44. Sarah Primrose, "The Attack on Planned Parenthood," *UCLA Women's Law Journal* 19, no. 165 (2012): 174.

45. Beisel and Kay, "Abortion, Race, and Gender," 506.

46. Storer, *Why Not? A Book for Every Woman*, 75.

47. Andrea Tone, ed., *Controlling Reproduction: An American History* (Wilmington, DE: SR Books, 1997), 65.

48. Smith-Rosenberg, *Disorderly Conduct*, 242.

49. Leslie J. Reagan, "Linking Midwives and Abortion in the Progressive Era," *Bulletin of the History of Medicine* 69, no. 4 (1995): 569.

50. DeLee, "Progress Towards Ideal Obstetrics," 408.

51. Horatio Storer and Franklin Fiske Heard, *Criminal Abortion: Its Nature, Its Evidence, and Its Law* (Boston: Little, Brown, 1868), 58, quoted in Goodwin, *Policing the Womb*, 53, 19.

52. Pomeroy, *Ethics of Marriage*, 83.

53. Montrose Pallen, "Foetecide," *Medical Archives* 3 (April 1869): 199.

54. Walter Channing, "Effects of Criminal Abortion," *Boston Medical and Surgical Journal* 60 (1859): 139, quoted in Smith-Rosenberg, *Disorderly Conduct*, 238.

CHAPTER EIGHTEEN

1. *New York Times*, April 2, 1878.

2. "List of the Principal Diamonds and Diamond Owners in New York," *Philadelphia Evening Telegraph*, March 20, 1867.

3. *New York Times*, December 10, 1878.

4. Edith Wharton, *The Age of Innocence* (Overland Park, KS: Digireads, 2011 [1920]), 15.

5. William J. Stern, "How Dagger John Saved New York's Irish," *City Journal*, Spring 1997.

6. Sr. Elizabeth Ann, SJW, "Dagger John" Catholic Heritage Curricula, https://www.chcweb.com/catalog/files/daggerjohn.pdf, 2001.

7. Stern, "How Dagger John Saved New York's Irish."

8. *Sunbury (PA) Gazette and Northumberland County (PA) Republican*, March 1, 1851.

9. *Lancaster (UK) Gazette*, April 27, 1878.

10. John R. G. Hassard, *The Life of the Most Reverend John Hughes, D.D., First Archbishop of New York, with Extracts of His Private Correspondence* (New York: D. Appleton, 1866), 331.

11. *Buffalo Evening News*, August 1, 1889.

12. *Lancaster (UK) Gazette*, April 27, 1878.

13. *Merchant's Magazine and Commercial Review* 37, no. 6 (December 1857): 660.

14. *New Orleans Times-Picayune*, April 6, 1878.

15. Hassard, *Life of the Most Reverend John Hughes*, 403.

16. *Lancaster (UK) Gazette*, April 27, 1878.

17. *Nashville Tennessean*, October 30, 1868.

18. *Chicago Tribune*, September 12, 1865.

19. *Pacific Commercial Advertiser* (Honolulu), July 17, 1869.

20. *Daily Milwaukee News*, May 31, 1865.

21. *Daily Milwaukee News*, May 31, 1865.

22. Eric Homberger, *The Historical Atlas of New York City: A Visual Celebration of 400 Years of New York City's History*, 2nd ed. (New York: Henry Holt, 2005), 73.

23. *Nashville Tennessean*, October 30, 1868.

24. *Daily Milwaukee News*, May 31, 1865.

25. *Daily Milwaukee News*, May 31, 1865.

26. *Daily Kansas Tribune*, September 24, 1865.

27. *Daily Meridian (MS) Clarion*, April 1, 1866.

28. *Leavenworth (KS) Times*, August 31, 1871.

29. F. D. Huntington, *Restel's Secret Life: A True History of Her from Birth to Her Awful Death by Her Own Wicked Hands* (Philadelphia: Old Franklin Publishing House, 1897), 5.

30. *Buffalo Sunday Morning News*, September 10, 1882.

31. Huntington, *Restel's Secret Life*, 3.

CHAPTER NINETEEN

1. *Brooklyn Daily Eagle*, April 15, 1861.

2. George Brown Tindall and David Emory Shi, *America: A Narrative History*, 7th ed. (New York: W. W. Norton, 2006), chap. 15.

3. John Lockwood and Charles Lockwood, "First South Carolina. Then New York?" *New York Times*, New York, Jan 6, 2011.

4. *New York Daily Herald*, November 1, 1860.

5. Nicole Gaudiano, "DeVos Compares Abortion Rights Debate to Slavery," *Politico*, January 23, 2020.

6. *Richmond (VA) Dispatch*, May 8, 1854.

7. *New York Times*, April 13, 1861.

8. *New York Daily Herald*, April 14, 1861.

9. Dale Cockrell, *Demons of Disorder: Early Blackface Minstrels and Their World* (Cambridge: Cambridge University Press, 1999), 116.

10. James L. Crouthamel, *Bennett's New York Herald and the Rise of the Popular Press* (Syracuse, NY: Syracuse University Press, 1989), 112, 117.

11. *New York Times*, July 27, 1861.

12. Benjamin Justice, "Historical Fiction to Historical Fact: Gangs of New York and the Whitewashing of History," *Social Education* 67, no. 4 (2003): 214.

13. *Brooklyn Daily Eagle*, June 27, 1867.

14. Bruce I. Bustard, "Spirited Republic," National Archives, https://www.archives.gov/files/publications/prologue/2014/winter/spirited.pdf, Sep 12, 2016.

15. Frederick Marryat, *A Diary in America with Remarks on Its Institutions*, vol. 1, pt. 2 (London: Longman, Orme, Brown, Green, and Longman's, 1839), 124, 126.

16. W. J. Rorabaugh, *The Alcoholic Republic: An American Tradition* (Oxford: Oxford University Press, 1979), 96.

17. Susanne Schmid and Barbara Schmidt-Haberkamp, eds., *Drink in the Eighteenth and Nineteenth Centuries* (London: Routledge, 2014), 144.

18. Testimony from Major Francis Pruyn, January 22, 1866, Albany, New York, image available at Fold3, www.fold3.com/image/301310572.

19. "History of Andersonville Prison," Andersonville, National Historic Site Georgia, National Park Service, www.nps.gov/ande/learn/historyculture/camp_sumter_history.htm.

20. "Captain Henry Wirz," Andersonville, National Historic Site Georgia, National Park Service, www.nps.gov/ande/learn/historyculture/captain_henry_wirz.htm.

21. Greg Bailey, "Why Does This Georgia Town Honor One of Americas Worst War Criminals?," *New Republic*, November 10, 2015.

22. F. D. Huntington, *Restel's Secret Life: A True History of Her from Birth to Her Awful Death by Her Own Wicked Hands* (Philadelphia: Old Franklin Publishing House, 1897), 3.

23. Huntington, *Restel's Secret Life*, 28.

24. *New York Times*, April 2, 1878.

25. Anne de Courcy, "'Husband Hunters' Is a Tale of Strong Women Getting What They Want," *Australian Financial Review*, June 9, 2017.

26. *Daily Milwaukee News*, May 31, 1865.

27. *New York Times*, April 2, 1878.

28. *New York Times*, April 2, 1878.

29. *New York Times*, April 2, 1878.

30. *New York Daily Herald*, December 11, 1878.

31. *Centralia (MO) Fireside Guard*, October 28, 1871.

32. *New York Times*, April 2, 1878.

33. *Chicago Tribune*, April 6, 1878.

34. "Obituary: Charles Robert Purdy," *Brooklyn Times Union*, January 31, 1922.

35. *Chicago Tribune*, April 6, 1878.

36. *New York Times*, April 2, 1878.

CHAPTER TWENTY

1. *New York Times*, December 18, 1870.

2. *Brandon (VT) Gazette*, February 2, 1860.

3. *Illinois State Journal*, April 10, 1878.

4. *Daily Meridian (MS) Clarion*, April 1, 1866.

5. Quoted in Allen Guelzo, "Did Religion Make the American Civil War Worse?," *Atlantic*, August 23, 2015.

6. Quoted in Guelzo, "Did Religion Make the American Civil War Worse?"

7. Allen C. Guelzo, *Fateful Lightning: A New History of the Civil War and Reconstruction*, 493, 108.

8. *New York Daily Herald*, May 31, 1868.

9. "A Palace of Blood," *Rutland (VT) Weekly*, June 29, 1865.

10. *Monmouth Democrat* (Freehold, NJ), June 8, 1865.

11. *Hartford (CT) Courant*, May 29, 1865.

12. Denis Tilden Lynch, *"Boss" Tweed: The Story of a Grim Generation* (New Brunswick, NJ: Transaction Publishers, 2002 [1927]), 182.

13. *Daily Milwaukee News*, May 31, 1865.

14. Lynch, *"Boss" Tweed*, 118, 183.

15. Lynch, *"Boss" Tweed*, 118.

16. *Brooklyn Union*, November 12, 1870.

17. *Belmont Chronicle* (Saint Clairsville, OH), August 1867.

18. Lynch, *"Boss" Tweed*, 182, 178.

19. Alexander B. Callow Jr., *The Tweed Ring* (New York: Oxford University Press, 1969), 250.

20. Lynch, *"Boss" Tweed*, 183.

21. "Death of Prince Hal," *San Francisco Examiner*, September 7, 1889.

22. "Are His Days Numbered? Harry Genet—'Prince Hal'—of the Old Tweed Ring," *Lancaster (WI) Teller*, September 20, 1888.

23. Lynch, *"Boss" Tweed*, 183.

24. Lynch, *"Boss" Tweed*, 183.

CHAPTER TWENTY-ONE

1. Madame Restell, "A Card," *New York Times*, December 29, 1866.

2. Restell, "A Card."

3. Restell, "A Card."

4. *Nashville Republican Banner*, January 6, 1867.

5. *Louisville (KY) Daily Courier*, October 28, 1868.

6. *Titusville (PA) Herald*, December 29, 1870.

7. *Ebensburg (PA) Cambria Freeman*, June 2, 1870.

8. *Louisville (KY) Daily Courier*, October 28, 1868.

9. *Chicago Tribune*, August 31, 1871.

10. *Scranton (PA) Tribune*, August 31, 1871.

11. *Burlington (VT) Democrat*, December 14, 1871.

12. *Norfolk Virginian*, September 4, 1871.

13. *Chicago Tribune*, September 3, 1871.

14. *Norfolk Virginian*, September 4, 1871.

15. *New-York Tribune*, September 8, 1871.

16. *New York Times*, October 29, 1871.

17. *New York Sun*, November 5, 1871.

18. *Fort Scott (KS) Daily Monitor*, September 3, 1871.

19. *Chicago Tribune*, September 3, 1871.

20. *Norfolk Virginian*, September 1, 1871.

21. "The Infant Murderers of New York," *Des Moines Register*, September 6, 1871.

22. "Infant Murderers of New York."

23. "The Evil of the Age," *Leavenworth (KS) Weekly Times*, August 31, 1871.

24. "The Evil of the Age."

25. Clifford Browder, *The Wickedest Woman in New York: Madame Restell, the Abortionist* (Hamden, CT: Archon Books, 1988), 133.

26. "A Versatile Swindler Arrested," *New York Times*, September 7, 1871.

27. Marvin Olasky, *The Press and Abortion, 1838–1988* (New York: Laurence Erlbaum Associations, 1988), 31, 29.

28. *New-York Tribune*, September 7, 1871.

29. Victoria Clafin Woodhull, "A Speech on the Great Social Problem of Labor & Capital," speech delivered at Cooper Institute, New York City, May 8, 1871.

30. *Neodesha (KS) Citizen*, September 22, 1871.

31. Victoria Woodhull, letter to the editor, *Hartford (CT) Courant*, December 2, 1871.

32. *New-York Tribune*, September 7, 1871.

33. *New-York Tribune*, September 7, 1871.

34. *New York Daily Herald*, April 8, 1878.

35. *New-York Tribune*, September 7, 1871.

36. *New-York Tribune*, September 7, 1871.

37. Olasky, *Press and Abortion*, 29.

38. Browder, *Wickedest Woman in New York*, 135.

39. *New York Times*, November 25, 1873.

CHAPTER TWENTY-TWO

1. Devin Leonard, "The Life And Times of a True American Moral Hysteric," LitHub, May 2, 2016, https://lithub.com/the-life-and-times-of-a-true-american -moral-hysteric/.

2. Anna Louise Bates, *Weeder in the Garden of the Lord: Anthony Comstock's Life and Career*, rev. ed. (Lanham, MD: University Press of America, 1995).

3. Amy Sohn, "How Anthony Comstock, Enemy to Women of the Gilded Age, Attempted to Ban Contraception," Literary Hub, July 20, 2021, https://lithub .com/how-anthony-comstock-enemy-to-women-of-the-gilded-age-attempted-to-ban -contraception.

4. Amy Sohn, *The Man Who Hated Women: Sex, Censorship and Civil Liberties in the Gilded Age* (New York: Farrar, Straus and Giroux, 2021), 22.

5. Sohn, *The Man Who Hated Women*, 24.

6. Anthony Comstock, *Traps for the Young* (New York: Funk and Wagnalls, 1883), 154.

7. Sohn, *The Man Who Hated Women*, 23.

8. Devin Leonard, *Neither Snow nor Rain: A History of the United States Postal Service* (New York: Grove Press, 2016), 70.

9. *New York Daily Herald*, February 26, 1870.

10. "Law Intelligence: The Sunday Liquor Traffic—*Comstock vs. Chapman*," *Brooklyn Union*, November 18, 1871; *Brooklyn Daily Eagle*, July 3, 1868.

11. "A False Witness on the Blunder and Scandal," *Brooklyn Daily Eagle*, November 23, 1872.

12. "Anthony Comstock and the War upon Indecency," *Stockton (CA) Daily Evening Herald*, June 20, 1872.

13. *Cincinnati Enquirer*, December 10, 1872.

14. "Anthony Comstock and the War upon Indecency."

15. *Colorado Springs Weekly Gazette*, December 12, 1872.

16. Sohn, *The Man Who Hated Women*, 31.

17. Sohn, *The Man Who Hated Women*, 61.

18. New York Society for the Suppression of Vice, *Annual Report* 36 (January 1910).

19. Brandon R. Burnette, "Comstock Act of 1873," in *The First Amendment Encyclopedia: Presented by the John Seigenthaler Chair of Excellence in First Amendment Studies*, Middle Tennessee State University, www.mtsu.edu/first-amendment/article/1038 /comstock-act-of-1873.

20. Sohn, *The Man Who Hated Women*, 72, 73.

21. Elizabeth Hovey, "Obscenity's Meaning, Smut-Fighters, and Contraception, 1872–1936," *San Diego Law Review* 29, no. 13 (February 1992): 19.

22. Kat Long, "The Forbidden Apple: Dastardly Do Gooders, 1873–1913," *New York Times*, April 3, 2009.

23. Original ink drawing for *A Dreadful Predicament* by Samuel D. Ehrhart, shown at "Puck, Anthony Comstock, and the 'Suppression of Vice' in Chicago," Driehaus Museum, November 16, 2015, https://driehausmuseum.org/blog /view/puck-anthony-comstock-the-suppression-of-vice-in-chicago.

24. Robert Minor, *Anthony Comstock (1844–1915), American Reformer*, cartoon, 1915, Granger Historical Picture Archive.

25. "Anthony Is Shocked," *New Ulm (MN) Review*, August 16, 1893.

CHAPTER TWENTY-THREE

1. *New York Daily Herald,* June 17, 1874.

2. Christopher Gray, "An 1871 Building with a Plaque Honoring a Visitor," *New York Times,* April 22, 2001.

3. *Knoxville (TN) Journal and Tribune,* May 25, 1886.

4. *Olney (IL) Daily Ledger,* December 2, 1875.

5. Christopher Gray, "Apartment Buildings, the Latest in French Ideas," *New York Times,* July 11, 2013.

6. *Chicago Inter Ocean,* May 8, 1880.

7. *New York Daily Herald,* December 11, 1878.

8. Christopher Gray, "An Architectural Barometer," *New York Times,* September 1, 2011.

9. "French Flats and Apartment Houses in New York," *Journal of Carpentry and Building* 2 (January 1880): 2.

10. "French Flats and Apartment Houses in New York," 2.

11. Christopher Gray, "Madame Restell's Other Profession," *New York Times,* October 13, 2013.

12. "French Flats and Apartment Houses in New York," 2.

13. "Apartment Houses," *Real Estate Record and Builder's Guide* 24, no. 65 (October 18, 1879): 822.

14. "French Flats and Apartment Houses in New York," 2.

15. "French Flats and Apartment Houses in New York," 2.

16. "Apartment Houses," 822.

17. "Apartment Houses," 822.

18. "Apartment Houses," 822.

19. "French Flats and Apartment Houses in New York," 2.

20. *Knoxville (TN) Journal and Tribune,* May 25, 1886.

21. Nathaniel Hawthorne, *Love Letters of Nathaniel Hawthorne to Miss Peabody* (Frankfurt: Outlook Verlag, 2020), 12.

22. *Hartford (CT) Courant,* April 3, 1878.

CHAPTER TWENTY-FOUR

1. *New York Daily Herald,* December 10, 1878.

2. "Mme. Restell's Money," *Chicago Inter Ocean,* May 8, 1880.

3. "Mme. Restell's Money," *Chicago Inter Ocean,* May 8, 1880.

4. "Mme. Restell's Money," *Chicago Inter Ocean,* May 8, 1880.

5. "Mme. Restell's Money," *Chicago Inter Ocean,* May 8, 1880.

6. "Mme. Restell's Money," *Chicago Inter Ocean,* May 8, 1880.

7. *Chicago Tribune,* April 4, 1878.

8. *New York Daily Herald,* December 10, 1878.

9. *Chicago Tribune,* April 4, 1878.

10. *Salt Lake City Deseret News,* April 2, 1878.

CHAPTER TWENTY-FIVE

1. Devin Leonard, "The Life and Times of an American Moral Hysteric," LitHub .com via Grove Press, May 2, 2016, https://lithub.com/the-life-and-times-of-a-true -american-moral-hysteric/.

2. Anthony Comstock, *Traps for the Young* (New York: Funk and Wagnalls, 1883), 155.

3. "Suppressing Vice—a Raid on Madame Restell," *Saint Paul (MN) Globe*, February 16, 1878.

CHAPTER TWENTY-SIX

1. *Boston Post*, February 13, 1878.

2. "The Tainted Millions of Madame Restell," *Fort Wayne (IN) Journal-Gazette*, June 9, 1918.

3. *Brooklyn Daily Eagle*, April 2, 1878.

4. "Suppressing Vice—a Raid on Madame Restell," *Saint Paul (MN) Globe*, February 16, 1878.

5. "Suppressing Vice—a Raid on Madame Restell."

6. "Suppressing Vice—a Raid on Madame Restell."

7. "Suppressing Vice—a Raid on Madame Restell."

8. "Suppressing Vice—a Raid on Madame Restell."

9. *New York Sun*, February 12, 1878.

10. "Suppressing Vice—a Raid on Madame Restell."

11. *New York Sun*, February 13, 1878.

12. *New York Sun*, February 13, 1878.

13. "A Vile Business Stopped," *New-York Tribune*, February 12, 1878.

14. *New York Sun*, February 13, 1878.

15. *New York Sun*, February 13, 1878.

16. *New York Sun*, February 13, 1878.

17. "Suppressing Vice—a Raid on Madame Restell."

18. "Suppressing Vice—a Raid on Madame Restell."

19. *New York Sun*, February 13, 1878.

20. *New York Sun*, February 14, 1878.

21. *New York Sun*, April 2, 1878.

22. *New York Times*, February 15, 1878.

23. *New York Times*, February 15, 1878.

24. *New York Times*, February 16, 1878.

25. *New York Daily Herald*, March 2, 1878.

26. *New York Times*, February 16, 1878.

27. *Brooklyn Daily Eagle*, February 24, 1878.

28. *New York Daily Herald*, March 2, 1878.

29. *New York Daily Herald*, March 2, 1878.

30. *New York Daily Herald*, March 2, 1878.

31. *New York Daily Herald*, March 2, 1878.

32. *New York Daily Herald*, March 6, 1878.

33. *New York Daily Herald*, March 6, 1878.

34. *New York Daily Herald*, March 6, 1878.

35. *New York Daily Herald,* March 6, 1878.

36. *New York Times,* April 2, 1878.

37. *New York Sun,* April 2, 1878.

38. *New York Sun,* April 2, 1878.

39. *New York Daily Herald,* December 10, 1878.

40. *New York Sun,* April 2, 1878.

41. *New York Sun,* March 30, 1878.

CHAPTER TWENTY-SEVEN

1. *New York Times,* April 2, 1878.

2. *Boston Globe,* April 2, 1878.

3. *New York Sun,* April 2, 1878.

4. *Boston Globe,* April 2, 1878.

5. *New York Times,* April 2, 1878.

6. *Boston Globe,* April 2, 1878.

7. Anthony Comstock, *Traps for the Young* (New York: Funk and Wagnalls, 1883), 155.

8. Clifford Browder, *The Wickedest Woman in New York: Madame Restell, the Abortionist* (Hamden, CT: Archon Books, 1988), 182.

9. "The Tainted Millions of Madame Restell," *Fort Wayne (IN) Journal-Gazette,* June 9, 1918.

10. *New Orleans Times-Picayune,* April 2, 1878.

11. *York (PA) Daily,* April 8, 1878.

12. *New York Daily Herald,* April 8, 1878.

13. *Carlisle Valley (PA) Sentinel,* October 4, 1878.

14. Geoffrey Stone, "'Sex and the Constitution': Anthony Comstock and the Reign of the Moralists, *Washington Post,* March 23, 2017.

15. *Fort Wayne (IN) Journal-Gazette,* June 9, 1918.

16. *Buffalo Morning Express and Illustrated Buffalo Express,* May 13, 1878.

17. *Scranton (PA) Republican,* November 13, 1878.

18. *Buffalo Morning Express and Illustrated Buffalo Express,* May 13, 1878.

19. *Salt Lake City Deseret News,* April 2, 1878.

20. *Brooklyn Daily Eagle,* April 2, 1878.

CHAPTER TWENTY-EIGHT

1. *Boston Globe,* April 5, 1878.

2. *Boston Globe,* April 5, 1878.

3. *Harrisburg (PA) Daily Independent,* April 4, 1878.

4. *Boston Globe,* April 5, 1878.

5. *Daily Arkansas Gazette,* July 21, 1918.

6. *Chicago Tribune,* April 7, 1878.

7. *Philadelphia Times,* March 2, 1879.

8. *Philadelphia Times,* March 2, 1879.

9. *Brooklyn Daily Eagle,* April 3, 1878.

10. *New York Sun*, April 2, 1878.

11. *Boston Globe*, April 5, 1878.

12. *Minneapolis Star Tribune*, April 8, 1878.

13. *Chicago Tribune*, April 7, 1878.

14. *Saint Paul (MN) Globe*, April 12, 1878.

15. *Boston Globe*, April 5, 1878.

16. *Chicago Inter Ocean*, May 8, 1880.

17. *Saint Paul (MN) Globe*, April 12, 1878.

18. *Saint Paul (MN) Globe*, April 12, 1878.

19. *Cincinnati Enquirer*, May 26, 1888.

20. *New Orleans Times-Picayune*, September 1, 1879.

21. *Buffalo Evening News*, August 1, 1889.

22. *Fort Wayne (IN) Journal-Gazette*, June 9, 1918.

EPILOGUE

1. Julie Husband and Jim O'Loughlin, *Daily Life in the Industrial United States, 1870–1900*, 2nd ed. (Santa Barbara, CA: Greenwood, 2019), 145.

2. Sarah Primrose, "The Attack on Planned Parenthood: A Historical Analysis," *UCLA Women's Law Journal* 19, no. 165 (2012): 175.

3. Primrose, "Attack on Planned Parenthood," 175.

4. Helena Huntington Smith, "They Were Eleven," *New Yorker*, June 28, 1930.

5. Primrose, "Attack on Planned Parenthood," 180.

6. Law Library, American Law and Legal Information, *New York v. Sanger*, https://law.jrank.org/pages/24655/New-York-v-Sanger-Door-Opened.html.

7. Caroline Kitchener, "The Next Frontier for the Antiabortion Movement: A Nationwide Ban," *Washington Post*, May 2, 2022.

8. Nicholas Confessore, "What to Know About Tucker Carlson's Rise," *New York Times*, April 30, 2022, www.nytimes.com/2022/04/30/business/media/tucker-carlson-fox-news-takeaways.html.

9. Andrew Gabbat, " 'Unparalleled in Intensity'—1,500 Book Bans in US School Districts," *Guardian*, April 7, 2022.

10. Ewan Palmer, "Judge Esther Salas Returns to Work After Son Killed at Home, Her Safety Warning Unheeded," *Newsweek*, March 1, 2021.

11. Natalie Colarossi, " 'Incel' Violence, Misogynistic Extremism on the Rise, Secret Service Warns," *Newsweek*, March 15, 2022.

12. "Childhood Food Insecurity in Texas," No Kid Hungry Presentation, https://capitol.texas.gov/tlodocs/86R/handouts/C4102020100500001/c59c0c56-b290-4f5c-86dd-83aa4fd5f9a0.pdf.

13. Gretchen Livingston and Deja Thomas, "Among 41 Countries, Only U.S. Lacks Paid Parental Leave," Pew Research Center, December 16, 2019, www.pewresearch.org/fact-tank/2019/12/16/u-s-lacks-mandated-paid-parental-leave.

14. Roosa Tikkanen, Munira Z. Gunja, Molly FitzGerald, and Laurie Zephyrin, "Maternal Mortality and Maternity Care in the United States Compared to 10 Other Developed Countries," Commonwealth Fund, November 18, 2020, www.commonwealthfund.org/publications/issue-briefs/2020/nov/maternal-mortality-maternity-care-us-compared-10-countries.

15. "Can I Buy Life Insurance for My Child Before They Are Born?," US Insurance Agents, August 13, 2012, www.usinsuranceagents.com/answers/can-i -buy-life-insurance-for-my-child-before-they-are-born.

16. Natalia Megas, "The Agony of Ending a Wanted Late-Term Pregnancy: Three Women Speak Out," *Guardian*, April 18, 2017.

17. Megas, "The Agony of Ending a Wanted Late-Term Pregnancy."

18. Andra H. James, MD, MPH, Jerome J. Federspiel, MD, PhD, and Homa K. Ahmadzia, MD, MPH, "Disparities in Obstetric Hemorrhage Outcomes," *Research and Practice in Thrombosis and Haemostasis* 6 (Jan 2022).

19. Mary Beth Flanders-Stepans, PhD, RN, "Alarming Racial Differences in Maternal Mortality," *J Perinat Educ* 2000 9, no. 2 (Spring 2000): 50–51.

20. Reuters Fact Check, "Fact Check-Termination of Pregnancy Can Be Necessary to Save a Woman's Life, Experts Say," Reuters, December 27, 2021, https://www .reuters.com/article/factcheck-abortion-false/fact-check-termination-of-pregnancy -can-be-necessary-to-save-a-womans-life-experts-say-idUSL1N2TC0VD.

21. Carrie Feibel, "Because of Texas Abortion Law, Her Wanted Pregnancy Became a Medical Nightmare," *Morning Edition*, NPR, July 26, 2022, www.npr.org /sections/health-shots/2022/07/26/1111280165/because-of-texas-abortion-law -her-wanted-pregnancy-became-a-medical-nightmare.

22. Anne Luty (@anneluty), Twitter, June 24, 2022, https://twitter.com /anneluty/status/1540397362362941441.

23. Haley BeMiller, "Who Can Be Charged? What About Ectopic Pregnancy? What to Know About Ohio's 6-Week Abortion Ban," *Cincinnati Enquirer*, June 28, 2022, https://www.cincinnati.com/story/news/2022/06/29/ohio-abortion-law-what -know-six-week-ban-ectopic-pregnancy/7748045001/.

24. Brent D. Griffiths, "GOP Rep. Jim Jordan Deletes Tweet Calling the Story of a 10-Year-Old Girl Being Raped 'Another Lie' After Ohio Authorities Charged a Man in the Case," *Business Insider*, July 13, 2022, www.businessinsider.com/jim -jordan-deletes-tweet-10-year-old-abortion-another-lie-2022-7; Editorial Board, "An Abortion Story Too Good to Confirm," *Wall Street Journal*, July 13, 2022, www.wsj .com/articles/an-abortion-story-too-good-to-confirm-joe-biden-ten-year-old-girl -indiana-ohio-caitlin-bernard-11657648618.

INDEX